D1595868

LIBERATION THEOLOGY
IN LATIN AMERICA

RELEASE

ST. JOSEPH'S UNIVERSITY

3 9353 00231 9075

JAMES V. SCHALL, S.J.

LIBERATION THEOLOGY
IN LATIN AMERICA

With selected essays and documents

BT
83.57
.S323
1982

IGNATIUS PRESS   SAN FRANCISCO

Calligraphy by Victoria Hoke

With ecclesiastical approval
© Ignatius Press 1982
All rights reserved
0–89870–006–X
Library of Congress Catalogue Number 80–82266
Printed in the United States of America

CONTENTS

PART III
DOCUMENTS ON LIBERATION THOUGHT

ACKNOWLEDGMENTS

The author wishes to acknowledge his gratitude to the Scaife Foundation for its generous assistance which made possible the publication of this book. Special thanks are also due to the Ethics and Public Policy Center in Washington D. C.

The Introduction was prepared at the suggestion of Professor Ernest Lefever at the Ethics and Public Policy Center.

The essays and documents are reprinted by permission of the respective journal or source from which they are each taken. The exact source is cited at the beginning of each selection.

I

LIBERATION THEOLOGY
IN LATIN AMERICA

INTRODUCTION

In the Acts of the Apostles, Peter and John were ordered
to cease preaching. On September 5, 1978, Father Pedro
Maria Belzuniqui, a Spanish Franciscan priest, was expelled from a then-turbulent Nicaragua because he had
presumably violated the local Constitution. Was he, like
Peter and John, merely preaching the Good News? Well, in
a way. According to reports, he seems to have had a cache
of "contact bombs and Molotov cocktails" in his rectory.

Meanwhile, the Costa Rican priest Padre Jose Maria
Pacheco Vasquez was also expelled. In his rectory also, it
appears, were discovered "Garand rifles, carbines, hand
grenades, ammunition magazines, and a large quantity of
subversive literature". The latter "literature", evidently,
was not the New Testament. Or was it? Maybe, as some
have been arguing ever since the Colombian priest martyr-
rebel Camilo Torres, Christianity means active revolutionary participation. We just have not been interpreting the
Gospels correctly. Are these latter priests who are apparently caught with weapons, or even killed because of them,
merely isolated exceptions, are they merely doing what
Peter and John would have done had they been confronted
with the situation in Latin America?

Yet, no one particularly wants to praise the police of the
now-deposed Mr. Somoza or believe without questioning
the charges of his security forces. On the other hand,
priests, nuns, even occasionally bishops are active in movements that would be called "violent" in any other time or
place and if not always violent, certainly "political". In an
excellent survey, "The Gospel as a Handbook for Revolutionaries", Peter Hebblethwaite wondered about the rejection of social collaboration with existing governments:

3

> Would you go to Communion alongside General Pinochet (the Chilean ruler)? On the whole, they answer no. He is a class enemy. But if someone raises the objection that Christians are commanded to love their enemies, the theologians of liberation do not demur: but they go on to produce a whole casuistry which enables them to combine class war with, so to speak, a postponed love of enemies.[1]

Thus, the obvious doctrines of Christianity seem turned upside down by many of its diligent and official practitioners. This is something more than the just war theory or the right to kill a tyrant of medieval theory. There is not only the evidence of a few clerics participating in political and revolutionary movements or abetting them. There are even rumors that some bishops, such as the Mexican Sergio Mendes Arceo or Leonidas Proaño in Ecuador, are definitely "leftish" in sympathy, if not in doctrine.

Thus, the past decades have been full of remarkably curious incidents at great odds with the pious belief that Latin America is a stable, "Catholic" culture. Indeed, much evidence would suggest that its "Catholicism" may be the cause of its present radicalism, something critics of religion have warned would happen all along. European and North American priests and nuns, then, have been regularly expelled from various Latin countries either for supposed "subversive" political activities in sympathy with such left-sounding ideas or, in their views, for fighting injustice. They have thereby often become sort of folk heroes and heroines. The American or European multi-national corporation, furthermore, has become for many religious people, almost as a dogma, the direct cause

[1] Peter Hebblethwaite, "The Gospel as a Handbook for Revolutionaries", *Religion and Freedom* (London, July 1978) 11.

of dictators and poverty. The U.S. or European governments are interpreted as little more than tools of such
"capitalism", the word now emotionally nearest to the old
notion of "sin".

Speaking in Costa Rica, for instance, the Nicaraguan
priest Ernesto Cardinal attacked the easily attackable
Somoza government of his homeland. Padre Cardinal is a
well-known poet and lecturer, a friend of Fidel Castro,
with whose regime he has never publicly found any fault.
What does he preach? "Christians are not only able to be
Marxists but, on the contrary, to be authentically Christian, they ought to be Marxist."[2] This seems somewhat
unsophisticated, no doubt, but that it is said at all already
emphasizes a change in social atmosphere in a Church
whose condemnation of communism still officially stands,
a position doubly interesting in the present light of a Polish
pope.

But, is Latin America really so full of Christian Marxists
as the rightist regimes there stoutly maintain? Is this just
smoke? The Guatemala Jesuit Cesar Jerez gave a moving
Commencement Address to the students at Canisius College in Buffalo in 1978. In classical rhetorical style, he
asked these typical American college graduates:

> Do you plan to follow in the footsteps of Dean Acheson
> and John Foster Dulles, of Richard Nixon and the CIA . . .
> who kept silent in the face of the plot by sinister forces to
> destroy a *new beginning*, a *new creation*, an attempt never be-
> fore made in that part of the world known as Chile to
> achieve *Socialism with liberty and without violence?*
>
> Do you plan to earn your degrees by your own efforts and
> not in an honorary capacity and then to use them for your

---

[2] *Denuncia* (January, 1978) 8.

own profit. . . ? Will you end up with General Motors or Morgan Trust, with Chase Manhattan or Abbott Laboratories, with Goodyear or Boeing? [Italics added]

Such premises and questions, of course, are revealing in their own right, with presupposed values themselves evidently immune from criticism. Here is the recurrent socialist dream of a perfect world, the one that never exists, the use of Scriptural terms to describe a political movement (*new creation, new beginning*), the implication that profit and corporations are *ipso facto* evil or corrupt.

These latter propositions about the "sinful" nature of capitalism and profit are perhaps the closest things to "dogmas" that exist in parts of the Christian world today. Thus, one of the leading analysts of Latin America has written: "In the decade since Medellín (1968 Conference of Latin American Bishops), the distortion of the economy of every country but Cuba has escalated. Capitalist intensive production techniques mean less work and more hunger in the cities."[3] The little phrase "but Cuba", of course, reveals the theory governing the analysis. So these are *a priori* doctrines, ideas of "distortion" and "production" that reveal little of Latin America but much about the ideology of the writers. Indeed, I will argue that, intellectually, very few of the writers on Latin American religious questions of this newer liberation school have ever really "been" in Latin America, even if born there or with very Latin American names. The intellectual tools are still European.

No one with any sensitivity, of course, has the slightest doubt about the seriousness of poverty in the world or in South America, in particular. This is a cause of human

---

[3] G. MacEoin, "The Stakes at CELAM", *The Commonweal* (August 4, 1978) 496.

anguish of the greatest concern. There is undoubtedly too much nationalism there, too much "national security state", as the radicals like to call the existing order, though it is disastrous to underestimate the values and worries nationalism reacts against. However, depth of feeling in either case is not necessarily a measure of intelligence or the best guide to a correct and effective program designed to change a difficult and tragic situation. The German President, Walter Scheel, rightly said in his response to the Apostolic Delegate:

> The gulf between rich and poor nations is the social issue of our age. It must be resolved in consideration of the vital interests of the developing countries and of the industrial countries alike, for only in a world in which all can lead a life worthy of man can peace be presumed.[4]

While ignoring too much, perhaps, the fact that slaves can be well-fed and clothed and the Aristotelian-Augustinian notion that the greatest political evils arise not from poverty but prosperity, still Scheel recognized that the world unit cannot best be conceived as a congeries of hostile nations but as a common whole. Even Michael Harrington, in *The Vast Majority: A Journey to the World's Poor*, has argued that the destruction of "capitalism" would make things much worse for the poor of the world. And several recent studies, from Barrington Moore's *On the Causes of Human Misery and Certain Proposals to Alleviate It* to Willard Gaylin's *"Doing Good": On the Limits of Benevolence*, even begin to suggest that uncritical zeal for helping others may be one of the major causes of poverty and absolutism.

And further, we need to be careful about deprecating what is being done, about exaggerating and isolating truly

---

[4] *The Bulletin* (Bonn, January 17, 1978).

difficult problems of the world community. The 1978 *World Development Report* of the World Bank, in this context, served to emphasize factors that will be most often absent, as we shall see, in the Latin American theories of liberation theology designed to improve the situation. These are: 1) Vast development has and is taking place. All is not bleak. 2) Many poor still remain, especially the poorest. 3) The growth and continued growth of all sectors are necessary for the poor to have any chance at all. 4) The very poor deserve special attention.[5]

[5] "The past quarter century has seen great progress in developing countries. In virtually all of them, income has risen faster than population, with a consequent rise in income per person. Economic growth has been accompanied by a rapid expansion of education systems, growing literacy, improvements in nutrition and health conditions, increasing technological sophistication, and structural changes, including a growing industrial base and greater urbanization. Progress on such a wide front and the steadily growing capacity of developing countries to manage their economies effectively are impressive achievements.

But much remains to be accomplished. Most countries have not yet completed the transition to modern economies and societies, and their growth is hindered by a variety of domestic and international factors. Moreover, about 800 million people still live in absolute poverty. . . .

Past experience has served to create a broad consensus about the goals for the future. The development effort should be directed toward the twin objectives of rapid growth and of reducing the numbers of people living in absolute poverty as rapidly as possible. Most developing countries have moved, or are moving, toward these objectives in designing their development strategies, and industrialized countries increasingly see them as the basis for defining their contribution.

Rapid growth and alleviating poverty are inextricably linked. Most of the absolute poor live in the poor countries of Asia and Africa, where economies have grown relatively slowly. In some of the more rapidly growing economies, the incomes of the lower groups have been raised substantially. Special action programs to improve the quality of life of the poor should be an integral part of a development strategy, but they

The issue that remains has to do with how and why the remaining poor are poor, and how and why this situation can be changed. Clearly, religion, economics, politics, and technology all have their place and contributions. The question to which this discussion will principally address itself is this: Does the Christian religious analysis currently gaining dominance in Latin America explain either why the poor are poor or how to alleviate their condition? Further, does it retain the central beliefs and ideas and practices Christianity is committed to preserve and hand on? I hold that it does not explain the poverty of the poor, nor even less make a positive contribution toward its alleviation. It does maintain that it changes no central Christian doctrine or practice, though this is questioned. In any case, it interprets Christianity radically so that it appears to be a this-worldly doctrine whose principal tendency is an economic and political one, explained in a fashion that would reunite religion and politics. This does not mean that we are not dealing mostly with sincere people, nor that problems of corruption and ignorance and political power do not exist. But it does mean that concern for the poor in Latin America and elsewhere is not best served by the present kinds of analysis we find formally presented as the answer to the questions of the human condition there.

---

need to be accompanied by growth in productivity and incomes to expand the resources available to raise living standards." *World Development Report* (Washington, D. C.: The World Bank, 1978) Chapter I.

CHAPTER I

CONCERN OVER LATIN AMERICA

Particularly in South America . . . Catholics . . . ask themselves whether the Church should not take an active initiative in the elimination of the established order.

–Concilium General Secretariat, Nijmegen, Netherlands, *"Peace through Revolution"*, The Social Message of the Gospels, *ed. F.Bockle, Concilium, no. 35 (New York: Paulist, 1968) 151.*

We have no right to expect that Christian principles will work in practice in the simple way that a political system may work. The Christian order is a supernatural order. It has its own principles and its own laws which are not those of the visible world. . . .

–Christopher Dawson, Beyond Politics *(London: 1939).*

We are living in an age in which the whole world proclaims freedom of conscience and religious freedom. We are also in an age in which the struggle against religion, which is defined as "the opium of the people", is waged in such a way as not to create new martyrs—as far as possible. Thus the programme of the age is persecution, but, appearances being saved, persecution does not exist and there is full religious freedom. What is more, all this programme has given many people the impression that they are on the side of Lazarus against the rich man, and, therefore, the same side as Christ; whereas they are, above all, against Christ.

–Karol Cardinal Wojtyla [*John Paul II*], Vita e Pensiero *(Milano, 1977),* L'Osservatore Romano *(November 9, 1978) 8. English Edition.*

In a famous and still continuing controversy, Max Weber once suggested, in *The Protestant Ethic and the Spirit of Capitalism*, that changes in economic structures did not determine changes in religious ideas—the Marxist thesis —but rather changes in religious ideas portended changes in economic and political institutions. Anyone familiar

11

with the kind of religious ideas becoming popular, sometimes even official, in Latin America today will, if he be
wise, be prepared for radical changes in civil structures.
What are these new ideas, if new they really be? Are they
necessary, wise? What are their political and economic
consequences for the United States, Europe, the Marxist
states, and the rest of the Third World? Have the Latin
Americans finally succeeded in forcing us to take them
seriously?

In a sense, all this recent interest in Latin America seems
strangely familiar. The history of the lands to the south of
the United States seems replete with the names of priests
and friars and bishops. And in spite of a century or so of a
Latin-styled anti-clericalism that seems so annoying today,
suddenly priests, ministers, nuns, Jesuits, and bishops are
again making intellectual and political headlines. In the new
Nicaragua, a priest is even Foreign Minister. Dom Helder
Camara, the peppery bishop of Recife in northeastern
Brazil, is easily the most well-known Latin American intellectual outside his own continent, while few reports
from Buenos Aires or Santiago or Bogata fail to mention
the local cardinal in a political context. The Throne and the
Altar appear to be reuniting in a mystique of the Left rather
than the traditional Right, wherein we are more accustomed to unite them. And as there were Dominicans who
accompanied Pizarro to Inca lands, so there were Franciscans, Mercedarians, and diocesan clergy with all the
great conquistadores. We should be little surprised to discover their heirs side by side in the new conquest, the new
revolution that we are told is now happening in Latin
America.

If all of this seems, at first sight, bizarre, perhaps we do
well to recall what Professor J. Lloyd Mecham wrote,

somewhat enigmatically to be sure, from the University of Texas in his *Church and State in Latin America* (1966): "The clergy of Latin America are quite different from the priesthood in the United States. This fact must be borne in mind if the Latin American religious situation is to be understood."[1] When Professor Mecham wrote these lines, he was not intending to compliment the Latin American clergy. But neither did he imply a diversity of belief, rather only a different attitude or approach. Today, the question can at least be posed whether the same credal faith is still shared. This, for instance, is a recent account of Latin American history:

> With 1492 . . . began the conquest, colonization and "evangelization" of the region, gradually forging what has come to be called Colonial Christendom.
>
> In 1808 the struggle for political independence from Spain and Portugal began, a time of political decolonization, civil wars, and the rise of nation states. A new Christendom then took shape inside the new colonial situation which was dependent first on England and later on the United States.
>
> In 1959 the first socialist revolution in Latin America succeeded in Cuba, representing an historical break, a new beginning which has been taken up as a sign, a program, and a hope for the whole continent. In the 1970s there began a structural crisis in neo-colonial and dependent capitalism, and, at the same time, a profound crisis in the structures of neo-Christendom and the church linked to it.[2]

Such an analysis is able to read history, finding an evolution of prophecy from efforts to free Indians in the 16th

[1] J. Lloyd Mecham, *Church and State in Latin America* (Chapel Hill: University of North Carolina Press, 1966) 419.

[2] Pablo Richard, "The Latin American Church, 1959–1978", *Cross Currents* (Spring, 1978) 35.

century with Fray Bartolome de las Casas, to free Mexico with the priests Hidalgo and Morelos, to the present prophecy. And what is to be freed?

> And now, at the beginning of our third great stage, we again witness the rise of a similar group of Christians, politically committed to the struggles of the people against capitalism and the neo-Christendom which has developed within it, and for a socialist liberation of the continent.[3]

Evidently, political problems are still seen as religious ones in Latin America no matter what the language used.

As René Descartes was the most famous former student of a Jesuit college in the 17th century, so today this not unmixed blessing must probably go to Fidel Castro. José Miguez Bonino, the Argentinian Protestant theologian, began his book *Christians and Marxists* with a rather witty remark of the popular Cuban dictator, who confessed honest consternation because, suddenly, "the theologians are becoming communists and the communists are becoming theologians." And thus, everyone from a Texas professor to the Cuban leader is confused over these different priests of Latin America. Twenty years ago, Latin American priests were condescendingly advised to "Go north" to learn about religion. Today, however, North American clerics sent south quickly return with instructions to change their own back yard first, usually away from "capitalism".

All of this is hard to account for. After all, did not the good Archbishop of Guatemala write in a not untypical Pastoral Letter as recent as 1954:

> The words of your Shepherd are meant to lead Catholics toward a just, national, and dignified campaign against

[3] Ibid., 36.

communism. The people of Guatemala must rise as one man to fight the enemy of God and of their country. Our fight against communism, therefore, must be based upon a nationalistic and a Catholic attitude. Let us undertake the campaign against communism in the name of God. . . .[4]

This was written at the time of a Yankee-inspired overthrow of a leftist government. What is now to be noted is that God has evidently, if we are to believe the current rhetoric, changed sides. The case for socialism, if not communism, is argued in mostly religious–political terms.

In this past quarter century, then, the passionate style of Latin American religious–political expression has not altered much. What has changed is the object against which it is employed. Until recently, writers from the European or United States tradition tended to look upon Latin American experience under the lenses of church and state, because this was the interest and focus of liberal, secularized thought. If church and state are still a major problem, it only concerns how the two can work together to solve another kind of problem, that which is called "oppression" and "poverty". Claude Geffré wrote of this tendency:

It is the Holy Spirit who inspires the activity of the Christian community and who shows Christians the substance of evangelical charity in this or that historical situation. We should juxtapose a theology based on revelation to one based on practice. God also reveals himself through, in and by liberation struggles undertaken by all the poor of the South American continent.[5]

[4] Letter translated in F. B. Pike, *The Conflict Between Church and State in Latin America* (New York: Knopf, 1964) 178.

[5] Claude Geffré, "A Prophetic Theology", *The Mystical and Political Dimensions of the Christian Faith* (New York: Herder and Herder, 1974) 11.

And so we often receive the impression from such literature that only these institutions, church and state, without any of that fear of their union which has been of concern in United States tradition, are really qualified to confront this issue. The value of religion has, consequently, come to be placed not so much on transcendence as on a specific, very narrow, and highly visible function—namely, what religion can do in this world for the world's problems.

In this context, if we read many of the pastoral statements coming from Latin America, such as that produced by the Peruvian bishops in 1971, there is a heavy overtone of contemporary ideology.

> Like other nations of the Third World, we are victims of systems that exploit our natural resources, control our political decisions, and impose upon us the cultural domination of their values and consumer civilization. This situation which was denounced at Medellín, Colombia (Bishops' Conference of 1968), is reinforced and supported by the internal structures of our nation. Economic, social, and cultural inequality is increasing, while politics are so perverted that instead of serving the common good, they favor a tiny minority.[6]

How is it possible that the Church once famed for its conservatism is now seen to be the most radical on earth? And this is especially to be wondered at when we recall that the one Catholic country in Europe under an imposed Marxist regime, the Poland of John Paul II, is clearly the most conservative in practice. And Poland is so precisely in order to be able to retain its religious heritage. Can Catholicism, then, mean anything at all in the light of such divergencies? Why is it, therefore, that many nations of

[6] Reprinted in *IDOC-North America*, no. 51 (March, 1973) 21.

Central and Latin America, nations which themselves often
gained their political independence only a few years after
1776 and under its inspiration, our "good neighbors", as a
famous American President once called them, why are
these lands so apparently anti-Yankee, perhaps even more
than anti-European?

On the surface, Americans north of the Rio Grande
should rejoice over this unexpected alteration of attitude
by these same Latin Americans. For years, we have been
preaching that there is something radically wrong and
amiss in the political and religious environment of the
Southern Continent. We were not slow to suggest that the
Latins unfortunately missed the Reformation. More than
one has suspected that a good dose of Calvinism might
have helped. Further, in their tradition of Roman and
French law, we felt they lacked that solid English Common Law sensibility, its taste for compromise, its practical-
ity in knowing how compromise and politics work.

In our view, then, the Latin Americans historically confused passion and party, mañana and a two-o'clock ap-
pointment, siesta and progress. The Spanish and Indian
traditions, concerned with human rights in a way long before we were, were thought to be radically incapable of
confronting the modern world. And it is not insignificant
that, just as most Third World political leaders were educated at the London School of Economics or at the Sor-
bonne, so most of the new Latin American theologians
studied under Italian, French, Spanish and German—
sometimes even North American—theologians.[7] Further,
no one would argue that Marxism itself is indigenous to

[7] Cf. Daniel Patrick Moynihan, "The United States in Opposition",
Commentary (March, 1975) 31–44.

Latin America. So, paradoxically, we seem to be confronted with a new kind of unacknowledged intellectual neo-colonialism designed to prove, "scientifically", that Latin America is not an out-of-the-way backwater of the world.

Latin America, however, for all its persistent claim to be the Christian intellectual leader of the new Third World, is a very different place from Asia or Africa, not only because its Christianity and nationalism are more pervasive and usually older, but also because its Christianity remains a living reality. Pierre Bigo, the noted French Jesuit commentator on Catholic social thought, recently wrote from Colombia, where he had been teaching:

> I am notably struck by the enormous difference between Latin America and Europe from the point of view of the Christian faith. One still lives here in a Christian milieu. This is no longer the case in France. . . . In the French spiritual melange, each one strives after a fashion to believe as he can: one believes yet in Christ, another only in God, but he does not know if this is good or bad, and another does not believe in anything. . . .
>
> In Latin America, on the other hand, we walk in a Christian atmosphere. One can base himself on the faith. Unbelief is the exception.[8]

Such remarks suggest, I think, that the central issue in Latin America is not so much one of faith *against* atheism, which would place the two in radical opposition, but rather one of how atheism can be used for the ends of faith. That the ever pragmatic, "authentic" Marxists ask precisely the opposite question, there can be no doubt. Yet,

[8] Pierre Bigo, Letter, in *On the Service of Faith and New Cultures* (Rome: Jesuit Curia, May, 1978) 32.

this does not lessen the impression that liberation theology, as this movement styles itself, is present on the stage of Latin America as an authentic Christian world view, one with definite apostolic purpose. Whether it is or not in fact remains to be seen both in terms of analysis and performance. And this should be on the grounds of its own theology, for its two most used words are "critique" and "practice". Nevertheless, to understand it adequately, it is well to see something of how it presents itself.

The long-range social and political effects of most theologies, Christian and otherwise, are usually not immediately obvious. Indeed, as Christopher Dawson, the distinguished English Catholic historian of culture, wrote of the initial effects of the life of Christ himself: "From a worldly point of view, from the standpoint of a contemporary secular historian, it was not only unimportant, but actually invisible."[9] Scholars have only lately begun to assess the relations between modernity and the view of classical religions. And even here, scholars are often wrong. Few governments and agencies, furthermore, have specialists on this subject, one which clearly may be the source of the profoundest public consequences. Certain secular ways of looking at religion actually make it impossible to govern. And even fewer corporations and businesses whose very future may well be most affected by ideas rooted precisely in a "liberation" ethos seem prepared to tackle such apparently obtuse material. This is especially shortsighted in the case of this Latin approach whose very premises presuppose methodologically that corporations and certain kinds of national states, often including their own, not to mention our own, are the main causes of evil in the world.

[9] Christopher Dawson, *Beyond Politics* (London: Sheed and Ward, 1939) 128.

If, then, the 19th century was the era of individual guilt
as well as of individual enterprise, we will soon become
aware that the 20th century, as it reaches its end, still flirts
with the terrible idea of collective guilt and collective enterprise, this even after the horrors of the 1930s. Our universities, furthermore, have to all intents and purposes
excluded any serious study of religion, especially Christianity, on its own terms, so that our general capacity to
comprehend the origins and consequences of theological
ideas and movements is absurdly deficient, reduced to a
kind of superficial sociology that hardly understands itself,
let alone religion. Our established secular humanism has
lopped off our spiritual heads, so to speak, when it comes
to grips seriously with a theological movement that claims
direct political and economic consequences. In such a context, the choice of a sound policy vis-à-vis such a religious
movement would lack depth and depend mostly on luck
for results. And it is the thesis of these remarks that, at
present, this is precisely where our capacity to act in relation to liberation thought does lie: with luck, not with intelligence about its implications.

No one, moreover, will appreciate the often virulent
anti-U.S. attitude coming from Latin American theological
circles unless he realizes the connection between the "life"
issue—the first part of our own Declaration of Independence
—and the ease with which Latin Americans are choosing a
kind of Marxism as a tool to achieve what they call liberation from oppression. For many, not without warrant,
Marxism appears to be the lesser evil. We are told over and
over that the main problem is too many Latin Americans,
a theme thinly disguised in birthrate discussions. Latin
America is flooded with abortion and anti-natal devices

from myriads of well-financed U.S. agencies, foundations and corporations. The deep anti–Christian roots that justify such an "anti–life" view of life make it only the more logical for Latin Americans to opt for the most prominent social philosophy which insists, in theory at least, that life and people are not at fault, but only structures and dominant systems. In this sense, the United States is only reaping the whirlwind of its own cultural values.

The liberation movement purports to be first of all a very moral system in the name of and for the poor, the very ones many of our theorists tell us ought not to exist in the first place. The deep and concerned estimation of the poor is surely a permanent emphasis of this kind of theology, one that is of great spiritual depth. Liberation theory does accept the fundamental principle, stressed by Popes Pius XII, John XXIII, and Paul VI, repeated by John Paul II, that the end, center, and purpose of social and political life is the existing human person, whoever he be, whatever his condition. Insofar as the United States' instrumentalities and values are seen to violate this principle, it becomes remarkably easy and tempting to condemn outright the whole U. S. system, pejoratively called "capitalism", to look elsewhere. We would understand very little of the moral force of this movement if we did not acknowledge this central fact about it. There is not a little irony in the belatedly growing realization that a good part of our own future labor force must come from other peoples, especially those south of us. We are indeed seeing only the beginning of the immigration problem with the arrival of more and more young people often motivated with ideas located in the liberation outlook. These seek work and eventual citizenship.

This passionate concern of the Latin American Church, however, does deserve our intelligent comprehension. I will argue here, substantially, that it often opts for the wrong means to a good end, that its poignancy and greater danger lie in once again leaving the Church open to the accusation that it is confusing absolutism and even totalitarianism with liberty in the name of some vast theoretical rationalization. The main objection is empirical, pragmatic —the theory does not work. As this movement progresses, more and more of these old fears that religion supports an absolutist system will arise. To say the least, it must strike us as strange to find a vision of a future world order, promoted by presumed Christians, clothed in the conscious terms of the most powerful absolutism of our times, an absolutism again and again condemned by the very Church itself.

Though I do not propose to press the point much here, the use of the term "liberation" to describe this theology and its surrounding ideology seems most confusing, at least against the background of United States political traditions. In his essay on the Third Conference of Latin American Bishops (Puebla, Mexico, February, 1979), Alfred Hennelly began and ended his essay with a quotation from John Courtney Murray, the well-known Jesuit architect of contemporary United States approaches to church and state. These quotations carried the implication that the kind of liberation or liberty Murray stood for was somehow a natural and logical predecessor to contemporary liberation theology.[10] In a truer sense, Murray's *We Hold These Truths* stands at almost the opposite pole to that of liberation

[10] Father Hennelly's article is in *America* (May 27, 1978). Cf. also his "Courage with Primitive Weapons", *Cross Currents* (Spring, 1978) 8–19.

thought.[11] Murray rather belonged, like Jacques Maritain, the French Thomist philosopher, in his *Reflections on America*, to that stream of political theory which holds that the United States in many ways comes close to that vision of classical political theory, that of the best practical form of government.[12] Needless to recall, liberation thought will have none of this approach. In strict analytical terms, then, the actual content and structure of what is called liberation theology would be best described as "equalization" theology in English, did not the term "equalization" connote something to do with liquor control.

The kind of socialized and corporative thinking espoused by professed liberation theology has little in common except the name with what is generally meant by either economic or political liberty. A reading of, say, Norman Macrae's *America's Third Century* reveals a passion for helping the poor equally as vivid as anything in liberation theory but with none of the socialist or egalitarian presuppositions of the theory typical of Latin America.[13]

[11] Several statements such as the Hartford Statement (see document no. 5) were designed to restate the central line of Christian reflection in the light of a too great concern with worldly politics. *Against the World for the World* (New York: Seabury, 1976).

[12] "The model of the 'New Christendom' (as elaborated by Jacques Maritain), which stressed the autonomy of the temporal sphere with regard to the church, is also rejected; for it often masked a tacit alliance of the church with oppressive regimes and appeared to be a totally inadequate response to the enormous misery and injustice everywhere evident in Latin America." Hennelly, *Cross Currents* (Spring, 1978) 13. This statement, of course, is the clearest one for a foundation of the reabsorption of politics into religion, or vice versa.

[13] Norman Macrae, "America's Third Century", *The Economist*, Survey, London (October 25, 1975); George Gilder, *Wealth and Poverty* (New York: Basic, 1980); Paul Johnson, *Can Capitalism Survive?* (Washington: Ethics and Public Policy Center, 1979).

Thus, the sorting out of the intellectual background of liberation thought produces some strange bedfellows. In a way, *Unam Sanctam*, the famous Bull of the early 14th-century Pope Boniface VIII, the one that came closest to identifying society and church, seems nearer to the kind of religious tendencies we find in liberation theorists than does anything in James Madison or Maritain or the Murray-inspired *Document on Religious Liberty* of Vatican Council II. The economic and political theories that have taken liberty seriously historically, the ones most responsible for a real economic development in modern times, are generally conceived to be what is most opposed by liberation theory, which often seems curiously blind to development on any other terms but its own.

Thus, to attempt an understanding of this new Latin American concern over its own plight is not only intel-lectually stimulating and often original, but politically nec-essary. "Ideas have consequences", almost every philoso-pher who has ever lived has told his skeptical students. True to some of the strands of Marxist inspiration, many Latin American theorists are now suggesting that actions produce ideas. And as these same theorists are often also theologians, what they see ultimately being produced is the action of God in our history. This becomes a moral and religious enterprise by being a political and economic one. Anyone brought up in the United States is naturally going to be more than skeptical about such an easy association of ideas which, it would seem, ought to be kept more separate and distinct.

None the less, it remains true that the turmoil in Latin America does have direct European and American roots. We are the very ones who have chided and often ridiculed the Latin Americans' performance. Too often we have done this because we could not understand their faith. If the Latin American today tends to rejoice in a theory that seems to explain his lowly status in terms of Yankee faults and greed, we should not underestimate the force of envy and frustration in history, something as old as Plato and Aristotle. The ultimate purpose of an analysis and critique of liberation theology, however, is to achieve a common goal we all can agree on and work for, one that solves the cultural problem at hand without, at a minimum, making things worse.

At the beginning of this chapter, I cited the historian Christopher Dawson. He warned us not to identify too quickly political and religious hopes. The ways of God and the ways of man, we have been taught since Isaiah, are not necessarily the same. Liberation theology does bring up the question of what Christianity is about and is at least tempted to bind together the two poles Isaiah set asunder. The classical criticism of religion, including Christianity, has been that it absorbs the energies of men so that they have no time or spirit for the important things of the world. As a result, religion is said to further the suppression of the presumably bright hopes of mankind. Little wonder that contemporary academic political modernization theories often seem to want to identify the energies evoked by religion with the accomplishment of the earthly, political task.[14] That Latin American theologians are reacting strenuously against this classical accusation, there can be little doubt. And yet, if Christianity introduced any revolution into the political world at all, and it did, it was that the things of God are not those of Caesar.

[14] Cf. D. Apter, *The Politics of Modernization* (Chicago: University of Chicago Press, 1965). Cf. also Neil Jacoby, "Some Principles of Development", *Dialogue*, no. 4 (1974) 60–63.

To conclude in this context, then, it is no accident, as a reading of such a work as José Porfirio Miranda's *Marx and the Bible* (1974) would show, that liberation theology is heavily Old Testament oriented. Its emphases are largely milk and honey in the land, the "people", prophecy, justice, judgment. The action of God is seen to demand just structures and almost visible results. Enemies of the political vision tend to become enemies of God. And so in order to appreciate the meaning of liberation thought, we must see it against a Judaeo-Christian background. The largest body of Roman Catholics in the world today is in Latin America. Some 18% of the world population is Catholic; of these 61% are on the two American continents, of these latter only 18% are north of the Texas-Arizona-California southern boundaries. No major change in their thought or condition can be indifferent to us, either as U.S. citizens or as Christians. I take it as obvious, then, that the argument is not so much over whether our sympathies and help ought to be with the poor, whether in Latin America or elsewhere, but rather over how best to analyze the causes of their poverty and how to alleviate it.

CHAPTER II

WHAT LIBERATION THEOLOGY MAINTAINS

Liberation is a term which expresses a new posture in Latin America. . . . Among more alert people today, what we have called a new awareness of Latin American reality is making headway. They believe that there can be authentic development for Latin America only if there is liberation from the domination exercised by the greatest capitalist countries, especially the most powerful, the United States of America. This liberation also implies a confrontation with these groups' natural allies, their compatriots who control national power structures. It is becoming more evident that Latin American peoples will not emerge from their present status except by means of a profound transformation, a social revolution.

–Gustavo Gutierrez, S.J., A Theology of Liberation *(Maryknoll: Orbis, 1971) 88.*

Ever since Hegel in his famous *Lectures on the Philosophy of History* taught modern man to look for the presence of the "Absolute Spirit", as he called it, in a particular state, in a particular era, the various nations, classes, races and continents have conceived themselves to be the bearers of world-historic missions and justifications. Eventually, everyone would have his turn in the public light. No doubt since the famous voyages of Christopher Columbus from Spain, in a year that coincided with the fall of Granada and the decline of Islamic dominance, voyages which discovered both North and South America, Europe has stood at the center of the world.

Within this same Europe, furthermore, after the revival of commerce and the Crusades in the late Middle Ages, the center shifted from Venice, Florence and Genoa westward to the Lisbon of Prince Henry and the Court of Ferdinand

and Isabella, then north to Amsterdam and Antwerp, then to Paris, London and Berlin. And all of these traditions recognized roots in Athens and Rome. But in the thirties of the last century, a perceptive Frenchman by the name of Alexis de Tocqueville startled the world by writing in his famous book on democracy that the dominant forces in the 20th century would be the two continent-sized nations, the United States and Russia. Indeed, he even went on to hold that the very quality of "liberty" would ultimately be decided by which one of these nations finally came to dominate.

Historians and philosophers have long wondered about changes in political power and civilizational decay. Spengler, Toynbee, and Sorokin even tried to reduce this reflection to a sort of science. Undoubtedly, one of the greatest intellectual stimuli that gave rise to this kind of consideration, besides Gibbon's famous *Decline and Fall of the Roman Empire*, was this: Why did modern science, with its commercial and industrial revolutions, arise in Europe and not elsewhere? Were the Europeans somehow superior even in the theory of equality they bequeathed to the rest of the world, or were they just lucky, agents of a transformation that might have happened anywhere? Further, was it the European *stock* or the European *beliefs* that founded it all? The arrival of Japan in particular on the world scene, with her diligence and selective imitations, seemed to argue conclusively for the latter. Beyond this, moreover, the French and American Revolutions raised the issue of the proper "form" of modern government. Was there some basic connection between economic growth and modernization such that the proper political form was necessary?

In all this context, Latin America appeared before the world horizon in two rather unfavorable lights. First, it was a colony of Spain or Portugal, both of which countries were apparently bypassed by modern science and industry. To be sure, the Spanish and Portuguese colonies were much more successfully transformed into the quasi-likeness of their mother countries than other European colonies in Asia or Africa. The United States, Canada, and Australia did not count, for they really seemed to be not so much colonies as somehow physical extensions of European peoples, especially the northern ones.

Secondly, Latin America, at its distance, seemed to have nothing new or unique to teach. Its Inca or Aztec or Indian backgrounds were interesting no doubt, even exotic, but the melting pot that became Latin America—in a sense one of the great founts of human rights tradition in another context—seemed to be merely poor imitations of a civilization already out-of-date. The results of the rather advanced political revolutions staged in Latin America in the 19th century only seemed to prove something more basic was at issue.

For a long time, then, modern intellectuals were convinced that the backwardness of southern, especially Latin, Europe was due to its religion. The famous thesis of Max Weber and R. H. Tawney, in spite of the caveats of Amintore Fanfani and George O'Brien, put this in structural form. It sought to find, as against Marx, the real reason for scientific and industrial development in changes in theology, not in material production. Whatever the limitation of such views, they served to brand the economic and political structures of the Latin, and especially Iberian, world as retarded, especially because of its particular religious, cultural, and social forms. The seed was then planted and is still bearing fruit, the seed that implied that the only way for this Latin world to achieve modern development would be for it to change its religion.

Thus, Spain, once the most powerful country in Europe,

quickly lost out to the northern European states because it
did not know how to use all the wealth of Latin America to
found a viable modern society. It did not possess the secret
of productivity and enterprise, largely because its religion
oriented it to less worldly issues. Consequently, if one
spurned the agnostic or atheist alternatives, which the
Iberian peoples generally did, only two alternatives seemed
logically open: either to become Protestant or to change
Catholicism into a directly worldly force.

Latin America, in a sense, then, suffered doubly and
seemed to be a proof of the thesis about the restrictive nature of the Latin religion. For even though Latin America
formally received its political independence very early, before Germany or Italy or, in a way, even before Spain, it
still seemed not to know what to do with either political
or economic institutions in the so-called modern world.
Rightly or wrongly, Latin America—in fact, a huge, diverse, rich, dynamic continent in so many ways—came to
be looked upon in a most condescending fashion. It was
just one more proof of the incapacity of Catholicism to
enter modernity. This was a view shared by liberal and
secular intellectuals, Latin American included, which may
explain why they are not in the forefront of the present
movement. Thus, one could either reject the modern world
to go back to the virtues of the pre-Columbian era or try to
change the religion. Liberation theology is a version of this
latter alternative. It is an effort to change Catholicism while
paradoxically still keeping it in order to achieve the kind of
modernization said to be lacking on the southern continent.

South America, then, simply did not exist on the stage
of world history. Even today, in spite of ship, plane, satellite, and television, in spite of dire threats of the consequences of its neglect, Latin America hardly attracts the attention of most of the world, since it is isolated geograph-

ically in a way that the other continents are not. The distance from San Francisco to Yokohama, for instance, is 4536 nautical miles, while it is 5140 to Valparaiso, Chile. From Chicago to Berlin is 4414 air miles, but to Rio, it is 5282 miles.

Yet, a small group of Latin American intellectuals, mainly clerics, are now claiming to have discovered a way to place Latin America precisely at the heart of world history. "Would we be out of line in suggesting," Juan Luis Segundo, the Uruguayan Jesuit, asked in *Our Idea of God*, "that Latin America has its own special destiny today? Would we be wrong to suggest that it is meant to give voice to the crisis which foreshadows and proclaims a new understanding of the history that has passed for occidental civilization, and that formulated the idea of God in its own categories?"[1]

Needless to say, this is no small claim. Neither the proposition that Liberation Theology is quite new nor the view that it is something uniquely Latin American should be accepted uncritically, of course. There is, as Père André-Vincent wrote in *Nouvelle Revue Théologique*, rather too much of this, in spite of protestations to the contrary, that bears the mark "Made in Germany". The South American flavor has heavy Germanic terminology.[2] Yet, he also noted that "the ambition of these liberators is nothing less than the creation of a new theology in its totality, one entirely Latin American. Nationalism and revolution, the two powers of Latin America, are exploding in the old edifice in order to reestablish it."[3] But, of course, there have been many theological revolutions in the past, so why

[1] Juan Luis Segundo, *Our Idea of God* (Maryknoll: Orbis, 1974) 34.

[2] André-Vincent, *"Les Théologies de la libération"*, *Nouvelle Revue Théologique* (February, 1976) 110. See essay no. 4, below.

[3] Ibid., 109.

should this one demand the attention of men of affairs and
public leaders elsewhere? No one has paid much attention
to Latin American thought before. Why should anyone
now?

Perhaps no one should. The leading Marxist economic
historian, Eric Hobsbawm, recently wrote in this connection:

> The churches are now left free to move left, for neither
> the right nor the state can any longer protect them against
> erosion. Some Christians may thus hope to retain, or more
> doubtfully, regain the support of the masses believed to be
> identified with the left. It is a surprising development.
> Conversely, parties of the Marxist left, seeking to widen
> their support, are more inclined to abandon their traditional
> identification with active opposition to religion. And yet,
> whatever the political attitudes of religious peoples or bodies,
> religion remains mainly a conservative factor. . . . The
> strongest religion remains the old-time religion.[4]

Thus—and this is the mark of much criticism of Latin
American liberation thought—it is not so very unique
after all. The proposed changes within the interpretation of
Catholicism are really as conservative as ever, even for the
authentic Marxists. They are merely a change from a right
to a left orthodoxy. And this is most likely to keep Latin
America in the same backwardness in which it has always
seen itself. The empirical causes of development and change
are still not realized.

European and American critics, to be sure, have always
chided Latin America, especially its supposedly conservative Church, for its failure to help reform the culture. Ironically, liberation theology is an effort to respond to this

[4] Eric Hobsbawm, "Religion and the Rise of Socialism", *Marxist
Perspectives* (Spring, 1978) 28.

charge, perhaps even by taking it more seriously than it should. Practically all writers note that this is itself largely a clerical movement, born of men who studied largely in Europe. It is not really spontaneous. At least some wonder if it is not just another form of clerical isolation. As C. Wolcott Parker remarked:

> In a prognosis of the forces and events that will be extant during the next 24 years, it is patently clear that the Latin American must come to grips with the dichotomy of counter-productive nationalism and the increasing need for technology and capital. He taps his feet to flamenco guitars and to martial music. Nevertheless, every nuance of the Latin American intellect that I have come to know over 23 years tells me that, in the matter of business, his pragmatic sense overrides his romantic nature.[5]

Consequently, if and when it is shown that the economic and social analysis of this theology is itself distorted or dangerous, something that is being shown, this will mean a further isolation and reaction against the ecclesiastical circles that proposed it. None the less, liberation theology presents itself as new. More often than not, it is reflective of some form of Marxist structural analysis, even though frequently, though not always, there is an effort to purge Marxism of its anti-Christian aspects. That this latter can be accomplished is practically a matter of faith in the liberation theorists. In the main empirical area where this kind of debate is most acute, between the Russian dissidents or their Eastern European relatives and the Latin Americans, the argument seems to be definitive that such a purgation is impossible in actual practice.

[5] C. Wolcott Parker, "Technolitics: Latin America 2000 AD", *Vital Speeches* (February 1, 1977) 256.

In this light, therefore, liberation theology proposes to rewrite or reinterpret all the major elements and themes of Christianity. This does not take the classic form of "heresy" or "protestantism" because it does not claim to deny classical Christianity. Rather, it claims to explain what Christianity "really" believes if it only knew its mind. Moreover, liberation thought accepts all or part of the Marxist analysis as being "scientifically" true. The conclusion from this is that Marxism is necessarily conformable with Christianity. To what degree this renovation is at all compatible with traditional Christianity is subject to considerable debate. There is a delicate and nuanced sparring going on between papacy, episcopacy, and theologians in this whole area. The trip of John Paul II to Mexico and Brazil has revealed the papacy's most complete analysis of the movement. Some unofficial commentaries like the Hartford Statement were addressed to certain basic exaggerations in this overall movement.[6] The statement of the International Theological Commission, an advisory body to the Holy Father, is also an effort to place some evaluation on the movement.[7] The periodical literature in the field is now obviously quite massive.

What is to be noted here first, however, is that probably few United States or European observers would disagree totally with the generally expressed goals of liberation thought insofar as they concern improving human life for the poor peoples of Latin America. Commonly, it is agreed that poverty in Latin America is a serious, agonizing issue,

[6] Cf. P. Berger and R. Neuhaus, *Against the World for the World* (New York: Seabury, 1976). Document no. 5 below.

[7] "Human Development and Christian Salvation", *Origins* (November 3, 1977); cf. also R. Heckel, *"Foi et justice: théologie, magistère, spiritualité"*, *Fides et Justitia* (Rome, 1976) 42–60.

that it can be alleviated, that certain economic, political, even religious attitudes and institutions are required for this process, that every people has a right to its own autonomy and well-being. The disagreement arises over the explanation of why this imbalance came about in the first place, why it continues to exist, over what is to be done about it, and over who is really at fault.

Liberation theology, then, is an explanation of why Latin America is as it is and what specifically is to be done about it. It has allowed rather few options for itself. In a sense, the situation appears to its authors not unlike that of Rome in the decades after the Emperor left for Byzantium, when the Church gradually came to fulfill essentially secular roles because, apparently, no one else could or would assume them. And although there is an adamant rejection of any "neo-Constantinianism" in liberation thought, any effort to establish a new worldly-religious union, still there is a similar presupposition that the key to success in the worldly order has something to do with this new evaluation of Catholicism. There is everywhere the influence of Marx's famous aphorism that the purpose of philosophy is not to understand the world but to change it. There is a heavy emphasis on action over against thought. Needless to recall, several passages in Scripture seem to bear a similar import, so the language of this effort is sophisticated and is replete with terms drawn largely from Christian theology, the Old Testament, and Marxism.

We would, however, err to doubt that liberation theology is a reaction to, and complement for, the various kinds of criticisms directed at Latin America in recent times. Thus, this theological response has to it a kind of missionary enthusiasm. Its spokesmen are all over the world zealously bearing its message to universities and seminaries.

By ignoring the pertinence of the Russian and Eastern European experience to the issue, we have no empirical laboratory except Cuba and the memory of an idealized Chile under socialism. The situation in Nicaragua remains yet to be seen. Gutierrez's *Theology of Liberation*, for instance, is said to be by far the most widely read book by Philippine clerics, though they can be presumed to have still some vague traditional connection with the Latin world.

The feeling exists, then, that now most of the basic answers and explanations of poverty are in, at least theoretically. All that is left to do is to put them into practice according to analytical forms now called "praxis", practice. Deliberately, then, little room is left for further thought, since part of the analysis is that action is to be effected in the world soon. Men are to be sensitized to their situation. The word most often used is from the Brazilian educator Paolo Freire—"conscientization".[8] People need actually to be taught, in this view, to understand the "objective" situation of their lives, especially the poor, understand in the sense of hating or disliking it enough to do something about it.

The initial starting point of this theology, therefore, as we have seen, is the condition of the poor. This is said to be the key with which to open both the meaning of Scripture and the way to change the situation of these same poor. The report of Father Gutierrez's remarks at the June 7–10, 1978, Catholic Theological Association meeting is typical of this viewpoint:

> Theology must come from the poor. . . . The Church needs the poor's reflection. They know death on an intimate level no intellectual can know. . . . The starting point

    [8] Cf. P. Berger, "The False Consciousness of 'Consciousness Raising' ", *Worldview* (January, 1975) 33–38.

of liberation theology is commitment to the poor, the "non-person". Its ideas come from the victim. . . . Commitment to the poor is the very place for spiritual experience. In commitment to the poor. . . , one encounters God. [Gutierrez] acknowledged that God is not the main subject in liberation theology, but added, "We're working on it." . . . Liberation theology is not optimistic. It speaks often of sin and sin situations. "We are not sure of another society, but we are sure the present society is not possible and we must change it.[9]

However, as it has been recognized from almost the beginning that poverty itself can be an unclear and relative term, some pains are taken to account for it.

If we read carefully the Medellín (1968 Latin American Bishops') documents and other discussions of the subject, it is clear that poverty is looked upon as an evil that ought not to exist. The poor being always with us is not the favorite Scriptural passage in these treatments. All the sympathy for the poor is not designed to keep them that way. The often-encountered tradition in Christianity that, spiritually, poverty is much safer than riches, is not stressed. The voluntary and exemplary poverty of Church and religious is designed to serve the poor and enable them to improve their lot. The assumption is that the reason the poor are poor is mainly because of the attitudes and ideas of the rich.[10]

This latter idea needs further explanation, of course. This is where the earlier analysis of the Latin American situation comes back in. The poverty of Latin America is now said to be caused by its "dependence". Astonishingly little attention in this literature is paid to Latin America's

[9] Report of E. Ginthoff, *The Monitor*, San Francisco (June 16, 1978).
[10] Basic Medellín Documents are in *The Gospel of Justice and Peace* (Maryknoll: Orbis, 1976) 445–76.

economic successes, which are not negligible. Yet the explanation of the poverty of Latin America is seen to be almost exclusively in terms of foreign and domestic "exploitation". If this be so, and it now seems to be taken for granted in the literature of this movement, then another kind of world and national society is required. This results in the famous "option for socialism", which is said to be required by these circumstances and the force of liberation logic. This will naturally mean that fighting for socialism will be equivalent to fighting for justice, since justice cannot exist in the present order of things. Liberation theology maintains that such an analysis is necessary because of the supposed failures of alternative approaches, especially the Alliance for Progress, North American developmentalism, and European Christian Democracy. These were all tried, thoroughly, it is claimed, during the 1950s and 1960s. Things only became worse. So liberation theology arose from the "scientific" necessity of embracing a quasi-Marxist type of analysis as the *only* way to alleviate the lot of the poor.

Poverty - Dependence - Exploitation - Conscientization - Revolution-Socialism—this is pictured as the natural sequence so that any other view which might propose a different logic to the same end is more or less equivalent to rejecting the dire needs of such peoples.[11] Chesterton's witticism that Christianity has not been tried and found wanting, but tried and found difficult seems pertinent here. In any case, in the light of such an analysis of the Latin American situation, a massive effort is made to reshape Christian Scripture and thought according to the liberation

[11] Cf. F. Stewart and P. Streeten, "New Strategies for Development: Poverty, Income Distribution, and Growth", *Oxford Economic Papers* (November, 1976) 381–405.

premises. No one should underestimate the diligence and persistence that have gone into these enterprises.

Essentially, the tendency of the theory consists in identifying the purposes and mission of God, his Kingdom, with the effort to improve the lot of the poor.[12] This lies behind the refusal of liberation thought to conceive its mission to be an individual or religious effort, but rather to be frankly a political and economic one. No longer is there much hesitation about politics, no effort to see it as "natural" over against the supernatural. The area of politics, once given to outer darkness in Augustine or to reason in Aquinas, is now the very locus of ongoing revelation since, it is assumed, no other way exists to help the poor. This is what God wants politics to be used for. The effect of this methodology and theology is intended to result in salutary action. And since both church and state institutions must be transformed soon, no one is free to escape the effort of "justice" in this program. Justice has thus largely replaced the older Christian idea of charity. Aquinas, to be sure, held that there could be no real charity without justice, but it is doubtful if he meant this to be put in temporal sequence. Probably he meant the opposite, that justice results from charity.

Here, then, the newly proclaimed critical function of the Church is to be found. The function most characteristic of religion is to align itself on the side of the poor, explaining why they are dependent and what they must do about it. Violence is treated gingerly, but not excluded. Indeed, it is often advocated as a sad necessity. What has to be done, for most advocates, has to be done. This latter is a proposition that used to be regarded as right-wing in Christian circles.

[12] Cf. the author's "From 'Catholic Social Doctrine' to the 'Kingdom of God on Earth' ", *Communio* (Winter, 1976) 284–300.

But this is not cynical. Rather it is held as a conclusion of the exploitive situation. This is what is at fault. In this context, one cannot help but notice the sensitivity of the leaders of the Church to the abiding radical charge that they are upholders of the status quo for the rich.

Furthermore, to add to the semantic confusion, the general rationale that this reaction to present economic and political order takes is that of human rights. This too is a position more stressed by less Marxist elements in the Church and one with certain appeal to pre-Reagan United States foreign policy.[13] One of the main efforts of many bishops in Latin America is to be able to criticize military regimes without being accused of communism. Many would frankly like a position that would clearly set them off from the obviously Marxist-type analysis in much liberation thought. As the Medellín bishops said:

> This situation demands all-embracing, courageous, urgent, and profoundly renovating transformations. We should not be surprised, therefore, that the "temptation to violence" is surfacing in Latin America. One should not abuse the patience of a people that for years has borne a situation that would not be acceptable to anyone with any degree of awareness of human rights.[14]

Such sentiments, of course, are not unlike those of the Declaration of Independence. Unfortunately, the real policy issue today is whether they demand the kind of solution proposed in the Latin American liberation view.

In any event, liberation theology maintains that the plight of Latin America is not of its own making. Structures of injustice are said to be imposed largely from the

---

[13] Cf. A. Bono, "Catholic Bishops and Human Rights in Latin America", *Worldview* (March, 1978).

[14] Medellín Documents, *Gospel of Justice and Peace*, 460.

outside, usually identified with the multi-national corporation. These are the causes of poverty, the removal of which
is the major burden of Judaeo-Christian revelation. The
anti-Americanism in liberation theology—and it is very
prevalent and basic—results from this kind of analysis. It is
due to presupposed intellectual causes.

> The capitalist form of organization of economic life is, I
> suggest, an innovation in human history which emanates
> from the cultural matrix of western Europe—particularly
> from those countries which broke with the Roman Catholic
> Church and which blessed the successful exercise of per-
> sonal gain and self-interest with the sanction of moral legiti-
> macy. Fragments of Europe were transplanted to other parts
> of the globe by European colonists. The fragment which
> took root in New England has flourished into the world's
> most powerful, dynamic, and expansionist capitalist metro-
> pole. The United States is the home of most of the world's
> largest multi-national corporations.[15]

Since the poor bear a moral, sinful burden in their oppression, this kind of analysis easily converts itself into a
crusade, born of an ethical superiority. The oft-repeated
accusation of "elitism" against liberation theology is not
without its point. The assumption is that ideological capitalism still exists in almost a pure form. This capitalism
clearly, in this view, possesses no relation to the solution of
the world's and Latin America's poverty problems.[16] The
belief is that a never-yet-existing socialism can do a better

[15] K. Levitt, "Multinational Corporations and the Third World",
IDOC-North America, no. 50 (February, 1973) 35.

[16] Cf. "The Church Right or Left?", North American Congress for
Latin America (September-October, 1978) 42–43; M. Novak, ed.,
Liberation North, Liberation South (Washington: American Enterprise
Institute, 1980); Jeane Kirkpatrick, "U.S. Security and Latin America",
Commentary (January, 1981).

job of production, distribution and protection of human rights, something the empirical records do not bear out in practice.[17]

Liberation theology, then, is not only an effort to incorporate classic Christian notions of original sin, redemption, hope and final beatitude in terms of political and economic movements in this world designed to effectuate a better, if not a perfect, worldly order; it is also a "spirituality".[18] Formerly, Christian spirituality made a relatively clear distinction between God and the world, whereas current liberation thought, as exemplified by writers like Segundo Galilea, seek to translate the transcendent realities into historical actions wherein God is said to be present to aid the poor in a direct political or economic sense. This spiritual aspect obviously is of some importance as it often leaves little space for liberation thought to speak of God in any other than political categories judged in a theory of "the poor", a theory not in itself ideologically totally neutral.

Father José Magaña, a Mexican Jesuit, wrote:

> . . . The conviction [exists] that the concrete, political, historical events of today are the place of fundamental encounter—a theological place—such that God not only

[17] Cf. P. Johnson, "Has Capitalism a Future?", *Wall Street Journal* (September 29, 1978); M. Novak, "In Defence of Democratic Capitalism", *Worldview* (July/August, 1977) 9–12; Irving Kristol, *Two Cheers for Capitalism* (New York: Basic Books, 1978); M. Novak, ed. *The Denigration of Capitalism* (Washington: American Enterprise Institute, 1979).

[18] Cf. Segundo Galilea, "Liberation as an Encounter with Politics and Contemplation", in *The Mystical and Political Dimension of the Christian Faith*, ed. Geffré/Gutierrez (New York: Herder and Herder, 1974) 19–33.

speaks above the Latin American man but from his geo-
graphy, from the facts and questions received from the
people—profound and silent. . . . If the soul and justice are
inseparable and if they ought to go out into practice necessarily, we then have politics. If it is not the only way of liberation, it is still the major evangelical experience of the
Christian today.[19]

Most of such thinking would not deny the transcendence
of God nor the need of grace, of divine help in the sense of
St. Paul. On the other hand, it would appear almost as if
God's will could be read from history, even though God's
will is strictly speaking unknown to us this way.[20] The
point to emphasize, however, is that politics in this model
has again taken on a religious enthusiasm and earnestness,
a kind of divine assurance that it has been the effort of
modern thought, including Christian thought, to deny to
it. This will mean in practice dealing with political and
economic questions as if they were directly religious ones.
This has the effect of converting politics and economics
back into a kind of morality that no longer tolerates the
kind of autonomy once thought necessary to their proper
functioning, the kind that actually seems best designed to
relieve the very poor.

Liberation theology, thus, can recommend itself to us as
an awakening in Latin America to its plight, to the condition of its poor. Few, if any, religious or ideological or
political movements would count this realization as a loss.
Moreover, it is undoubtedly true that political and economic attitudes, ideas and institutions do relate directly to

[19] José Magaña, "*Ejercicios como Espiritualidad de Liberación*", *Manresa*
(January–May, 1976) 13, 17.

[20] Cf. J. Laishley, "The Theology of Liberation", *The Way*, London
(April, 1978) 128–40.

how this poverty is to be best confronted. Clearly, liberation theology admits that in the past certain ways of conceiving Christianity itself may have been contributory to this current situation. Furthermore, this theology maintains that a cause exists for the evils in Latin America, and there is a logic and a rationale for action to remove them. The assumption that these analyses and programs are directly related to the proper way to read Scripture, to the way to conceive God and our relation to him, however, can be separated from the earnestness of the concern. It can also be doubted if the liberation way is the only way to read a religious concern for the actual poor.

The claim that there is a clear and proper analysis in this theology, valid on its own grounds as it interprets the "science" of radical sociology, surely allows too little room for alternative methods and ways. Undoubtedly, the danger of liberation theology is to make its analysis the only one, to fail to see the dangerous tendencies contained in its own system. The question is whether in the name of something quite laudable, a whole continent is not being led to commit itself to a system in which the presumed elimination of poverty will rather result in the elimination of freedom, with only a minimal attack on poverty. Such a liberation would be ironical indeed, especially in the name of God.

CHAPTER III

WHERE LIBERATION
THEOLOGIES LEAD

Ours is at the moment the most rational of all religions.

–G. K. Chesterton, The Thing: Why Am I a Catholic? *(New York: Dodd, Mead, 1930) 192.*

Theologians are men-women who "speak about God". As a punishment for my sins, I have been constrained in recent weeks to spend a considerable amount of time with these folk. I discovered a lot of them would sooner speak about anything else but God.

. . . [Thus we have what is] called "political theology" or "liberation theology" or "prophetic theology". It has nothing to do with God and much to do with denouncing people because they are Americans (especially citizens of the "northern hemisphere") and (especially if the theologian happens to be Catholic) with denouncing Church authority—an activity which is now about as original and as courageous as popping away at the ducks in the old galleries at Riverside.

–Father Andrew Greeley, "Political Liberation Theology for the Masses", The Presbyterian Layman *(November, 1977).*

When the political theologian of Europe requires Latin Americans to put forward a project for a socialist society which will guarantee in advance that the evident defects of known socialist systems will be avoided, why do we not demand of Christ also that before telling a sick man that he will be cured . . . he should give a guarantee that that cure will not be followed by even greater illnesses?

Historical sensibility to hunger and illiteracy, for example, calls for a society where competition and profit will not be the law and where the provision of basic food and culture to an underdeveloped people will be regarded as a liberation.

–Juan Luis Segundo, "Capitalism-Socialism", The Mystical and Political Dimension of the Christian Faith, *ed. by Geffré/Gutierrez (New York: Herder and Herder, 1974) 120–21.*

Rudolf Augstein, the editor of the German journal *Der Spiegel*, recently and belatedly discovered that many professedly Christian theologians and intellectuals do not in fact teach or profess what the Church has traditionally maintained on a number of basic points. This German innocence and surprise can, doubtless, be excused, though others besides German journalists wonder about it also. Nevertheless, "the most rational of the religions" has suddenly seemed to be overtaken by a kind of bewildering intellectual chaos, one that cannot but have profound political consequences. The relation between political change and intellectual vision is by no means a new problem. Professor Hans Schmidt has traced the relation of political forms and the concept of Christ in various ages to see how they were related.[1] Indeed, in a broader context, it can be argued that fundamental changes within the religious concepts and expectations of the great faiths—Hinduism, Confucianism, Judaism, Islam, Buddhism, and especially Roman Christianity—constitute the main causes of instability in the public order, This means that judges, presidents, and prime ministers, as well as dictators, and commissars, would do well to be briefed daily in theology as in economics and foreign affairs. Iran, if not Nicaragua and El Salvador, has recently taught this lesson vividly.

Ever since Ananias and Sapphira dropped dead because they kept some of the revenue of a dubious land deal in the Acts of the Apostles, Christians have been bickering and arguing about what Christianity means. The cynics of history, of course, have claimed that these controversies were mere abstractions and senseless disputes. But in truth, they almost invariably touched something basic about how

[1] Hans Schmidt, "Politics and Christology: Historical Background", *Concilium*, no. 36 (New York: Paulist Press, 1968) 72–84.

human life and its destiny ought to be conceived. This is why we can legitimately wonder why things exist or do not, why they exist in one way rather than another. And we discover that these reasons more often than not depend upon a slight nuance or change in religious definition. The Church, to its credit or infamy, has historically been acutely aware of the narrowness of what separates sanity and insanity, health and moral disease.

The early Church, to recall, was full of heresies, such as Gnosticism, Arianism, Monophysitism, Nestorianism, Manicheanism, Donatism, Docetism, Semi-Arianism and Pelagianism to but begin. How the Church was none of these very often popular movements is one of the great intellectual dramas of history. In the Middle Ages, there were Begards and Beguines, the Catharists, the Albigensians and the Spiritual Franciscans, whom Chesterton once remarked were not unlike the modern communists. We saw the Quietists and the Diggers, the Levellers and the Jansenists, Febronians, Erastians, and even "Old Catholics" in the more modern period. Thus, it should come as no ultimate shock that today there are Christian Marxists, Christian Maoists, Christian Trotskyites, Christian Socialists, and Christian Castroites. At times, it must seem that Christianity is able to embrace just about anything that comes on the political scene.

Yet, as the German Jesuit theologian, Karl Rahner, said in his essay "On Heresy", Christianity instinctively wants to confront ideas and movements at variance with itself, especially if these have, as does Marxism, some basically Christian overtones in their original mixture. And it would be highly unlikely if some Christians, at least, were not attracted by the most pervasive ideologies of their times.[2]

[2] Karl Rahner, *On Heresy* (Montreal: Palm Publishers, 1964).

On the other hand, Christianity does have a stable content, serious deviation from which does change how a person or a people may act in the world. And while politics is incompetent in the area of religious truths, still the public order is immediately affected by the status of religion among its professed believers.

Thus, if significant numbers of Christian leaders or peoples can be converted to Marxism or one of its variants, or even if they merely decide it is just another social option, as it is often called, then we are bound to take another look at their politics to see how they decide to act in a socially significant fashion. The consequences and possibility of such a change have been commented upon in the past. John Henry Newman, the great English cardinal and writer of the 19th century, in the conclusion to his monumental study, *The Arians of the Fourth Century*, wrote:

> And so of the present perils, with which our branch of the Church is beset, as they bear a marked resemblance to those of the fourth century, so are the lessons, which we gain from that ancient time, especially cheery and edifying to Christians of the present day. Then as now, there is the prospect, and partly present in the Church, of an Heretical Power enthralling it, exerting a varied influence and a usurped claim in the appointing of her functionaries, and interfering with the management of her internal affairs. . . .[3]

Newman went on to find comfort in the ability of ecclesiastical authorities to hold their own against deviations in their own ranks.

Nevertheless, as the state influence on episcopal appointments in Eastern Europe and the various radical priests in

[3] John Henry Newman, *The Arians of the Fourth Century* (London: Longmans, 1908, 1st ed. 1833) 393–94.

Latin America suggest, many objective minds are beginning to wonder if this danger of a new heretical power
"enthralling" itself into the heart of the Church is not
becoming a reality. Even some Marxist theoreticians are
wondering if their historical opposition to religion might
not best be dropped to entice this power to their side. There
is no doubt, indeed, that in more and more seminaries, various brands of political and liberation theologies are being
taught as quasi-house doctrines. As I have often remarked
previously, twenty years ago, young army officers and
Roman Catholic seminarians were among the most difficult to convert to a Marxist orientation, while today they
are often perhaps the easiest in many parts of the world,
ironically in mostly those areas wherein Marxists do *not*
officially control the state.

Interestingly too in this regard, since so much liberation
thought deals with christology—that is, who was Christ?
—and the civil power, we do well to remember that these
same Arians of whom Newman wrote were concerned to
demote the divinity of Christ. And they did control
many Church offices, while supporting the current secular
power. Jean Guitton, the French philosopher, made these
pertinent remarks in this context:

> The Arian crisis is no doubt the most remarkable from
> both the dogmatic and political point of view. It could be
> called eminently theologico-political: it introduced an era in
> which theology and politics will always be more or less
> closely linked.
> Toward the year 380, the Church barely missed turning
> semi-Arian overnight. The mystery of the Incarnation was
> being put in question. . . . Christ was merely this super-
> man, this saint, this "chief of mystics" who ought to be
> taken for the "dim goal of evolution".

> . . . I should add that Arianism, which began as a theo-
> logical hypothesis and a plausible system, did in the end
> become established state doctrine. . . . Perhaps it was more
> liable than other doctrines to lead to Caesaro-Papism, or at
> least to the confusion of the spiritual and the temporal.
> Reducing Christ to the proportions of man, it was in har-
> mony with the hidden desires of worldly power. And it was
> easily put to use.[4]

The great danger or temptation of liberation thought,
paradoxically, lies apparently along such lines—in its use of
christology—in its being itself used by a certain kind of
state.

Anyone who follows liberation thought realizes that it is
directly related to recent more radical theological controversies. However much liberation theology appears to
be an indigenous South American product, it is inevitably
reflective of the general cultural climate of the West. While
the Third World may have some cohesion, still the African
and Asian do not speak like the Latin American, except,
significantly, when each speaks in those terms wherein a
common western ideology is employed. The major intellectual phenomenon after World War II in Europe centered around what is called "existentialism" with a kind of
revival of humanism in its light. This was a philosophical
movement itself reacting against the totalitarianism of the
30s and the consequences of mass armies and societies.
Behind it there was also a struggle against the imper-
sonalism of liberalism and the collectivism implicit in the
Hegelian tradition.

Existentialism, consequently, deprecated the public order
to emphasize personal relationships, doubt, anguish, subjec-

---

[4] Jean Guitton, *Great Heresies and Church Councils* (New York: Harper,
1965) 21, 95.

tive values and personal commitment. "I-Thou"—a phrase the Jewish philosopher Martin Buber popularized from Feuerbach, Marx's predecessor—became the catchword of a generation of thinkers who realized the sovereign individual of the classical tradition was nothing without otherness. In large part, the movements that have followed and reacted to this individualist reality–there are atheist and Christian advocates–have tended to stress the corporate and public rather than the private and subjective which latter have often become viewed as inimical to human well-being, whereas they originally were seen in modern thought as its main promoter.

The next pertinent movement was that of the so-called "death of God" theology or "secularization" theology, during the middle fifties and early sixties. Earlier post-war theology, more open perhaps, had tried to stress the positive notion of the "terrestrial realities". Such "death of God" positions, however, became notorious for wondering about such recondite things as "How to be a Christian in a godless world?" Nietzsche and modern science were said, almost without argument, to have killed the religious God by defining reality through scientific methodology in such a manner that nothing was left over for God to be or do. For a time, "atheist Christians" were the curious vogue, while secularized Christianity meant transcendence was no longer important because we could supposedly now answer for ourselves all the classic questions thought once to be the exclusive province of religion—even problems of life, death, and human order. The "deification" of man that had been implicit in the modern project at least since the Enlightenment seemed at hand. Vatican II, in a way, was designed to confront and evaluate these theologies which came mainly from the experience of the developed world and the powerful presence of science.

Suddenly, however, another theology was discovered during the late 60s and early 70s that practically inverted the old atheism. There had been a long tradition of "civil religion" since Roman times. But everything in the modern era seemed against this tradition. The "separation of church and state", so much discussed in Vatican II, began to appear obsolete almost immediately after the Council. Were not after all the early Christians considered to be "atheists" by the Romans because they doubted all the gods of the Pantheon?

Then, the ecologists came along to discover that Christianity had "secularized" nature, something the Death-of-God school had been pointing to as a virtue. But the Christians cut down the sacred groves and thereby allowed nature to be "exploited". This curious Marxist word came to take on all the pejorative overtones once attributed to original sin. The humanizing of nature was destroying it. As a result, Christianity found itself attacked for being at the origins of science and technology, now seen as the cause of our evils, whereas for the previous three hundred years, religion had been accused of being against science in the rationalist scheme of things. Marxism from this angle often found itself on the side of Christianity in holding for the value of the world found in science and technology.

This controversy, variously described as ecology or the "limits of growth", after a notoriously biased pseudo-study by the Club of Rome, was behind the approaches that came to dominate Third World discussions. One maintained that industrial society was at fault, its size, ethos, progress. Mankind could be saved only by austerity and the social reorganization of its wants. This was something to which certain strands of religion seemed to gravitate much too readily. Did not religion preach mortification and were not the rich really the big spenders? When it was discovered by naive statisticians that six percent of the world's population consumed forty percent of its resources, the case seemed open and shut to the unreflective who never understood what "resources" might mean, or whether such "resources" might ever have existed without the productivity of the six percent.

Herman Kahn's *The Next 200 Years* seemed like a voice in the wilderness. Yet such a voice was disturbingly in the air for all who wanted to believe that we were about to disappear tomorrow morning. Moreover, Norman Macrae's sober warning that if this same six percent stopped their producing and consuming, the poor two-thirds of the world would be just that much closer to starvation and destitution, seemed merely incomprehensible. The productivity of the upper one-third of the productive nations alone was what gave hope to the other two-thirds.[5] However, the Third World itself suddenly woke up to the fact that they were the first ones proposed to be sacrificed to these same supposed "limits of growth". International congresses soon echoed the charge that the ecological enthusiasm of the rich was but a plot to keep the poor poor.

Thus, in such a context, a third look at a tired old Marxism, whose productivity record was comparatively as miserable as it was, seemed to many to be quite logical. Did it not preach "exploitation" of the poor by the rich as the cause of their ills? Could not its simple and easy to understand theory explain all essential facts? Did it not advocate the strong state everyone in the Third World seemed

[5] Cf. N. Macrae, "America's Third Century", *The Economist*, London (October 25, 1975); M. Novak, *The American Vision* (Washington, American Enterprise Institute, 1978); and Novak's forthcoming *A Theology of Democratic Capitalism*; see also R. Heckel, essay no. 14, below.

to be looking to justify? What was needed was "redistribution", the old socialist panacea, an idea that even reap-
peared in a sophisticated form in Harvard Professor John
Rawls' *A Theory of Justice*. The normal drives and values
of the "people" were not at fault as the ecologists argued
but rather political and economic structures conveniently
lumped together under the hated "capitalism". Theologians suddenly revived a form of the almost diabolical
theory of collective guilt and baptized it as "sinful structures". All the modern economy needed was a proper
"re-ordering", a phrase that always seemed to have overtones of but one specific ideology, the Marxist one, however much some kinds of reordering might prove advisa-
ble. The Marxists were already missionaries for their belief
and the ecologists were not far behind, making one wonder again about their ultimate and respective theological
origins. Everyone apparently wanted to save mankind
either from itself or from present exploiting society.

The rise of the self-styled theologies of "hope", "revolution" and "politics" in Europe during the 60s and early
70s was formulated against such a background. For a time,
it appeared evident to the West that the way to assist the
poor peoples of the world would be for them to imitate, in
their own fashion to be sure, the patterns and processes of
growth that once took place in Europe, North America
and Japan. Indeed, the few countries that actually did this
seriously—South Korea, Taiwan, Singapore and Brazil
—were among the most rapidly growing in the world.
Probably one of the reasons these countries were attacked
so strongly was precisely due to their laboratory effect
against the worldwide socialist failures and assumptions. In
any case, economic development and political modernization theories abounded.

A kind of modernized international Marshall Plan was always in the background; a vast program of self-help was hopefully possible. Yet, the results of the various plans actually tried seemed more and more dubious. Almost inevitably and invariably, socialist economic models were chosen, usually on *a priori* ideological grounds stemming from the European education of many Third World leaders. And these plans usually insured, as P. T. Bauer has argued, a failure to develop quickly and normally.[6] Often, the major objective of newly formed Third World leadership was in fact merely to retain power, to control people who did not presuppose the values and ideas that motivated most development theories. This demanded evidently another kind of political theory.

The dogmatic theory that prosperity, the product of development, would lead to democracy became questionable. Theories such as those of David Apter in *The Politics of Modernization*, arguing that freedom would itself be the best foundation for prosperity, were rejected. The path to development seemed to require an absolute form of government to discipline the people and direct progress. Mao's China, almost the reverse of every conceivable liberal and humanitarian value, came to be praised by many Christians and liberal people on the grounds that there was order and a better life there. No wonder, then, on the 200th Anniversary of the Declaration of Independence, Daniel Moynihan wrote sadly in *The Public Interest* that only a couple of dozen democracies remained in the world community, even though all nations nominally called themselves by that

[6] P. T. Bauer, "Western Guilt and Third World Poverty", *Commentary* (January, 1976); T. W. Schultz, "The Economics of Being Poor", *Journal of Political Economy*, no. 4 (1980) 639–51; P. T. Bauer, "Breaking the Grip of Poverty". *Wall Street Journal* (April 18, 1979).

noble name. Democracy is a thing of the past, not the future. But then, almost as if to grant Moynihan's point, it was possible to mean by democracy a "collective freedom", something to be achieved only after the revolution. And it was possible to think this way in both Marxist and limits-of-growth traditions. Individual freedom became opposed to "public" freedom in these notions.

And so within this context, revolution and politics became popular in Christian circles. This reversed dramatically the previous trend which seemed to want to legitimize politics by withdrawing it from religious organization and practice. The older Christian tradition, particularly the Jesuit one that arose at the beginnings of the modern state in the 17th century, did have a theory of the right to change governments in extreme cases of misrule by resort to force. This theory was usually discussed under the heading of tyrannicide. In a sense, modern democratic methods of electing and changing political leaders grew out of a need to eliminate this sort of violent necessity. However, since modern constitutional democracy in a Marxist-type analysis at least could be looked upon as an exploitative superstructure, the old liberal values that guaranteed it were rejected. Thus, "gradualism", "compromise" and "development" became almost dirty words. Nothing could be done until existing structures were radically changed. Since this latter attitude prevented working with any present government, politics often consisted in preventing any governmental success except one with revolutionary control.

But such changes to improve things, it was next argued, the capitalists would never allow to happen in any case. Chile became a myth. Fidel Castro's armies roaming Africa "by invitation" were but getting rid of imperialists, aiding the legitimate revolutions. Meanwhile, in South America, revolution was advocated and even joined in by priests like Camilo Torres in Colombia, who was to become something of a martyr of the left. Theologians began to wonder if the machine gun could not somehow be sanctified, or at least justified. A theology of "revolution" had analysts like the Belgian priest Joseph Comblin who was for a long time stationed in Latin America. This was not the main line of the Latin American Church, of course, but such ideas gained respectability as a direct result of the supposed necessity to embrace socialism and reject developmentalism.

Meantime, in Germany, where many Latin American theologians had studied, a formal "political theology" was itself evolving with both Protestant and Catholic versions. Indeed, in this area, old-fashioned denominational lines are no longer as pertinent as the degree to which one accepts the new social theories about poverty. J. B. Metz, Jürgen Möltmann, Dorothy Sölle, among others, became prominant figures. "Political theology", as it was called, was by no means a new term. It was directly related to the Roman notion of civil religion, to "Christendom", to Rousseau's remarks on civil religion in the *Social Contract*, to Saint-Simon's "Essay on New Christianity", to the political theologies of the Catholic Restoration in the 19th century responding to the French Revolution, to Carlo Schmitt's efforts during Hitler's time to establish a public religious justification.

In the current German context, political theology is a reaction against humanism and existentialism, against what is called the "privatization" of faith and religion that leads men to be excessively concerned about salvation and personal holiness. This is argued against the background of modern industrial society and modern German metaphysics.

In this view, no Christian society has existed or can exist. On the other hand, formal religion should have an effect in the world. This must logically be a political one since that is what the world is about. And as values in religion are real and meant to affect men where they are, religion must free itself from every particular political form to be able to "criticize" what goes on in politics in the light of religion's objectives. This view, in theory at least, acknowledged the autonomy of politics. As Johannes Metz put it:

> In a pluralistic society, it cannot be the socio-critical attitude of the Church to proclaim one positive societal order as an absolute norm. It can only consist in effecting within the society a critical, liberating freedom. The Christian task here is not the elaboration of a system of social doctrine, but of social criticism. The Church is a particular institution in society, yet presents a universal claim; if this claim is not to be an ideology, it can only be formulated and urged as criticism.[7]

Such political theology tends to stress not how difficult it is to live in and support any existing society, but concentrates on all the defects and imperfections in the light of some utopian or future norm.

In more classical Christian theories, by comparison, there was not too much expectation that politics would yield overly much. Christians were given spiritual reserves and resources to suffer and endure what "had to be". Aquinas always advised law not to expect men to be perfect. The political theologies, on the other hand, arose out of a fear of compromising themselves with the realities

---

[7] J. B. Metz, "The Church and the World in the Light of a 'Political Theology' ", *The Theology of the World* (New York: Herder, 1969) 122–23. See the author's *Christianity and Politics* (Boston: St. Paul Editions, 1981).

and necessities of any *de facto* worldly order, so their critical force came down upon what was yet left to be done. In the older structure, bishops and popes were expected to realize the difficulties of political orders in particular and the human condition in general. Now, the political theologies were set apart from any more conservative appreciation of the difficulty of doing anything positive at all in this world. The older view expected a kind of practical paralysis when nothing but the perfect critical position was taken by religion.

Political theology, however, is not exactly identical with the Latin American intellectual movements. The background and thought patterns diverge. Germany is a most developed country. In a sense, it is a model of development, both in its own first industrial revolution under Bismarck when it imitated the British, in its World War I state-organized economy, with which Lenin was so impressed, and finally in its remarkable record after World War II. The German model has always tended to stress the use of the state combined with individual initiative and social security in a mutually supportive fashion. The Nazi experience, however, must always condition German thought about the dangers of the omnipotent state. This latter strain of thought especially seems lacking in Latin American revolutionary Christian thought.[8]

Political theology in a way rejected a compromise political philosophy or practice, one based on a more realistic view of what was possible. And it did this in the name

---

[8] Cf. F. L. Fiorenza, "Political Theology: An Historical Analysis", *Theology Digest* (Winter, 1977) 317–34; Jeane Kirkpatrick, "Dictatorships and Double Standards", essay no. 3, below; M. Dodson, "Prophetic Theory and Political Theory in Latin America", *Polity* (Spring, 1980) 358–408.

of a future that would presumably come to be. Thomas
Aquinas' view of politics—that we cannot expect too high
a level of virtue from most ordinary men in politics—
seemed to be strangely forgotten. The focal point became
not so much the present but the on-going history of men
who are not seeking a private salvation for themselves—
the only possible one for an Augustine—but something
more, something in the nature of a public order that would
justify and mediate their salvation. The notion of a "holy"
society was to be rejected verbally, yet the idea seemed
implicit.

One of the major tasks of political theology, then, was
not to allow Marxism the public world to itself. This
meant, paradoxically, that the denial of a specifically Christian politics tended to result in reuniting religion and politics in a new fashion, whereby their real objects involve the
same processes and ultimate goals. To be orthodox, of
course, political theology usually maintained the gratuity
of the Kingdom of God in an ultimate sense. This German-
oriented background served as a kind of justification and
position against which liberation theology found its intellectual content.

The Latin American versions of political theology were
deliberately called "liberation theologies". While the two
ideas are obviously similar, they are not exactly the same in
origin or emphasis. Alfredo Fierro's remarks are worth citing in this context:

> A similar [to Germany] turn toward politics soon ap-
> peared in Latin America. Its peculiar situation was a general
> one of inequality within a country and dependence vis-à-vis
> the outside world. This fostered a new kind of theological
> reflection cut off from the earlier dogmatics and essentially
> found in the process of liberation in connection with ex-

ploited peoples. This new theology was usually presented as
a "theology of liberation". It was rooted in the social context of Latin American Christians and their public *praxis* and
embodied as critical awareness of their faith. As such it was
fully autonomous and autochthonous, not merely a reflection of European theology.[9]

The distinctiveness and general importance of this Latin
American social thought are, in its own terms, to be measured by its practical effects. This would logically have a
criterion of its success from within history as well as a
judgment of religion about its performance.

Yet, as Fierro also noted, this newer theology does not
appear as original and as independent as it likes to pretend:

Historical materialism has been the overt or covert inter-
locutor of the most recent theology—that is to say, of the
theologies . . . which, by virtue of their clear involvement
in the realm of the *polis*, can be described as political
theologies. In some authors, however, acceptance of the
historical-materialist analysis of socio-economic relationships has moved to the forefront and decisively shaped their
theological position. That is the case of those theologies
that accept the fact of class conflict and the consequent need
to opt for some class.[10]

In this light, then, it is possible to judge the comparative
performance of this Latin American movement. The arguments for this newer system, its roots, and its ambitions
seem rather clear enough at this stage. Of course, it has not
really produced as yet, if it ever will, a viable political
power on the basis of which we can actually judge performance. However, there is perhaps another way to ascertain

[9] A. Fierro, *The Militant Gospel* (Maryknoll: Orbis, 1975) 15.
[10] Ibid., 16.

its value and validity. This would not only be to question the degree in which the classical doctrines and practices of Christianity remain themselves, but also to wonder if the analyses used actually conform to the professed goals better than other systems. In this sense, liberation thought seems strangely distant from the actual ambitions and dreams of the poor themselves, this in spite of its repeated insistence that the poor are the origins of its enthusiasm and analysis.

CHAPTER IV

THE LIBERATION PERPLEXITY:
INTENTIONS AND RESULTS

. . . Some Christians have come to see that man, his future, and transforma-
tion of the Earth, are primary concerns. . . . [Dietrich] Bonhoeffer [the famous
German theologian killed by the Nazis] was more a prophet than a theologian
of the new form of engagement: "We do not occupy ourselves with the world to
come, but with this world. What is spoken of in the Gospel as beyond this
world, we propose to locate in this world." In other words, the world is a pri-
mary (ultimate) concern.

—Ruben Alves, *"Theses for a Reconstruction of Theology"*, IDOC-North
America *(October 31, 1970) 13.*

Libertas Ecclesiae [The Liberty of the Church] . . . *has always implied*
a community, the Church, not to be identified with any transitory political
form. . . . Libertas Ecclesiae *meant that, whatever its positive legal guar-*
antees might be, the Church understood itself to have its own divine mission
to fulfill—a mission that set it apart as different from and ultimately independent
of, the world and the world-historical structures, civil and cultural.

—Heinrich Rommen, *"The Church and Human Rights,"* Modern Catholic
Thinkers, *ed. A. R. Caponigri (New York: Harper Torchbooks, 1960)*
vol. 2, 392.

How ought liberation theology to be judged then? Fun-
damentally, I think, the only just evaluation is that we have
here a world view with much heart and very little real
hardheadedness about the world. Not only is the road to
hell paved with good intentions, but even more so is
the road to utopia. Undoubtedly, the most difficult thing
about the human condition is the agonizing dichotomy
between dreams of betterment which we can earnestly
conceive and the actual programs to achieve them, with the
empirical results we achieve when we finally have the

power to do what we conceive. This is so because there is a structure to life, laws of the human being that remain even in their breach. Experience itself limits our visions, and this is the best thing that can happen to many of our visions. Aquinas' instinct from Aristotle that a small error in the beginning would lead to a huge error in the end was meant to teach us that we cannot afford to neglect the import of ideas, no matter how small or unimportant they might seem initially.

Many American and European intellectuals and clerics have decided—and it is that, a "choice", not a necessity—that this seemingly novel liberation critique of the ills of the Third World, even though there are others perhaps more cogent, is basically valid. Thus, these, along with various token Marxist professors now featured regularly in American university faculties—these latter are not yet in full control as they are in too many western European faculties—conceive it their sacred mission to advocate that no more missionaries should be sent south until they are first converted to this new ethic. Better yet, they are often advised to stay at home and preach in their own houses. The structural analysis of liberation thought, as we have suggested, puts most of the faults and sins in the First World, especially in the United States. Logically, this means that there is really no drama in the confrontation of "good" and "evil" in Latin America anyhow, since the causes of both lie elsewhere. Paradoxically, liberation thought again makes South America theoretically insignificant since it claims that the real fault is in the North. This is happening at a very time when so-called neo-capitalism makes the Southern Hemisphere more and more important.

There are many sources for a "liberation" analysis of American and South American society.[1] Here, an attempt is made to inflict the so-called "Third World guilt" on the consciences of the developed countries. This is seen as a methodology to change their structures; it is argued in the name of a kind of social science. The Latin American hierarchy in general, evidently, has not accepted the ideological background of this sort of analysis. Rather it has taken a more pragmatic, human-rights, common-good position that is free to criticize, while recognizing the dangers of greater evils and the difficulties of doing anything at all.[2]

Furthermore, the vast intellectual effort to come to terms with Marxism as the main way to help the poor is not wholly unexpected.[3] There is probably no task so crucial for the world's well-being than the slow or, preferably, rapid evolution within Marxism to something with which

[1] Cf. J. Holland, "Marxian Class Analysis in American Society Today", *Theology in America* (Maryknoll; Orbis, 1976) 317–28; Fathers E. Toland, M.M., T. Fenton, M.M., and L. McCulloch, M.M. "World Justice and Peace: A Radical Analysis for American Christians", *IDOC-North America* (Summer, 1973) 1–8; in Europe, Father Giulio Girardi serves a similar function, cf. his "Christianity and the Class Struggle", *IDOC-North America* (November 14, 1970) 5–18, and his *Christianesimo, Liberazione Umana, Lotta di Classe* (Assisi: Citadella, 1972); A. F. McGovern, *Marxism: An American Christian Perspective* (Maryknoll: Orbis, 1980); P. Lernoux, *Cry of the People* (New York: Doubleday, 1980).

[2] Cf. Bishops of Argentina, "National Security vs. Individual Rights", *Origins* (June 2, 1977); the results of the III Episcopal Conference of the Latin American Bishops in Puebla, Mexico, in 1979 also are a basic source to see where the bishops stand on most of these questions. See document no. 2, below.

[3] Cf. R. Coste, *Analyse marxiste et foi chrétien* (Paris, 1976).

we can live more comfortably and humanely. The hostility towards, or at least avoidance by liberation theology, of the kind of thought represented by Alexander Solzhenitsyn and the Russian and East European dissidents over the precise Christian evaluation of Marxism is probably the most important controversy in this area. In so many words, if a Solzhenitsyn is right, liberation theology is disastrously wrong in many of its premises and perspectives. Undoubtedly the arrival of a Polish pope in the Vatican has had a welcome and powerful effect on many of the extremes of liberation thought in regard to its Marxist and socialist orientations. What the liberation school and a Solzhenitsyn do share, however, and this is important, is a strong critique of the West for many of its moral failures and positions. Yet, the main failure that Solzhenitsyn sees in the West seems to be precisely the toleration of those views most advocated as the solution for South American ills by the liberation schools.

Writing in 1971, Edward J. Williams at the University of Arizona argued that the effects of the changes in the Latin American Church to that time, and hence their significance for policy, had to do with the strengthening of the secular nation-state:

> The most salient characteristic of the present polity-religion equation in Latin America highlights the increasing cogency of Latin American Catholicism's role as legitimizing nation-builder. As the religion has updated and re-defined itself, it has emphasized elements that contribute to the emergence of the secular nation-state. . . . Secular reforms issuing from secularizing national governments elicit the blessing of Church and religion as both necessary and legitimate. . . . Latin American Catholicism legitimizes the secular nation-state by repudiating its traditional totalistic

orientations. By redefining itself as a minority creed and positing the essential secularity of contemporary society, Latin American enthusiasm propels the secular nation-state into a position of primacy.[4]

Such an analysis strikes one today as almost totally missing the point of the direction of liberation theology in Latin America, which is totalistic and tending to transform rather the secular into a quasi-religious element of sacral history, a trend probably not so clear in 1971. The liberal, secular nation-state, in a sense, hardly exists for liberation theology, as it did not for classical socialism. The secular state seen in terms of the national security state is, indeed, seen as the main thing to be eliminated.

However, if we are to estimate the main origins of the intellectual confusions that ground and presumptively justify liberation thought, insofar as it is not merely a growth of the central line of Catholic social doctrine, which it does not claim to be, we shall have to look at what it means by a growing "gap" between rich and poor, at its analysis of profit and incentive, at its empirical perception of modern economic institutions, and most importantly at its use of the idea of the poor. The basic view that shall be argued here is that liberation theology is, in its essential outlines, itself a cause of continued underdevelopment, that its eventual growth and success would institutionalize in Latin America a life of low-level socialist poverty enforced by a rigid party-military discipline in control of economic enterprise and the movement of peoples.

The danger for the Catholic Church resulting from this kind of thought is, moreover, very great, as it risks being

[4] Edward J. Williams, *The Emergence of the Secular Nation-State and Latin American Catholicism*, Tucson, Arizona, University of Arizona, Research Paper no. 7 (1971) 21–22.

identified again with an authoritarian or totalitarian movement. No one argues that the present authoritarian regimes are paragons of virtue or justice. But there are degrees of evil and corruption which any realistic politics or religion must keep in mind. It is clear that the present situation has elements that need changing. But it is dubious whether the models and notions proposed in liberation thought are at all better in the long run. And to maintain that something is not better than the present is not necessarily to say that the present situation is ideal. This is why classical political philosophy insisted on treating all forms of possible government, arranging them in an order of hierarchical principle and practical performance.

Perhaps some indication of the validity of these hesitations about the potential efficacy of the socialist-orientated liberation approaches can be seen if we refer to a recent essay in *The Economist* of London:

In 1972–78 the 240m people of the five ASEAN countries (Thailand, Malaysia, Singapore, Indonesia and the Philippines) plus the 60m people of three neighbours (Taiwan, Hongkong, South Korea) have achieved between 6% and 11% average annual growth in national gnp; this is now the only group of countries in the world in which real gnp is doubling every 7–12 years. It is nonsense to say the benefits are going only to the rich. In all these eight countries life expectancy is lengthening dramatically, in most of them mugging rates and drug-trafficking have been cut, in each the sense of national and regional self-confidence is growing. . . . In the genuinely free elections which none of these eight peoples is allowed to have, the proportion who would freely vote communist is now probably not much more than it is in Glasgow, certainly much less than it is in Milan. . . . The purely economic burdens on the ordinary man from corruption in these governments is less than the burden on him from bureaucracy in countries which take much more from him than the 15% of national income in taxes, and then do not get the economic growth.

... If ASEAN continues to double its gnp each decade, the rich capitalist one-quarter of the world will soon center on three groups with 200–250m people each (the United States, EEC, ASEAN), plus one group (Japan) with half that number. Of the coming world's big four, ASEAN has the most valuable recent experience in achieving economic policies that work, together with political set-ups that are just tolerable, in the mine-strewn ideological background over which the poor three-quarters of the world are soon to advance.[5]

With even China recently tending to wonder if some imitation of the Japanese model is not a better way for it to go, this kind of an analysis becomes even more striking.

In the context of Latin America, moreover, it is most important to come to terms with this more progressive kind of development, for it belies graphically the seemingly iron-clad argument that poor nations cannot become rapidly richer. Furthermore, it argues against the idea that socialism is the best method for the poor countries to use. The one Latin American nation that has been developing as rapidly as the ASEAN ones is probably the most important one, Brazil. And it is interesting to note the double standard applied to it in liberation literature about its successes and failures as compared to those of socialist systems.[6] In a real sense, the Latin American Left has a vested interest in seeing to it that Brazil fails to become the world power it seems to have every potential of becoming.

[5] See *The Economist*, London (May 13, 1978); N. Macrae, "Must Japan Slow", *The Economist*, Survey (February 23, 1980).

[6] Cf. D. Moynihan, "The United States in Opposition", *Commentary* (March, 1975) 31–44.

Actually, the total number of liberation theologians is not particularly large. The strength of the liberation system seems to be overly argued in terms drawn largely from European Marxist sources. An example of this is perhaps the use of the so-called "gap" theory, one popular in many even non-socialist sources, one with a definite historical origin. Again, the argument ought not to be conceived as being over which group has greater sympathy for the poor. Rather it is over what kind of analysis really applies to the situation.[7]

Is the "gap" between rich and poor growing every day? And if it is, does that mean the poor are getting "poorer"? This thesis is an old one. Reaction to it goes back to Edouard Bernstein and the revisionists, who found that European workers in the 19th century were not in fact getting poorer, but richer. Lenin's *Imperialism*, whose inspiration comes largely from an English economist on this point, sought to save the theory by arguing that the "workers" in the colonies were getting poorer instead of the workers in Europe. However, the idea that an increasing gap means that the poor are actually getting poorer is, of course, quite unclear and illogical. Growth proceeds at different rates at different times. The idea of linear growth that so often dominates population and development studies needs great circumspection. If the poor are getting poorer, we have some explaining to do in the light of a statement such as this:

> Latin America's growth rate in 1973 was 7.4 per cent, thus giving an average of 6.8 per cent for the period of the

[7] Cf. "The Moving Frontier", *The Economist*, London, Survey (September 2, 1972); "On, Brazil", *The Economist*, Survey (August 4, 1979).

present decade which has so far elapsed. The rise in per capita income in the same year was 4.5 per cent, which is quite a high figure considering the big population increases recorded for the region as a whole.[8]

We could say, to be sure, that the rich are getting all of this so it is a structural problem. But there is no real evidence that the poor are themselves getting objectively poorer in any place on earth except in societies with seriously mismanaged or overly ideological institutions. Usually, a resort to a "gap" explanation is necessary to uphold the thesis that the poor are getting poorer, an *a priori* thesis that arises from other sources than evidence. Furthermore, the gap thesis does not even begin to approach the problem of whether an egalitarian and controlled distribution system can provide motives for any growth at all.

For the most part, then, everyone is getting richer, even the so-called Fourth World, but at widely differing rates. And these rates usually follow a pattern such that a country basing itself on work and enterprise usually achieves a higher growth rate. The ASEAN example clearly suggests that the poor can become richer and relatively quickly, something that Japan and Germany proved twice each in modern times, but only if they imitate the proper way and adapt to their own situation the ideas and institutions that cause growth. Furthermore, as Herman Kahn argued in his *The Next 200 Years*,

. . . by the year 2000 perhaps a quarter of mankind will live in emerging post-industrial societies and more than two-thirds will have passed the levels of $1000 per capita.

[8] Enrique V. Iglesias, "Latin America and the Creation of the New World Order", *Economic Bulletin for Latin America*, U.N., no. 1 and no. 2 (1974) 1.

By the end of the 21st century almost all societies should have a GNP per capita greater than $2000 and be entering some form of post-industrial culture. The task is not to see that these societies proceed along the same path as Europe, North America and Japan, but rather that each should find its own way. However, even in the year 2100 there may be large income gaps. Today per capita GNP ranges from about $100 to $10,000, and it would not at all surprise us if the range at the end of the 21st century were still rather large, perhaps from a basic minimum of a few thousand dollars to a maximum of ten to 20 times greater.

As far as we can tell, arithmetic differences (as opposed to ratios) in per capita product will generally increase for the next 100 years, with of course many exceptions. But this should not be disastrous either morally or politically since there are very few peasants, workers, or even businessmen in developing countries who care much about gaps (whether arithmetic or geometric), no matter how much intellectuals, academics, and some businessmen profess to. The major objective of most people is to increase their own safety and improve their own standard of living and their own capabilities. When they make comparisons, it is usually with others at their socioeconomic level or with those who have recently been at their own or a lower level.[9]

The "growing gap" theory and its implications, then, must be mostly rejected as a hypothesis, if it implies that the poor are getting poorer by some absolute standard. This is why the theory must present itself as psychological, that someone feels himself getting comparatively poorer.

[9] Herman Kahn, *The Next 200 Years* (New York: Morrow, 1976) 48–49. Ben Wattenberg makes this same kind of point in *The Real America* (New York: Capricorn, 1976); H. Kahn, *World Economic Development* (New York: Morrow, 1979).

But this is clearly a spiritual and not a factual problem, clearly at the roots of why Plato and Aristotle were so concerned with envy as a factor in politics.[10]

The next essential element of liberation thought holds that the rich are rich *because* they are exploiting the poorer nations. Again, this is a fundamental tenet of liberation thought, usually accepted as methodologically and empirically true. The recent remarks of Philip Scharper, editor of Orbis Books, prime publisher of liberation theology in English, a noted lay commentator, serve to illustrate how this notion is used.

> Gunnar Myrdal has estimated, for example, that United States corporations, directly or indirectly, control or decisively influence between 70 and 90 per cent of the raw materials of Latin America, and probably more than half of its industry, banking, commerce, and foreign trade. . . . [Development failed so that] the developed nations continued to grow at the expense of the underdeveloped. . . . The "have" nations are not about to change patterns of trade in order to benefit the "have-nots". . . . History seems to show . . . that effective altruism is seldom found in nations or groups possessing wealth and power.[11]

This latter idea of altruism would also be Augustine's and Reinhold Niebuhr's political realism. But in that case, all

---

[10] Cf. D. Vree, *On Synthesizing Marxism and Christianity* (New York: Wiley, 1976); cf. *Solzhenitsyn at Harvard* (Washington: Ethics and Public Policy Center, 1980).

[11] Philip Scharper, "Toward a Politicized Christianity", *The Commonweal* (June 16, 1978) 395. Cf. in this context, Irving Kristol's "Human Nature and Social Reform", *The Wall Street Journal* (September 18, 1978); N. Macrae, "The Brusque Recessional", *The Economist*, London, Survey (December 28, 1979).

groups would have to be included, including socialist and radical ones, so that it is unfair to imply that only American corporations have this tendency. However, this is an interesting example of a tendency found in much liberation thinking to apply an essential spiritual category (effective altruism) to particular institutions under fire for political purposes.

The core of the issue here, however, has to do with the idea that business and commerce necessarily "exploit" when they operate for a profit to do large-scale, worldwide business which would not exist without the profit incentive. This is the other side of the question of the nature of profits and incentives themselves, something many modern clerics and intellectuals are reluctant to understand. The following example might, perhaps, be illustrative of this point:

> "Every time the word 'profit' comes up in that room, you can feel it," the Rev. William J. Inderstrodt said . . . slowly clenching his fists as he stood outside the Economic Education Conference for Clergy. . . . "You can feel the tension."
>
> . . . "If you look at the preparation they get in the seminaries," said Edward L. Hamblin . . . "they don't have much insight on the economic sources which move society, if they are called upon to interpret these forces from the pulpit. The very basic elements we're talking about are how the market functions, and what the pay-offs are, like the creation of wealth. This group is particularly sensitive to the equity factor. . . ."
>
> "How are you going to deliver food to these people when agriculture is run on a profit basis?"[the Rev. John B. Ferra] asked.
>
> "To say food is for people and not for profit, would eventually preclude all of you from having food," coun-

tered Luther E. Stearns of the American Farm Bureau
Federation. . . .

"We never talk in the churches about incentives." [Mr.
Inderstrodt] said. . . . "Most business executives look at the
clergy as softheaded, and most clergy look at business
executives as less than used-car salesmen."[12]

The claim is often made, moreover, that business operates
differently in Latin America. But again the question must
be posed against the culture that accepts and limits its op-
erations. Business has probably recognized long before the
moralist or politician the complexity of dealing with governments or unions that demand bribes to continue any sort
of operation at all. Furthermore, the failure of Marxist-
socialist analysis to grasp the meaning of the profit incentive and its relation to freedom has long been noted.

Catholic social thought has traditionally articulated the
danger of abuse of profits, beginning with Leo XIII. But it
has always recognized their meaning and legitimacy, as
well as the close relationship they bear to incentive and the
capacity of the free person to act on the world. The essential point, then, is that profits do not represent automatically "exploitation". That is, they do not take away from
someone what is his. Rather they create something that is
new, that would never otherwise have existed. When they
fail to do this they are, properly speaking, abuses. Professor
P. T. Bauer put this issue well:

> Many of the assertions concerning western responsibility
> for poverty in the Third World express or reflect the belief
> that the prosperity of relatively well-to-do persons, groups,

[12] M. L. Wald, "Clergymen Get Short Courses in Economics", *The
New York Times* (June 21, 1978); cf. P. Johnson, "Capitalism's Futures",
Wall Street Journal (January 22, 1981).

> and societies is always achieved at the expense of the less well-off, i.e., that incomes are not generated by those who earn them, but are somehow extracted from others, so that economic activity is akin to a zero-sum game, in which the gains of some are always balanced by the loss of others. In fact, incomes (other than subsidies) are earned by the recipients for resources and services supplied, and are not acquired by depriving others of what they had.[13]

If this be basically true, as it seems to be, the whole basis of the exploitation analysis is undermined, and a truer picture of the world is open for consideration. This newer one would have a more proper place for incentive, abundance, growth, and alleviation of poverty in a system that demands not the struggle of class against class, as liberation thought insists, but rather the operative competition and intelligence of all, for an objective good, one called by the central line of Catholic social thought "the common good".

Norman Macrae has often and forcefully argued that one of the best institutions for the rapid transferal of skills, capital, and production to the Third World is the much criticized multi-national corporation.[14] Almost by instinct, liberation theology, which on this score betrays little of the famous 16th- and 17th-century Spanish Jesuit moral pragmatism at the advent of capitalism over the question of

[13] P. T. Bauer, "Western Guilt and Third World Poverty", *Commentary* (January, 1976) 36.

[14] Cf. Norman Macrae, "The Future of International Business", *The Economist*, Survey (January 20, 1972); "America's Third Century", *The Economist*, Survey (October 25, 1975). Cf. also Michael Novak's *The American Vision: An Essay on the Future of Democratic Capitalism* (Washington: American Enterprise Institute, 1978); I. Kristol, "No Cheers for the Profit Motive", *Wall Street Journal* (February 20, 1979).

usury, has zeroed in on this so-called sinful structure of the corporation as its main target. This has entailed a rejection of the famous and still worthy thesis of Jacques Maritain in his *Reflections on America* about how such economic institutions, imperfect as they might be, really work, guided by law and custom and public opinion.

John Kenneth Galbraith, never a full fan, has even found it necessary to say a few kind words of the multi-national corporation:

> If to be a part of the Third World is to be a hewer of wood and a supplier of food and natural produce, the United States and Canada are, by a wide margin, the first of the Third World countries and should vote accordingly in the United Nations.
>
> International trade always had to be defended against those who saw only its costs, never its advantages; who saw only the intrusions of foreign competition, never the resulting efficiency in supply or products or the reciprocal gains from greater exports. The multi-national corporation comes into existence when international trade consists of modern, technical, specialized or uniquely styled manufactured products. Accordingly, it should be defended as international trade was defended, for its contribution to efficiency in production and marketing, to living standards, and to reciprocal opportunities in other lands for the enterprises of the host country. . . .
>
> . . . Critics allege that multi-national corporations export jobs, capital, and technology. This is one of the few matters on which the multi-national enterprise has developed a defense. It holds that, in one way or another, it cares most about the home country and its labor force—these are its primary interests. It should hold more often than it does that, as it goes abroad, others from abroad should come in. The aggregate result is a more rapid spread of technology, a

better international division of labor, greater productivity, greater aggregate employment.[15]

Again, such observations serve as a corrective for the implicit theory which holds that because business in a foreign country produces and makes a profit, it only "takes" from that country and that the same or better level of development would be possible without it and its innovations.

The final and perhaps most serious defect of formal liberation thought is what is called its "manichean" tendency. This is a temptation to divide good and evil according to rich and poor. The whole exploitation analysis is open to this danger. The Brazilian-based Dominican François Lepargneur pointed out the problem:

> One can beautifully reinterpret the gospel as he wishes, but if he will remain honest, he will recognize that the construction of the Kingdom of God is founded essentially on personal conversion and not on an intellectual dialectics of force. And ideology, even if it present itself under the title of theology, which rests essentially on the accusation of someone else as the author of all evil, is not to be confounded with a viable interpretation of Christianity which is, in its very principle, an appeal to the conversion of him who receives the call of grace, of salvation. Otherwise, one does not speak of the same salvation, of the same God, of the same religion.[16]

[15] John Kenneth Galbraith, "The Defence of the Multinational Company", *The Harvard Business Review* (March-April, 1978) 85, 88, 89; cf. also S. Brennan and E. Molander, "Is the Ethics of Business Changing?". *The Harvard Business Review* (January-February, 1977) 57–71; T. J. Purcell, "Management and the 'Ethical' Investors", *Harvard Business Review* (September–October, 1979).

[16] François Lepargneur, "*Théologies de la liberation et théologie tout court*", *Nouvelle Revue Théologique*, Louvain (February, 1976) 167–68.

And this thesis of liberation theology, that it speaks for the poor who are implicitly the "good" against the rich who are "bad", this endeavor to see all through the eyes of the poor, needs further attention.

Fortunately, both Jacques Ellul and Hannah Arendt have called our attention to the erroneous and one-sided way "the poor" are used in modern thought. Ellul, the French Protestant sociologist-theologian, sharply pointed out in his *The Betrayal of the West*, how selective the precise denomination of the poor really has been. The poor become much too often, and in an unacknowledged way, those who conform to the theoretical exigencies of ideological demands, not those who really suffer for justice or poverty. This is usually seen in the selective way the poor are denominated in a given system. Poverty is used surprisingly often as a tool and ideological weapon for achieving a certain kind of society and that alone.[17]

Hannah Arendt, in her *On Revolution*, has reminded us of the curious connection between the radically different notions of the poor in the American and French Revolution. The intellectual significance of this is very important.[18] Essentially, she argued that the "passion for compassion" which dominates the discussion comes from the French Revolution, wherein essentially political and social questions were confused. The notion of poverty was transformed into part of a necessitarian program in the Hegelian

[17] Jacques Ellul, *The Betrayal of the West* (New York: Seabury, 1978) Chapter II, "The Truly Poor and the End of the Left", 87–146; cf. M. Krauss, "Social Democracies and Foreign Aid", *Wall Street Journal* (September 12, 1979).

[18] Hannah Arendt, "The Social Question", in her *On Revolution* (New York: Viking, 1965) 53–110.

tradition so that all revolutions were supposed necessarily to follow the path of the French Revolution. This path had to be built into any revolutionary project. Thus, the terror and poverty were logically joined together through an idea or tradition; they do not imply one another. "The poor" again became signs in such an analysis, tools for a societal process.

Hannah Arendt's observations are remarkable in the light of liberation theology's self-proclaimed priorities and values which place the poor at such a central point:

> In this stream of the poor, the element of irresistibility, which we found so intimately connected with the original meaning of the word "revolution", was embodied. . . . All rulership has its original and its most legitimate source in man's wish to emancipate himself from life's necessity, and men achieved such liberation by means of violence, by forcing others to bear the burdens of life for them. This was the core of slavery, and it is only the rise of technology, and not the rise of modern political ideas as such, which has refuted the old and terrible truth that only violence and rule over others could make some free.
>
> *Nothing we might say today could be more obsolete than to attempt to liberate mankind from poverty by political means; nothing could be more futile and more dangerous.* For the violence which occurs between men who are emancipated from necessity is different from, less terrifying, though often not less cruel, than the primordial violence with which man pits himself against necessity, and which appeared in the full daylight of political, historically recorded events for the first time in the modern age. The result was that necessity invaded the political realm, the only realm that can be truly free.
>
> The masses of the poor, this overwhelming majority of all men, whom the French Revolution called *les malheureux,*

whom it transformed into *les enragés*, only to desert them and let them fall back into the state of *les misérables*, as the nineteenth century called them, carried with them necessity, to which they had been subject as long as memory reaches, together with the violence that had always been used to overcome necessity. Both together, necessity and violence, made them appear irresistible. . . .[19]

What can be stressed from these remarks of Ellul and Arendt, then, is that the peculiar force and manner in which "the poor" are reiterated and used in most liberation theology have an intellectual structure closer to this French Revolutionary kind of analysis than to anything in Scripture or classic Catholic social thought. This is the ultimate root, too, of the otherwise inexplicable anti-Americanism in most liberation approaches. This is something, as Arendt suggested, that must go back to the basic differences between the French and American revolutions.[20] In this light, consequently, the theses on the growing "gap", on the necessity of violence, on profit, on the poor all flow from this intellectual background and explain why it is not able to take the more pragmatic—and more philosophical —avenues found in the American tradition, in much papal analysis, in Maritain, Kahn, Macrae, Bauer, and others who are looking also at real poverty and what relieves it.

Hans Urs von Balthasar, the noted Swiss theologian, suggested that this would be an appropriate attitude to take to liberation theology:

> I feel that the combined efforts of theology in the United States and Europe should also be directed toward helping the Latin American theology of liberation, which often becomes self-seeking and confused. I mean helping to clarify

[19] Ibid., 110. Italics added.   [20] Cf. ibid., 62–68.

it with a sympathetic understanding of its genuine claims. Teilhard de Chardin (the French Jesuit philosopher) saw the future of theology as supranational, global, but he did not recognize the concerns of liberation theology. We must include them in our theological thinking, but in doing so, we must show greater discernment than our South American brothers do. Usually, their analysis of the social situation is based impulsively on Marxist categories of "exploiting" and "exploited" countries. . . . The tragic situation is more complex and we must show them that.

. . . The exponents of this third (liberation) direction must learn—with all due regard to their justified claims— that the Kingdom of God cannot be coerced into existence by any amount of social or political effort. It remains the gift of God and of the returning Lord to a world that cannot perfect itself by its own efforts.[21]

These words of von Balthasar suggest why the movement of Christians Arising in Latin America is mostly an "impractical *praxis*". For it seems constantly to confuse the goal for a mere aid and means, while ignoring the real means available for the goal it does profess, the elimination of poverty. The ironies of the situation, of course, are many; but Latin America is now thinking of the United States and Europe, and these countries are thinking of it. How each thinks of the other remains the vital question for both. For it is still mostly what men think that determines what they shall endeavor to put into effect.

[21] Hans Urs von Balthasar, "Current Trends in Catholic Theology", *Communio* (Sprint, 1978) 84–85; see also essay no. 1, below.

CHAPTER V

PUEBLA AND ITS CONSEQUENCES

. . . When some 2000 years ago God sent his Son, he did not wait for human efforts to eliminate all kinds of injustices. Jesus came and began to share our human condition, its sufferings, and difficulties, even death, before transforming the daily life of the people.

—Pope John Paul II, to workers at Monterrey, Mexico (January 31, 1979).

The whole context of liberation theology, its tendencies, and its varied claims changed quite drastically by the time the Third Conference of Latin American Bishops finally opened in Puebla, Mexico, on January 27, 1979, after having been postponed twice because of the deaths of two popes. The election of John Paul II, a Pole, from a Marxist-controlled country, moreover, could not have provided a more graphic way to contrast the issues presented by the theories of development and society being promoted by various Christians in Latin America. With the hindsight provided by the new Holy Father's visits to Mexico, Brazil, Africa, the Philippines and Poland and the record of his performance in the papacy, it seems now possible to place the Latin American context in some proportion. At least at the religious level, there is now a pope quite willing and capable of attending to specifically theological aberrations, even though a good deal is left to be desired in analyzing just what it is that "develops".[1]

[1] See also the Holy Father's first Encyclical, *Redemptor Hominis* (St. Paul Editions, 1979). See also the author's commentary on this in *Homiletic and Pastoral Review* (October, 1979); cf. also John Paul II, *Dives in Misericordia* (St. Paul Editions, 1980); and *Laborem Exercens* (St. Paul Editions, 1981).

Generally speaking, liberation theology had been almost completely silent, to many even blindly so, about the very real oppression that existed outside the Latin American orbit, especially about that caused by Marxist regimes. All of the anguished and oftentimes implausible affirmations by Latin American apologists, that "Marxism" in theory was radically different from what actual Marxists did when they reached power, seemed less than defensible before this new pope, who seemed quite aware of the types of real oppression in fact existing in the world, more so than the proponents of this theology themselves.[2] Thus, such a movement, however varied it might be, could not but be placed on the defensive before a Roman pontiff who knew Marxism intimately, one who had lived and survived under it, yet a pontiff with an extraordinary intelligence and an even more charming and vigorous personality.[3] Before John Paul II, it was really quite difficult to think of anything more newsworthy than the firm orthodoxy he insisted upon.

[2] "This century has so far been a century of great calamities for man, of great devastations, not only material ones but also moral ones, indeed, perhaps above all, moral ones. Admittedly, it is not easy to compare one age or one century with another under this aspect, since that depends also on changing historical standards. Nevertheless, without applying these comparisons, one still cannot fail to see that this century has so far been one in which people have provided many injustices and sufferings for themselves." *Redemptor Hominis*, no. 17, p. 35.

[3] Cf. Leopold Tyrmand, "Poland, Marxism, and John Paul II", *The Wall Street Journal* (December 6, 1978) 18. These are the remarks of *Time* on the Polish visit: "Charisma was not the word to describe what had happened. Returning to his homeland for the first time since he was chosen Pope last October, Karol Wojtyla, John Paul II, stirred an outpouring of trust and affection that no political leader in today's world could hope to inspire, let alone command. . . ." "A Triumphal Return", *Time* (June 18, 1979) 28.

Before his arrival in Mexico, Latin American clerics were heard to claim that "the people" were with them. But after the Pope's visit, it was clear that this was mere rhetoric. The evident popularity of John Paul II served to require another kind of approach, if this movement were to survive, one, as it developed, which would maintain that he said nothing different from what the Latin American theorists had been saying all along. Yet, it was the honorable merit of John Paul II that his tack with the dissenting Latin American clerics was a thoroughly generous one, one full of wisdom and concern. He was not in principle out to drive people away. He made a serious theological effort to grant what could be granted within the confines of Christian orthodoxy to this pressing Latin mentality. At the same time, he sought to present a broad theological and spiritual canopy under which those who wished could both save face and reaffirm the basic Christian truths that seemed in jeopardy by certain positions proposed for the salvation of Latin America.

What did John Paul II, then, decide at Puebla? There were, not unexpectedly, two extreme views of John Paul's visit—one that he totally rejected Latin liberation thought, the other that he simply reconfirmed the Medellín tendencies. After the Holy Father's initial address in Mexico, *The New York Times* wrote a severely critical editorial about John Paul II—one intellectually most curious and self-revealing about the journal's own presuppositions. The Pope was said to have "spoken flatly" against a view which held that Scripture justifies political action. He was said to have restricted the role of religious men and women to prayer and traditional norms.

> It was a disappointing speech. A group of priests has announced disagreement with its message. Prayer alone,

they say, is not enough. The clergy must do more than create a spiritual climate for social reform. The Pope's stand directly contradicts that taken at the Latin American Bishops' Conference at Medellín ten years ago which gave impetus to a decade of activism.[4]

This is a "curious" editorial from this source since *The Times* now seemed to encourage clerical interference in politics, a position long criticized by liberal thought in other areas.[5] By setting up certain selected priests against the Pope as an editorial device, it seemed to give the impression that these were of equal value. Finally, the editorial gave no intimation of the precise kind of ideological presuppositions that the Pope might see behind the type of political and economic activism being promulgated in Latin America, an ideology *The Times* itself usually criticized in other contexts.

Columnist Coleman McCarthy echoed this kind of analysis. Writing in the *Washington Post*, McCarthy charged that ". . . in aligning his authority with the right wing of the Latin American Church, the Pope dampens the vibrant spirit of economic and political reform begun ten years ago. . . ."[6] John Paul II was thus pictured in some of the American press as hostile to the poor and the causes that might help them. As the Pope continued to speak and the crowds coming to see him continued to grow, it became clear that the kind of criticism espoused by *The Times* and Coleman McCarthy was quite incorrect. The poor loved the Pope. Moreover, this position failed to understand

[4] Editorial, "A Voice Against Liberation Theology", *The New York Times* (January 30, 1979) D18.

[5] See Letters to Editor in document no. 6, below.

[6] Coleman McCarthy, "Papal Blandness", *The Washington Post* (February 3, 1979) A19.

what religion is as well as the content of the view the Pope was criticizing. No attempt was made to recognize that, however bad the situation in Latin America might be, it could be worse if, in addition to poverty and various autocracies and oligarchies, there was added a complete totalitarian system.

Midway in the Pope's visit, then, many liberal writers and reporters began to argue that the Pope was merely slapping the hands of a few extremists of the liberation movement. The Pope himself, furthermore, was moved by the crowds to modify his stand, so he made it clear that the poor have a cause. But in fact, he even more insisted that they have souls and faith. The reporters of *The New York Times*, writing from Mexico itself, began to tone down somewhat the extreme of their journal's editorial. "Evangelism is still widely interpreted as a process of winning converts to the Church," Kenneth Briggs wrote.

> But beginning with Paul VI, the term has been given broader meaning, underscoring the need to save people from tyranny and brutality in addition to saving their souls. . . . The difficulty with this agenda—and with the Pope's similar guidelines—is the paucity of strategies for achieving the stated aims. In the last speech in Mexico, for example, the Pope, appealing before a group of workers for a new world order, said it was their "fundamental human right freely to create organizations to defend and promote their interests."
>
> The speech lacked specifics as to how this could be achieved, but it contrasted with his admonitions to priests to steer clear of politics. . . .[7]

---

[7] Kenneth Briggs, "John Paul II Has No Easy Answers for Latin America", *The New York Times* (February 4, 1979) E7.

There is no hint here, of course, of the classic Catholic social doctrine about the difference between laity and clergy in the very matter of social and political organization, not a hint about the difference between principle and application of principle, nor a realization of the consequences of not allowing such distinction.

George Vecsey also wrote:

> The 218 bishops have been meeting here since January 28, when Pope John Paul II addressed them in a speech that was interpreted by some as warning clerics to stay out of politics. However, most activist bishops here have insisted that the Pope was merely cautioning them not to become involved with politics or ideology. The two reports indicate that most bishops agree with this interpretation.[8]

What both of these remarks—on the lack of "specifics" and the cautioning of extremes—indicate is that the Pope operated with quite different purposes and values than the ones assumed by his critics who insisted on interpreting him in only a political or economic role.

Thus, if the Church, contrary to its tradition of social thought, were to claim for itself an active role in formulating economic and political "specifics", it would both violate the autonomy of the social order and define the Church's essential role as fostering productivity and public order in this world. John Paul II was careful to keep the distinctions and values of the Christian social tradition before him so that he be not judged by Marxist, socialist, or liberal values as if these determined the validity of the Christian contribution. George Will probably underscored better than many the more basic context in which the trip of John Paul to Mexico ought to be seen.

[8] George Vecsey, "Support of Bishops for Action", *The New York Times* (February 12, 1979) A 13.

John Paul II is a formidable philosopher who understands, as a result of hard thinking and hard living, the great
struggle of the century, the struggle between the totalitarian
state and all rival allegiances. The time is ripe for such a
toughened intellectual as the Pope. Secular enthusiasms
have lost their allure. No one still believes that the "death of
God" would mean the birth of an age of reason. Only the
willfully ignorant believe that a "new man" is being shaped
in Russia or China or Cuba. And the papacy, the oldest
western institution, is more likely than any secular regime
to last another 2000 years.[9]

In this context, it could well be argued that Latin America
serves as a sort of spiritual last gasp for the validity of
socialism and Marxism in our time. Even the Marxists
know that Russia is a tyranny, that there is no freedom in
China, that Cuba is presently the most imperialist nation in
the world, Cambodia and Vietnam slaughterhouses.

The pains taken in liberation thought to distinguish itself
from the admitted Marxist failures in Europe or Asia,
consequently, reveal that the "new man" is felt to be alive
and well in Latin America, that here is at last a hope for
Marxism also to be ethical. What John Paul II did, however, was to make sure that the ideological overtones of
Marxism be not confused with Christianity, that the temptation to worldly enthusiasm be rejected even by the Christian community. Many critics have held that the Catholic
Church is itself a totalitarian system. For a time, in Latin
America, under the impetus of liberation thought, it began
to look as if the Church there might itself, willingly even,
out of its own resources, accept as a norm the most totalitarian system of our time as its own model. This is why
many lovers of real freedom have been so concerned that

[9] George Will, *Newsweek* (October 3, 1978) 112.

religion seemed to be succumbing to precisely that to which it claimed itself immune. In this sense, the experience and intelligence of the Polish Pope seem particularly providential.

John Paul II's initial address to the Latin American bishops was noteworthy in the care taken in it to identify exactly what things are questionable in liberation thought from the viewpoint of the Church's conception of itself.[10] For Catholicism, doctrinal truth is not an indifferent matter. Catholics in this sense are not liberals who base their theory of liberty on the unknowability of truth. The Church has always recognized that careful attention to truth, to what is being taught, is a necessary part of its task, for revelation is also and properly revelation *to* human intelligence. There is a characteristic tendency to downplay this aspect of religion in many areas of Christianity and in the modern mind itself. This is why continued attention precisely to doctrine is one of the signs of the Church's own claim to truth and therefore to credibility. Needless to say, there is a way of conceiving religion that would believe that we should shove all these hairsplitting dogmas aside and just love our neighbor and help the poor.[11] But while not underestimating the importance of our love of neighbor and our help of the poor, the Church has always been sensitive to the fact that political and social theories of how these good ends come about are not themselves always religiously neutral. Ultimately the controversy about liberation theology in Latin America is over this very point. Are there, in other words, elements in it

[10] See this address in document no. 1, below.
[11] For a critique of this approach, cf. Dorothy Sayers, "The Shattering Dogmas of Christian Tradition", in *Christian Letters to a Post-Christian World* (Grand Rapids: Eerdmans, 1969) 13–48.

that are contrary to Christian doctrine and practice? John Paul II, clearly yet delicately, held that there were.

The first thing John Paul II told the bishops, consequently, was that they should "be watchful for purity of doctrine", which meant that they were to be "teachers of the truth, not a human and rational truth, but the truth that comes from God".[12] He reiterated that this is what the Church in its popes and bishops has taught about itself from the very earliest of centuries.[13] Much of what John Paul said, then, was based upon this claim, upon this insistence that liberation be not reduced from the full content given in the sources of faith. Naturally, however, what ought to be of particular interest to a pope is whether the advocacy of any political or social thesis involves an open or subtle attack on some basic element of defined Christian doctrine.

Within the modern socialist-Marxist tradition there has always been a theme of collective self-redemption for the human race.[14] This meant the challenging of the Christian doctrine of the divinity of the man Christ. This divinity undermined any "atheist" premise which sought to base human brotherhood on values other than those taught by Christ. Attempts to "re-read" the Gospels in this way, then, the Pope found to be of particular danger. He was quite aware of what happens when such dubious ideas are passed on "under the guise of catechesis, to the Christian

[12] Introduction to Address. In addition to the text in the Documents section of this book, this address can also be found in *The Tablet*, London (February 3, 1979) and *The Pope Speaks*, vol. 24, no. 1 (1979) and *L'Osservatore Romano*, English (February 5, 1979). All John Paul II's Mexican Addresses are in *Puebla: A Pilgrimage of Faith* (Boston: St. Paul Editions, 1979).

[13] Ibid., I, 1.

[14] See the essays of O'Donohue and Belda, no. 6 and no. 9 below.

Communities."[15] Simple people need correctness of Christian teaching and do not always see when essential shifts are being made. Thus,

> in some cases, either Christ's divinity is passed over in silence, or some people in fact fall into forms of interpretation at variance with the Church's faith. Christ is said to be merely a "prophet", one who proclaimed God's kingdom and love but not the true Son of God, and therefore not the center of the very gospel message.[16]

This center became a class, the proletariat, or struggle itself, or some other usually collective substitute, which often replaced the suffering Christ with the suffering masses. This was the most important correction the Pope had to make, for the aberration went to the very structure of Christianity. The attempt to replace Christ by an elevation of a social class or to place the poor at the center of Christianity, to make it mainly of this world, was rightly seen as a threat to basic Christian dogma.

The second consequence of this de-divinizing Christ was the effort to make him unique not as the true Son of God incarnated into this world, but merely as a model representative of a political revolutionary, who would justify ideological presuppositions and tactics.[17] Jesus was thus made out to be exactly the opposite of what is portrayed by the Gospels.

> People claim to show Jesus as politically committed, as one who fought against Roman oppression and the authorities, and also as one involved in the class struggle. This idea of Christ as a political figure, a revolutionary, as the subversive man from Nazareth, does not tally with the Church's catechesis. By confusing the insidious pretexts of Jesus' accusors with the—very different—attitude of Jesus himself,

[15] Initial Address, ibid., I, 4.   [16] Ibid.   [17] Ibid.

some people adduce as the cause of his death the outcome of a political conflict, and nothing is said of the Lord's will to deliver himself and of his consciousness of his redemptive mission.[18]

These two errors, along with a rejection of a class analysis as the proper way to look on the community, were, in a sense, the most serious items the Pope had to deal with in Mexico. The Church must always take care to make clear what it is about. Any theory or movement which obscures or changes fundamental aspects of this mission will prevent attention to the more fundamental aspects of the Church's purpose. The Church is not unmindful of political or social realities and problems, but it cannot be reduced to a dependency upon them.

The Holy Father, then, was first to insist upon the essential truth of Christianity as it saw itself. The fact that there was great confusion here required a straightforward confrontation, which the Pope did not hesitate to make. More often than we care to realize, "heresy" in the twentieth century has been a function of social analyses and political presuppositions. Quite often the severest criticism of the Pope came precisely from philosophic positions that did not allow for the essentials of faith. The Pope, therefore, continued:

[Jesus] does not accept the position of those who mixed the things of God with merely political attitudes. He unequivocally rejects recourse to violence. He opens his message of conversion to everybody, without excluding the very publicans. The perspective of his mission is much deeper. It consists in complete salvation through a transforming, peacemaking, pardoning and reconciling love. . . .[19]

[18] Ibid.   [19] Ibid.

John Paul, then, defined the faith which all the Church including Latin America affirmed: "Jesus Christ, the Word and Son of God, becomes man in order to come close to man and to offer him, through the power of his mystery, salvation, the great gift of God."[20] The confusion of the word "liberation" with the word "salvation" made it seem often that the Church was placed in the world merely to supply or direct what was lacking in the political or economic orders. Such reductionism was what John Paul most vigorously opposed.

Perhaps the classic example of the effort to reduce the Pope himself to the confines of mere humanism, to make him into a rather pale liberal, is Tad Szulc's analysis in *The New York Times Magazine*, when the Pope was about to return to Poland:

> If there is a common element among all these [various] aspects, it is John Paul's utter obsession with the terrestrial destiny and dignity of the human being. He speaks infrequently of the hereafter, or of the immortal soul: it is man on Earth, always man, who concerns him—man's human rights, his mental processes, and his sexuality and sensuality in the context of holy matrimony.[21]

What is of interest in such an analysis is not that John Paul is interested in man's terrestrial destiny. But rather that the very thing the Pope saw most clearly in need of correction—the exaggerated interest and emphasis upon this world—is minimized or rendered innocuous. In so capturing John Paul for humanism, he is rendered harmless when the human is judged insufficient. Only if the Holy Father's is a humanism based upon some transcendent reality that is rooted in the Incarnation can he be said to be a

[20] Ibid., I, 5.
[21] Tad Szulc, "Homecoming for the Pope", *The New York Times Magazine* (May 27, 1979) 22.

force for this era. And it is this latter that the Pope claimed to be.

The effect of this "overhumanization" leads to another error which John Paul II was quick to point out, that of confusing the Kingdom of God with movements of justice, or the reduction of the Church to a role of mere prophecy for social action.[22] Reading carefully the Documents the Latin American bishops presented to him, the Holy Father commented:

> Allusion is made . . . to the separation that some set up between the Church and the Kingdom of God. The Kingdom of God is emptied of its full content and is understood in a rather secularist sense. It is interpreted as being reached not by faith and membership in the Church but by the mere changing of structures and social and political involvement, and as being present wherever there is a certain type of involvement and activity for justice.[23]

The Pope rejected this view along with the idea that there are "two churches", one official and the other of the poor. The prayerful and sacramental Church is not to be conceived as contrasted to a mystical political church of the people.

John Paul II did, of course, stress a proper Christian anthropology. Again he insisted that the truth about men be taught. But this is not known exclusively in the human sciences.

> The truth that we owe to man is, first and foremost, a truth about man. As witnesses of Jesus Christ, we are heralds, spokesmen and servants of this truth. We cannot reduce it to the principles of a system of philosophy or to pure political activity.[24]

[22] Cf. the author's "From Catholic 'Social Doctrine' to the 'Kingdom of God on Earth' ", *Communio* (Winter, 1976) 287–300.
[23] Initial Address, ibid., I, 18.   [24] Ibid., I, 9.

The truth about man received from Jesus Christ is such that a complete social philosophy will include it. The Church "has the right and duty to proclaim the truth about man she learned from her teacher Jesus Christ."[25] So when the Church teaches, it claims something more, though nothing contrary, to authentic human science, social or physical.

> This complete truth about the human being constitutes the foundation of the Church's social teaching and the basis also of true liberation. In the light of this truth, man is not a being subject to economic or political processes, these processes are instead directed to man and are subjected to him.[26]

This fullness also requires an intellectual attention to the Church's teaching, not to some other ideological source, as its basic orientation to the truth about man.

And this kind of emphasis, furthermore, is directed to the whole Church. "In this matter everybody in the ecclesial community has the duty of avoiding magisteria other than the Church's magisterium, for they are ecclesiastically unacceptable and politically sterile."[27] Again, this is an acute awareness that other "teaching authorities", or magisteria—Marxism, for example—have been cited as justifications for certain kinds of values and activities. On the contrary, Christians have their own value and action system which is itself more adequate and complete than opposing ones. There has been in Europe and Latin America a widespread view that there is no such thing as a Christian social philosophy, so that Christians are free to choose other social systems.[28] This position is rejected in no uncertain terms:

[25] Ibid.   [26] Ibid., I, 9.   [27] Ibid., II, 2.
[28] Cf. the author's "On the Non-Existence of Christian Political Philosophy", *Worldview* (April, 1976) 26–30; "The 'Non-Catholic' Revival of Catholic Social Thought", *The Month* (March, 1977) 93–97.

The Church's action in earthly matters such as human advancement, development, justice, the rights of the individual, is always intended to be at the service of man, and of man as she sees him in the Christian vision of the anthropology she adopts. She therefore does not need to have recourse to ideological systems in order to love, defend and collaborate in the liberation of man: at the center of the message of which she is the depository and which she proclaims she finds her inspiration for acting in behalf of brotherhood, justice and peace, against all forms of domination, slavery, discrimination, violence, attacks on religious liberty and aggression against man, and whatever attacks life.[29]

The Pope recognized that human life, from its beginning before birth to its actual existence in any society, has a dignity independent of any state.

There are, then, very many violations against man. In a Solzhenitsyn-like passage, reflecting on Puebla with a General Audience in Rome shortly after he returned from Mexico, John Paul remarked:

It is necessary to call by their name injustice, the exploitation of man by man, or the exploitation of man by the state, institutions, mechanisms of systems and regimes which sometimes operate without sensitivity. It is necessary to call by name every social injustice, discrimination, violence inflicted on man against the body, against the spirit, against his conscience and against his conviction.[30]

Undoubtedly, the theme closest to the Holy Father's heart is that of the violation of religious and human freedom by political states, though he is quite aware that other evils exist which ought not to be neglected.

[29] Initial Address, ibid., III, 2.
[30] Address of February 21, 1979, in *L'Osservatore Romano*, English (February 26, 1979) 1. Also document no. 7, below.

He listed such violations: "Who can deny that today individual persons and civil powers violate basic rights of the human person with impunity: rights such as the right to be born, the right to life, the right to procreation, to work, to peace, to freedom, and to social justice, the right to participate in the decisions that affect people and nations."[31] "The right to be born" may be new, but it emphasizes the close connection between dangers arising from violations of social justice with those arising from areas of population control. This latter was not strongly touched by the Pope, but he showed clear awareness of the connections: "Think of the campaign in favor of divorce, of the use of contraceptive practices, of abortion, which destroy society."[32]

What has been most characteristic of Latin American analyses is the idea that the continent's problems are due to a malfunctioning international order and unethical international political societies. The Pope did not disagree that serious distortions existed at both levels.[33] However, reverting to the essential Christian principle that economic and political "laws" are not mechanical but ethical, he insisted that the causes of these disorders required an approach that would take into consideration man's moral nature. Moreover, he was quite aware that justice itself requires in practice a higher value than itself.

There is no economic rule capable of changing these mechanisms by itself. It is necessary, in international life, to call upon ethical principles, the demands of justice, the primary commandment which is that of love. Primacy must

[31] Initial Address, ibid., III, 2.
[32] Ibid., IV, A. See also the author's *Christianity and Life* (San Francisco, Ignatius, 1981).
[33] Ibid., III, 4.

be given to what is moral, to what is spiritual, to what springs from the full truth concerning man.[34]

In this sense, there was a reaffirmation of a specifically ethical and Christian concept about the very nature of the social sciences and the legal systems that presume to deal with man in society.

To the accusation that the Pope dealt only in spiritual or general principles—an accusation that generally ignores the subtle nature of the theoretical distinction between faith and reason upon which the refusal of the Church to give "concrete" programs is built—the Pope in his Mexican journey consistently emphasized values and principles that would not allow Catholics as citizens to be indifferent to real solutions. To the peasants at Oaxaca, John Paul reiterated the basic position of all Catholic social thought about property from *Rerum Novarum* to *Quadragesimo Anno*, *Mater et Magistra* and *Populorum Progressio*:

> The Church does indeed defend the legitimate right to private property, but she also teaches no less clearly that there is always a social mortgage on all private property, in order that goods may serve the general purpose that God gave them. And if the common good requires it, there should be no hesitation even at expropriation, carried out in due form.[35]

The Pope does not refer here, because of the nature of this audience, to the fact that the government may also be overly concentrated and that its own inefficiency and nature may be the major cause of the plight of the poor. The

[34] Ibid.

[35] Speech of January 29, 1979, in *L'Osservatore Romano* (February 12, 1979) 7.

Pope reemphasized, also, the traditional idea of the common good, as many in the liberation schools had questioned or rejected this idea in the name of the class struggle. The Pope even worried that the peasants were too "individualistic".

The Pope, clearly, showed great compassion for the lot of the peasant:

> The peasant has a right to be respected and not deprived, with manoeuvres which are sometimes tantamount to real spoilation, of the little amount he has. He has the right to be rid of the barriers of exploitation, often made up of intolerable selfishness, against which his best efforts of advancement are shattered. He has the right to real help—which is not charity or crumbs of justice—in order that he may have access to the development that his dignity as a man and as a son of God deserves.[36]

This dignity, moreover, is already given to man. It does not depend upon some future social structure.

In Guadalajara, the Pope stressed the right to organize, the dignity of work itself. "It is not enough for the Christian to denounce injustice; he is asked to be a real witness and promoter of justice. He who works has rights that must be defended legally, but he also has duties which he must carry out generously. As Christians, you are called to be architects of justice and of real freedom as well as forgers of social charity."[37] The Pope's concept was again rooted in a social theory that is not exhausted by science but includes the truth of the whole man, with its particular roots in Christ.

[36] Ibid.
[37] Speech of January 30, 1979, in *L'Osservatore Romano* (February 12, 1979), 11.

John Paul I, whom John Paul II has often recalled with affection,[38] said in a General Audience:

> . . . It is a mistake to claim that political, economic and social liberation are identical with salvation in Jesus Christ: that the Kingdom of God is identical with the Kingdom of man, and that "Where Lenin is, there is Jerusalem".[39]

John Paul II did not hesitate to cite and emphasize this passage. Liberation theology has the merit of suggesting that the faith has worldly effects, even though this has always been part of Christianity. But worldly order is not the faith. No pope can be silent about this really more basic truth. To do so would be equivalent to affirming that the Christian faith ought to be treated as a political movement, since that is what it claims to be in such a view. The Pope was, consequently, quite severe on the clergy, warning them in particular not to confuse their religious role with a political one.[40]

> You are priests and religious; you are not social or political leaders or officials of a temporal power. . . . Let us not forget that temporal leadership can easily be a source of division, while the priest must be a sign and agent of unity and brotherhood. Secular functions are the specific field of the action of laymen, who have to improve temporal matters with the Christian spirit.[41]

[38] Initial Address, ibid., I, 8.

[39] John Paul I, Address of September 20, 1978, *The Pope Speaks*, vol. 23, no. 4, 324.

[40] Cf. Speeches of January 26, 1979, *L'Osservatore Romano* (February 5, 1979) 10 and January 27, 1979, *L'Osservatore Romano* (February 12, 1979) 4.

[41] Ibid. (January 27, 1979) 4; see also document no. 4, below.

These words are of rather great significance in the modern tradition of the Church relating to Vatican II's Declaration on Religious Liberty.

This is so, then, because liberation theology may be the only movement in recent years that is praised by secular liberals for encouraging the clergy to become politically active at least in the case of a certain concept of the structure of the temporal order.[42] Modern Catholic tradition has, in fact, been going in the opposite direction, towards minimizing the role of the clergy in secular affairs and enhancing that of the laity. However, the clergy in this recent controversy are encouraged only when they themselves espouse a concept of society that has ideological origins, which seem to challenge, if not undermine any general Christian world view. When the Pope was directly called upon to sort out this issue, he quite rightly recalled that the clergy had a religious function to perform even in the most totalitarian society—even in the best one, for that matter. Indeed, John Paul II's constant worry seems to be that inattention to the specifically religious aspects of faith— cult and doctrine—will especially make Christians weak, both in free and in absolutist societies.[43]

Whether John Paul II succeeded in his mission of correcting the errors of liberation theology, while not alienating its zealous proponents, remains to be seen. The combination of his personality, teaching and popularity, however, did serve to make this kind of necessary yet difficult work at least seem possible of success. As Pope, he was concerned most directly with serious doctrinal errors which he

[42] See document no. 6, below.

[43] Cf. John Paul II's Address to U.S. Bishops, November 9, 1978, *The Pope Speaks*, vol. 24, no. 1 (1979) 39–42.

did not hesitate to underscore. As a Pole, he knew the dangers inherent in the kinds of proposals that were, almost naively, being proposed as Christian solutions to economic and social problems. At the same time, he knew that many things were wrong that could not be condoned but needed identification and correction. As the inheritor of a specific Catholic social philosophy, he saw that its independent and religious sources and attitude were necessary to improve the whole anthropology of modern man.

Probably it is no exaggeration to say that almost single-handedly John Paul II called the attention of an essentially good and dynamic people to the foundations of their Christian faith, ones they obviously shared with him. What he left them with was a choice of prudence and political wisdom that in Christian social theory could not be imposed on an autonomous people. In very little of the literature on liberation theology is there any real awareness of the kind of non-Marxist, free, productive and innovative development that comes from the pragmatic rejection of the ideologies of our time. The tragedy of the Latin American theological movement is that it does not know the case for a non-Marxist development, even though this lack of knowledge is too often itself the result of an ideological presupposition. Statistically, Latin America is the most Christian of continents. The Pope realized the importance of its staying this way as well as the effects if it chose freely an ideological solution at variance with the essentials of the Christian faith. The drama of Puebla, then, was not just economic or political. This is why a pope went there, first to teach about Christianity.

CHAPTER VI

LIBERATION IN JOHN PAUL II

So, liberation, then, is certainly a reality of faith, one of the fundamental biblical themes, which are a deep part of Christ's salvific mission, of the work of Redemption, of his teaching. This subject has never ceased to constitute the content of the spiritual life of Christians. . . .

Christ himself links liberation particularly with knowledge of the truth. . . . Liberation means man's inner transformation, which is a consequence of the knowledge of the truth. . . . Truth is important not only for the growth of human knowledge, deepening man's interior life in this way; truth has also a prophetic significance and power. . . . The theology of liberation must, above all, be faithful to the whole truth on man, in order to show clearly, not only in the Latin-American context but also in contemporary contexts, what reality is this freedom "for which Christ set us free".

–John Paul II, General Audience, February 21, 1979.

The least that can be said about "liberation theology", its background and meaning, is that, after the advent of John Paul II, a pope of remarkable philosophical perception and political insight, it will never be quite the same again. In a real sense, the Pope has given it legitimacy by situating it precisely within the context of Christian belief. Since much of the notoriety accruing to this movement was based on those elements within it most contrary to Christian thought and practice, this proper "situating" has in itself been a most important service. The most striking characteristic of John Paul II has surely been his instinctive capacity to make precise any issue of doubt or controversy that has arisen within the Church or in contemporary society. He does not hesitate to speak to a problem where the problem actually exists, yet in a context of sympathy, reconciliation, and an abiding fidelity to the truth of the matter. His wide-ranging travels, as he has explained them, have produced a vast corpus of original yet classically Christian analyses designed to exercise the Christian's religious freedom to present Christianity and its views on human and world problems.[1] He has recognized that the nature of the papal office requires his own teaching and witnessing, his own urgings and comfortings about man's purpose and condition before God in the world.

Perhaps no social issue except the family has been more watched to gauge Pope Wojtyla's views than that of "liberation". Coming himself from a Marxist-controlled country, he was quick to appreciate the potentially dangerous directions and religiously distorted implications often contained in many widely propagated and popular ideas generally gathered under the rubric of "liberation". None the less, John Paul II has been forthright in scrutinizing objective imbalances and deviations in every political and economic system, without opting arbitrarily for an explanation of them deriving from contemporary ideologies, Marxist or liberal, ecological or conservative, about development and underdevelopment, taken as a description of man's position in this world.

This is why, in his address on the subject at Puebla, Mexico (January 28, 1979), before the Latin American bishops and often repeated since (February 21, 1979; Rio, July 2, 1980), he has reaffirmed that there is such a thing as Catholic social doctrine, which does not depend on sources outside Christianity's own traditions, including in that tradition the classical philosophies and the accumulated Christian experience of man. This Christian social doctrine

[1] Cf. Address of John Paul II to General Audience, May 21, 1980, on his journeys.

thus has its own reasons to be concerned with man's human condition, its own norms by which to judge what man is in his freedom and dignity. This reaffirmation takes on double significance in the light of strenuous efforts made during recent years to give Catholic doctrine a predominantly Marxist hue, or at least to classify Catholic thought as so wholly neutral before contemporary ideologies that Christians are simply free to "select" what ideology seems best.[2] In essence, John Paul II has firmly rejected these latter efforts and analyses, while at the same time subjecting the serious human problems that do exist to a wide-ranging analysis based upon specifically Christian approaches. In so doing, he has broken the liberal or Marxist stranglehold often declared to be "scientifically" necessary for thinking about political, social and economic problems. He has done this, furthermore, upon the essentially broadening basis of philosophical realism and the freeing effect of truth itself on man.[3] Indeed, as he argued in his Encyclical *Redemptor Hominis*, the truth about man, his whole truth, includes religious truth so that any restrictive ideology must necessarily be too narrow to conceive the real forces that are at human disposal.

John Paul II has approached the subject of liberation, and the theology that seeks to use the term, in a very original and surprising way. Pedagogically, he has recognized that the best way to correct a widespread misuse of a term is not to reject it altogether, but to refashion it carefully so

[2] Cf. M.-D. Chenu, *La "Doctrine Sociale" de l'Eglise* (Paris: Cerf, 1979).

[3] Cf. John Paul II's Address to the Angelicum University on St. Thomas, November 17, 1979. Cf. also Andrew Woznicki, *A Christian Humanism: Karol Wojtyla's Existential Personalism* (New Britain, CT.: Mariel, 1980).

that it means what the context of truth requires of it. This is an essentially Thomist approach which tries to save the truth in any usage insofar as possible. As words connected with "liberation" have been common in modern economic and political theory and constitutional practice, as well as in contemporary philosophy and ideology, the effort to use the term properly within a Christian context is doubly important. Roger Heckel has summarized the approach of the Pope to the theme of liberation in this way:

> . . . One reason for [John Paul II's] prudent and discreet use of the word *liberation* [is that] he is not the type of person prone to follow changing currents. . . . The Pope's attitude can be explained by his evident concern to avoid the ambiguities which, he is aware, have marked the use of the word *liberation*. Therefore, he is careful to qualify the word properly when he uses it. His attitude is usually critical.
>
> The principal ambiguity would seem to be the following: the theologians of liberation invoke the religious and biblical resonance of the word but give it a more immediate meaning in terms of the various social, economic, political and cultural liberations pursued by contemporary persons and peoples. The ambiguous point is therefore in the bond which people too quickly establish between these political expressions of *liberation* and *liberation by Jesus Christ*. This bond does exist, but it must be discerned and qualified in a very clear way in order to avoid all sorts of false conclusions and confusion. This represents an even more serious problem since the most radical currents usually dominate the scene and sweep along others in their wake whether they like it or not.[4]

There are three points John Paul makes to avoid these difficulties.

[4] Roger Heckel, *The Theme of Liberation* (Rome: Pontifical Commission on Justice and Peace, 1980) 21.

1) He uses the word [liberation] with discretion, and when he does so almost always explains its meaning.

2) He systematically gives greater emphasis to the specifically *religious* sense of the word.

3) In his perspective of evangelization, the Pope considers political liberation (economic, social, cultural) as dependent on religious liberation by Jesus Christ.[5]

This is the originality of John Paul II's analysis of liberation.

Roger Heckel went on to draw these conclusions about John Paul II's analysis of liberation:

> In the truly Christian sense (biblical, theological), liberation is the work of God, the work of Jesus Christ. . . . The word is therefore normally linked in an explicit way to the more common words of salvation and redemption in Christian and biblical theology. They represent, and this can bear repetition, the ordinary terminology used by the Pope. . . .
>
> This liberation is beyond human strength and is the forgiveness and the gift of God. . . . The Pope frequently stresses . . . the fact that this liberation affects the interior person, the very centre, the heart, the very source of one's being, and that each person experiences this *liberation* (the theological virtues of faith, hope and charity) from that moment on, even before other expressions of liberation have become tangible. From that moment on, each of us is free in Christ. . . .
>
> . . . This personal and interpersonal liberation received from God tends to penetrate all the concrete aspects of social existence, where the history of the individual and mankind unfolds. . . .
>
> The Pope is fully aware of the nature of social structures

[5] Ibid.

and the importance of sound social structures for personal development. However, in the context of the Church's specific contribution to human efforts, he constantly refers to the divine and gratuitous sources of that contribution.

He issues a warning against the dangers of confusion and reductionism. Human works (the liberation pursued by women and men) are never the fully adequate sign in themselves, nor even less are they the specific source of the growth of the Kingdom of God.

Finally, within the realm of their real but relative independence, in order to be authentic, the various concrete expressions of liberation cannot be guaranteed by ideologies which do not fully respect all the constituent dimensions of the human person. To an even lesser extent can they claim to liberate us when they subject us to any type of structure, make truth dependent upon *praxis*, or ultimately claim to free us from faith in God.[6]

From this, it is clear that, for John Paul II, the essential task is the constant reassertion of religious meaning, truth, and value whenever a movement uses ideas or practices that touch upon man's basically religious meaning. For liberation theology has appeared in the secular realm as an effort to evaporate the content of Christian ideas while using Christian organization and terms for essentially economic or political purposes as understood in ideological terms. Religion has thus tended to become subordinated to, interpreted within, those ideological analyses and programs which propose public issues to be the major, indeed the only, factors in human life.

John Paul II, however, has carefully and consistently argued that not only are religious issues valid and basic in themselves, not requiring justification by a political or

[6] Ibid., 22–23.

economic criterion, but that even the goal of objectively better human economic, social, or political conditions will not be accomplished without the newer freeing initiatives, graces and motives that arise within man's religious reality. The first task, then, for the Pope is to orient man to the religious truth about himself, the ultimate meaning of his conception, birth, growth, work, thought and death. Since the word "liberation" is often used as a substitute for an expression of the Christian terms redemption or salvation, John Paul II is careful to use the term liberation only when defining it within its proper religious usage, which specifically refers to Christ's salvific action for men. In this sense, liberation does not mean something political or economic in the first place. On the other hand, the Pope maintains that the same human person who is the recipient of salvation in Christ is also and properly active in this world, so that now he has motives of love, sacrifice, justice and courage which ought properly to result in love for the neighbor and just institutions. This does not involve denying man's tendency to sin and to abuse every good institution or motive. Thus, Christianity does not locate ultimate happiness for each person in this life, nor does it even deny that ill-formed or ill-developed institutions can, with proper experience and motivation, become rather better than many abstractly ideal formulae.

John Paul II has addressed himself to the frequent objection that this Christian religious concern deflects man from accomplishing anything in this world.[7] Far from admitting any truth to such an accusation, the Holy Father has turned the argument around. What primarily *prevents* a better world is rather the belief that there is *only* this world. Since

[7] Cf. John Paul II's Address at Pomezia, September 13, 1979.

there is a unity between man's ultimate end—the personal vision of God in eternal life, something properly trans-political—and the kind of being man is created to be—one actually capable of such a transcendent goal—the very reality of man contains forces or impulses or knowledge that flow forth into human life. But these cannot be confined to or even properly measured by the various scientific methodologies or ideologies which would reduce man to only the exterior or socially measurable part of his reality. Since this life of God is offered freely to mankind and since it is a reality within each person's life, to be chosen or rejected, it will follow that there exists in the world a possibility of changing the interior tendencies and external structures so that men really can meet their difficulties. These latter are not only the results of a lack of knowledge or the condition of finiteness proper to humanity but correspond to real spiritual issues about how and why men are to act towards one another. It is this that stands at the basis of John Paul II's confidence and, likewise, of his realism.

What is behind the Holy Father's careful attention to the terms in which liberation thought is presented as a political force is the tendency of that thought to obviate the peculiar terms of Christian redemption. Social ideology has proposed a way of "salvation" or "liberation" in modern times that contains characteristics and positions distinctly at odds with Christianity. Essentially, again, these are the views that 1) man wholly liberates himself from any presumed bondage or restriction, 2) that this is a collective effort which subordinates the individual to the group, 3) that this is achieved by hatred, violence, or class struggle, 4) that therefore Christ is either not necessary or merely a model of a revolutionary person, and 5) that the goal of liberation is a perfect worldly order.

John Paul II has met these positions in a twofold fashion. First, he has clearly restated the fact that Christ is true God and true man, the sole savior or "liberator" of mankind from sin and death, the main bondages. This means, as it were, that men are saved by a unique "man-God", so they do not save themselves in the humanist or atheist context which would exclude the gift context of redemption. Thus, there may have possibly been other ways to save man, but the Church in its belief and structure is bound to the specific way God chose in Christ. This orients Christianity to a primarily sacrificial, not political, mode of redemption. This is why eventually Christianity will come to understand governmental authority as service and not merely as rule or force. The consequence of this is that, in a real way, even the legitimately political comes to be seen in the light of the sacrificial, which deals with the particular destiny of each man or woman, no matter in what age or political system. In his homily for the slain Italian journalist and politician, Vittorio Bachelet, John Paul II said:

> Christ was aware that his sacrifice was necessary for the salvation of the world. . . . In God's plan, it was established that it was not possible to save man in any other way. No other word, no other act would have sufficed to do so.
>
> The word of the Cross was necessary; the death of the Innocent One was necessary, as the definitive act of his mission. It was necessary "to justify man. . . ," to shake hearts and consciences, to constitute the definitive argument in that conflict between good and evil, which accompanies the history of man and the history of Peoples.
>
> The Sacrifice was necessary. The death of the Innocent One. (February 28, 1980)

The Holy Father, thus, recognizes at this fundamental level that respect for man's truth and freedom, for the kind of being he is, one personally created for eternal life, implies that all of human reality is transformed by this notion of sacrifice, of something beyond political or economic justice at the heart of the kind of persons we are.

Having made this clear, John Paul II can then return to the subject of serious imbalances in the world. He does this first by insisting that the clergy in the Church do not have direct political responsibility.[8] On the other hand, when public policies or social practices violate the truth about man, particularly his religious truth, there is a corresponding requirement that these conditions be precisely defined, responsibility located, and prudently confronted by means that do not themselves violate man's purpose or dignity. This negative function, as it were, of taking the part of the poor or those who lack freedom is a logical consequence of encouraging human justice, freedom, and peace. Moreover, John Paul II has been remarkable, particularly when addressing himself to questions of culture, as at UNESCO (June 2, 1980), in stressing the universality of truth and doctrine while emphasizing that this same truth can find many diverse expressions, that it is proper and normal for this wide diversity to occur. John Paul II, then, has emphasized various "national ways" of Christianity. This is, in a sense, the Church's definitive response to the notions that truth tends to unity while freedom to diversity, yet both are contained within one and the same religious reality. John Paul II's address to intellectuals in Rio de Janeiro is worth much attention here:

The meeting place between the Church and culture is the world, and in it man, who is a "being-in-the-world", a subject of development for both of them, by means of the

[8] Cf. John Paul II's Address at Puebla, January 28, 1978; Address to Latin American Bishops, Rio de Janeiro, July 2, 1980; Addresses in Philippines, February, 1981, and Germany, November, 1980.

word and grace of God on the part of the Church, and by means of man himself, with all his spiritual and material resources, on the part of culture.

True *cultura animi* is a culture of freedom, which springs from the depths of the spirit, from lucidity of thought and from generous disinterestedness of love. Apart from freedom there can be no culture. The real culture of a people, its full humanization, cannot be developed in a system of coercion.

Culture cannot be subjected to any coercion of power, either political or economic, but must be helped by both in all those forms of public and private initiative which are in conformity with real humanism and with the tradition and true spirit of every people. Culture which is born free should also spread in a free system.

Now man cannot be fully himself, he cannot fulfill his humanity completely, if he does not recognize and does not live the transcendence of his own being over the world, and of his own relationship with God. (July 1, 1980)

This is part of John Paul II's constant reiteration of the primacy of the free person to all social structures, within the person's relation to the truth and being of God.[9]

In the much-disputed area of church and state, John Paul II's contribution is not merely to have placed religious liberty at the center of all human rights, something in a way original with him, but he has also, on the basis of his resolution of the "liberation" question, insisted upon the mutual concern and accord between religious and civil authorities. To the President of Zaire, John Paul II thus emphasized that his journey had essentially a "religious character", yet one that permitted a genuine meeting with

[9] Cf. Roger Heckel, *The Human Person and Social Structures: Texts of John Paul II* (Rome: Pontifical Commission on Justice and Peace, 1980).

civil authorities which was more than a formality. "I also attach great importance to conversations with those who hold civil power", he stated to President Mobutu Seko Sese.

> There are many opportunities for exchanging views, in a constructive way, on the most fundamental problems for man, his spiritual dimension, his dignity and his future, on peace and also harmony among peoples, on the freedom the Church requests to proclaim the Gospel in the name of the respect of consciences that is contained in most constitutions or organic laws of states. (May 2, 1980)

The primary "liberation" for the Pope remains the freedom to present Christian truth after the manner in which alone truth can be communicated, that is, in real cultural freedom.

This transcendent religious freedom corresponds in the Pope's view, then, with the mutual need which each different nation and culture has for other cultures and nations. The result of freedom is the authenticity of different political and economic forms and a simultaneous liberation of each from a too narrow dependence on its own parochial values or outlooks. What John Paul II said of Africa can be said of every culture and can be taken as the touchstone of his approach to how men can be freed by a religious liberation that enables them to see beyond themselves:

> I am convinced myself that, while African questions must be the business of Africans, and not be subject to pressures or interference from any bloc or interested group whatsoever, their successful resolution cannot fail to have a beneficial influence on other continents.

> But for this purpose it would also be necessary for other peoples to *learn to receive* from African peoples. It is not just material and technical aid that the latter need. They need

also to give: their heart, their wisdom, their culture, their
sense of man, their sense of God, which is keener than in
many others. (May 2, 1980)

This is a powerful statement which follows from John Paul
II's reinterpretation of liberation. Now it is not so much a
question of setting one culture against another but a mutual
recognition of the depth of human variety and need.

The idea of liberation has been connected, in a curious
way, with the proper modern formula for making peoples
richer, for the proper understanding of poverty. The questions of why the poor are poor, of how to remind them of
their dignity while at the same time proposing a betterment of their lot, has concerned John Paul II in this context. In Brazil, he has again demonstrated his first thesis
that human value and dignity are independent of economic
categories, such that poverty itself does not deprive any
person of his transcendent worth. Moreover, poverty witnesses to a sense of human priorities which, when understood, can serve to foster the kind of economic improvement that would be of real service.

> To the poor, to those who live in want, [the Church]
> says that they are particularly close to God and his king-
> dom. But, at the same time, she says that they are not
> allowed—as no one is allowed—to reduce themselves and
> their families arbitrarily to poverty. It is necessary to do ev-
> erything that is lawful to ensure themselves and the mem-
> bers of their families all that is necessary to life and mainte-
> nance. In poverty it is necessary above all to maintain
> human dignity and also that magnanimity, that openness of
> heart to others, that availability, which are precisely the
> characteristics of the poor, the poor in spirit. (July 2, 1980)

What is to be stressed here is that, as in the case of cultural
diversity and exchange, John Paul II does not set rich

against poor but stresses their common worth and obligations toward each other. It is here that he explicitly rejects any ideological approach that would argue for human equality by violence of one group against another as a proper means of economic or political action.

To the relatively prosperous, then, John Paul II went on:

> Take advantage of the fruits of your work and lawful industry, but, in the name of Christ's words, in the name of human brotherhood and solidarity, do not shut yourselves up in yourselves. Think of the poorest. . . . Share in a pragmatic and systematic way. (July 2, 1980)

The Holy Father here recognized that spiritual values and human initiative are both required as well as a proper economic approach. There are ways that stress egoism or deny liberty that do not work for the poor. To the wealthy, the Pope remarked in the same spirit: "You must think how to give, how to organize social and economic life and each of its sectors in order that this life will aim at equality among men and not at an abyss between them." Yet, the Church "is not the Church of one class or caste. . . . The Church of the poor does not wish to serve what causes tensions and the explosion of conflicts among men. . . . The Church of the poor does not wish to serve immediate political purposes, struggles for power, and at the same time she very diligently sees to it that her words and her acts are not used for this purpose. . . ." (June 2, 1980) The Pope has managed both to preserve an authentic space for politics and economics and, at the same time, to show how the whole human person includes these areas in the light of man's religious nature and end. Thus, there is no arbitrary or absolute separation that would reduce Christianity to a pure abstraction or a purely political movement.

The "liberation" of man, then, if that term be used, can be placed within a proper Christian context. But that is the issue, namely, that Christianity does not itself mean just anything at all, but itself contains certain basic truths and an authority charged with a responsibility not to let words and ideas be evaporated of their real religious meaning. The danger of contemporary liberation thought is that it can easily do just this. George Will's observation was well stated:

> The Roman Catholic Church's claim that its teaching in matters of faith and morals is providentially guaranteed against error is not new and is really not what rankles many people about today's Pope. The reason the Pope stirs uneasiness, and the reason his example is of political as well as theological interest, is that it makes vivid a timeless and awkward truth about communities, political or religious. That truth is that any community must have a core of settled convictions and any community determined to endure must charge some authority with the task of nurturing, defending and transmitting those convictions.[10]

But the Pope does not, from his side, merely argue that all communities need some living authority but that the particular truth of Christianity is the whole truth of man without which man will not be free.[11]

Roger Heckel has stated this position in another way:

> In the secular climate of some countries the words "man" or "to speak to the human person" are immediately under-

[10] George Will, *Newsweek* (June 23, 1980) 92.

[11] This is one of the principal burdens of John Paul II's Encyclical *Redemptor Hominis*. See the author's *The Whole Truth about Man: John Paul II to University Faculties and Students* (Boston: St. Paul Editions, 1981).

stood to mean that the religious dimension is to be excluded, that the aim is to determine a common denominator which so limits the human condition as to exclude the religious dimension. This is not John Paul II's approach nor does it reflect his horizon. The human being of which he speaks and to whom he addresses his message is basically defined by openness to God, a quest for the Absolute. . . .

Social teaching takes up a good amount of his teaching, but is not all of it. . . . It does not become the center around which everything else is expected to rotate or the controlling idea which would weaken the proper nature of other elements and manifestations of ecclesial life. The Pope does not feel the pressing need to speak always about social problems. . . . The Pope never gives the impression that the unfathomable mystery of God exhausts itself in social work or that the spreading of the Kingdom finds its adequate expression and full realization—even less its specific impulse —in the progress of civilization. The work of God, the work God has entrusted to the Church, is that all men and women believe in Jesus Christ.[12]

Clearly, any ideology or philosophy which would seek to "liberate" men from this religious dimension—and many specifically modern ones do have this element—must be rejected.[13] Indeed, John Paul II sees the need of a thorough philosophical analysis which would reject any philosophical system closed in on man alone.[14]

The importance of John Paul II in the discussion of liberation theology, then, is fundamental. He has, as it were,

[12] Roger Heckel, *General Aspects of the Social Catechesis of John Paul II* (Rome: Pontifical Commission on Justice and Peace, 1980) 11–12.

[13] Cf. John Paul II, Address of November 17, 1979.

[14] This was the main theme of *Redemptor Hominis* and the addresses of November 17, 1979, and December 15, 1979, to the Angelicum and Gregorian Universities.

managed to save liberation from itself. The Pope, however, admits that he is not competent in technical economic
or political issues.[15] He can urge creativity, concern, responsibility, love, intelligence. He can point out what
seems to be wrong. But he recognizes that the particulars
of what each people choose and do ought to be left primarily to themselves.[16] John Paul II has emphasized often the
primacy of the human person to social systems.[17] This is,
in part, why he is essentially optimistic in believing that
human needs can be defined, met, and bettered, without at
the same time embracing a this-worldly utopianism or denying the reality of the consequences of the Fall. He is not
stuck in a kind of impasse that requires vast structural
changes before men can act. The Christian philosophy he
embraces is itself based on a correct understanding of the
relation of persons and institutions, of persons and things,
so that, however important institutions may be, the Pope
recognizes that change begins within man himself, in persons who can act also out of transcendent motives to meet
the real needs of mankind.

In this sense, then, John Paul II, in restoring the terms of
proper discussion to their religious center, has freed politics
and economics from the bondage of the ideologies while
teaching men that their very being is destined to eternal life,
a destiny that frees them from the sin and death that are
their first bondage. Without this sense of clarification by
John Paul II, liberation theology no doubt stood in danger
of obscuring religious truths and using religion as a tool to

[15] This was the theme often in John Paul II's addresses to political
leaders in Africa in May, 1980.
[16] Cf. Roger Heckel, *Self-Reliance* (Rome: Pontifical Commission on
Justice and Peace, 1978).
[17] See footnote no. 9.

impose ideological systems upon many peoples, systems that generally, by their own historical records, have compromised either freedom or growth, usually both. There is, of course, no assurance that John Paul II's teaching will be followed, but he has served notice that liberation on any other terms but those he has argued will most certainly not be Christian and will probably end up being used against man.

CONCLUSION

There is a vocabulary now current in Christian circles which implies that freedom can be assured by rejecting all constraints as "domination". In reality, human freedom among individuals and people must be achieved by acknowledging, by coming to terms with and humanizing life's inevitable constraints: to deny this is both unrealistic and useless. The interdependent growths of freedom cannot do without organized solidarity which implies institutional constraints and power.

—Bishop Roger Heckel, S.J. (Former Secretary, Pontifical Commission on Justice and Peace), "The Church's Social Doctrine and Practice", Lumen Vitae (Louvain, no. 1, 1978) 59. See essay no. 10, below.

Everyone agrees, in conclusion, that Latin America presents a moral, religious, economic, cultural, and political challenge first to itself, then to men of our era. Liberation theology, as a new movement of religious thinkers in Latin America, has been presenting one way to interpret and change this situation. Indeed, it often argues that it is the only way. Here, we have essentially argued that the analysis as it is presented by this influential school deviates at crucial points from some of the emphases of classical Christianity. The presence and presentation of John Paul II at Puebla served to underscore this. Moreover, with regard to the chosen problem at hand, it neither analyzes the causes of poverty properly nor does it advocate the means best designed and tested to remove them. The result of this seems to be that liberation theology is itself a major cause of underdevelopment because it deflects energy and intelligence from the real causes and best means to aid the poor, not merely in their poverty but in their total persons. Both religion and politics, the very heart of the lives of the poor, suffer from this confusion, however well-intended its advocacy.

The argument with these Latin American thinkers is not about whether we should be concerned with the poor. Nor is it whether things in their economic or political systems need improvement. We need not be chauvinistic to agree with them that they do. Rather the argument is over with what model, or analysis, men choose to improve them. Behind this mutual reflection is the recognition on all sides that something can be done. The age of passive conformity or acceptance on all sides is over. On the other hand, the very notion of the possibility of change forces the recognition that things can also be worse. Poverty in fact is worse in parts of Asia or Africa than in Latin America as a rule. Furthermore, there are things worse than poverty. Poverty, as Christianity taught, has its salutary aspects. The poor state is not the worst kind of moral state available to men.

This realization of the possibility of something worse, however difficult that may be to understand, of something worse in human moral terms, gives considerable pause to arguments which imply that *anything* would be an improvement. There are certainly political systems, since the very New Testament itself, that Christian sensibility has taught us we must be most cautious about.[1] This probably lies at the basis, too, of the hostility between the liberation school and a Solzhenitsyn. In any case, Christian social documents have traditionally seen in most Marxist systems the definite possibility of being worse than poverty systems, even though these same documents will find poverty a difficult environment in which to practice virtue.

[1] Cf. Heinrich Schlier, "The State According to the New Testament", *The Relevance of Christianity* (New York: Herder and Herder, 1968) 215–38; Oscar Cullmann, *The State in the New Testament* (New York: Scribner's, 1956).

The key to the religious hesitation with liberation theology is undoubtedly the latter's tendency to use religion as a modernization force for a kind of civil improvement. This goes against most of what the West has learned about religion and its delicate autonomy in the world. The tendency to make worship and faith depend on a largely political and economic purpose contains clear dangers. In this sense, too, there is a danger in taking away from the poor themselves the one thing all men in all societies— good or bad—need most, a sense of their personal destiny which transcends every social order. Making liberation a kind of unified program between this world and the next only confuses this issue.

The other side of the objection to liberation thought, and probably in a way the more important one as it argues on the ground upon which liberation thought itself has chosen to take its stand, is precisely on the worldly, empirical side. This kind of theology translated into action evidently cannot deliver what it promises. The argument for the alternative is probably best stated in this way:

A democratic capitalist society does not promise salvation. It does not even promise the development of a higher human type (like the "new man" of socialist ideology). It does promise that each individual human being will have, by constitutional right and even by a certain minimal economic opportunity, freedom to think and to act, to aspire, to improve himself and his lot, and to move, go about, and make an almost unlimited series of choices about how to spend his or her life. The system does not promise that each person will, in fact, make out of himself or herself what he or she would like. But it does, in fact, give ample room for each person to experiment and to try. Most citizens, it appears, do in fact better their own lot over the course of their lifetimes. But not all do. In a perfectly free system, a realist would not expect all to succeed equally, nor each to avoid some measure of failure.[2]

The position here is that the alleviation of poverty lies best in the direction of freedom, freedom with constitutional restraints and order, but with each person's potential clearly at work for and within his own dignity.

No one denies that much is wrong with Europe, Japan, and the United States, particularly in their values concerning the right of life. Here Latin America teaches much and is often rightly repelled by what it sees to the north. The moral and religious divisions of men are, however, never to be defined mainly geographically. The poor are not all good, the rich are not all bad. On the other hand, a creative use of North American, European, Japanese, and ASEAN experiences, as opposed to dogmatic socialist models so often chosen for theoretical reasons by the liberation school, would better enable those nations of Latin America to alleviate their poverty, retain so much that is unique and valid in their culture, and protect the rights and duties of religion and public freedom. In spite of all protestations to the contrary, it is precisely this approach that has not been considered by Latin American liberation thought. Paradoxically, what liberation thought seems most in need of is precisely a theory and practice of liberty.

[2] Michael Novak, *The American Vision: An Essay on the Future of Democratic Capitalism* (Washington: American Enterprise Institute, 1978); see below, essay no. 11.

II

CRITICAL ESSAYS

INTRODUCTION

The following fourteen essays are designed to give serious and reflective attention to the nature and meaning of liberation theology and its orientations. Some essays are quite scholarly, others more journalistic and popular. The authors are various responsible theologians and essayists who have looked carefully at the essential aspects of this movement. For some time it has been difficult to find in one place sufficient critical attention that would cover the theological, ideological, political, and ethical aspects of the controversies in Latin America about the structure of society and religion. This section is designed to meet this need. It is conceived both as a source and as a survey of the kinds of problems that liberation theology presents to Christian and democratic society.

Though at first sight, discussion of liberation theology might seem overly theological and technically Catholic, the fact is that the forces and dangers that could arise on a national or international scale do so because of the changes in these sometimes esoteric areas. Too often, politicians, journalists and other media people have too little sophisticated knowledge to see the import of even slight or obscure changes in man's spirit. And as I have argued in the Introduction, changes need not be bad, but the option for a certain kind of change, a socialism with its own intellectual and practical tradition, is the major problem with this newer theology. The heavily ideological overtones need to be examined, as several essays point out.

The essays of von Balthasar (1) and Galot (2) are designed to present the theological background of the main issue presented by liberation thought, namely, the use of

Christianity to foster a political change in society. The essays of Heckel (14), André-Vincent (4) and Lepargneur (5) survey and organize from different angles the content of the liberation proposals. O'Donohue (6) gives a critical analysis of the broader nature of the socialist claim which lies behind so much of liberation thinking. The editorial of *Civiltà Cattolica* (7), the authoritative Jesuit Roman journal, analyzes the exact purposes and intentions of John Paul II's presentation at Puebla in the context of the Latin American issues. Vree (8), Novak (11), Kirkpatrick (3) and Smith (12) present analyses of this movement from outside the specific theological circles, while Heckel (10), Belda (9) and Finnis (13) deal with the relation of Catholic social thought to Marxism and the nature of public society in the Christian tradition.

I

HANS URS VON BALTHASAR

LIBERATION THEOLOGY IN THE LIGHT OF SALVATION HISTORY

Translated by Erasmo Leiva

A. PRELIMINARY REMARKS

This subject could be approached from many different angles. We could take our departure from a traditional dogmatics with its various treatises in order to see what liberation theology could contribute to it. But in this case we would be disappointed, since this theology either disregards the traditional *loci theologici* or reduces them to the one privileged *locus* which is its own. And we would also be committing an injustice against liberation theology, since it strives for a radical simplification of theology and has developed its own standpoint by bypassing most of what has become traditional and by reading Scripture in a way that amounts to a wholly new start. We would like to share these concerns of liberation theology as much as possible by letting our encounter with it occur, not under the strictures of unchanging dogmatic treatises, but within the wide-open context of a Christian theology of history which has as its center the unity of the Old and the New Testament and which does not lose from sight the perennial relevance of the transition from one to the other.

Nevertheless, it seems to us that three very general demands may be made of a theology which considers itself Catholic —prerequisites which remain valid both at present and in the future for any "re-interpretation" (*relecture*) of Christian revelation, regardless of how radical it may be. The first of these

Originally published under the title "Heilsgeschichtliche Überlegungen zur Befreiungstheologie" in *Theologie der Befreiung* (Einsiedeln: Johannesverlag, 1977). Reprinted by permission.

demands concerns the form of Catholic theology; the second
concerns its content, and the third, its method.

1. Catholic theology (and this is a tautology) has universal
validity. This does not, of course, rule out the possibility of
theologies with a particular coloration according to given epochs
or cultures: indeed, because of the inexhaustible richness of the
Catholic principle, such theologies *must* come to be, since Catholic truth is "symphonic". But this does mean that it is the characteristic of sects and heresies to define themselves and begin
to spread starting from a given national sphere. Any theology
which is colored by a specific culture or epoch must, if it is
Catholic, be acceptable in its central concerns to all other local
churches. A theology of liberation can be no exception to this
Catholic prerequisite. It must be so shaped that, in essence, it
could be considered relevant and be proclaimed in every satellite
of the Soviet Union or of the People's Republic of China.

Catholic theologies colored by specific epochs and cultures
take their departure from particular images and receive their
orientation from certain central concepts; but these images and
concepts must be open to and commune with one another within
the universe of the *Catholica*. No culture can raise for its own
standpoint such a claim to absoluteness that it thereby formally
refuses to commune with other Catholic central concepts. "Liberation" is, doubtless, a central point of revelation; but revelation
would suffer a drastic contraction if everything without exception were to be traced back to the concept of liberation.[1] Non-
Catholic Christian theology is primarily national. It can be
organized "internationally" (World Council of Churches); but
Catholic theology is always supra-national in principle: it comes
to be as the *communio* of all countries and epochs.

2. Catholic theology begins its reflection with the central facts
of salvation, and it never loses sight of the mutual circumin-
cession of these facts. Thus we have the unity of Old and New

[1] Cf. P. M. Manzanera, S.J.: "The Bible can be explained and understood only
with this hermeneutic of liberation"; every other interpretation "is in its very
roots a secret siding with the *status quo*" and, therefore, discriminatory. "Die
Theologie der Befreiung in Lateinamerika und ihre Hermeneutik", in *Theologische
Akademie* 12 (Knecht, 1975) 58, 61.

Testament, with its peculiar trajectory. So, too, the unity between the hidden and the public life of Jesus and between his
dying and rising, again with its peculiar trajectory. And the
mandate of the Catholic Church to proclaim to the world the
liberation of this same world from the powers of injustice, sin
and death—a liberation which has in essence been completed in
Christ. The Church does this in word and sacrament, but likewise through holiness of life in the ecclesial community and
through a commmitment to an earthly justice through all means
that can be justified by a Christian.

Individual members of the Church have in this their special
charisms, which can focus on different spiritual centers according
to the mission received. But all charisms have their validity only
within the one Body—through it and for it—in such a way that
they commune among one another. A more "synoptic" charism
stands in perfect communion with a more "Pauline" or a more
"Johannine" charism, as was already clearly evidenced in the
primitive Church. In the same way, the different aspects of
Christology become integrated in the New Testament to form
one whole.

3. Catholic theology must never lose sight of God's self-
interpretation in Jesus Christ, and of the fact that the God who
interprets himself has enough might to make himself comprehensible to men of all times: that is, to deliver his own hermeneutic.
To be sure, God's revelation encounters created man both as an
unchanging and a changing subject, that is, a subject with its
permanent (mostly philosophical) and its changing (cultural)
presuppositions, which man brings to bear as aids in his attempt
to interpret revelation. But, as a believer, man has to be primarily
a hearer of the Word, and he must let this Word finish speaking
without abruptly interrupting with his ready-made notions. Man
must allow his presuppositions to be criticized and modified by
God's Word, in the knowledge that no human thought-model is
sufficient to capture the fullness of divine grace and truth.

Whether they are of a more personal or a more social nature,
schemas for the interpretation of human existence as a whole
often stand in the service of a non-Christian or an anti-Christian
ideology, and they are, therefore, to be tested with double care
for their "neutrality" and possible usefulness for the Christian

explanation of the world. The bias of such a filter or screen can quite distort God's self-interpretation in Christ to the point of unrecognizability.

B. MILESTONES OF SALVATION HISTORY

I. Liberation and Salvation in the Old Testament

1. The salvation history of the people in the Old Testament begins with God's formation of them as a people at the time he led them out of Egypt. According to the universal understanding of the Old Testament, this leading out is no self-liberation, but remains God's "great deed".

It is not a valid objection against this truth to say that God calls forth certain men for this work of liberation. For these men at times rebel in the extreme against their calling (Moses), or they demand signs as a guarantee (Gideon).

2. Israel will always ascribe its first liberation and all later liberations to God's free initiative.

This is particularly evident in the manner in which God is invoked for salvation, redemption, liberation in times of oppression and injustice—invoked either by individuals, whether kings or simple people (cf. the Psalms),[2] or by the whole people's cries for help, as portrayed by the writers of the historical books.

3. The first liberation, in the covenant on Sinai and the cult promulgated with it, has as immediate goal a more than political salvation.

The Exodus tradition and the Sinai tradition are interconnected from the outset (de Vaux). There is in Israel no understanding of salvation which does not include more than political and economic welfare. The covenant with Yahweh implies an interior participation in the holiness of God. It is at once a gift and a moral demand.

---

[2] See especially N. Lohfink, "Heil als Befreiung in Israel", in: L. Scheffczyk, ed., *Erlösung und Emanzipation, Quaestiones Disputatae* 61 (Herder, 1973) 30–50.

4. The "salvation" which is directly promised to the right covenant attitude reveals its eschatological components ever more strongly in the course of history.

As prophecy, the teaching of the Wisdom Books and apocalyptic succeed one another, the content of the concept of salvation becomes ever more inclusive: God, the liberator of Israel, is at the same time Creator of the world and Lord over all peoples intended to participate in his salvation. In its world mission, Israel transcends itself ever more consciously, without nevertheless transcending this world (not even in the doctrine of the two eons). Thus, on the one hand, a certain preliminary understanding is created upon which Jesus will build. But, on the other hand, the permanent end-time messianism sets up an obstacle to the world's definitive transcendence of itself in the act of liberation at the Cross and in the Resurrection.

5. As response to God's deed there is demanded of Israel, in the intercourse among men, a "willingness to liberate" corresponding to God's own liberating attitude.

Israel's ethics and legislation, being interpersonal, are theomorphic: they must be an answer, a correspondence and an echo of God's Word and active behavior. The implications in the economic sector (towards poor members of one's race, migrant workers, etc.) result directly from this, and they are inculcated by the Law and the Prophets.

6. When they fall away from the covenant, the people lapse back into an "Egyptian" situation (Hos 8:13).

God's punishment for those who do not keep the covenant is drastic and consists above all in the loss of the freedom God had wrought (servitude under the great powers, deportation, diaspora, etc.). This punishment is a sign of God's fidelity to his covenant-word. The slaves' labor which is imposed, therefore, is not an "alienating" event, but one which "reminds": it is precisely in the Exile that the decisive meditation on the Law, the culmination of prophecy (the "servant of God"), the writing of history, the full formation of the cult, etc. take place. The time after the Exile is likewise intended to make ever clearer the preponderance of the religious element over the purely political.

II. The Structure of Israel and the Structure of the Church

1. Israel is a people both in the ethnic and in the theological sense, something which cannot be said of the Church.

The Church of the New Covenant is referred to as a "people" only in quotes or references to the old Israel. This expression, when applied to the Church, is just as symbolic as the terms "house", "body" and "bride". This already shows that in the Church the political element receives a new meaning and valuation. From being primarily ethnic, the call in the New Testament becomes primarily personal, which is not to say that the call becomes "privatized". For the personal character of a charism is ordered to the whole "body" of Christ, the whole *Civitas Dei* with its mission to the world. A Christian's expropriation for God and his work for mankind is (through baptism into Christ's obedient death) even more thoroughgoing than being chosen for God in the Old Testament (through circumcision, for instance).

2. In this unity lies Israel's greatness—it has been chosen from among all other peoples—but also its limitation. In contrast to the Church, Israel cannot be universalized, being of ethnic constitution.

Israel has often attempted to explain its special paradoxical position as a role exemplary for all of mankind (Philo, M. Buber); but the ethnic boundary cannot be crossed even by proselytization. Israel's movement remains centripetal (cf. Zionism and its present-day results). Through his death and Resurrection, Jesus Christ is universalized in his Eucharist. Already as the Word of God become man, he addresses himself to every person. Being his disciple within the Church is, therefore, essentially a centrifugal thing: "As the Father has sent me, so do I send you."

3. For this reason, Israel's religious concerns remain political and its political concerns religious, even in the area of its eschatological (chiliastic) hope (cf. I, 4).

The monistic construction of religion–politics, which is a part of Israel's very constitution, has always been disastrous for the Church in all its forms (caesaropapism, *Cujus regio* . . . , etc.) and remains such. With its role in warfare, Qumrân can at once expect two messiahs for the earthly battle at the end of time, a worldly one and a spiritual one. Theologically speaking, the Crusades remain a pious misunderstanding, for in the light of the New Testament there can be no "Holy Land" in a theological sense.

4. In this, Israel is both a positive and a negative *type* of the Church: positive, because of the transcendence of its hope and because of its ethical obligation to give an answer to the God of the covenant; negative, on account of the temporarily unfulfilled state of the promise. For the Church, mankind's bonds of death have been shattered by Christ's Cross, Resurrection and sending of the Spirit, and the negative aspect of these bonds has received a meaning which is positive in an interior sense: the Passion and the death are, beyond all activity possible in this world, an atoning liberation of the world from the enslaving powers, of which the final and the strongest is death.

The salvation bestowed in the New Testament fulfilled the promises of the Old Testament in an extravagant manner (*super-abundanter, eminenter*). For this reason, such salvation must also contain within itself in an eminent manner the positive and typical elements of the covenant. The hope for the definitive (messianic) coming of God's salvation for Israel and for the world as a whole gains a new intensity through what has already been accomplished by Christ's deed and through the "down-payment" of the Holy Spirit for what already is to be had in inchoate form; Israel's answer to God, as an "attitude of liberation among men", becomes in the Church an even more urgent matter due to the perfect convergence of love of God and love of neighbor which results from the Incarnation of God's Word (Mt 25 ff); the old cult is surpassed and supplanted by a new cult which is at the same time mystical (the Eucharist means that the Church and its members are sacrificed together with Christ) and existential (day-to-day service to the world is the completion of the liturgy).

5. The intertwining of religion and politics in the Old Testament is thus transcended in favor of a diastasis. For the Church is

sent out into the structures of the world as a whole, structures which are not identical with its own (sacral) structures but within which it must carry out its activity. On the other hand, the Church is enriched interiorly with a new social dimension un-known in the Old Testament: this is the Communion of Saints, with its own laws and effects which cannot be calculated in worldly terms and which rest on the action of Christ in the paschal mystery.

The dissolution of the Old Testament amalgam of religion and politics in no way implies that the Christian is dispensed from ethico-social action, or even (according to a particular charism) from political action. The Old Testament's political element, which was primarily bound up with the people of Israel, is transposed in a positive manner into the Church's mission to the whole world. By converting hearts to their political responsi-bility, something like the "conversion of structures"[3] can be effected. Beyond this, in the New Testament the paschal mystery becomes the center of Christian activity. Jesus' miracles of heal-ing and feeding the multitudes are not an end in themselves; they are efficacious signs of God's love as it reveals itself unsurpassably on the Cross, liberating man. The Church's corporal works of mercy, including their political dimension, are, moreover, re-minders of the perfect efficaciousness of God's grace on the Cross and forms of his real presence in the world. This is why the Christian norm is not found primarily in external political efficacy, but in the proximity of a given action to Christ's self-denying and obedient attitude, which is what provides the genuine standard for all fruitfulness in the Kingdom of God. Political liberation of the poor and the oppressed, where it is possible, is one of the signs demanded of the Christian to pro-claim the deeper liberation from the power of sin and death by

---

[3] Eberhard Müller, *Bekehrung der Strukturen: Konflikte und ihre Bewältigung im Bereich der Gesellschaft* (Theologischer Verlag, Zürich—Furche Verlag, Hamburg, 1973). It should be noted that the "Church [consists] of Jews and pagans" and that, therefore, from these, its origins, it inherits both things: sacral structures for itself (and this not *only* as an inheritance from Judaism, but because the incarnate Word himself has structure) and profane structures which are outside of itself but to which it is essentially ordered in its mission to the world.

means of the Cross. Christian evangelization can and, indeed, should always begin with the direct proclamation to the poor of this deeper liberation, and with a corresponding pronouncement to the rich and the oppressors. From this point onwards, and as far as possible without violence, following the example of Christ, progress can be made to political and social liberation as well (cf. the Letter to Philemon). This does not preclude the contrasting principle that in situations of extreme social misery a drastic reorganization of living conditions could be the absolute prerequisite for fruitful evangelization.

III. The Secularization of Old Testament Messianism as a Theological Principle in World History

1. With the promises and the hope of the Old Testament there irrupts into history a "utopian" element which breaks up ("demythologizes") the tight interdependence between the order of the polis and the order of the cosmos, and which releases a dynamism that had already seemed a threat to the "heathen" even before Christ and that in the Christian era forcibly becomes part of a ghetto mentality.

The Book of Esther, the Third and Fourth Books of the Maccabees, Philo's *Legatio ad Caium*, etc. bear witness to pre-Christian anti-Semitism. In the Christian era, believing Jews derived their living faith from meditation on the Torah and on messianic expectation; but in so doing they developed a gnosis (the cabala) which grew in its influence upon Christian thought after the Renaissance. In Hasidism this gnosis showed its utopian traits and (through Solomon Maimon) exerted considerable influence even on the German Idealists.

2. With the (post-Christian) Enlightenment and the emancipation of a great portion of enlightened Jewry, Israel's prophetic-utopian pole became detached from the other pole, constituted by the Torah. The result was a great impulse in the direction of man's total liberation (Marx's *Selbsterschaffung*, i.e., man's self-creation and self-determination). Hegel's genial analysis of "master and slave", which is but a single step within the total development of his phenomenology, was raised to an absolute

hermeneutical principle. Yahweh then appeared, first, as the tyrant who imposes his law from above and from whom man must liberate himself. And the conclusion of this trend of thought was that God is the projection of earthly oppression, the abolition of which will result in man's liberation from his alienation.

Several dominant hermeneutics today betray the unmistakable presence of a theological principle at work in the world's history, and this principle is but a secularized aspect of Israel's heritage. Examples of this kind of hermeneutic are: Marx, Freud (human brotherhood based on initial parricide, analysis of the liberation from a fictitious and oppressive super-ego), Bloch (God's Incarnation as the end of his divinity), Kafka (Torah as an oppressive verdict of guilt pronounced on man from without), Wiener (cybernetics as a secularized cabala, cf. Weinreb), Bergson-Simmel-Scheler (vital *élan* as the power governing every form), etc.

3. Whenever a form of Christianity which considers itself enlightened forgets that Christ's Cross and Resurrection have wholly fulfilled the Old Testament's "utopian" promise ("God with us"), the result is not a lapsing back into paganism (which, in any event, is irretrievable), but a drifting into a Judaizing mentality that now reads the New Testament through the filter of a master-slave ideology and which, consequently, takes into its own control the business of mankind's total politico-religious liberation, entirely contrary to the Old Testament's original understanding of Israel.

There was, of course, a long pre-history to the Enlightenment and the idea of a progressive "education of human kind" (Lessing) and a self-liberation of the spirit through historical process (the Idealists)—it included the secularization and rationalization of salvation that occurred within Christianity itself. (Joachim of Flora). In the course of this transformation, the advancing deterioration of the Christian "flesh" laid bare the "skeleton" of the Old Testament. The possibilities of modern technology seemed to foster the goal of a "self-creation" of freedom; at a deeper level, however, they drew their justification from theological potentialities within history, which by now had become unconscious. This state of affairs should warn us to be extremely wary and, indeed, on the lookout for ideological biases whenever theologians, using secularized theological analyses, read and interpret social structures in such a way that these are made to exact certain equally secularized theological actions.[4]

4. The task of subjecting the earth to himself, which was imposed on man by creation, is inscribed in his human nature quite apart from any self-revelation by God. He is to struggle with the powers of the cosmos without any guarantee that he will ever come to terms with them. The order to be established is not, in the final analysis, a social order; according to Plato, justice is the (cardinal) virtue that includes all the others. The Old Testament enhances this striving with a wholly new motif: the anthropological struggle for order is now to become theomorphic (cf. 1,5), and to this end the God of the covenant bestows on man a firmly founded hope in eschatological success. But Israel's provisional role does not allow it to include in its eschatological ideal either the abolition of death or the retroactive justification of all the suffering and injustice accumulated by mankind on its long road. In this sense, Israel remains a "foreshadowing" and an "announcement" (not a mere "sign") of the definitive salvation that appeared in Christ's Cross and Resurrection. Established firmly on this salvific event, Christian hope does not lag behind Old Testament expectation, but rather surpasses it: Christian salvation is not simply "ahead", but rather encompasses the whole course of history.

This is why the hope of the Old Testament, insofar as it aims at a future kingdom of peace and at nothing else, has to be abrogated as something provisional and made to yield to a Kingdom of God which intersects the direction of history, existing in hidden form and suddenly "flaring up" from within it (W. Benjamin). In the end, therefore, only two things stand face to face: mankind as it struggles for order and justice, and God's deed in Christ, announcing the totality of salvation. And this yields the following for the situation of the Christian.

[4] John Chrysostom can stand as an example of the motivation of the fight for social justice without the aid of any extraneous filter of interpretation. Moreover, his "practical" struggle, waged with every fiber of his being, in no way prevented him from being one of the greatest "theoretical" interpreters of the word of God.

IV. Christian Commitment
within Autonomous Worldly Structures

1. Since it aims at the end of time, the message of salvation as lived and proclaimed by Jesus cannot be brought into a wholly univocal relationship with the structuring of the world's future within time.

This is the "eschatological proviso" (Käsemann), which allows neither a monism nor a dualism to exist between history and the Kingdom. The Kingdom of God is eschatological insofar as it is founded, in the end, on Jesus' death and Resurrection and can only be indirectly reflected in the inner-worldly events of history (it is not "observable", Lk 17:21). Deeds that conform to Christ externally can be objectionable because of an interior attitude (Pharisaism). What belongs to God cannot be added to the things of this world as any finite thing can, nor can it be subtracted from them. This is why a pure dualism (between "culture" and "the Kingdom") would also make the Church (as a separate *societas perfecta*) and its mission to the world appear to be something aloof from mankind's own mission to the world, and this would contradict God's becoming human.

2. Insofar as the world as a whole is advancing to its death, it cannot be regarded as an immanent reflection or an anticipation of the Kingdom of God, nor can we hope that the world will become the Kingdom.

All worldly progress is ambivalent, consisting in both gain and loss. There is an entropy of culture, too. "De-velopment" is a loss of tension in the springs that are unwinding. Examples of technical domination of time and space, of industrialization and cosmopolization, etc., are blatant and speak against any utopia that envisions a linear history of liberation.[5] A "total transforma-

---

[5] Aid to the underdeveloped thus favors the "Third World" with questionable boons, which can be useful for an initial period of relief but soon reveal a satanic cloven foot. In his socialistic period, Péguy distinguished sharply between *misère* (distress) and *pauvreté* (poverty): the first is to be remedied at all costs, the second can be a person's and a Christian's normal situation. The difficulty is that those means which seek to remedy *misère* also inject the poor with an appetite for wealth

tion" of mankind, as hoped or postulated by theologians of
liberation, can be conceived only as the definitive entanglement
of the individual in the mesh of the "just" socialistic systems of
distribution.

3. In particular, the world cannot be regarded as such an anticipation of the Kingdom because the scandal of the Cross is an
ever more unbearable provocation to the enclaves of worldly
power as they become increasingly more condensed as a result of
technical progress. The Cross thus necessarily polarizes people's
stances and world views.

Our only prospect on the world's future is given us by
revelation in the apocalyptic tradition (from the Old Testament
to the intertestamental literature, to the Gospels, Paul's letters,
and the Book of Revelation). Especially the New Testament
literature points to an increase in the tensions within the "history
of freedom" unleashed by Christ: the "anti-Christs" (1 Jn) and
the beasts as powers in the Apocalypse appear only after the birth
of the Messiah (Rev 12), and the whole event culminates in a
battle to the death (Rev 19). It appears from this that the Church
is apportioned a path through history which is analogous to the
path of its Lord (cf. Lk 18:8, "Will he find faith on earth?").

4. But Christians must form their attitudes and options as
followers and imitators of Christ. Thus, it is their duty to make
them effective, as far as possible, within the structures of this
world and inside the autonomy of these structures.

Jesus sides with the poor, fulfilling the Old Testament's pronouncements concerning God's saving actions. But the promised
Kingdom is to be universal, and thus Jesus' option does not
constitute the founding of a party in opposition to the wealthy:
these are not cursed, but rather invited to conversion. The tax
collectors with whom Jesus associated were materially rich, but
spiritually they were marginal: like the pagan officers, they
belonged to the class of "oppressors". Among the Pharisees there

---

and prosperity. Péguy the Christian will discover a deeper *misère* in man: that of
sin and concupiscence, to which he will oppose his mystery plays of vicarious
suffering (*Jeanne d'Arc* and *The Holy Innocents*).

were some who "were not far" from the Kingdom of God. What is condemned is egotistic satedness ("the poor Lazarus"), greed ("the rich fool", Lk 12:13 ff.), spiritual oppression (Mt 23:13). The Beatitudes addressed to the poor and others look towards their total salvation, which is inseparably spiritual and material.

The Church, too, must by preference side with the poor: its best members have always done so. But this option cannot compromise the universality of the Church's offer of salvation to all, in such a way that it becomes a political party. It cannot, therefore, celebrate its Eucharist only with those who are materially poor, or limit its Catholic unity to the "party" of the poor, or extend its unity to all only after a victorious "class-struggle".

Above all, the Church must not think in terms of utopias, but of realities. Three things result from this:

a) The Church today is less than ever a superpower in a position to change the basic structures of world economy and world politics. It can only attempt to shape people's opinions within the limits of the possible. It can try to educate in its spirit professionals who can then exert a real influence on the changing of structures.

b) The Church must affect the worldly structures; but these possess their own form, and it would be utopian to want to transform the state into a "superchurch" (cf. Schleiermacher). There is no state without coercion, and the more justice is institutionalized, the more coercion is required for this end (Horkheimer).

c) Following the Christian social teaching and opposing all fascisms of either the right or the left, the Church will not lose sight of the ideal of the *integration* of all men into a worldwide work-process, in which all depend on all. This ideal is in direct opposition to an abstract class-ideal, which has until now failed universally in its application. The Church will, therefore, promote the ideal of an education of all to the acceptance of personal responsibility in state and society—a *democratic* frame of mind which alone overcomes from within dictatorships steered from the left or the right.

C. FINAL REFLECTIONS

The Christian Within "Sinful Structures"

1. At the Medellín Bishops' Conference there was much talk of *estructuras injustas y opresoras* (1,2 and *passim*), of *situación de injusticia* (1,1 and *passim*) and *situación de pecado* (2,1). Now, societal situations can be unjust, but in themselves they cannot be sinful. Only those persons can be sinful who are responsible for the existence of such situations and who continue to tolerate them even though they could abolish or ameliorate them.

2. The New Testament basically recognizes only two contrasting forms of existence: the one subject to *hamartia* and the other freed from *hamartia* by Christ. It does not, therefore, appear to give a direct answer to the question of how Christians can and should live within worldly structures which, even in the best of cases, are only relatively just or least unjust, or to the question of whether they are affected by the inadequacy of these structures. According to Paul, Christians are compelled to live "in the world" (1 Cor 5:10), and at the same time they are told to withdraw spiritually from the world and not to be "yoked" together with unbelievers (2 Cor 6:14). In the Apocalypse they are "sealed" with the sign of the Lamb. A "living space", as it were, is provided for them in the "interstices" between the great powers (Schürmann), but they can also "be defeated" by the superior might of the demonic powers (13:6). For the situation of Christians in an un-Christian world of politics and economics, one will scarcely (with R. Niebuhr) appeal to the principle of *simul peccator et justus*, but rather to the gradations of fidelity to Christ as we find them in the circular letters of the Apocalypse and also in Paul's epistles. The actual influence an individual Christian exerts on a total economic system remains very different in different cases. But each one can help to boycott luxury by a personal attitude of poverty, not only by one's visible example before others but also invisibly by the fruitfulness of one's stance before God.

3. Christians can share guilt in social injustice without actually realizing it, whether because of pure ignorance (cf. G. B. Shaw's play *Mrs. Warren's Profession*) or because of an education that holds certain class privileges to be right which objectively are not so considering society as a whole. In such circumstances, the Church—both clergy and laity—has the duty to sensitize public opinion and thus usher in a more just balance of goods, without, for all that, globally condemning as "sinful" such a highly complex economic system as "capitalism".

4. Today more than ever competent Christians should become active in the social, economic and political sectors of society, where one necessarily confronts hard contradictions and struggles, and where compromise always represents the best solution ("Politics is the art of the possible"). The evangelical "peacemaker" has to set up shop precisely between parties in conflict, between employers and employees, political factions and economic interest groups. Only by the—dramatic!—collaboration of all will the structures be "converted" from their "sinfulness" and changed more effectively than by violent overthrows or brutal nationalizations behind which there are very often goals sought in utopian and unrealistic fashion.

5. The urgency of the practical concerns of liberation theology is not called into question by any criticism that may be made of it. But the totality of God's revelation to the world can in no way be reduced to political and social liberation, nor even to the general concept of liberation. Liberation theology has its specific place in a theology of the Kingdom of God. It is *one* aspect of the whole of theology and, in practical terms, it demands the Church's commitment to the shaping of the world as a whole in a manner conforming with Christ.

II

JEAN GALOT

JESUS AND THE PLAN FOR A SOCIETY OF BROTHERLY LOVE
Translated by Pamela Joseph Benson

Because he wanted the Kingdom of God to be established among
mankind on earth, Jesus instituted his Church as the beginning of
the transformation of society. Without elaborating any precise
plan for this transformation, he established the bases on which
society should be developed. In this sense the general plan for a
fraternal society can be found in the Gospels. Our aim here is not
to apply this plan in a practical way, but simply to try to
understand Jesus' intentions better by rediscovering them in the
Gospels. As we have noted elsewhere,[1] the notion of the Kingdom of God is authentically Jesus'; its authority is demonstrated
by its appurtenance to the Jewish tradition and by the radical
novelty of the meaning Jesus gave it. This novelty is not just a
new description of old ideas; it involves all the profound thought
of the one who brought men a divine design for a new life.
Without doubt, Jesus is the greatest revolutionary of the spiritual
and religious order, but he began with the state of human society
as he found it. He wished the new spirit to modify the legacy
received from the past in a gradual way so that society would be
able to evolve without damage or destruction.

Love That Passes All Limits
Because It Comes from God

In the evangelical view the Kingdom of God is the Kingdom in
which love of God is spread and manifested in the love of men for
each other. This principle is revealed in the prayer Jesus taught.

Originally published under the title "Gesù e il progetto di una società fraterna"
in La Civiltà Cattolica (18 November 1978) 342–53. Reprinted by permission.
[1] Cf. J. Galot, "Gesù ha predicato un regno di Dio 'politico'?", in Civ. Catt. III
(1978) 105–18.

The disciples are invited to ask the Father to let his Kingdom come. The only precise indication about the manner in which to establish it derives from the following request: forgive us our debts as we also forgive our debtors (Mt 6:12). The Kingdom of the Father cannot come except on the condition that we forgive those who have wronged us. We cannot ask the Father to forgive our faults if we ourselves do not assume this attitude of sincere forgiveness toward others. Obviously, this does not mean that we must be the first to pardon. It is above all the Father who pardons, but his pardon cannot extend to us in the concrete if we also do not pardon others. There would be an internal contradiction between the divine grace of the pardon and our behavior if we refused to pardon each other.

If Jesus spoke of this pardon it is because he attached great importance to it. He knew the difficulty that men would have had in pardoning and the temptation that would have pushed them to stress and also to aggravate the wrongs they received from others. This temptation occurs not only in individual life but also in the life of society. Exacerbated nationalism concentrates its gaze on the wrongs, on the lacks and the injustices, of other nations. The spirit of the class war stimulates hatred, indicting the wrongs of a social class, reducing to a system the denunciation of exploitation or of oppression and attributing them exclusively to others and to a collective category. Although a few liberation theologians have tried to introduce this fight into the presentation of the Gospel message,[2] it is necessary to say that this is in manifest conflict with Jesus' precepts and outlook. In preaching this attitude that consists of forgiving the trespasses of those who trespass against us, Jesus does not ask that we ignore the injuries received: he desires that we attempt to put an end to unjust actions since he himself wants a society that is held together by relationships of love and respectful of the rights of everyone: he requires a true and complete pardon that excludes feelings of hatred or rancor or desire for revenge.

This pardon is expressly recollected in the Our Father as a sign of the boundless love that must characterize the reign of the

[2] Cf. G. Gutiérrez, *Teologia della Liberazione* (Brescia: Queriniana, 1972) 272–77.

Father; the universality and limitlessness of love are signs of the divine. For Jesus, the Kingdom of God signifies the kingdom of unbounded love.

It is precisely in this field of forgiveness that Jesus wished to show that all limits must be surmounted. To Peter, who maintained that offenses ought to be pardoned a maximum of seven times, he prescribed pardoning "up to seventy times seven" (Mt 18:22). The rule of unlimited forgiveness is given for all his disciples, but the fact that such a principle was formulated for the future head of the Church demonstrates to what extent it must be applied in the Christian life, so insolubly joined to membership in the Church.

The recommendation found in Matthew (Mt 18:5–18) to attempt reconciliation to the bitter end works in the same way. It has often been misinterpreted, since men have believed to find a justification for excommunication in it, whereas it aimed principally at putting into play all means for reestablishing good relations.[3] When the means provided by law or custom are shown to be insufficient, it is necessary to have recourse to other means, as is done in relations with publicans and pagans. Whatever one tries to do in the efforts of union and of reconciliation, in conformity with the established rules or outside them, it is always approved in heaven. Jesus, therefore, invites us to overcome all laws that limit charity.

The Moral Revolution Accomplished by Jesus

In the formulation of his precepts, Jesus gives an example of going beyond the past when he opposes a new law to the ancient one that circumscribes love of one's neighbor within reasonable limits: "You have heard that it was said: love your neighbor and hate your enemy. But I say to you: love your enemies, pray for those who persecute you" (Mt 5:43–44). One might say that it is in this love for one's enemies that all the force of the moral and spiritual revolution worked by Christ in humanity is expressed: a revolution consciously and deliberately provoked, as is demon-

[3] Cf. J. Galot, "Un messaggio sconvolgente di riconciliazione," in *Civ. Catt.* II (1975) 42–51.

strated by the conflict between that which the Jewish law enjoined and the "but I say to you"; revolution so radical that it would encounter many difficulties in guiding Christian conduct.

The liberation theologians who have allowed or encouraged the class war have in effect wished to return to the ancient law: "You shall love your neighbor and hate your enemy." They have attempted to justify their positions on every sort of pretext, as though, for example, in ordering the love of enemies Jesus admitted that one could have enemies; or again, that the best way to love them is to combat them.[4] Certainly the fact of having enemies was assumed by the commandment; but if no one can prevent others from hating and from behaving like enemies, the Christian must behave in such a way that there is no hostility on his part. Moreover, love that one owes to enemies must be a sincere love that translates into benevolent action in practice and not into a fight to annihilate others: "Do good to those who hate you" (Lk 6:27).

In order that no loopholes or illusions may be encountered, Jesus specifies the attitudes that love for one's enemies requires: beyond the good that is to be done for those who are moved by hostile feelings, it is a question of blessing those who curse us, praying for those who calumniate us. Even the last refuge of hatred and revenge, that which in the Old Testament consisted in praying God to take revenge himself on those who made one suffer, is now forbidden: prayer must not express anything other than the sincere desire to obtain benefits for those who do evil.

It is therefore in the deepest attitudes of spirit and heart, as well as in external behavior, that love for one's neighbors must exist. Those who believe themselves to be revolutionaries because they feed the hostility of one social class toward another do nothing but follow the old paths of human instinct; in reality, in the eyes of Christ's moral law, they are not revolutionary enough. True revolution is produced in the heart of the man who responds to hatred with love.

The true principle for the change in social relations as Christ planned it for the future of humanity is found there, in this heart. Such a change cannot come from anywhere but above; according

[4] Cf. G. Gutiérrez, op. cit.

to what Jesus tells us, it comes from the Father: "Love your enemies . . . that you may be sons of your Father who is in heaven, who makes his sun rise over the wicked and over the good and makes the rain fall on the just and the unjust" (Mt 5:44–45). The celestial Father wishes to communicate his own goodness to his children: this goodness consists in granting to everyone, friends and enemies, the gifts of creation; when he ascertains the ruin produced by wickedness and injustice, he does not destroy the "system", but he seeks to conquer the evil with love. He makes those who resist him and offend him benefit from his creative activity and his providence. This divine perfection of universal and limitless love must be reflected in those who are his children: "Therefore be perfect as your heavenly Father is perfect" (Mt 5:48). Luke's version is more explicit: "Therefore be merciful as your Father is merciful" (Lk 6:36). The perfection of the Father is evident in his merciful love; and it is this perfection that must be revealed in Christian conduct.

The transcendent origin of love for one's enemies makes it understandable that no merely human doctrine has attained the formulation of this principle. But there is more, the moral doctrines that limit their horizons to the mere level of relations between men run the risk of opposing such an elevated recommendation, likening it to weakness or passivity before the forces of evil. Only Christ has broken the chains of human hostilities that reinforce one another and prolong themselves indefinitely. He caused this rupture by bringing the Father's message and making us see the living image of the paternal face, the first source of love.

"As I Have Loved You"

The simple announcement by the Father's messenger would not have sufficed. The discovery of God's merciful love could have been an indication and a stimulus, but it still would not have been capable of giving the decisive force necessary to change human feelings. The principle of this new society was established with the Savior's absolute engagement in the way of love.

It is useful to discern clearly all that is innate in the "new commandment". The precept "Love each other" is presented very directly as a principle of social life and not only as a rule of individual life: it is a question of reciprocal love that depends on the cooperation of everyone. The words "as I have loved you" established the model to follow. Jesus had spoken of another model: in fact, we have seen how he recommended that his disciples imitate the perfection of the Father. But this perfection retains something of the invisible, even in its own manifestations. The love witnessed by the Savior is the full and visible revelation of the Father's love for men, a revelation expressed with a human love. Jesus demonstrated how it is possible to love in all the circumstances of his earthly existence.

His love reached out particularly toward those who needed help, and with this he showed, in a definitive manner, an orientation that will never lack charity: a predilection for the poor and unfortunate. Note, in fact, that "the poor, the crippled, the blind, the lame" (Lk 14:21) are invited into the Kingdom of Heaven. The attention paid to the most unfortunate testifies above all that they are destined to receive the first places in the Kingdom. At the same time it encourages Christians to interest themselves in the welfare of those who find themselves in a position of indigence or misfortune so that they may help them as much as possible in both the political and social arenas. Here it is a question of going far beyond social justice, since, whatever the successes of this justice may be, the world will always have poor or unfortunate people. An imbalance of justice naturally exists in certain cases, and these require a supplement of effective love.

The predilection for the less favored takes an even more universal form in Jesus' behavior because of the benevolence he shows toward all those who are cast aside by society, or those toward whom there is public reprobation, and especially toward those who are classified as sinners. Among these sinners are the publicans, considered to be collaborators with the occupying power and exploiters of the people in the collection of taxes. Jesus has the audacity to mix with them and to praise their disposition to conversion (Lk 18:10; Mt 12:31). He does not fear to challenge the murmurs of the crowd when he announces to Zacchaeus, head of the publicans, that he has decided to ask for his hospitality; and because of his graciousness, he obtains the conversion of this man who promises him that he will behave completely differently: "Behold, Lord, I will give half of my goods to the poor" (Lk 19:8). In this way, Jesus demonstrates that he refuses to participate in the condemnations and exclusions practiced by his society. He opens his love to all without exception, and in a few cases, like that of the repentant prostitute or the head of the publicans, the effectiveness of this love that transforms unexemplary conduct is manifested in a very significant manner.

In the sacrifice, Christ's love takes on all its real dimension. When he proposes his love as a model of charity, Jesus refers to his sacrifice. The words "as I have loved you" indicate the greatest love, which consists of sacrificing one's own life for one's friends (Jn 15:13). Now, this model, indicating the sacrifices which one must be prepared to make for the love of others, shows the price Jesus paid to secure the liberation of the human heart and the triumph of love in humanity.

Here again Jesus turns the dominant conceptions of his time upside-down. We know that his contemporaries dreamt of a glorious messianism, an earthly kingdom in which all human desires would be satisfied. In contrast to these presentations of a paradisiac society, Jesus lays down the principle of love that accepts suffering and offers it up to make the building of a better society, where love will never be purely pleasure. This new humanity cannot be generated except in pain; love that must spread through the community of men necessarily involves a painful, a sacrificial aspect. It is redemptive love.

Every social doctrine that would seek to propose a form of terrestrial paradise would be an illusion, according to this measure. It would be a return to myth. The society of brotherly love cannot be built except at the price of profound renunciations.

Liberation

Christian charity and a society of brotherly love begins in a liberating sacrifice. Christ brings authentic liberation to humanity, a liberation for which the Son of man gives his life in redemption for many (Mk 10:45; Mt 20:28). Other projects for liberation could have tempted the Jews of his time, like the zealot movement that was preparing violent revolutionary action; in the course of history, various projects of national and social liberation have not ceased to find adherents.

Of what has the liberation effected by Christ consisted, then? It has been a liberation from the essential servitude which alienates the human personality, that servitude of sin: "Whoever sins is a slave" (Jn 8:34). Sin is simultaneously separation from God and division among men, so that liberation must reconcile man with God and men with each other. Man must become himself again in relations of friendship with God and in social relations of mutual love; but to attain this, man must be saved from his own alienation. Thus, according to the affirmation of Saint John, "Jesus had to die . . . to bring together the dispersed sons of God" (Jn 11:51–52). The dispersion was the fruit of sin; unity could not come except from the Savior.

Christ's sacrifice has liberated man from the egoism to which he was a slave; at the same time it has earned him the gift of the power of superior love, that love which comes from God and is communicated by means of the gift of the Holy Spirit. The construction of a society of brotherly love is based, therefore, on this liberation and on this gift of divine love. Liberation permits man to overcome all the obstacles that he meets inside himself, and transcendent love allows him to surpass all the limits that his brothers may attempt to put on his gift.

As for the political and social liberation proposed by the Marxist vision as an essential objective to be reached, let us observe that the liberation procured by Jesus is more fundamental, more universal, and has more important consequences in all areas of human life, including the political and social spheres.

It is a fundamental liberation since it frees man to the extent that he is man and in his most profound inclinations. The construction of a society of brotherly love cannot be achieved except by a "new man", he who has been newly created by the Savior in the image of God. If the liberation of the human heart had not occurred, every other liberation would remain external, superficial, and ineffective in the end. For what would it serve to change the structures of economic life and social relationships if man were not freed from the rule of his egoism? In this change of structure, exploitation and oppression would continue to be exercised in some other way. The only path to building a more just, more humane society is that which passes by way of the liberation of the depths of man; and this has only been effected by Christ, and it produces its effect in those who open themselves to the liberating action of the Savior.

On the other hand, the liberation offered to humanity by Christ is universal in scope: it is not simply the liberation of a social class. All men need it as all are subject to sin.

Finally, it is destined to have consequences in all fields of human activity: in the order of individual psychology it is expressed in liberation from the emotions of fear and from other inclinations that hinder love; in the order of social relations, it permits a fuller expansion of fraternal love; in political activity, it tends to liberate men from the thirst for power and to render them capable of wanting to serve their brothers sincerely rather than to make themselves be served by them, seeking honors and profits.

Jesus Confronted with Violence

Some liberation movements have based their hopes on violence; and "liberation theology" has sought for indications in favor of this violence in the Gospels. However, the liberation effected by Christ is characterized by a renunciation of violence. According to the Gospels, those who use violence are those who want to usurp the Kingdom in order to annihilate it. Thus the Kingdom "suffers violence", being a victim of persecution (Mt 11:12).

This Gospel text has been interpreted as a justification for violence, as if Jesus had recommended violence as a way of entering the Kingdom.[5] But, according to the version of St. Matthew, it is probably a question of hostile action that had already been spreading since the time of John the Baptist; thus it is the violence of those who persecuted Jesus and his work and impeded men from entering the Kingdom. Neither does Luke's sentence (Lk 16:16), which speaks of violence as a means of entering the Kingdom, aim at violence employed against others.

[5] Cf. G. Gutiérrez, op. cit., 229.

What is certain is the general behavior of Jesus, which excludes any recourse to material force.

As weapons in his conflicts with adversaries, Jesus knew only truth and goodness. Always answering accusations and cavils in a way that brought new clarity, he counted on the power of truth. He constrained no one to adhere to the faith; he simply proposed a doctrine capable of sustaining this adhesion in men of good will. In his trial, as in all his public life, he gave testimony and left it up to each person to appreciate its value: he even shunned the use of intellectual violence to impose his message. The coercion is found on the side of the adversaries, who did not allow those who would have liked to enter the Kingdom to do so (Mt 23:13). Contrarily, referring to the liberty and responsibility of the human person in welcoming the good news, Jesus shows himself to be a liberator. He proposes a principle destined to be of considerable influence upon the life of society, in the sense of the opening up, the blooming, of liberty, and of the suppression of intellectual constraints. His message cannot be discussed, diminished, or altered; it may only be taken or left, but everyone receives it or refuses it freely. The strength of the attraction of truth, made more potent by the illuminating action of the Spirit, is destined to triumph without abolishing human liberty.

In conflicts imposed on him by the hostility of his adversaries, Jesus wanted to base his victory, not only on truth, but on goodness. In seeking to convince, he presented himself with an attractiveness that never allowed itself to be overwhelmed by disappointments. Not wishing to make the good news penetrate except by the power of love, he applied this principle to the fullest extent, refusing to oppose violence with violence. He did not resist those who came to arrest him, or those who condemned him to death. He let himself be crucified without the least reaction of force. His only answer to the hatred of his enemies was an entreaty for pardon, in which he tried to exculpate them. The Cross could have been a platform for him, from which, in his capacity as sovereign judge, he could have denounced the injustice and exposed the guilt of those responsible for the crucifixion. Far from making this denunciation, Jesus sought the extenuating circumstances in favor of those responsible and solicited for them, not punishment, but pardon.

In this way, the development of love in the human heart and the creation of a society of brotherly love are not only objectives of the liberation he worked in humanity; this liberation is already complete in the full realization of the love he wishes to institute. Jesus never wished to use violence with the aim of then being able to establish a community of love; he himself followed this unique way of love, so that his liberating sacrifice would constitute the definitive model of love carried to an extreme—the immaculate, irreproachable principle of the new human society.

Evangelic Instructions about Social Behavior

If the essential liberation brought to humanity by Christ puts a heavy emphasis on the social behavior of Christians, what instructions about this love that must transform society do we find in the Gospel texts?

We know that Jesus showed himself to be very sensitive to the misery that he met in the society of his time and we know how much he would have liked to remedy it. He expressly wished that his disciples have an analogous attitude. The context of universal judgment illuminates the religious meaning of this attitude. Above all, the fact that judgment is passed on behavior toward unfortunates is already an indication of the importance of this social attitude. We must not think that judgment is based exclusively on this attitude because we must keep in mind other words of Jesus, especially those that record judgment on the testimony of the faith: "Whoever will recognize me before men, I also will recognize him before my Father who is in heaven (Mt 10:32; cf. Mk 8:38; Lk 9:26; 12:8–9). Men, therefore, will also be judged on their faith; the fact remains, however, that love toward unfortunates is a main factor in judgment.

Jesus emphasizes the mysterious significance of this love that touches him personally: "you did it to me" (Mt 25:40). It is present even in those whom we might be tempted to overlook or disdain: "All that which you have done to one of the least among my brothers, you have done it to me." This presence of Jesus is not tied to the moral value of those who must be helped, since it is also verified in those who are in prison: one can be incarcerated unjustly, as in the case of the persecuted, but one can also have merited it by criminal conduct. The presence of Christ is assured in all, whoever they may be; thus an act of love toward them is received by Christ in person.

The presence of Christ in every unfortunate person confers, therefore, a superior significance to love. It equally shows that no pretext can exist for excluding anyone from the duty to help in an efficacious way. Moreover, the examples listed by Jesus have a notable social value. They belong to the context of the Jewish society of that epoch, but they continue to be strikingly topical. "I was hungry": thus Jesus posed the problem of world hunger, and with it the more general problem of poverty: "I was naked." The problem of immigrants and of the harmonious relations between the races emerges from the affirmation, "I was a foreigner." All aspects of cures requested by sick people at home or in hospitals are mentioned: "I was sick." The declaration, "I was a prisoner", calls attention to the problem of delinquency, to the reeducation of prisoners and their reinsertion into society. In Jesus' design, this enumeration is only suggestive and does not intend to list all the unfortunate cases in need of help. The principle, presented in a general fashion, is not restricted only to individual relations, but concerns all the problems that society must face in order to keep in mind the needs of all those who are less fortunate.

The importance of this social help, nevertheless, does not hide the essential value of human destiny, which does not consist in creating an opulent earthly society; what is decisive is the acquisition of heavenly life for eternity. The eternal society is being built now with that love which unfolds in earthly relations, since entrance to the heavenly realm is granted to those who have helped the unfortunate.

The parable of the rich captive (Lk 16:19–31) can be understood in this same way; it, too, calls attention to social behavior. This parable points out the scandal of the coexistence of wealth and poverty. It does not present a case of exploitation, nor of injury done to others; it puts under our eyes, however, the figure of a rich man who enjoys his goods abundantly, refusing to give anything to a poor man. In our present situation, it evokes the contrast between immense fortunes and extreme forms of poverty. What truly is in question is the redivision of earthly goods: it is intolerable that considerable wealth and extreme poverty should exist together. The parable depicts only an individual situation, but it is evident that the lesson it imparts reaches much farther. It should be applied to the nexus of social connections to bring about a more equal division of goods. Today the most urgent application must be on an international plane, to suppress the excessive inequalities that exist between rich and poor nations.

The obligation to share is not bounded by the perspective of earthly goods, but, as a final goal, it is oriented toward the happiness of the beyond. Those who have not benefited from this equal participation during earthly life will receive a superior compensation in eternal beatitude: only the future world will level all the inequalities and put an end to all unjust situations.

Is there hope that the rich may understand their responsibilities? Jesus condemns no one; he does not exclude them from the Kingdom, but he makes it clear what a great obstacle their wealth presents. At the end of the parable a path of liberation and conversion is suggested, but with the appearance of the hypothesis "If one were to rise again from the dead" (Lk 16:31). The resurrected Savior will have the power to free the rich from their egoism on the condition, however, that they allow themselves to be convinced.

What Jesus condemns is an attachment to money to the extent of making it an idol, an absolute that must be served: the service of money and the service of God are incompatible (Mt 6:24; Lk 16:13). This attachment is encountered more easily among the rich, but it also occurs in those who make acquisition of earthly goods the goal of their life. A certain detachment is necessary, and it must help social relations and arouse the intention to share everything with one's less fortunate brothers.

Justice and Love

A wish to go beyond strict justice emerges from the references to social behavior that we have surveyed: help for the poor and the sharing of goods must surpass the requirements of justice and be animated by generosity and love. In his preaching, John the Baptist called to mind a few rules of justice, those that consisted in never doing wrong to anyone and in giving everyone what he deserves (Lk 3:10–14). Jesus goes beyond this and insists on the necessity of not claiming one's rights and of not contenting oneself with the minimum in one's own duties. Untiring pardon for offenses and love for one's enemies are expressions of this surmounting of justice.

Christian charity is often reproved for wanting to substitute itself for justice. If one reduces charity to alms, if one conceives of it as a disposition that dispenses with doing what is just and one tries to replace his obligations to impartiality with arbitrary and gratuitous generosity, then one has not understood the meaning of the authentic love instituted and recommended by Jesus. This love must take upon itself all the obligations of justice and, in particular, must promote social justice. Far from restricting the meaning of justice, it must be applied with great conviction. But it is necessary to do more.

Only love can assure the building of a society of brotherly love. Jesus wanted to found more than a well-regulated society in which the laws of justice would be promulgated and respected. After his liberating sacrifice, he called his disciples "my brothers", indicating the supreme source of this brotherhood: "My Father and your Father" (Jn 20:17). He communicated to men his divine origin and he instituted the community of those who have become brothers through being sons of the same celestial Father. This fraternal community responds to the deepest aspirations of humanity; it satisfies them by surpassing them with its transcendent foundation, divine filiation.

In the light of this superior principle, one can better understand why everyone must recognize in the least of his brothers the face of the one who is the first-born brother. Thanks to him, human brotherhood has become a brotherhood of men with God. Social justice without brotherly love would be a soulless structure. Changes in structure can produce only a new judicial system or institutions of different kinds. But what must be improved in society is the spirit which must govern social relations.

Brotherly love introduces a new mentality. It expresses a solidarity that wants to overcome all economic and social conflicts, looking for true harmony. It imparts a more positive orientation to the fight against injustice, making it avoid the danger of purely egoistic claims or hostilities full of rancor. It completes and corrects the inevitable insufficiencies in the social order and relieves the unfortunate situations that no measure of justice and social laws can succeed in suppressing.

It is true that Jesus did not prescribe a social or political system, but he established a superior principle of social life and, from this point of view, one can say that he left his disciples a plan for society that is superior to those that could be conceived and experienced after him. This plan is the plan of God himself, the plan of the Kingdom of God: the Christian's responsibility is to translate it into concrete achievements.

III

JEANE KIRKPATRICK

DICTATORSHIPS
AND DOUBLE STANDARDS

The failure of the Carter administration's foreign policy is now clear to everyone except its architects, and even they must entertain private doubts, from time to time, about a policy whose crowning achievement has been to lay the groundwork for a transfer of the Panama Canal from the United States to a swaggering Latin dictator of Castroite bent. In the thirty-odd months since the inauguration of Jimmy Carter as President there has occurred a dramatic Soviet military build-up, matched by the stagnation of American armed forces, and a dramatic extension of Soviet influence in the Horn of Africa, Afghanistan, Southern Africa, and the Caribbean, matched by a declining American position in all these areas. The U.S. has never tried so hard and failed so utterly to make and keep friends in the Third World.

As if this were not bad enough, in the current year the United States has suffered two other major blows—in Iran and Nicaragua—of large and strategic significance. In each country, the Carter administration not only failed to prevent the undesired outcome, it actively collaborated in the replacement of moderate autocrats friendly to American interests with less friendly autocrats of extremist persuasion. It is too soon to be certain about what kind of regime will ultimately emerge in either Iran or Nicaragua, but accumulating evidence suggests that things are as likely to get worse as to get better in both countries. The Sandinistas in Nicaragua appear to be as skillful in consolidating power as the Ayatollah Khomeini is inept, and leaders of both revolutions display an intolerance and arrogance that do not bode well for the peaceful sharing of power or the establishment of constitutional governments, especially since those leaders have made it clear that they have no intention of seeking either.

Reprinted by permission from *Commentary* (November 1979); all rights reserved.

It is at least possible that the SALT debate may stimulate new scrutiny of the nation's strategic position and defense policy, but there are no signs that anyone is giving serious attention to this nation's role in Iranian and Nicaraguan developments—despite clear warnings that the U.S. is confronted with similar situations and options in El Salvador, Guatemala, Morocco, Zaire, and elsewhere. Yet no problem of American foreign policy is more urgent than that of formulating a morally and strategically acceptable, and politically realistic, program for dealing with non-democratic governments who are threatened by Soviet-sponsored subversion. In the absence of such a policy, we can expect that the same reflexes that guided Washington in Iran and Nicaragua will be permitted to determine American actions from Korea to Mexico—with the same disastrous effects on the U.S. strategic position. (That the administration has not called its policies in Iran and Nicaragua a failure—and probably does not consider them such—complicates the problem without changing its nature.)

There were, of course, significant differences in the relations between the United States and each of these countries during the past two or three decades. Oil, size, and proximity to the Soviet Union gave Iran greater economic and strategic import than any Central American "republic", and closer relations were cultivated with the Shah, his counselors, and family than with President Somoza, his advisers, and family. Relations with the Shah were probably also enhanced by our approval of his mani-fest determination to modernize Iran regardless of the effects of modernization on traditional social and cultural patterns (includ-ing those which enhanced his own authority and legitimacy). And, of course, the Shah was much better looking and altogether more dashing than Somoza; his private life was much more romantic, more interesting to the media, popular and otherwise. Therefore, more Americans were more aware of the Shah than of the equally tenacious Somoza.

But even though Iran was rich, blessed with a product the U.S. and its allies needed badly, and led by a handsome king, while Nicaragua was poor and rocked along under a long-tenure presi-dent of less striking aspect, there were many similarities between the two countries and our relations with them. Both these small nations were led by men who had not been selected by free elections, who recognized no duty to submit themselves to searching tests of popular acceptability. Both did tolerate limited opposition, including opposition newspapers and political parties, but both were also confronted by radical, violent opponents bent on social and political revolution. Both rulers, therefore, sometimes invoked martial law to arrest, imprison, exile, and occasionally, it was alleged, torture their opponents. Both relied for public order on police forces whose personnel were said to be too harsh, too arbitrary, and too powerful. Each had what the American press termed "private armies", which is to say, armies pledging their allegiance to the ruler rather than the "constitution" or the "nation" or some other impersonal entity.

In short, both Somoza and the Shah were, in central ways, traditional rulers of semi-traditional societies. Although the Shah very badly wanted to create a technologically modern and powerful nation and Somoza tried hard to introduce modern agricultural methods, neither sought to reform his society in the light of any abstract idea of socal justice or political virtue. Neither attempted to alter significantly the distribution of goods, status, or power (though the democratization of education and skills that accompanied modernization in Iran did result in some redistribution of money and power there).

Both Somoza and the Shah enjoyed long tenure, large personal fortunes (which were no doubt in large part appropriated from general revenues), and good relations with the United States. The Shah and Somoza were not only anti-Communist, they were positively friendly to the U.S., sending their sons and others to be educated in our universities, voting with us in the United Nations, and regularly supporting American interests and positions even when these entailed personal and political cost. The embassies of both governments were active in Washington social life, and were frequented by powerful Americans who occupied major roles in this nation's diplomatic, military, and political life. And the Shah and Somoza themselves were both welcome in Washington, and had many American friends.

Though each of the rulers was from time to time criticized by American officials for violating civil and human rights, the fact that the people of Iran and Nicaragua only intermittently enjoyed the rights accorded to citizens in the Western democracies did not prevent successive administrations from granting—with the necessary approval of successive Congresses—both military and economic aid. In the case of both Iran and Nicaragua, tangible and intangible tokens of U.S. support continued until the regime became the object of a major attack by forces explicitly hostile to the United States.

But once an attack was launched by opponents bent on destruction, everything changed. The rise of serious, violent opposition in Iran and Nicaragua set in motion a succession of events which bore a suggestive resemblance to one another and a suggestive similarity to our behavior in China before the fall of Chiang Kai-shek, in Cuba before the triumph of Castro, in certain crucial periods of the Vietnamese war, and, more recently, in Angola. In each of these countries, the American effort to impose liberalization and democratization on a government confronted with violent internal opposition not only failed, but actually assisted the coming to power of new regimes in which ordinary people enjoy fewer freedoms and less personal security than under the previous autocracy—regimes, moreover, hostile to American interests and policies.

The pattern is familiar enough: an established autocracy with a record of friendship with the U.S. is attacked by insurgents, some of whose leaders have long ties to the Communist movement, and most of whose arms are of Soviet, Chinese, or Czechoslovak origin. The "Marxist" presence is ignored and/or minimized by American officials and by the elite media on the ground that U.S. support for the dictator gives the rebels little choice but to seek aid "elsewhere". Violence spreads and American officials wonder aloud about the viability of a regime that "lacks the support of its own people". The absence of an opposition party is deplored and civil-rights violations are reviewed. Liberal columnists question the morality of continuing aid to a "rightist dictatorship" and provide assurances concerning the essential moderation of some insurgent leaders who "hope" for some sign that the U.S. will remember its own revolutionary origins. Requests for help from the beleaguered autocrat go unheeded, and the argument is increasingly voiced that ties should be established with rebel leaders "before it is too late". The President, delaying U.S. aid, appoints a special emissary who confirms the deterioration of the government position and its diminished capacity to control the situation and recommends various measures for "strengthening" and "liberalizing" the regime, all of which involve diluting its power.

The emissary's recommendations are presented in the context of a growing clamor for American disengagement on grounds that continued involvement confirms our status as an agent of imperialism, racism, and reaction; is inconsistent with support for human rights; alienates us from the "forces of democracy"; and threatens to put the U.S. once more on the side of history's "losers". This chorus is supplemented daily by interviews with returning missionaries and "reasonable" rebels.

As the situation worsens, the President assures the world that the U.S. desires only that the "people choose their own form of government"; he blocks delivery of all arms to the government and undertakes negotiations to establish a "broadly based" coalition headed by a "moderate" critic of the regime who, once elevated, will move quickly to seek a "political" settlement to the conflict. Should the incumbent autocrat prove resistant to American demands that he step aside, he will be readily overwhelmed by the military strength of his opponents, whose patrons will have continued to provide sophisticated arms and advisers at the same time the U.S. cuts off military sales. Should the incumbent be so demoralized as to agree to yield power, he will be replaced by a "moderate" of American selection. Only after the insurgents have refused the proffered political solution and anarchy has spread throughout the nation will it be noticed that the new head of government has no significant following, no experience at governing, and no talent for leadership. By then, military commanders, no longer bound by loyalty to the chief of state, will depose the faltering "moderate" in favor of a fanatic of their own choosing.

In either case, the U.S. will have been led by its own misunderstanding of the situation to assist actively in deposing an erstwhile friend and ally and installing a government hostile to American interests and policies in the world. At best we will have lost access to friendly territory. At worst the Soviets will have gained a new base. And everywhere our friends will have noted that the U.S.

cannot be counted on in times of difficulty and our enemies will have observed that American support provides no security against the forward march of history.

No particular crisis conforms exactly with the sequence of events described above; there are always variations on the theme. In Iran, for example, the Carter administration—and the President himself—offered the ruler support for a longer time, though by December 1978 the President was acknowledging that he did not know if the Shah would survive, adding that the U.S. would not get "directly involved". Neither did the U.S. ever call publicly for the Shah's resignation. However, the President's special emissary, George Ball, "reportedly concluded that the Shah cannot hope to maintain total power and must now bargain with a moderate segment of the opposition . . ." and was "known to have discussed various alternatives that would effectively ease the Shah out of total power" (Washington *Post*, December 15, 1978). There is, furthermore, not much doubt that the U.S. assisted the Shah's departure and helped arrange the succession of Bakhtiar. In Iran, the Carter administration's commitment to nonintervention proved stronger than strategic considerations or national pride. What the rest of the world regarded as a stinging American defeat, the U.S. government saw as a matter to be settled by Iranians. "We personally prefer that the Shah maintain a major role in the government," the President acknowledged, "but that is a decision for the Iranian people to make."

Events in Nicaragua also departed from the scenario presented above because the Cuban and Soviet roles were clearer and because U.S. officials were more intensely and publicly working against Somoza. After the Somoza regime had defeated the first wave of Sandinista violence, the U.S. ceased aid, imposed sanctions, and took other steps which undermined the status and the credibility of the government in domestic and foreign affairs. Between the murder of ABC correspondent Bill Stewart by a National Guardsman in early June and the Sandinista victory in late July, the U.S. State Department assigned a new ambassador who refused to submit his credentials to Somoza even though Somoza was still chief of state, and called for replacing the government with a "broadly based provisional government that would include representatives of Sandinista guerillas." Americans were assured by Assistant Secretary of State Viron Vaky that "Nicaraguans and our democratic friends in Latin America have no intention of seeing Nicaragua turned into a second Cuba", even though the State Department knew that the top Sandinista leaders had close personal ties and were in continuing contact with Havana, and, more specifically, that a Cuban secret-police official, Julian Lopez, was frequently present in the Sandinista headquarters and that Cuban military advisers were present in Sandinista ranks.

In a manner uncharacteristic of the Carter administration, which generally seems willing to negotiate anything with anyone anywhere, the U.S. government adopted an oddly uncompromising posture in dealing with Somoza. "No end to the crisis is possible," said Vaky, "that does not start with the departure of Somoza from power and the end of his regime. No negotiation, mediation, or compromise can be achieved any longer with a Somoza government. The solution can only begin with a sharp break from the past." Trying hard, we not only banned all American arms sales to the government of Nicaragua but pressured Israel, Guatemala, and others to do likewise—all in the name of insuring a "democratic" outcome. Finally, as the Sandinista leaders consolidated control over weapons and communications, banned opposition, and took off for Cuba, President Carter warned us against attributing this "evolutionary change" to "Cuban machinations" and assured the world that the U.S. desired only to "let the people of Nicaragua choose their own form of government."

Yet despite all the variations, the Carter administration brought to the crises in Iran and Nicaragua several common assumptions, each of which played a major role in hastening the victory of even more repressive dictatorships than had been in place before. These were, first, the belief that there existed at the moment of crisis a democratic alternative to the incumbent government: second, the belief that the continuation of the status quo was not possible; third, the belief that any change, including the establishment of a government headed by self-styled Marxist revolutionaries, was preferable to the present government. Each of these beliefs was (and is) widely shared in the liberal community generally. Not one of them can withstand close scrutiny.

Although most governments in the world are, as they always have been, autocracies of one kind or another, no idea holds greater sway in the mind of educated Americans than the belief that it is possible to democratize governments, anytime, anywhere, under any circumstances. This notion is belied by an enormous body of evidence based on the experience of dozens of countries which have attempted with more or less (usually less) success to move from autocratic to democratic government. Many of the wisest political scientists of this and previous centuries agree that democratic institutions are especially difficult to establish and maintain—because they make heavy demands on all portions of a population and because they depend on complex social, cultural, and economic conditions.

Two or three decades ago, when Marxism enjoyed its greatest prestige among American intellectuals, it was the economic prerequisites of democracy that were emphasized by social scientists. Democracy, they argued, could function only in relatively rich societies with an advanced economy, a substantial middle class, and a literate population, but it could be expected to emerge more or less automatically whenever these conditions prevailed. Today, this picture seems grossly oversimplified. While it surely helps to have an economy strong enough to provide decent levels of well-being for all, and "open" enough to provide mobility and encourage achievement, a pluralistic society and the right kind of political culture—and time—are even more essential.

In his essay on *Representative Government*, John Stuart Mill identified three fundamental conditions which the Carter administration would do well to ponder. These are: "One, that the people should be willing to receive it [representative government]; two, that they should be willing and able to do what is necessary for its preservation; three, that they should be willing and able to fulfill the duties and discharge the functions which it imposes on them."

Fulfilling the duties and discharging the functions of representative government make heavy demands on leaders and citizens, demands for participation and restraint, for consensus and compromise. It is not necessary for all citizens to be avidly interested in politics or well-informed about public affairs—although far more widespread interest and mobilization are needed than in autocracies. What *is* necessary is that a substantial number of citizens think of themselves as participants in society's decision-making and not simply as subjects bound by its laws. Moreover, leaders of all major sectors of society must agree to pursue power only by legal means, must eschew (at least in principle) violence, theft, and fraud, and must accept defeat when necessary. They must also be skilled at finding and creating common ground among diverse points of view and interests, and correlatively willing to compromise on all but the most basic values.

In addition to an appropriate political culture, democratic government requires institutions strong enough to channel and contain conflict. Voluntary, non-official institutions are needed to articulate and aggregate diverse interests and opinions present in the society. Otherwise, the formal governmental institutions will not be able to translate popular demands into public policy.

In the relatively few places where they exist, democratic governments have come into being slowly, after extended prior experience with more limited forms of participation during which leaders have reluctantly grown accustomed to tolerating dissent and opposition, opponents have accepted the notion that they may defeat but not destroy incumbents, and people have become aware of government's effects on their lives and of their own possible effects on government. Decades, if not centuries, are normally required for people to acquire the necessary disciplines and habits. In Britain, the road from the Magna Carta to the Act of Settlement, to the great Reform Bills of 1832, 1867, and 1885, took seven centuries to traverse. American history gives no better grounds for believing that democracy comes easily, quickly, or for the asking. A war of independence, an unsuccessful constitution, a civil war, a long process of gradual enfranchisement marked our progress toward constitutional democratic government. The French path was still more difficult. Terror, dictatorship, monarchy, instability, and incompetence followed on the revolution that was to usher in a millennium of brotherhood. Only in the twentieth century did the democratic principle finally gain wide acceptance in France and not until after World War II were the principles of order and democracy, popular sovereignty and authority, finally reconciled in institutions strong enough to contain conflicting currents of public opinion.

Although there is no instance of a revolutionary "socialist" or Communist society being democratized, right-wing autocracies do sometimes evolve into democracies—given time, propitious economic, social, and political circumstances, talented leaders, and a strong indigenous demand for representative government. Something of the kind is in progress on the Iberian peninsula and the first steps have been taken in Brazil. Something similar could conceivably have also occurred in Iran and Nicaragua if contestation and participation had been more gradually expanded.

But it seems clear that the architects of contemporary American foreign policy have little idea of how to go about encouraging the liberalization of an autocracy. In neither Nicaragua nor Iran did they realize that the only likely result of an effort to replace an incumbent autocrat with one of his moderate critics or a "broad-based coalition" would be to sap the foundations of the existing regime without moving the nation any closer to democracy. Yet this outcome was entirely predictable. Authority in traditional autocracies is transmitted through personal relations: from the ruler to his close associates (relatives, household members, personal friends) and from them to people to whom the associates are related by personal ties resembling their own relation to the ruler. The fabric of authority unravels quickly when the power and status of the man at the top are undermined or eliminated. The longer the autocrat has held power, and the more pervasive his personal influence, the more dependent a nation's institutions will be on him. Without him, the organized life of the society will collapse, like an arch from which the keystone has been removed. The blend of qualities that bound the Iranian army to the Shah or the national guard to Somoza is typical of the relationships—personal, hierarchical, non-transferable—that support a traditional autocracy. The speed with which armies collapse, bureaucracies abdicate, and social structures dissolve once the autocrat is removed frequently surprises American policy-makers and journalists accustomed to public institutions based on universalistic norms rather than particularistic relations.

The failure to understand these relations is one source of the failure of U.S. policy in this and previous administrations. There are others. In Iran and Nicaragua (as previously in Vietnam, Cuba, and China) Washington overestimated the political diversity of the opposition—especially the strength of "moderates" and "democrats" in the opposition movement; underestimated the strength and intransigence of radicals in the movement; and mis-estimated the nature and extent of American influence on both the government and the opposition.

Confusion concerning the character of the opposition, especially its intransigence and will to power, leads regularly to downplaying the amount of force required to counteract its violence. In neither Iran nor Nicaragua did the U.S. adequately appreciate the government's problem in maintaining order in a society confronted with an ideologically extreme opposition. Yet the presence of such groups was well known. The State Department's 1977 report on human rights described an Iran confronted

> with a small number of extreme rightist and leftist terrorists operating within the country. There is evidence that they have received substantial foreign support and training . . . [and] have been responsible for the murder of Iranian government officials and Americans. . . .

The same report characterized Somoza's opponents in the following terms:

> A guerrilla organization known as the Sandinista National Liberation Front (FSLN) seeks the violent overthrow of the government, and has received limited support from Cuba. The FSLN carried out an operation in Managua in December 1974, killing four people, taking several officials hostage . . . , since then, it continues to challenge civil authority in certain isolated regions.

In 1978, the State Department's report said that Sandinista violence was continuing—after the state of siege had been lifted by the Somoza government.

When U.S. policy-makers and large portions of the liberal press interpret insurgency as evidence of widespread popular discontent and a will to democracy, the scene is set for disaster. For if civil strife reflects a popular demand for democracy, it follows that a "liberalized" government will be more acceptable to "public opinion".

Thus, in the hope of strengthening a government, U.S. policy-makers are led, mistake after mistake, to impose measures almost certain to weaken its authority. Hurried efforts to force complex and unfamiliar political practices on societies lacking the requisite political culture, tradition, and social structures not only fail to produce desired outcomes; if they are undertaken at a time when the traditional regime is under attack, they actually facilitate the job of the insurgents.

Vietnam presumably taught us that the United States could not serve as the world's policeman; it should also have taught us the dangers of trying to be the world's midwife to democracy when the birth is scheduled to take place under conditions of guerrilla war.

If the administration's actions in Iran and Nicaragua reflect the pervasive and mistaken assumption that one can easily locate and impose democratic alternatives to incumbent autocracies, they also reflect the equally pervasive and equally flawed belief that change *per se* in such autocracies is inevitable, desirable, and in the American interest. It is this belief which induces the Carter administration to participate actively in the toppling of non-Communist autocracies while remaining passive in the face of Communist expansion.

At the time the Carter administration came into office it was widely reported that the President had assembled a team who shared a new approach to foreign policy and a new conception of the national interest. The principal elements of this new approach were said to be two: the conviction that the cold war was over, and the conviction that, this being the case, the U.S. should give priority to North-South problems and help less developed nations achieve their own destiny.

More is involved in these changes than originally meets the eye. For, unlikely as it may seem, the foreign policy of the Carter administration is guided by a relatively full-blown philosophy of history which includes, as philosophies of history always do, a theory of social change, or, as it is currently called, a doctrine of modernization. Like most other philosophies of history that have appeared in the West since the eighteenth century, the Carter administration's doctrine predicts progress (in the form of modernization for all societies) and a happy ending (in the form of a world community of developed, autonomous nations).

The administration's approach to foreign affairs was clearly foreshadowed in Zbigniew Brzezinski's 1970 book on the U.S. role in the "technetronic era", *Between Two Ages*. In that book, Brzezinski showed that he had the imagination to look beyond the cold war to a brave new world of global politics and inter-dependence. To deal with that new world a new approach was said to be "evolving", which Brzezinski designated "rational humanism". In the new approach, the "preoccupation" with "national supremacy" would give way to "global" perspectives, and international problems would be viewed as "human issues" rather than as "political confrontations". The traditional intellectual framework for dealing with foreign policy would have to be scrapped:

> Today, the old framework of international politics . . . with their spheres of influence, military alliances between nation states, the fiction of sovereignty, doctrinal conflicts arising from 19th-century crisis—is clearly no longer compatible with reality.[1]

Only the "delayed development" of the Soviet Union, "an archaic religious community that experiences modernity existentially but not quite yet normatively", prevented wider realization

[1] Concerning Latin America, Brzezinski observed: "Latin American nationalism, more and more radical as it widens its popular base, will be directed with increasing animosity against the United States unless the United States rapidly shifts its own posture. Accordingly, it would be wise for the United States to make an explicit move to abandon the Monroe Doctrine and to concede that in the new global age geographic or hemispheric contiguity no longer need be politically decisive. Nothing could be healthier for Pan-American relations than for the United States to place them on the same level as its relations with the rest of the world, confining itself to emphasis on cultural-political affinities (as it does with Western Europe) and economic-social obligations (as it does with less developed countries)."

of the fact that the end of ideology was already here. For the U.S., Brzezinski recommended "a great deal of patience", a more detached attitude toward world revolutionary processes, and a less anxious preoccupation with the Soviet Union. Instead of engaging in ancient diplomatic pastimes, we should make "a broader effort to contain the global tendencies toward chaos", while assisting the processes of change that will move the world toward the "community of developed nations".

The central concern of Brzezinski's book, as of the Carter administration's foreign policy, is with the modernization of the Third World. From the beginning, the administration has manifested a special, intense interest in the problems of the so-called Third World. But instead of viewing international developments in terms of the American national interest, as national interest is historically conceived, the architects of administration policy have viewed them in terms of a contemporary version of the same idea of progress that has traumatized Western imaginations since the Enlightenment.

In its current form, the concept of modernization involves more than industrialization, more than "political development" (whatever that is). It is used instead to designate ". . . the process through which a traditional or pre-technological society passes as it is transformed into a society characterized by machine technology, rational and secular attitudes, and highly differentiated social structures." Condorcet, Comte, Hegel, Marx, and Weber are all present in this view of history as the working out of the idea of modernity.

The crucial elements of the modernization concept have been clearly explicated by Samuel P. Huntington (who, despite a period at the National Security Council, was assuredly not the architect of the administration's policy). The modernization paradigm, Huntington has observed, postulates an ongoing process of change: complex, because it involves all dimensions of human life in society; systemic, because its elements interact in predictable, necessary ways; global, because all societies will, necessarily, pass through the transition from traditional to modern; lengthy, because time is required to modernize economic and social organization, character, and culture; phased because each modernizing society must pass through essentially the same stages; homogenizing, because it tends toward the convergence and interdependence of societies; irreversible, because the direction of change is "given" in the relation of the elements of the process; progressive, in the sense that it is desirable, and in the long run provides significant benefits to the affiliated people.

Although the modernization paradigm has proved a sometimes useful as well as influential tool in social science, it has become the object of searching critiques that have challenged one after another of its central assumptions. Its shortcomings as an analytical tool pale, however, when compared to its inadequacies as a framework for thinking about foreign policy, where its principal effects are to encourage the view that events are manifestations of deep historical forces which cannot be controlled and that the best any government can do is to serve as a "midwife" to history, helping events to move where they are already headed.

This perspective on contemporary events is optimistic in the sense that it foresees continuing human progress; deterministic in the sense that it perceives events as fixed by processes over which persons and policies can have but little influence; moralistic in the sense that it perceives history and U.S. policy as having moral ends; cosmopolitan in the sense that it attempts to view the world not from the perspective of American interests or intentions but from the perspective of the modernizing nation and the "end" of history. It identifies modernization with both revolution and morality, and U.S. policy with all three.

The idea that it is "forces" rather than people which shape events recurs each time an administration spokesman articulates or explains policy. President Carter, for example, assured us in February of this year [1979]:

> The revolution in Iran is a product of deep social, political, religious, and economic factors growing out of the history of Iran itself.

And of Asia he said:

> At this moment there is turmoil or change in various countries from one end of the Indian Ocean to the other; some turmoil as in Indochina is the product of age-old enmities, inflamed by rivalries

for influence by conflicting forces. Stability in some other countries is being shaken by the process of modernization, the search for national significance, or the desire to fulfill legitimate human hopes and human aspirations.

Harold Saunders, Assistant Secretary for Near Eastern and South Asian Affairs, commenting on "instability" in Iran and the Horn of Africa, states:

> We, of course, recognize that fundamental changes are taking place across this area of western Asia and northeastern Africa—economic modernization, social change, a revival of religion, resurgent nationalism, demands for broader popular participation in the political process. These changes are generated by forces within each country.

Or here is Anthony Lake, chief of the State Department's Policy Planning staff, on South Africa:

> Change will come in South Africa. The welfare of the people there, and American interests, will be profoundly affected by the way in which it comes. The question is whether it will be peaceful or not.

Brzezinski makes the point still clearer. Speaking as chief of the National Security Council, he has assured us that the struggles for power in Asia and Africa are really only incidents along the route to modernization:

> . . . all the developing countries in the arc from northeast Asia to southern Africa continue to search for viable forms of government capable of managing the process of modernization.

No matter that the invasions, coups, civil wars, and political struggles of less violent kinds that one sees all around do not *seem* to be incidents in a global personnel search for someone to manage the modernization process. Neither Brzezinski nor anyone else seems bothered by the fact that the political participants in that arc from northeast Asia to southern Africa do not *know* that they are "searching for viable forms of government capable of managing the process of modernization". The motives and intentions of real persons are no more relevant to the modernization paradigm than they are to the Marxist view of history.

Viewed from this level of abstraction, it is the "forces" rather than the people that count.

So what if the "deep historical forces" at work in such diverse places as Iran, the Horn of Africa, Southeast Asia, Central America, and the United Nations look a lot like Russians or Cubans? Having moved past what the President calls our "inordinate fear of Communism", identified by him with the cold war, we should, we are told, now be capable of distinguishing Soviet and Cuban "machinations" (which anyway exist mainly in the minds of cold warriors and others guilty of over-simplifying the world) from evolutionary changes, which seem to be the only kind that actually occur.

What can a U.S. President faced with such complicated, inexorable, impersonal processes *do*? The answer, offered again and again by the President and his top officials, is, not much. Since events are not caused by human decisions, they cannot be stopped or altered by them. Brzezinski, for example, has said: "We recognize that the world is changing under the influence of forces no government can control. . . ." And Cyrus Vance has cautioned: "The fact is that we can no more stop change than Canute could still the waters."

The Carter administration's essentially deterministic and a-political view of contemporary events discourages an active American response and encourages passivity. The American inability to influence events in Iran became the President's theme song:

> Those who argue that the U.S. should *or could* intervene directly to thwart [the revolution in Iran] are wrong about the realities of Iran. . . . We have encouraged *to the limited extent of our own ability* the public support for the Bakhtiar government. . . . How long [the Shah] will be out of Iran, we have no way to determine. Future events and his own desires will determine that. . . . It is impossible for anyone to anticipate all future political events. . . . Even if we had been able to anticipate events that were going to take place in Iran or in other countries, obviously our ability to determine those events is very limited [emphasis added].

Vance made the same point:

> In Iran our policy throughout the current crisis has been based on the fact that only Iranians can resolve the fundamental political issues which they now confront.

Where once upon a time an American President might have sent Marines to assure the protection of American strategic interests, there is no room for force in this world of progress and self-determination. Force, the President told us at Notre Dame, does not work; that is the lesson he extracted from Vietnam. It offers only "superficial" solutions. Concerning Iran, he said:

> Certainly we have no desire or ability to intrude massive forces into Iran or any other country to determine the outcome of domestic political issues. This is something that we have no intention of ever doing in another country. We've tried this once in Vietnam. It didn't work, as you well know.

There was nothing unique about Iran. In Nicaragua, the climate and language were different but the "historical forces" and the U.S. response were the same. Military intervention was out of the question. Assistant Secretary of State Viron Vaky described as "unthinkable" the "use of U.S. military power to intervene in the internal affairs of another American republic". Vance provided parallel assurances for Africa, asserting that we would not try to match Cuban and Soviet activities there.

What *is* the function of foreign policy under these conditions? It is to understand the processes of change and then, like Marxists, to align ourselves with history, hoping to contribute a bit of stability along the way. And this, administration spokesmen assure us, is precisely what we are doing. The Carter administration has defined the U.S. national interest in the Third World as identical with the putative end of the modernization process. Vance put this with characteristic candor in a recent statement when he explained that U.S. policy vis-à-vis the Third World is "grounded in the conviction that we best serve our interest there by supporting the efforts of developing nations to advance their economic well-being and preserve their political independence."

Our "commitment to the promotion of constructive change worldwide" (Brzezinski's words) have been vouchsafed in every conceivable context.

But there is a problem. The conceivable contexts turn out to be mainly those in which non-Communist autocracies are under pressure from revolutionary guerrillas. Since Moscow is the aggressive, expansionist power today, it is more often than not insurgents, encouraged and armed by the Soviet Union, who challenge the status quo. The American commitment to "change" in the abstract ends up by aligning us tacitly with Soviet clients and irresponsible extremists like the Ayatollah Khomeini or, in the end, Yasir Arafat.

So far, assisting "change" has not led the Carter administration to undertake the destabilization of a *Communist* country. The principles of self-determination and nonintervention are thus both selectively applied. We seem to accept the status quo in Communist nations (in the name of "diversity" and national autonomy), but not in nations ruled by "right-wing" dictators or white oligarchies. Concerning China, for example, Brzezinski has observed:

> We recognize that the PRC and we have different ideologies and economic and political systems. . . . We harbor neither the hope nor the desire that through extensive contacts with China we can remake that nation into the American image. Indeed, we accept our differences.

Of Southeast Asia, the President noted in February:

> Our interest is to promote peace and the withdrawal of outside forces and not to become embroiled in the conflict among Asian nations. And, in general, our interest is to promote the health and the development of individual societies, not to a pattern cut exactly like ours in the United States but tailored rather to the hopes and the needs and desires of the peoples involved.

But the administration's position shifts sharply when South Africa is discussed. For example, Anthony Lake asserted in late 1978:

. . . We have indicated to South Africa the fact that if it does not make significant progress toward racial equality, its relations with the international community, including the United States, are bound to deteriorate.

Over the years, we have tried through a series of progressive steps to demonstrate that the U.S. cannot and will not be associated with the continued practice of apartheid.

As to Nicaragua, Hodding Carter III said in February 1979:

The unwillingness of the Nicaraguan government to accept the [OAS] group's proposal, the resulting prospects for renewal and polarization, and the human-rights situation in Nicaragua . . . unavoidably affect the kind of relationships we can maintain with that government. . . .

And Carter commented on Latin American autocracies:

My government will not be deterred from protecting human rights, including economic and social rights, in whatever ways we can. We prefer to take actions that are positive, but where nations persist in serious violations of human rights, we will continue to demonstrate that there are costs to the flagrant disregard of international standards.

Something very odd is going on here. How does an administration that desires to let people work out their own destinies get involved in determined efforts at reform in South Africa, Zaire, Nicaragua, El Salvador, and elsewhere? How can an administration committed to nonintervention in Cambodia and Vietnam announce that it "will not be deterred" from righting wrongs in South Africa? What should be made of an administration that sees the U.S. interest as identical with economic modernization and political independence and yet heedlessly endangers the political independence of Taiwan, a country whose success in economic modernization and egalitarian distribution of wealth is unequaled in Asia? The contrast is as striking as that between the administration's frenzied speed in recognizing the new dictatorship in

Nicaragua and its continuing refusal to recognize the elected government of Zimbabwe Rhodesia, or its refusal to maintain any presence in Zimbabwe Rhodesia while staffing a U.S. Information Office in Cuba. Not only are there ideology and a double standard at work here, the ideology neither fits nor explains reality, and the double standard involves the administration in the wholesale contradiction of its own principles.

Inconsistencies are a familiar part of politics in most societies. Usually, however, governments behave hypocritically when their principles conflict with the national interest. What makes the inconsistencies of the Carter administration noteworthy are, first, the administration's moralism—which renders it especially vulnerable to charges of hypocrisy; and, second, the administration's predilection for policies that violate the strategic and economic interests of the United States. The administration's conception of national interest borders on doublethink: it finds friendly powers to be guilty representatives of the status quo and views the triumph of unfriendly groups as beneficial to America's "true interests".

This logic is quite obviously reinforced by the prejudices and preferences of many administration officials. Traditional autocracies are, in general and in their very nature, deeply offensive to modern American sensibilities. The notion that public affairs should be ordered on the basis of kinship, friendship, and other personal relations rather than on the basis of objective "rational" standards violates our conception of justice and efficiency. The preference for stability rather than change is also disturbing to Americans whose whole national experience rests on the principles of change, growth, and progress. The extremes of wealth and poverty characteristic of traditional societies also offend us, the more so since the poor are usually *very* poor and bound to their squalor by a hereditary allocation of role. Moreover, the relative lack of concern of rich, comfortable rulers for the poverty, ignorance, and disease of "their" people is likely to be interpreted by Americans as moral dereliction pure and simple. The truth is that Americans can hardly bear such societies and such rulers. Confronted with them, our vaunted cultural relativism evaporates and we become as censorious as Cotton Mather confronting sin in New England.

But if the politics of traditional and semi-traditional autocracy is nearly antithetical to our own—at both the symbolic and the operational level—the rhetoric of progressive revolutionaries sounds much better to us; their symbols are much more acceptable. One reason that some modern Americans prefer "socialist" to traditional autocracies is that the former have embraced modernity and have adopted modern modes and perspectives, including an instrumental, manipulative, functional orientation toward most social, cultural, and personal affairs; a profession of universalistic norms; an emphasis on reason, science, education, and progress; a de-emphasis of the sacred; and "rational", bureaucratic organizations. They speak our language.

Because socialism of the Soviet-Chinese-Cuban variety is an ideology rooted in a version of the same values that sparked the Enlightenment and the democratic revolutions of the eighteenth century; because it is modern and not traditional; because it postulates goals that appeal to Christian as well as to secular values (brotherhood of man, elimination of power as a mode of human relations), it is highly congenial to many Americans at the symbolic level. Marxist revolutionaries speak the language of a hopeful future while traditional autocrats speak the language of an unattractive past. Because left-wing revolutionaries invoke the symbols and values of democracy—emphasizing egalitarianism rather than hierarchy and privilege, liberty rather than order, activity rather than passivity—they are again and again accepted as partisans in the cause of freedom and democracy.

Nowhere is the affinity of liberalism, Christianity, and Marxist socialism more apparent than among liberals who are "duped" time after time into supporting "liberators" who turn out to be totalitarians, and among left-leaning clerics whose attraction to a secular style of "redemptive community" is stronger than their outrage at the hostility of socialist regimes to religion. In Jimmy Carter—egalitarian, optimist, liberal, Christian—the tendency to be repelled by frankly non-democratic rulers and hierarchical societies is almost as strong as the tendency to be attracted to the idea of popular revolution, liberation, and progress. Carter is, *par excellence*, the kind of liberal most likely to confound revolution with idealism, change with progress, optimism with virtue.

Where concern about "socialist encirclement", Soviet expansion, and traditional conceptions of the national interest inoculated his predecessors against such easy equations, Carter's doctrine of national interest and modernization encourages support for all change that takes place in the name of "the people", regardless of its "superficial" Marxist or anti-American content. Any lingering doubt about whether the U.S. should, in case of conflict, support a "tested friend" such as the Shah or a friendly power such as Zimbabwe Rhodesia against an opponent who despises us is resolved by reference to our "true", our "long-range" interests.

Stephen Rosenfeld of the Washington *Post* described the commitment of the Carter administration to this sort of "progressive liberalism":

> The Carter administration came to power, after all, committed precisely to reducing the centrality of strategic competition with Moscow in American foreign policy, and to extending the United States' association with what it was prepared to accept as legitimate wave-of-the-future popular movements around the world—first of all with the victorious movement in Vietnam.
>
> . . . Indochina was supposed to be the state on which Americans could demonstrate their "post-Vietnam" intent to come to terms with the progressive popular element that Kissinger, the villain, had denied.

In other words, the Carter administration, Rosenfeld tells us, came to power resolved not to assess international developments in the light of "cold-war" perspectives but to accept at face value the claim of revolutionary groups to represent "popular" aspirations and "progressive" forces—regardless of the ties of these revolutionaries to the Soviet Union. To this end, overtures were made looking to the "normalization" of relations with Vietnam, Cuba, and the Chinese People's Republic, and steps were taken to cool relations with South Korea, South Africa, Nicaragua, the Philippines, and others. These moves followed naturally from the conviction that the U.S. had, as our enemies said, been on the wrong side of history in supporting the status quo and opposing revolution.

One might have thought that this perspective would have been undermined by events in Southeast Asia since the triumph of "progressive" forces there over the "agents of reaction". To cite Rosenfeld again:

> In this administration's time, Vietnam has been transformed for much of American public opinion, from a country wronged by the U.S. to one revealing a brutal essence of its own.
>
> This has been a quiet but major trauma to the Carter people (as to all liberals) scarring their self-confidence and their claim on public trust alike.

Presumably, however, the barbarity of the "progressive" governments in Cambodia and Vietnam has been less traumatic for the President and his chief advisers than for Rosenfeld, since there is little evidence of changed predispositions at crucial levels of the White House and the State Department. The President continues to behave as before—not like a man who abhors autocrats but like one who abhors only right-wing autocrats.

In fact, high officials in the Carter administration understand better than they seem to the aggressive, expansionist character of contemporary Soviet behavior in Africa, the Middle East, Southeast Asia, the Indian Ocean, Central America, and the Caribbean. But although the Soviet-Cuban role in Grenada, Nicaragua, and El Salvador (plus the transfer of MIG-23's to Cuba) had already prompted resumption of surveillance of Cuba (which in turn confirmed the presence of a Soviet combat brigade), the President's eagerness not to "heat up" the climate of public opinion remains stronger than his commitment to speak the truth to the American people. His statement on Nicaragua clearly reflects these priorities:

> It's a mistake for Americans to assume or to claim that every time an evolutionary change takes place in this hemisphere that some- how it's a result of secret, massive Cuban intervention. The fact in Nicaragua is that the Somoza regime lost the confidence of the

people. To bring about an orderly transition there, our effort was to let the people of Nicaragua ultimately make the decision on who would be their leader—what form of government they should have.

This statement, which presumably represents the President's best thinking on the matter, is illuminating. Carter's effort to dismiss concern about military events in this specific country as a manifestation of a national proclivity for seeing "Cuban machinations" under every bed constitutes a shocking effort to falsify reality. There was no question in Nicaragua of "evolutionary change" or of attributing such change to Castro's agents. There was only a question about the appropriate U.S. response to a military struggle in a country whose location gives it strategic importance out of proportion to its size or strength.

But that is not all. The rest of the President's statement graphically illustrates the blinding power of ideology on his interpretation of events. When he says that "the Somoza regime lost the confidence of the people", the President implies that the regime had previously rested on the confidence of "the people", but that the situation had now changed. In fact, the Somoza regime had never rested on popular will (but instead on manipulation, force, and habit), and was not being ousted by it. It was instead succumbing to arms and soldiers. However, the assumption that the armed conflict of Sandinistas and Somozistas was the military equivalent of a national referendum enabled the President to imagine that it could be, and should be, settled by the people of Nicaragua. For this pious sentiment even to seem true the President would have had to be unaware that insurgents were receiving a great many arms from other non-Nicaraguans; and that the U.S. had played a significant role in disarming the Somoza regime.

The President's mistakes and distortions are all fashionable ones. His assumptions are those of people who want badly to be on the progressive side in conflicts between "rightist" autocracy and "leftist" challenges, and to prefer the latter, almost regardless of the probable consequences.

To be sure, neither the President, nor Vance, nor Brzezinski *desires* the proliferation of Soviet-supported regimes. Each has asserted his disapproval of Soviet "interference" in the modernization process. But each, nevertheless, remains willing to "destabilize" friendly or neutral autocracies without any assurance that they will not be replaced by reactionary totalitarian theocracies, totalitarian Soviet client states, or worst of all, by murderous fanatics of the Pol Pot variety.

The foreign policy of the Carter administration fails not for lack of good intentions but for lack of realism about the nature of traditional versus revolutionary autocracies and the relation of each to the American national interest. Only intellectual fashion and the tyranny of right-left thinking prevent intelligent men of good will from perceiving the *facts* that traditional authoritarian governments are less repressive than revolutionary autocracies, that they are more susceptible of liberalization, and that they are more compatible with U.S. interests. The evidence on all these points is clear enough.

Surely it is now beyond reasonable doubt that the present governments of Vietnam, Cambodia, and Laos are much more repressive than those of the despised previous rulers; that the government of the People's Republic of China is more repressive than that of Taiwan, that North Korea is more repressive than South Korea, and so forth. This is the most important lesson of Vietnam and Cambodia. It is not new but it is a gruesome reminder of harsh facts.

From time to time a truly bestial ruler can come to power in either type of autocracy—Idi Amin, Papa Doc Duvalier, Joseph Stalin, Pol Pot are examples—but neither type regularly produces such moral monsters (though democracy regularly prevents their accession to power). There are, however, *systemic* differences between traditional and revolutionary autocracies that have a predictable effect on their degree of repressiveness. Generally speaking, traditional autocrats tolerate social inequities, brutality, and poverty while revolutionary autocracies create them.

Traditional autocrats leave in place existing allocations of wealth, power, status, and other resources which in most traditional societies favor an affluent few and maintain masses in poverty. But they worship traditional gods and observe traditional taboos. They do not disturb the habitual rhythms of work and leisure, habitual places of residence, habitual patterns of family and personal relations. Because the miseries of traditional life are familiar, they are bearable to ordinary people who, growing up in the society, learn to cope, as children born to untouchables in India acquire the skills and attitudes necessary for survival in the miserable roles they are destined to fill. Such societies create no refugees.

Precisely the opposite is true of revolutionary Communist regimes. They create refugees by the million because they claim jurisdiction over the whole life of the society and make demands for change that so violate internalized values and habits that inhabitants flee by the tens of thousands in the remarkable expectation that their attitudes, values, and goals will "fit" better in a foreign country than in their native land.

The former deputy chairman of Vietnam's National Assembly from 1976 to his defection early in August 1979, Hoang Van Hoan, described recently the impact of Vietnam's ongoing revolution on that country's more than one million Chinese inhabitants:

> They have been expelled from places they have lived in for generations. They have been dispossessed of virtually all possessions —their lands, their houses. They have been driven into areas called new economic zones, but they have not been given any aid.
>
> How can they eke out a living in such conditions reclaiming new land? They gradually die for a number of reasons—diseases, the hard life. They also die of humiliation.

It is not only the Chinese who have suffered in Southeast Asia since the "liberation", and it is not only in Vietnam that the Chinese suffer. By the end of 1978 more than six million refugees had fled countries ruled by Marxist governments. In spite of walls, fences, guns, and sharks, the steady stream of people fleeing revolutionary utopias continues.

There is a damning contrast between the number of refugees created by Marxist regimes and those created by other autocracies: more than a million Cubans have left their homeland since Castro's rise (one refugee for every nine inhabitants) as compared to about thirty-five thousand each from Argentina, Brazil, and

Chile. In Africa more than five times as many refugees have fled Guinea and Guinea Bissau as have left Zimbabwe Rhodesia, suggesting that civil war and racial discrimination are easier for most people to bear than Marxist-style liberation.

Moreover, the history of this century provides no grounds for expecting that radical totalitarian regimes will transform themselves. At the moment there is a far greater likelihood of progressive liberalization and democratization in the governments of Brazil, Argentina, and Chile than in the government of Cuba; in Taiwan than in the People's Republic of China; in South Korea than in North Korea; in Zaire than in Angola; and so forth.

Since many traditional autocracies permit limited contestation and participation, it is not impossible that U.S. policy could effectively encourage this process of liberalization and democratization, provided that the effort is not made at a time when the incumbent government is fighting for its life against violent adversaries, and that proposed reforms are aimed at producing gradual change rather than perfect democracy overnight. To accomplish this, policy-makers are needed who understand how actual democracies have actually come into being. History is a better guide than good intentions.

A realistic policy which aims at protecting our own interest and assisting the capacities for self-determination of less developed nations will need to face the unpleasant fact that, if victorious, violent insurgency headed by Marxist revolutionaries is unlikely to lead to anything but totalitarian tyranny. Armed intellectuals citing Marx and supported by Soviet-bloc arms and advisers will almost surely not turn out to be agrarian reformers, or simple nationalists, or democratic socialists. However incomprehensible it may be to some, Marxist revolutionaries are not contemporary embodiments of the Americans who wrote the Declaration of Independence, and they will not be content with establishing a broad-based coalition in which they have only one voice among many.

It may not always be easy to distinguish between democratic and totalitarian agents of change, but it is also not too difficult. Authentic democratic revolutionaries aim at securing governments based on the consent of the governed and believe that

ordinary men are capable of using freedom, knowing their own
interest, choosing rulers. They do not, like the current leaders in
Nicaragua, assume that it will be necessary to postpone elections
for three to five years during which time they can "cure" the false
consciousness of almost everyone.

If, moreover, revolutionary leaders describe the United States
as the scourge of the twentieth century, the enemy of freedom-
loving people, the perpetrator of imperialism, racism, colonialism, genocide, war, then they are not authentic democrats or,
to put it mildly, friends. Groups which define themselves as
enemies should be treated as enemies. The United States is not in
fact a racist, colonial power, it does not practice genocide, it does
not threaten world peace with expansionist activities. In the last
decade especially we have practiced remarkable forbearance
everywhere and undertaken the "unilateral restraints on defense
spending" recommended by Brzezinski as appropriate for the
technetronic era. We have also moved further, faster, in eliminating domestic racism than any multiracial society in the world or
in history.

For these reasons and more, a posture of continuous self-
abasement and apology vis-à-vis the Third World is neither
morally necessary nor politically appropriate. No more is it
necessary or appropriate to support vocal enemies of the United
States because they invoke the rhetoric of popular liberation. It is
not even necessary or appropriate for our leaders to forswear
unilaterally the use of military force to counter military force.
Liberal idealism need not be identical with masochism, and need
not be incompatible with the defense of freedom and the national
interest.

IV

PH.-I. ANDRÉ-VINCENT, O.P.

THE "THEOLOGIES OF LIBERATION"
Translated by Rev. James McCauley, S.J.

In the course of the last decade, Latin America has begotten an abundance of creative ideas and explosive myths, but the live wire linking all of them has been the "theology of liberation". The very juncture of the two words creates a shock. The theology in question was born at an hour of guerilla warfare, at the heart of battles for the "conscientization" of the masses in opposition to "capitalist oppression"—battles waged by students and the bourgeoisie rather than by workers and peasants: battles of an "intelligentsia". These committed intellectuals were men of action on the pattern of Camilo Torres and Che Guevara, men of thought like Gustavo Gutíerrez or Enrique Dussel. Many of them were priests. All of them had Latin America branded in their hearts and minds. They took the myth of liberation and provided it with a theology. Or perhaps one should say, they provided theology with a new life, one derived from the vigor of the liberation myth. The ambition of these *liberadores* was nothing less than to create an entirely new theology—and one entirely Latin American. Nationalism and Revolution, those two potent forces of Latin America, dynamited the old structures of theology in order to build its house anew.

The *liberadores* of theology are many and of very different types. From Hugo Assmann, fully committed to the Marxist class war, one passes to Gustavo Gutíerrez, cautiously maneuvering among the various levels of committed thought, and the scale of theologians of liberation produces a certain amount of discord. Its fundamental harmony must be found in its origin—a theological viewpoint which is essentially derived from a political

Originally published under the title "Les 'théologies de la libération' " in *Nouvelle Revue Théologique* 98 (1976) 109–25. Reprinted by permission.

analysis and political commitment. All these "theologies of liberation" have their origin in the philosophic revolution proclaimed by Marx: "Up to now philosophy has limited itself to contemplating the world; now it must transform the world." Will these theologians be the demiurges of the new society? Some of them seem to confuse theology with guerilla warfare, others with the "conscientization" which precedes it; all of them conceive theology in a setting of revolutionary struggle (whether violent or not) which will give birth to a new world. But the new theology makes no claim to direct this struggle. It acknowledges with Vatican II (and with St. Thomas) the proper sphere of the secular order, the autonomy of the political order. Now this autonomy is fitted to the dimensions of modern man, of man creator of himself and of society. This self-creation is identified with the course of history; it is the result of the "dialectic of history".

Liberation theology does not set itself in opposition to the Promethean ambition of modern man. Building the world is the political task of mankind grown to adulthood. "In the beginning was the Deed." Modern philosophy makes this poetic intuition of Goethe the first principle of the social sciences. The "dialectic of history" presupposes this primacy of action. German idealism is the lens through which the new science views the world, with Marx rounding out Hegel. The Thomistic renaissance having died away, the philosophy of being is left stranded on the river bank. The "theology of liberation" flows into the current of becoming.

In this view, theology comes into being only after political theory has evolved in consequence of political action. It is a reflection upon this action. Will this theology, like the bird of Minerva in Hegelian philosophy, be condemned to sing only in the twilight of history? It must always be pointed toward the dawn of a new day, but each day until the last will be primarily an engagement in action, a new immersion in the ever-new current of becoming which is history. Only with the last day will come the final synthesis: *the classless society, the promised land, the new heaven*. Might one not say that the theologies of liberation are the South American echo of the theological utopias born in sad old Europe? Progeny of resentment and revolt, they escape with

Metz and Moltmann into an avenging future. All their prophecies and all their faith is grounded in the hope of a "new earth". The theology of liberation is in the mainstream of modern philosophy, and it all carries the stamp "made in Germany".[1] But it wishes to claim a different source. It claims to be a child of Latin America, and, in its physical origins, so it is.

Latin American Theology. Medellín, 1968

The theology of liberation is primarily the cry of revolt of a sub-continent. It springs from the anguished consciousness of nations who achieved their independence a century ago but who see themselves still enchained. The Church has made this anguished consciousness her own. The assemblage of Latin American bishops at Medellín, denouncing neo-colonialism, took up the "cry for liberty" of the twenty republics. The theology of liberation claims Medellín as its own Vatican II. Now this "Latin American Vatican II" is a rather curious continuation of the Roman council. The conclusions of Medellín are born from a different perspective from that of the Council documents: a Church rooted in the world—in the Latin American world—has been substituted for the "timeless vision" of the "Church in the world" found in the constitution *Gaudium et Spes*. And the language which flows from this Church is the language of liberation.[2]

It is a new language in the history of the Church, a language welling forth from the living springs of the continent. The Gospel was planted in American soil four centuries ago and brought forth the fruit of liberty. The bishops of missionary Christianity encountered oppression. The pioneers of the Church in the New World took the side of the oppressed. In "New Spain", Zumarraga, Garcès, and Vasco de Quiroga laid the foundation of a hybrid Christianity by fighting for the rights of the Indians. At their sides, Dominicans and Franciscans shared the lot of the poor and denounced injustice throughout Spanish

---

[1] And a theology which had rediscovered history (after nineteen centuries) in Tübingen with Hegel and Mochler. Cf. Enr. Dussel., *Histoire et théologie de la libération* (Paris: Ed. Ouvrières, 1974) 66.

[2] Enr. Dussel, op. cit., 111.

Christendom. Las Casas was the "first Latin American prophet".[3]
Today Christendom no longer exists in the Americas. The theologians of liberation have been impressed by the failure of the
renewal which was ablaze at the turn of the century under
the auspices of neo-Thomism and Catholic Action. They have
buried the "new Christianity" of Maritain; and Christian Democracy, despite its Chilean springtime under Eduardo Frei, has
collapsed of its own accord. They see no hope in the "third way"
offered by populist movements nor in military coups d'état.
Only two alternatives remain for them: capitalism or socialism.
They have taken the socialist option without hesitation. Could
it not be said that their theology is nothing more than the
consequence of this option? The theology of liberation claims to
express the drama of Latin America. Accordingly, the socialist
option would be dictated by the historical processes of the continent in the perspective of liberation. This involvement is to be
forced upon a Church which is still—despite the secularization of
society—an intimate part of the history of Latin America. But is
not this Church still too closely bound up with the established
order? Breaking with this order and taking the part of the oppressed is the most urgent duty of the Church. It is also the first
condition for the establishment of a Latin American theology.[4]

Medellín represents the beginning of this break and this commitment by the Church. In denouncing neo-colonialism, the
bishops' declaration stigmatized this situation of injustice as
"institutionalized violence".[5] The entire document is developed
against the background of this situation of violence and is charged
with the necessity of liberation.[6] The theologians of liberation
glory in Medellín. They see in the document of October 1968
a moment of revelation, realized in history through the signs
of the times. This revelation goes on endlessly. The text of
Medellín must therefore undergo continual reinterpretation.
The hermeneutic of this theology is that of the "prophetic"

[3] Enr. Dussel, ibid., 78. Despite his prejudice against "colonial Christianity"
the author recognizes the evangelical freedom of the bishops of Latin America and
their value as examples to others—whatever one might say of the "managerial
class".

[4] G. Gutíerrez, *Teología de la liberación* (Lima: CEP, 1970).

[5] Medellín Conference, *Documentos*, sect. I, 72.

[6] G. Gutíerrez, op. cit., 140–42.

interpreters of the "signs of the times" of the "course of history". It interprets Medellín like Vatican II, by situating the event within the historical process. This viewpoint gives the advantage to Medellín. Vatican II dealt with the development of peoples; Medellín came at the hour of their liberation in a world "in full revolutionary process".[7]

Medellín reinterprets Vatican II. But the theology of liberation reinterprets Medellín. Texts grow obsolete quickly in the current of history. Are there no permanent values? "Many things abide unchanged because of their relation to Christ, who is always himself, yesterday, today and tomorrow," so says Vatican II.[8] But this vertical dimension is absent from thought plunged into the world of becoming; thought which has been reduced to a mere shifting path toward the Absolute to come. For such a theology, the texts of Medellín, like those of Vatican II, have less need of protection against erroneous interpretation than of deliverance from their own obsolescence. How is this to be done? By steeping them in that very stream of history which gave them birth: by illuminating them with the light of that great sign of the new times which the fathers of Medellín had acknowledged—the "process of liberation".[9] What is this "process" so celebrated by every soapbox orator of the theology of liberation? It is not the function of theology to define it or judge it but merely to recognize it and then to adhere to it as to its primordial datum. Is history then the revealed datum? History is the "locus of revelation", the very form of the creative and redemptive Word.[10]

History as the Locus of Revelation

The new theology sees history as the "locus of revelation" in the strongest sense of that term. When the masters of bygone ages used the term "theological loci", they were referring to their

[7] Ibid., 167. Vatican II provides the broad outlines for the renewal of the Church. Medellín represents a further stage, the transformation of the Church in function of her presence on a continent of poverty and injustice.

[8] *Gaudium et Spes* 10, sect. 2, citing Heb 13:8.

[9] G. Gutíerrez, op. cit., 168.

[10] The word (theological) "locus" must here be understood in the potent sense which it has held in theological tradition. This is the sense in which it is used by great authorities of the "New Church" to whom the theologies of liberation refer (in France, Chenu, Congar). See G. Gutíerrez, op. cit., 23.

hierarchical sources: Scripture, the apostolic magisterium and the Fathers. All this structure has been leveled. The current of history flows on. "There is nothing in the Bible which is not historical"; moreover there is nothing in history which is not the word of God.[11] Each moment in history is a new theological locus, a new source of revelation for one who can read the signs of the times. Now the present moment in history appears to this Latin American theology to be a "process of liberation".

In taking as its starting point the political situation in Latin America, the theology of liberation was obliged to work out a political analysis—or rather to accept one ready-made. Do these theologians wish to make themselves into polito-logians? They were already involved in the revolutionary struggle, their political analysis came ready made from the hands of others, they had perceived the process of liberation in the light of the "socialist option". The new theology begins with that option; it will develop its contents by reinterpreting the entire Christian faith from the point of view of "liberative praxis". A Marxist hermeneutic of the Bible is the natural consequence of this fundamental option which is reinventing Christianity. But what exactly is this option?

The Socialist Option

The socialist option is radically Marxist even if it claims to be something different.[12] It flows from a Marxist reading of the movement of history, a movement reduced to the dialectic between master and slave, between oppressor and oppressed. To take the side of the poor means involvement in the class struggle and the class struggle is the foundation of history and the mainspring of progress. Liberation will consist in the seizure of power by the oppressed. In the dialectic of historical materialism, there is no possibility that power can play the role of arbitrator between

[11] This confusion between the interpretation of history and divine revelation is common to all the theologies of liberation. See the collected work *Fe cristiana y compromiso*, the texts of Scannone, 263 f. and of Assmann, 342–45.

[12] As has been noted by the bishops of Chile with regard to the movement, "Christians for Socialism". Document of the Bishops' Conference, May 1971, nos. 28–30.

classes. Power is an attribute of classes and is generated by the conflict between the dominant class and the dominated class. It is out of the question, therefore, that any power exist outside the conflict, above the class struggle. There is no third way: One must choose between bourgeois power and the worker's power. The choice between capitalism and socialism must be made: The poor, obviously, must choose socialism.

The socialist option is the Christian response to the "process of liberation" revealed by a Marxist reading of history. And the only one. It forces itself upon the Church as the Church's duty with regard to the poor. The various movements of liberation are concrete expressions of that cry of distress and of hope signalized in the documents of Medellín as "the sign of the times" for Latin America. The "liberating involvement" enjoined by this great document is therefore nothing other than the choice of socialism. Now this choice can be arrived at "scientifically" only by means of Marxist analysis; this involvement can be made real only within the dynamic of Marxism.[13] But in reinterpreting Medellín in a Marxist perspective, have the theologies of liberation revealed the true meaning of the document or have they betrayed it?[14]

Medellín was a document born of compromise, and like all such documents it is open to divergent interpretations. In order not to betray its meaning, one must hold all of its elements together, even—or especially—if they are contradictory. Was this not what the directors of the Latin American Episcopal Conference from the staff of CELAM tried to achieve? Bishop Pironio, President of CELAM from 1970 to 1975, was its secretary general in 1968, at the time when the text was being

---

[13] Following Bishop Lopez-Trujillo one could distinguish between the various branches of "liberation theology" on the basis of their strictness (more or less) in adherence to Marxist praxis—none is entirely free of Marxist method. See *Liberación: Diálogos en el CELAM, Documentos CELAM* 16 (Bogatá, 1974) 42, 50 ff.

[14] The fundamental importance of Marxist influence on liberation theology is perfectly described by F. Malley, *Bibliographie de la Libération*, introduction, 8. G. Gutíerrez, while carefully safeguarding the autonomy of the theologian, maintains that Marxism is the common denominator of all theologies of liberation. See further the letters of the bishops of Chile, May 1971 and April 1972.

laboriously hammered out. The present secretary general, Bishop Lopez-Trujillo, who was with him at that time, is making every effort to safeguard the interpretation of Medellín in fidelity to sound doctrine, maintaining at the same time a close dialogue with the theologians of liberation.[15]

Although it pushes its analysis of the conflict situation in Latin America very far, Medellín is careful to avoid making that conflict into a primary principle. The demand for justice and peace is above such conflicts and tends to dominate them, to go beyond them. Denunciation of injustice provokes conflict, but it is conflict for the sake of justice and for the sake of peace through justice. Did Medellín not encourage the involvement of Christians in the revolutionary struggle when it denounced "unjust situations and structures" and when it spoke of "institutional violence"? There is need for discernment here. Not every revolution in Latin America is Marxist. Not every "reform of structure" is a tool in the class conflict. Not every political involvement is a "socialist option". Medellín did not define the political conditions of involvement; CELAM left to each Christian the responsibility of making his own political analysis and his own option. Was an opening to socialism effected? Medellín did not reduce sin to social structures nor salvation to a revolution. The appeal of Bishop Pironio for an "integral liberation of man" is clearly opposed to any Marxist interpretation of Medellín. By this expression, the president of CELAM meant the work of the grace of Christ who alone "frees from sin and death".[16] This "integral liberation" cannot be reduced to any historical process whatever. The genesis of the Mystical Body of Christ is not to be confused with that of a Christian civilization and much less so with the genesis of some ideal society by means of the class struggle.

[15] The summit conferences of 1974 were part of the same effort—they were published in *Liberación* . . . (see note 13). So, too, was the foundation at that time of the review *Medellín. Teología y Pastoral para América Latina*. Review of the Pastoral Institute of CELAM, Medellín, 1975.

[16] Bishop Pironio, in the CELAM bulletin, April 1975, 9–15; and in *Liberación* . . . (See note 13) 20.

A theology involved in "liberative praxis" produces just this confusion. The theology of liberation is engendered by its praxis and molded to fit its dialectic.[17] Liberative praxis is the crucible of this new theology. This praxis is actually a "transforming action" taking in the entire world and all mankind—an action proportionate to the creative and redemptive action of God. Builder of a "different society", creator of a "new sort of human existence", this praxis is pregnant with "the new earth" and the "new heavens" which are to appear at the end of salvation history. The discernment of this history is the object of the theology of liberation. A new "understanding of the faith" is coming about in the light of this *praxis liberadora*.[18] A complete reinterpretation of divine revelation begins with the very act of its acceptance. Faith is no longer an adherence of the understanding to the First Truth but rather a willed involvement in the present moment of history in which this Truth is refracted. The faith is not primarily contemplative but active; it is not "theoria", but "praxis".[19] Does it still have God for its object? But God reveals himself only in terms of that historical salvation which man (with God?) achieves. Now there is no distinction between the history of salvation and that of the universe or of mankind. There is one single history, one single process adding up to the evolution of the species, and in that process, the genesis of humanity is the central axis, a genesis realized through the energy of conflict in the struggle for liberation, class against class. This truth is the primary object of faith.[20]

The perspective of *praxis liberadora* resembles the post-Hegelian theologies of Moltmann and Pannenberg in that it does away with the distinction between human history and sacred history

[17] G. Gutíerrez. "Evangelio y praxis", in *Fe cristiana* . . . (see note 11), 231 f.
[18] G. Gutíerrez, ibid.: "Se trata de una intelligencia de la fe hecha desde la Praxis liberadora, contructora de una sociedad distinta—forjadora de una nueva manera de ser hombre." Cf. Idem. "Teología y Política", in *Fe cristiana* . . . (see note 11), 20–27.
[19] "La fe es practica": Scannone, "Teología y Política", in *Fe cristiana* . . . (see note 11), 258; cf. 247–58.
[20] G. Gutíerrez, *Teología* . . . (see note 4), 183–225.

employed by Vatican II. This distinction rests on a distinction between two planes of human destiny, the natural and the supernatural; two orders of ends intimately united in human action by the sight of the ultimate end, but remaining distinct in their being, in their ontological and moral structure. The monism of "History" does away with this fundamental distinction between the two orders of nature and grace: human history is rendered sacred by the process of liberation at work within it; grace is commitment to that liberative process, salvation is labor within it. The act of faith is a political act.[21]

A Political Reinterpretation of Revelation

The political dimension is essential to faith, as it is to history.[22] The theology of liberation does not base this primal certitude upon abstract analysis but upon a direct perception of divine revelation in the concrete circumstances of history.

This hermeneutic pushes back into the shade the fundamental element of both the Old and New Testaments, the relation of man to God; the religious element fades away, and is lost in "the social". Sin is no longer separation from God but rather separation from one's oppressed brothers. Note again that the identity of the oppressed is determined by the "dialectic of history"; it is through the class struggle that the oppressed are defined. In the twentieth century, there are no oppressed persons within the socialist camp, just as there were none within the camp of Israel in the time of Joshua. In this "camp", one finds only liberation. To become involved is the primary duty; in short, there can be no sin except in relation to this involvement. Sin therefore is not an attribute of any personal act; it is an attribute of the oppressive structures of capitalist society. Original sin is nothing other than the evil nature of these structures. Liberation has its beginning in a battle against the established order. It continues under the

---

[21] "The concrete historical option of the Christian is always both a political option and an option of faith"—the two must neither be confused nor divided. Scannone, "Teología y Política" in *Fe cristiana* . . . (See note 11), 262. This indivisible union is the consequence of the practical character of faith, as is also the confusion between the two histories and two orders of being. Cf. ibid., 247–64.

[22] G. Gutíerrez, "Evangelio y praxis" in *Fe cristiana* . . . (see note 11), 235.

imperial force of an ever new utopia. A permanent revolution runs through all history in the name of the future society.[23]

Is the eschatological return of Christ together with the "new heaven and the new earth" at least the central axis of this dialectic of liberation? No, the Parousia does not come from on high; it proceeds from that same process of salvific liberation which is the work of history. This liberation has no source outside the world in which it produces its fruit. Liberation takes place within time. It is the fruit of time, it culminates in the advent, within eschatological time, of that which one may no longer call "the Eternal" but rather "the Future", or its biblical synonym, the Eschaton.[24]

This political and eschatological reading of the Gospel brings one back to the holy war of the Essenes of Qumrân and the messianic fever of the Jewish patriots. The object of faith is the promise of the Messiah and of the messianic age. In Jesus the promise was renewed rather than realized. Its realization is pursued within the same history of salvation by the same dialectic of conflict which sets oppressor against oppressed, class against class. The theology of liberation leads to a reinterpretation of social life in terms of conflict. The children of God realize themselves only within history and by means of history, and therefore only within conflict and by means of it. They can live as true children of God only by achieving an "actual identification with the interests of those who suffer oppression, with the struggles of the exploited classes." "Liberative praxis is the very life of faith." "Is there any other way to encounter Christ in the poor and to receive the power to become a son of God and a brother

[23] G. Gutíerrez, *Teología* . . . (see note 4), 284–94.

[24] Has not Jesus fulfilled the Promise? In him liberation has indeed become a reality, and the dialectic of history has been transcended, but only in virtue of that Resurrection which carried him directly to the end of time. In this historico-eschatological perspective, Jesus is not the Eternal, the Always-Present, but the Future. And if he becomes contemporary, it is only through his Church which is in time. The liberation is in the making always in time, and its objectives are born of the projection of the Eschaton into time. The relation of the Christian to the resurrected Christ is totally eschatological: it passes on through the totality of time. The vertical has disappeared in a history of salvation now identified with human history. The dimension of eternity has become an anticipation of the Eschaton, a projection of the world to come into present time.

of man than to enlist sincerely and effectively in the struggle
for liberation?"[25]

The only thing left is to ask the Marxist dialectic to provide a
definition of sin and grace. "Grace is the solidarity of the people,
sin consists in the failure to cooperate with that solidarity." Here
the reference was to the Chile of President Allende. But for any
other country, the same method will determine sin and grace by
tracing the "path to socialism".[26] Since the Marxist dialectic is the
supreme teacher of political analysis, it is by that very fact the
supreme teacher of faith. The whole life of faith is reinterpreted in
terms of one's involvement with the class struggle. For it is not
purely a question of recognizing that the class struggle exists but
of seeing in the class struggle the "fundamental reality" and the
mainspring of the dialectic of liberation.[27] Class solidarity lived
out within this conflict is the sole means of realizing the Christian
imperative of love in its true nature and in its universality. Let no
one object to the hatred which nourishes the class struggle!
One must revise the ancient love-hate dualism: hatred of the
dominating class is a part of true love—love of the dominated
class.[28] Should we not revise our notions of sin and violence
along the same line? All of this (together with the traditional idea
of God) is merely the superstructure of bourgeois society. The
substructure is liberation by means of the class struggle. Was
Medellín not inspired by these necessary principles of analysis?[29]

The "Integral Liberation of Mankind"

The watchers on the heights of CELAM are making every effort
to defend Medellín against Marxist interpretation. The past few
years have seen a dramatic dialogue between two versions of

[25] G. Gutíerrez. "Evangelio y praxis" in Fe cristiana . . . (see note 11), 244 f.

[26] J.-L. Segundo, in Fe cristiana . . . (see note 11), 208.

[27] The class struggle, the "fundamental fact", is the primary postulate of the
Declaration of the "Christians for Socialism" who met at Santiago, Chile, in May
1972. See G. Gutíerrez, Teología . . . (see note 4), 341–44.

[28] G. Gutíerrez, op. cit. 345; Hugo Assmann, in Fe cristiana . . . (see note 11),
343.

[29] Which are Marxist. . . . Segundo does not hesitate to go this far in his
interpretation of Medellín in Fe cristiana . . . (see note 11), 204 f.

Medellín. But the thrust of the debate goes far beyond textual exegesis. What is at issue is the essence of the Church and its unity. The touchstone of unity is the participation of Christians of different classes—and even of opposing "camps"—in the same Eucharist. If the class struggle is the substructure of religion, it would be a lie and almost a blasphemy for Christians of different classes or of opposing camps to participate in the same Eucharist. The bishops of Latin America have risen in opposition to this subversive interpretation of the faith. They have denounced this invasion of hatred. "One can arrive at the community of fraternal love only by the path of love."[30] Bishop Pironio and Bishop Lopez-Trujillo have sought an open dialogue with the theologians of liberation. The summit conferences of 1974 made evident once more the cleavage that exists between the two groups even when they use similar language. The president of CELAM is always ready to open his arms wide. Moreover, although it does include true political liberation, the "integral liberation of man", as he proclaims it, is incompatible with any theology which would reduce this integral liberation to the level of the political order alone. In the dialectic of historical materialism, there can be only one liberation in which the political and religious orders are indivisible. How can one escape from this reduction of the divine to the human and of the Church to the world?[31]

During the two years 1973 and 1974, at the time of the dialogues, the development of the synodal documents was in process and preparations were being made for the fifteenth regular meeting of CELAM, which was to be "celebrated" in Rome on the occasion of the World Synod of Bishops. In his statement of theologico-pastoral guidelines, Bishop Pironio proclaimed "the liberative work of evangelization" and "the involvement of the Church in Latin America" in "the liberation of the whole man and of all mankind". But these words were still laden with heavy

---

[30] Declaration of the Conference of Bishops of Chile, March 24, 1973.

[31] The summit conferences of 1974 brought together a group of theologians especially qualifed to treat the "theology of liberation" from G. Gutíerrez to P. P. Bigo, under the direction of Bishop Lopez-Trujillo. See *Liberación* . . . (see note 13).

ambiguity. The president of CELAM endeavored to dispel these ambiguities in his closing remarks.[32]

On the last day of the CELAM meeting in Rome, the Pope came and spoke, putting an end to all equivocation in clear and unmistakable language: "Authentic liberation is liberation from sin and death." The language of the Gospel is not to be confused with that of the world: "Liberation is not merely a fashionable word, it is also a word intimately familiar to the Christian. It is part of his vocabulary, and we are obliged to use it every day, whenever we refer to the redemptive work of Christ our Savior, through whom we have been granted reconciliation with God and through whom we have been reborn into a new life."[33] On the same day, November 3, at the time of the Angelus, the Pope forcefully returned to the subject of equivocation in the use of the word liberation: "We speak of 'liberation'. The Church esteems this term highly and makes it her own. In fact it is used most emphatically in her most fundamental teaching, the good news of that redemption which brings freedom from evil and sin. It is evil and sin which constitute the principal obstacles to the true freedom of the children of God, the main link in that dreadful chain of slavery which drags mankind into indescribable chaos, ever aggravated by the dialectic of egoism and the corruption of the passions."[34] This is the meaning of the word liberation in the language of the Gospel and of the Church, the full and primary meaning. The other meaning belongs to another language, full of equivocation when it tries to absorb the fuller sense into itself by reducing it "to an economic and purely social program, when it takes hatred and violence as weapons to show off its swift efficiency, when it so deludes itself as to place its hope *a priori* in systematic struggle among men and in revolution. This is not the way of the Gospel, not the way of the Church."

[32] For the work preparatory to the Synod, see *Aspectos de la evangelijación en América Latina*, in the CELAM bulletin, March-July 1974, 2 ff. Also the report of the Secretary General in his *Assessment of CELAM*. For Bishop Lopez-Trujillo's account and that of Bishop Pironio, see the CELAM bulletin, Jan. 1975, 1 ff., 11 ff.

[33] Paul VI's talk on November 3, 1974. *Doc. Cath.*, no. 1665 (12 Jan. 1974) 1001.   [34] Ibid., 1003.

Was the Pope ignoring the temporal involvement of the Church in Latin America? Was he rejecting it? On the contrary, he had ratified it but by making clear distinctions and by freeing it from the equivocal language of "liberation". In describing the Church's sense of involvement and the action which flows from this sense, the Pope did not use the now-ambiguous word "liberation", but spoke instead of "integral progress", "true freedom", "authentic justice". He made "social involvement" an obvious consequence of the transformation of persons by the life of grace. "It is by transforming man from within, by making him a conscious carrier of the values which faith and grace have engendered in his soul, by setting in his heart the dynamism of love, that one can infallibly achieve integral progress within society, a progress founded on true liberty and authentic justice."[35] The temporal involvement of the Church in Latin America is an involvement of Christians who know how to be truly free in their choices and in their action. "Prisoners only of the Gospel", they will be able "to make choices calmly, to make decisions courageously. knowing that 'the Lord opens wide the door' (cf. 1 Cor 16:9; 2 Cor 2:12) by which the Gospel can penetrate freely and decisively into mankind and its history, into society and its structures."[36]

The Pope commended confidence in the social magisterium of the Church to the bishops of Latin America as a means of bringing about this penetration of society by the Gospel.[37] He urged them to safeguard their "apostolic enthusiasm" against the double temptation of capitulation to "situations of injustice" and of "binding themselves to ideologies foreign to the Christian spirit or having recourse to violence, which is the source of evils even greater than those they seek to remedy."[38] The Pope recalled to their minds his teaching at Bogotá and also his more recent teaching on liberation as the salvation of the whole man: salvation in Jesus Christ, liberation from death and sin by the

[35] Ibid., 1001 f.   [36] Ibid., 1002.   [37] Ibid., 1001.

[38] Ibid., 1002. Here the Pope refers again to a controverted passage in *Populorum Progressio* (no. 31) as well as to his talk in Bogotá, August 24, 1968. In his Angelus address on November 3, 1974, he vigorously returned to the subject of these temptations to violence and the "warfare between systems", ibid., 1003.

grace of Jesus Christ. This "Christian liberation" must never become a mere instrument of political ends; it must not be reduced to mere political action. Moreover, Christian liberation is not compatible with every form of action; it spreads into social life by means of "Christian principles" which are a "light" and "an incomparable stimulus for steadfast work toward the regeneration of a modern and peaceful society living within a constantly renewed justice and a perpetual fraternal charity."[39] The Pope refused to use the word "liberation" to designate this action of justice and love. The warning to theologians of liberation was clear. But the word liberation covers a variety of political demands. Did the Pope reject them all? Did he reject Medellín?

Bishop Pironio placed the work of Medellín in its true light. Human liberation is a part of spiritual liberation. The first is included within the second, and not vice versa. The president of CELAM abstained from any political judgment when he insisted on the primacy of the spiritual, but he did make clear what must be the primary source of discernment when one is dealing with human liberation. He challenged Church members to achieve that inner and spiritual freedom without which no involvement in human freedom can itself be free.[40]

The liberation proclaimed by Bishop Pironio is not identified with any particular praxis; it leaves all political questions open. Is this a reason for reproaching him? His perspective on liberation does not exempt one from the urgency of action nor from the prudence it requires; it illumines them with a new light by making one requirement of any political system very clear: the requirement to give men space to breathe. Every human being

[39] Paul VI, Talk of July 31, 1974; Doc. Cath., no. 1660 (8/22-9-1974) 753. A little earlier the Pope had distinguished "wise, consistent, effective criticism of Christian social and religious principles" from "materialistic analysis".

[40] Promoted to the leadership of a great Roman tribunal, Bishop Pironio entrusted to his co-worker, Bishop Lopez-Trujillo, the further conduct of the dialogue which they had begun together with the principal "theologians of liberation". A thorny dialogue, in which one always comes at the end to opposite poles: Marxism or Christianity. But the president of CELAM, going far beyond the world of politics and dialectic, has shown the theologians the true path of their liberation: conversion to transcendence—and humble service to the truth.

carries within himself something which goes beyond human society. This "beyond" arises from his direct relationship to the Absolute; it is lived in filial relation to God.

Politics must stop short at the threshold of the Absolute; it is not the whole of man. And in this thought lies the first principle of any true liberation: liberationist totalitarianism stumbles at the very threshold. The theologians of liberation must liberate themselves from totalitarianism; theirs is the worst of all totalitarianisms because it hides itself under the mask of liberty. In doing so they will not be denying the political dimension of their passionate concern and love. Perhaps they must exile themselves for a time from the drama of this world but only in order to reenter it with a deepened faith guided by divine love, with a new and freer capacity for involvement in human history.

For the sons of the kingdom, contemplation precedes involvement. Theology is born from that source where the eternal penetrates time, where God comes clothed in the flesh of the world. Daughter of the Word, theology precedes history as the redemptive Incarnation precedes salvation. Theology is the light of salvation, finding its first source in the gift of the Spirit.

No fact of history, no drama of humanity, even be it worldwide, can be the root of a theology of the liberation effected among men by Christ our liberator. The political situation of the Third World, no matter how extreme the state of oppression, no matter how urgent the cry for justice, cannot be the ultimate foundation of a theology. A political situation determines political actions, undertaken in the light of political principles. The fact that the Gospel illuminates political principles does not make them a theology. The liberation which Christ brings is not limited to a social drama but pertains to the drama of man face to face with God.

V

FRANÇOIS HUBERT LEPARGNEUR

THE THEOLOGIES OF
LIBERATION AND THEOLOGY

Translated by Msgr. Henry Cosgrove

Liberation Theology: Its Exaggerations

1. Its highly extrapolated theory of dependence

We have indicated that one of the major components and principal sources of the theological-political movement of liberation
is the hypothesis of international economic dependence: this has
grown in theory and is regarded as proved in the eyes of many,
and as dogma for others.[1] At the present time statements about
development and help on the part of developed nations to the
developing peoples have appeared childish, false, dangerous, in-
jurious. The extrapolation of the theory of dependence has been
complete, passing from the economic to the political sphere and
thence to the theological level. The role of historical interpretation (of dependence) in Latin American theology of liberation is
parallel to the role which the human sciences in general tend to

---

Originally published under the title "Théologies de la libération et théologie tout court" in *Nouvelle Revue Théologique* 98 (1976) 147–69. Reprinted by
permission.

[1] "A good example of European methods which have caused economic dependence, in the rest of the world nowadays called 'under development', is the
colonization of Brazil": Marina Bandeira, member of the Brazilian commission "Justice and Peace". Other typical expressions are found in G. Gutíerrez:
"situation of dependence and oppression". "The poor man is the subproduct of
the system in which we live and for which *we* are responsible" (the *we* needs
interpretation). "Poverty, the result of social injustice . . . " (natural data are not
considered). "To opt for the poor man is to opt for one social class against the
other." "Material poverty is a sub-human situation . . ." (Are we not to distinguish between poverty and misery?).

play in European theology. In short much has been made in a few years of the truth suddenly revealed and enlarged into a myth: thus there has been opened a new epistomological field for *sacra doctrina*. It matters little in this regard to know in what degree or measure evidence is objectively founded; as always, where there is smoke there is fire. We have the impression, to say no more, of excessive manipulation.

The vogue of liberation theology has perhaps not been helpful, has in fact even been harmful to the development of the techniques which are directly linked to the traditional development of theology (exegesis, patristics, history of the Church, knowledge of the documents of the magisterium, the main medieval theological schools of thought and of their *Summae*, etc., to say nothing of archeology, of ancient languages, and of canon law): everything, in short, which is a part of the chain which we have indicated and which is a chain of alienation and captivity only if one chooses to make it so.[2] They say: This is a new way to do theology, with the newspaper in hand. But let us imagine, against all probability, that we are dealing here with a type which would come to an end in only a few years after perhaps one or two decades of domination in the market place. What would happen then? The almost two thousand year line of evolution would tend to continue; then it would be necessary to appeal to skills or competence which have never been improvised, and look for them wherever they will be found. This new plea for help would amount to an admission of failure; but let us not anticipate. We are talking of dependence; is theology of liberation the surest way of bringing it to an end in the theological domain itself?

[2] Once the chain has been broken, discontinuity in theological affirmation often resembles irresponsible sub-culture. The new theological formation permits young "theologians", who have only recently begun to be heard, to teach propositions such as: "Nothing done through love and with love is a sin"; "Individual confession: demand or request for pardon without obligation (*compromisso*)" [this word is a subtitle]; "Classical moral philosophy does not consider the social implication of personal acts, nor the consequences—in the individual life—of conditionings which are not subject to the human will." Attacks against "traditional theology" generally speaking, in this context result in caricatures due rather to ignorance than to ill will. But ought not liberation itself be liberation from error?

2. "We have done it": What have you done?

Like every great ideological current, liberation theology is founded on the strength of a dialectic, which in this case is in opposition, and with considerable lyric or dramatic quality, to the "non-man" (Hegel again), result of dependence, with regard to colonialism-imperialism coming from elsewhere and the enormous work of liberation carried out by the Latin Americans. They repeat: "Our theology is not an ideal or a new abstract conception, but an accomplishment. We have done it." What? If it were a case of a completely interior work, a transformation of the soul, no rigorous control would be possible; liberation theology would then resemble only too much its predecessors and would lose epistemological originality. Liberation theology points out insistently that its criteria belong to the historical and visible order, not just the order of the "lived" or of the socio-cultural, the economic, or the political. Therefore one must look more closely. Which are the countries whose theologians fuel liberation theology with the greatest fervor? Argentina, Uruguay, Chile, Peru, and Brazil—we hope the others will pardon us. Let us look at the history and the progress of these countries in the last ten years. We will not be so unkind as to insist, since the reader is sufficiently informed elsewhere: let him judge.

Liberation theology will not put up with mere foolish tales; it wishes palpable proofs; moreover, presupposes them. But in so doing it leaves itself open to the retort: Where then have you actually realized a world that is more just and less alienated? In which country? When? In reality there are no Christians of superior calibre: all conscious Christians struggle among other men of good will to improve the conditions of life, with varying and scarcely remarkable success, and in the bosom of an inevitable and healthy pluralism of tactics. We have immense respect for martyrs, for those who struggle according to their conscience, for those who live their faith in painful conditions; such heroes and believers exist everywhere; but blustering does not merit any consideration. When liberation theologians have freed their own country from the evil which history can overcome we will speak of it again; while waiting, the disorder is visible enough to need no commentary; while waiting it is only fair not to take its own desires for realities and not to award oneself a monopoly of efforts that are more or less in vain. By claiming that liberation theology is true because it works, one enters upon a very slippery road, a road which quickly leads to insoluble contradictions as soon as the law of the Cross intervenes, a law which is by no means favorable to visible success. How then to avoid the "excessive freedom" which was believed to have been surpassed? Frey and Howe, in their article about the Umbanda (Afro-Brazilian religion) and Pentecostalism, indicate that the originality of these religions consists in recruiting members on the basis of experiences or situations which arise from suffering or affliction. Liberation theologians at bottom are saying the same thing of their own movement. Let us then consult sociological and historical data to see which of these two contrary reactions (the differences, although important, which intervene between Umbanda and Pentecostalism may be passed over) has greater success in Brazil. In these latter years no religious thrust has had more success in growth among the truly poor, the people, especially in the shanty towns of the great cities, than the Umbanda and Pentecostalism.

3. Its politicization of religion

Gutíerrez seems not to understand that between the Gospel and the revolutionary option—however justified this may be—there intervenes an analysis of the situation the reading of which is ideological;[3] he accuses of blindness or bad faith millions of Latin American Christians who do not take the same option. This is extremely radical. The principal warhorse of the ideology of liberation is the *struggle against dualisms*. To eliminate them people close their eyes to the necessary articulations of the poles or extremes. No reality is simple in the socio-political universe in which the theology in question is located. Maritain showed more finesse by insisting on the principle "distinguish in order to unite". This is the normal path of speculative, analytic

---

[3] "The Gospel, deprived of all ideological elements which might have falsified a cruelly conflictual social reality, not only was not incompatible with the revolution, but, on the contrary, demanded it": G. Gutíerrez.

and scientific thought: analysis and synthesis, abstraction and return to the dialectical concrete.[4]

Some followers of liberation theology appear to apply the rules of dialectical materialism with a radicalism which exceeds the living currents of Marxism. This is a point of criticism at present which we would not mention if it did not seem to have some foundation: some Catholics involved in problems of progress adopt theories which are being abandoned by those who launched them or by their legitimate heirs. By casting all the blame for Latin American under-development on the shoulders of international capitalism, these believers are too ready to excuse the responsibility of Iberian Christianity and of its Latin American clerical representatives. Without denying the contribution of realism, which a socio-economic analysis, inspired by Marxism, frequently assures, one cannot honestly, without further qualification, impute to theology the hypotheses and deductions one believes ought to be drawn from the history of the continent, by claiming that this is where the future of Christian faith rests in these latitudes. To draw out the political consequences of faith and perceive that it has social obligations and links is an operation which is fully justified; but the confusion arising between the very ideological elaborations which are sometimes proposed and the theology really required by the continent, motivates the cry of alarm which we address to all those who accept the task of honestly studying the problem. One may be pleased by the turn to the left of a very active portion of Latin American Christians (less numerous than sometimes we are led to suppose),[5] and anxious about the lack of theological preparation among many of its leaders. The penetration of ideology into theology is a serious problem which we cannot treat here: the recognition of this penetration should not mean the reducing of faith to certain debatable interpretations, nor even a blocking of this same faith with fallible tactics. Let ideology be studied at its own level (it

[4] H. Lepargneur, "Continuidade e descontinuidade no pensamento de J. Maritain", *Convivium*, S. Paulo, XII-5 (1973) 401–403.

[5] Cf. D. Fregosi, "La nouvelle gauche dans cinq pays d'Amerique latine: Bolivie, Chili, Colombie, Pérou, Vénézuela" [Thesis] (Paris: University of Sociology, 1971).

would be a poor subterfuge to pretend that it is dead).[6] The influence of the master ideas of Christianity has already been revealed as relatively effective in Latin America, without need of extremist doctrines.[7] There is a risk of borrowing from the religious instinct its most suspicious component, that is, its propensity to fanaticism: the dramatic history of messianic movements in Brazil should however serve as a moderating force.

4. Its neo-triumphalism

Until the last council, Latin-American Catholicism was clerical and triumphalist among many of the clergy but pietistic and lacking sacramental formation in the ordinary classes. Has the situation changed very much in this regard? The development has been different among the partisans of the first group with the survival of certain elements of triumphalism when the better

[6] Cf. Elisco Véron (coord.), Nicole Belmont et al., El Proceso Ideológico (Buenos Aires: Ed. Tiempo Contemporaneo, 1971); J. P. Andric, "Idéologies et relations internationales en Amérique latine" [Unpublished Memorandum], (Droit: Clermont-Ferrand, 1972). Finally, from the official report presented by Msgr. Pironio to the episcopal Synod of 1974 on Latin America (no. 13): "Also in Latin America, certain risks appear of a superficial identification between evangelization and human promotion, reducing liberation to the field of the purely socio-economic or of politics or restricting this liberation to the limits of time."

[7] M. Ch. Paulus, "Le role de l'Eglise dans les transformations sociales en Amérique latine. L'exemple du Brésil" [Unpublished memorandum], (Paris: DES. Sc. Pol., 1970). Available in Thomas Bruneau, The Political Transformation of the Brazilian Catholic Church (London-New York: Cambridge University Press, 1974), [or in Portuguese: O Catolicismo brasileiro em época de transição (San Paulo: Ed. Loyola, 1974), furnished with an ample bibliography]. At Campina Grande, in May 1956, before liberation theology was a conscious force, the bishops of Northeast Brazil prepared a theoretical course of action against the physical and social troubles afflicting the area. In very correct terms they place the physical or temporal situation in the perspective of the Kingdom. Let us emphasize the following statement of the formal declaration (whose text, as far as we know, has never been published): "It is basic that we should show with absolute clarity that we cannot assume responsibility for the concrete formation of the plan of action stated here." Responsibility in its various ways is then clearly limited. In what degree is it necessary to re-examine the division of roles and responsibilities in the economic and socio-political fields?

informed or the more ambitious have passed from a scrupulously Roman formation to liberation theology, itself the heir—as has often been stated—of some minor avatars. It is said that the spirit of Christianity has finally been discovered (this proclamation does not have an entirely new sound for anyone who knows the European history of theology); finally it is also said that functional theology has been articulated (based on action and no longer upon being), at last also the secretly Christian needs of the contemporary world have been set forth in the language of the people. One might be tempted to give citations; however, the principle is not open to citation: the reactions of the base or core formed in the belief that Europe and twenty centuries of Christianity have little to say in the face of the inflated proclamations of the sons of Joel who tirelessly set forth the same message from one meeting to another, from one congress to the next, and from one review article or book to others. One thinks of Karl Marx: until his time philosophers were content to describe the world (or to contemplate it "Greek-wise"), henceforth its transformation has begun and its true reconstruction. Traditional Latin theology, the heir of Hellenic philosophy, now denounced as dualist, (in both its Platonic and Aristotelian currents; which would certainly give cause for astonishment to a Hellenist or a Thomist), had engaged in speculation: the new theology produces. Thomism is condemned without being heard, its monuments are relegated to the dusty corners of seminary libraries; certain indications suggest that it will be rediscovered by historians and philosophers. Like all neo-triumphalism this one too contains a good measure of scorn for those who do not belong to the current. The dialogue which it proposes is extra-ecclesial (with unbelievers, Marxists, animist-reincarnationists).

5. The Myth of the "people"

This is something which must not be forgotten in the system. The word "people" while somewhat pejorative in French is not so in Portuguese and Spanish. In connection with the promotion of the religious sentiment of the ordinary people and the valorization of the resources of the unwritten culture in the ideology which underlies the Paulo-Freire method, its prestige has continued to grow. It has become a myth, that is, something which is eventually subject to manipulation, something understood which needs no explication or proof. The "people" know, they think correctly, they are not mistaken, they are born without original sin; they are however perverted by scholars of all types and despoiled by the rich of all kinds; the people would lose their wisdom by going to college or university (that is the truest element of all, but there are very few who have seen or mentioned the absurdity of promising college or university to everyone). In short, society (the bourgeois) corrupts the "people" (one thinks of Rousseau) who are defenseless before the agents of international capitalism. In this sense, liberation theology seeks to express purely and simply popular dynamism; through liberation theology the voice of the silent is expressed and acts.

Unhappily the anti-speculative reflection attributed to the people is falsely anonymous; the same names keep reappearing constantly to proclaim what they think the "people" think. What is attributed to the people evidently does not always have the same content and oddly enough resembles the opinion of the authors who lend their voices to the "people". The idea that the people have practically nothing to receive from the scholars since they, the people, develop their theology of liberation on their own by putting it into operation, this idea (that it originates with scholars as is easy to prove) aims at reinforcing the standing of the savants who know how to read the views of the people (or at least pretend to translate this unthought thought), in opposition to the statements of those who understand nothing of the popular message. It is difficult not to believe that the expulsion of one theology by another covers some struggle for influence between academics. Who would dare to contradict the good, suffering people? Liberation theology links populism (very mishandled in the history of the Latin peoples, on the level of the conquest of power) to sophistication. It is equally difficult not to see in the schema reproduced here the transposition of Marxist relations which unite the directors of the Communist party to the proletariat and by it to the people.

Where is the creativity of the Latin American people headed when it is free to adopt its own religious language? Fr. Renato

Poblete, in citing the well-known theological study made about Pentecostalism in Chile and published under the title *El refugio de las massas*, observes: "Lalive d'Epinay (the author of this book) analyzes an apparently spontaneous movement born of the people which is the people's expression on a religious level; a movement in which at last, and contrary to what happens in the traditional churches, the man of the people acquires his own language. In spite of that, it is a movement which tends to go on record dangerously as an enclave of immobilism, impervious to the social and political changes in course."[8] Many of the liberation theologians claim that they are faithfully interpreting the spontaneity of the Christian people of Latin America in the convergence of its faith and its misery; attentive observation of the phenomenon will allow some doubts on this subject. Good or bad, liberation theology must be attributed to its own authors who are professors with a European formation, revolting—rightly or wrongly, often rightly—in the face of what appears to them to be the injustice of the Latin American condition.

Its Conclusions and False Options

1. *Revelation, nowadays, is especially history, our present history*

God speaks to men in history, our history; the signs of the times. This is the foundation of a theology that has been put back on its feet. We do not contest or dispute the valid sense in which a Fr. Chenu, a John XXIII, the last Council, have prudently and discreetly mentioned the necessary attention to the transformation of the modern world, the necessary reading of the signs of the times, in a Biblical sense. But never has a responsible theologian submerged the revealed sense of history in its equivocal materiality which carries along both the good seed and the cockle. The paschal mystery, apart from which there cannot be Christian theology, this paschal mystery, the seed of eschatology in history, is not completely homogeneous with history as

---

[8] *Les luttes de libération bousculent la théologie* (Paris: Editions du Cerf, 1975).

the phenomenon or appearance gives it to us. Fr. Teilhard de
Chardin, always so sensitive to the continuities of cosmic and
historic evolution, held it as a matter of faith to avoid treating
human progress as univocal.[9]

2. Towards a neo-Christianity of the left

Why not say simply: "Towards A Humanitarian Socialism"?
Because the struggle of liberation theology considers itself as
basically with a religious foundation: no one needs the Christian
faith to declare himself a socialist; finally if Communism itself has
not succeeded in implanting a totally secular Marxism unbur-
dened by any religious impulse (or anti-religious, the same force
being utilized), it has not been proved that another movement
will succeed in doing so. However, "there is only one history" is
the leit-motif of Christianity just as it is of all totalitarianism. The
rejection without qualification of "dualisms" introduces into
liberation theology a confusion on the order of that which is
imputed to medieval Christianity. A new antinomy: rejection of
the distinction between the spiritual and the temporal considered
as out-moded has introduced confusion between theology and
politics, a confusion judged, however, to be opportune. "What
is the socio-political schema which we must choose nowadays,
beginning with our underdevelopment, which would be simultaneously effective and coherent with the type of society which
we desire for Latin American people whom we know? This is the
question which we put to theology because, for us, it is a vital
question."[10] Who will answer the theological question if not the

[9] In a letter dated February 15, 1940, Fr. Teilhard indicated to Mlle. Mortier
that he regretted not having underlined sufficiently in *The Divine Milieu* that the
end or term of the efforts of convergence will be obtained only "in a gesture of
returning", in an eschatological "discontinuity" (*Le Christ cosmique*, p. 71). The
same idea reappears in other places; for example; "The world can reach God, *in
Christo Jesu*, only by a total re-founding in which it must *appear* to founder
completely, without *experimental compensation* (of an earthly order or type)":
P. Teilhard de Chardin, *Science et Christ* (Paris: Ed. du Seuil, 1972); *Sur la
souffrance*, ibid., p. 1974.
[10] J. L. Segundo, "Capitalisme-Socialisme, une croix pour la théologie", in
Concilium, French edition, no. 96 (June 1974) 98.

student? Who should reply to the question about the socio-political organization of the country, if not the citizen, in the exercise of his political rights? By stating that it is in the name of faith that one brings about socio-political options of a basic type one thereby establishes an intolerance which, because of changing direction, has no greater weight than those which preceded it.[11]

3. Is Christianity just simple moralism?

We bring up here a consequence of the secularization of religion which results in the theology of liberation. A preaching void of all mysticism (Fr. Segundo Galilea is an exception in this matter) turns fatally either to rubricism, which is not the case, or to moralism which is frequently verified. Christianity is reduced, in fact, to its moral; and this moral is reduced, in fact, to the socio-political dimensions of human action.[12] This is an aspect of the liberation movement which is more lived than made explicit,

[11] From the same author, J. L. Segundo: "Which leads us once more to the conviction that if we conclude that the Gospel has nothing to say on a problem as decisive as is the alternative capitalism-socialism it is clear that it could have only an absolute value, hence not functional . . . which amounts to saying no value at all": *Concilium*, no. 96. On the politicization of the Church, an observation of Jacques Ellul ("Politics is the greatest problem posed to the Church, the occasion of her greatest falls, her constant temptation, a trap which the Prince of this World lays for her ceaselessly") has prompted this comment of A. Fabre-Luce: "The long utilization of religion by the right has been heavily paid for in our time. The Church is now tempted to make peace with the left. The same danger reappears under an inverse form" (*La mort a changée* [Paris: Gallimard, 1966], p. 282). The third temptation of Jesus, in Matthew 4:8–13, cannot be avoided by any Christian theology.

[12] We share the distaste expressed by J. Daniélou with regard to any reduction of Christianity to a moralism, be it only in the name of secularization or interests which are really valid in the technical or political level (*Et qui est mon prochain?* [Paris: Stock, 1974] p. 175); this author has clearly seen that the pointed issue here is the concept of the transcendence of Christianity (ibid., pp. 172, 195, 237) and, by a reflex, the nature of the consecrated religious life: "I do not see what would justify the total gift which a young Jesuit makes when he pronounces his religious vows if it were simply a matter of advancing the interests of society in various sectors. His vocation gives testimony, beyond the social, political, and cultural phenomena, of a deeper reality, a more fundamental reality, of the permanence of a dimension of human history: the encounter of man with God through Christ by the intermediary of the Church" (ibid., p. 102).

but still very real. It in no way contradicts the following paragraph about Manichaeism: in the descriptions of liberation theology we almost find, in opposing camps dialectically speaking, the good and bad, the people and the imperialists, the poor believers and the capitalists, the good underdeveloped and the wicked "developed" nations (that is, those who would claim to be more advanced). In fact the social moral which is preached, is preached for others: the identification made of oneself with the good exploited poor man (the modern version of the *good savage*) apparently prevents the moralism which is preached from finding an immediate personal application. Personal morality will consist essentially in solidarity with the good people to whom justice has not been given: petitions, pamphlets, columns of protestations, etc. Experience shows constantly that it is not necessarily those (individuals or institutions) who shout the loudest against the injustices of this world who fulfill in a most scrupulous fashion their own duties in justice: the injustice against which they struggle is always the injustice of others, and freqently it prevents them from seeing where they are putting their own feet.

Are science and technology instruments of liberation and true progress?[13] The answer is debated[14] and certainly needs to be nuanced in various senses. In an underdeveloped country, a small elite is aware of this critical complexity, but most of the inhabitants aspire in fact to the consumer society without being aware of the exact cost of it, and sometimes without being willing to pay the cost (for example, it is easy to forget the centuries of

---

[13] M. Schooyans has observed that the man of the developed world sees in science and technology the instrument of a liberation, when in fact they make him a slave ("L'avortement, problème, politique", in *NRT* 96 [1974] 1034). Let us add that a new consciousness is appearing in the developed countries, where quite a few works have appeared denouncing this slavery; people of the underdeveloped countries, ignorant of this experience, still seek to enter upon the same path, namely that of the consumer society. But here the question of *dependence* should be reviewed: how to benefit from inventions without paying tribute to the inventors? How to gather the rose without the thorn? Has liberation theology protected the poor from jealousy of the rich, from imitation of the rich, and even perhaps from replacing them? In any case, where is there wealth without disastrous falls?

[14] J. Gray and D. Carrière, *Les Misères de l'abondance. Sept questions sur la croissance* (Paris, 1973).

restrictions, of hard work, and economies which occurred in Europe in order to pay for the dawn of a capitalism which, however, we do not intend by that fact to legitimize). It would be a simplification of the problem to pretend that the poverty of the others has been the only price for the acquisition of wealth: let us suggest to liberation theology more extensive study of the implications of medicine for all, of the university for all, of integral autarchy, etc. In any case these problems should remain secondary when the Church defines for herself the task which Christ has confided to her. If you withdraw from Christianity its belief in the afterlife, its cult and mysticism, then its moral will no longer have much weight.

4. *Its Manichaeism: All evil from the "Other"*

We have reserved for the end our most decisive criticism: the Manichaeism of liberation theology or at least of its representatives. We are the good guys, the oppressed.[15] The others are bad, the oppressors. Who are they? Principally the United States when it is a question of economics and hence of imperialism; Europe, when it is a question of cultural power; the coalition which they form with soviet Russia and capitalist Japan when it is a matter of international political structures. The dichotomy does not stop there; as evil exists evidently in the country, the identification of the good and the evil continues; between the rich profiteers of capitalism and the poor proletarians (here once again is the theme already mentioned, the people "hypostatized"), between the governed and the rulers. How does it happen that people who are so good and so richly endowed are constantly directed by such evil governments? There must be a formidable orchestration of this dichotomy to render it invisible to the critical minds who must, however, exist in the very heart of liberation theology.

[15] "This despoiled and oppressed continent, which profoundly aspires to liberation: Latin America. . . .": G. Gutíerrez. To shed light on the expression: *the guilty party is the other fellow*, read for example the criticism, available in French, which E. Dussel made of the "pedagogical domination" of European theologians (*Les luttes de libération bousculent. . .* , cited in note 2, p. 95, a page which is remarkable, to say the least. for its frankness), or the one which J. L. Segundo addresses to "professional theology" (ibid., p. 178), without forgetting number 96 of *Concilium*.

Since there is very little new under the sun, the lesson of colonialism has not been lost: the art of the colonizer consisted in forming a bad conscience in the ones colonized, who then came to grovel at his feet and ask pardon for being what they are (the Hegelian dialectic of the master and the slave). Liberation theology has renewed the arguments but preserved the structure of the operation: it is a matter now of forming a bad conscience in all those who are on the other side. Of course, he who acquires a bad conscience may *in fact* be guilty, a partner in some way with the guilty. We draw attention to the simplistic dialectic of the operation. On the one hand the good, on the other the bad: this is the eternal schema of the good conscience (at the very moment in which the confessional is being abandoned, the conscience of *the other* is being examined). North Americans and Europeans understand nothing of the things of Latin America: they will never begin to understand anything except by acknowledging that they are guilty. The process is not totally devoid of foundation, but extremely partial and clumsy: as always the cultural arms surrendered by the former master to the former slave permit the inversion of the roles. But by changing the partners, does one really correct the dialectic of oppression, if it is this which forms the essence of the sin of the world?

We would not speak of this point if it were the exception; it is general.[16] Not only are the classical theologies scorned and criticized without being known (obviously they had not been born in the Americas), but the religion attributed to the generation of the forties and fifties (the *good* generation follows the *wicked*) is summed up in caricatures which legitimize for

---

[16] "According to Msgr. Lopez Trujillo, there are two liberation theologies, one following a spiritual direction and originating in Latin America, and the other placing the emphasis on politics and originating in Europe. Only the first is valid, and not marked by foreign interventionism": *Informations Catholiques Internationales*, no. 481 (1–6–75) 11; in the same number , we learned that Dr. E. Dussel had been dismissed from the University of Mendoza by the "wicked" who dominate the University (this is the logic of the system, the powerful are the oppressors), but we are reminded also that in 1974 Dussel had been excluded from the Pastoral Institute of CELAM (cf. ibid. no. 443), which is much more disturbing as evidence of a split in the unity of the renewed Christianity of Latin America. In any case, we shall not try to teach Msgr. Trujillo about the influence of Marxism in Latin American thought on liberation theology.

many the revolt of the young to whom all good qualities are attributed.[17] Since 1958, it seems that mankind is born without original sin. The most skillful ones in this opposition between good (Latin American) theology and bad (European) theology are careful to put the Council on their side,[18] but, was Vatican II really the work of Latin America or of the Third World?

The schema must be analysed and judged on two levels: that of sane human equilibriums, by employing the tool of the human sciences and by trying to instill an ethical aspect; and on the evangelical level, which is indispensable since a "theology" is in question. a) On the psycho-social level, the development of the revolt may constitute a stage in the cure (*transfer* in psychoanalysis), on the condition that it be surpassed. Liberation theology may in effect be the Oedipus of Latin America: the problem then is to know how one resolves the Oedipus. May our

---

[17] One example: "*Analyse synthétique de la religiosité 'traditionnelle'*. . . . In the concrete, faith is simply changed into certain unintelligible formulas which often appear contradictory. And the only argument that is offered is submission to an authority, unconditional fidelity to this belief being the absolute guarantee of salvation. *God*: not a person but a Power necessary to explain the world. His supreme maxim: to reward and punish. . . . *Sin*: the violation of a law of this God, something like passing a red light in traffic. This results in the judgment passed by the young about the religion of preceding generations: "*excessively traditional*: purely habitual; childishly legalistic; ritualistic; without foundation; very negative and moralizing; very demanding and excessively circumscribed; gloomy and sentimental; supremely pietistic. . . ." On the other hand: "*characteristics of present day youth*: a great desire for sincerity and authenticity. . . ; exaltation of freedom. . . ; dignity and fraternal love, etc." "Actualização. Revista de divulgação teológica para o cristã de hoje", *Belo Horizone*, no. 68–69 (August–September 1975) 304 f. This morsel of bravura is representative and not exceptional. But then what is authenticity? respect for the other? sincere search for truth?

[18] "With regard to the eschatalogical *bona* we do not accept the divided vision, shared by a good portion of European theology, between a history which would be the work of man alone and an eschatology which would be the inroad of the work of God alone. According to conciliar theology, a majority of Latin American theologians conceives eschatology as interaction of two causalities: God's and man's": J. L. Segundo (Montevideo) *Perspectiva teológica* (revue de S. Leopoldo, Brazil) vii–13 (1975, second sem.) 164. What European theologian would recognize himself in the first position?

thoughts help for the consciousness-raising of the global process to produce greater serenity in the evaluations of the relationship of faith and world, or religion and history. In this perspective liberation theology is a highly expressive verbalization which must be taken seriously and respected even in its awkwardness: it is never easy to resolve one's Oedipus state or to complete one's transfer. Let us add in the same perspective that on the historical as well as the psycho-social level there is always a certain complicity in us with the evil which happens to us in the usual course. A line of good and evil passes radically through the marrow of each human being and is not reduced to a line separating class and class, nation and nation, continent and continent. Macro-analysis must not eliminate Micro-etiology, nor must utopia eliminate common sense or political economy the message of Revelation which remains as the foundation of all Christian theology worthy of the name. It seems unlikely that a people or nation would have no responsibility—on the internal level as well as the international level—for what happens to them in the course of a period of more than four centuries.

b) The level of the Gospel: charity will give us understanding without any false subterfuges or evasions before the exigencies of clarity which all fraternal charity implies. One may very well reinterpret the Gospel as desired, but if, however, one remains honest and straight-forward it will be recognized that the construction of the Kingdom of God is founded essentially on *personal metanoia* and not on learned dialectics of forces. *An ideology, even if it claims the title of theology, which rests essentially on accusation of the other side as the source of all evil cannot be confused with a valid interpretation of Christianity which is, in its very principle an appeal for the conversion of him who receives the call of grace, of salvation.* Otherwise, we are not speaking of the same salvation, of the same God, or of the same religion.

CONCLUSION

We reaffirm our sympathy in principle for a movement which will bring forth the fruits which we have the right to expect from it only if it is assisted by the clarity of its guides, and their critical and constructive spirit. The movement represented by liberation theology must rediscover the values of simplicity, lack of pretension, of service, of true and prudent faith which characterize the Latin American peoples in their actual history. In fact, the authors of this theology are for the most part theologians who have changed their attack after having received a theological formation of the classic type; they retain a traditional theological culture; but what will happen when "theologians" formed in the pure schemas of "liberation theology" as really practiced, have taken their place? We know that we are not alone in being disturbed about this. What is spoken today will be published tomorrow.

A very serious risk hangs over the whole enterprise: to create a "theory of practice" which will take the place of *practice* as the imaginary document or paper of a theory in the ordinary or petty sense of the word. It would be quite in conformity with the program of the Statement whose content would be exhausted in a kind of dance of words which the rules of their own grammar state for each other. Instead of accomplishing a move forward towards historical operativeness, and by that means towards the eschatological conclusion, they would be yielding to the nominalist current of empty, but structural, formalism.

We have tried to indicate the real point of a very promising debate. And after? Liberation theology, according to its own leaders, was claiming to save theology. We ask rather: will it save itself in order to become or remain a Christian theology? Let us cultivate theological pluralism. Furthermore we have a right to require that a Christian theology be theological and not simply political, that it be Christian[19] and not just clever or brilliant,[20] and of easy commercialization. Will liberation theology be able

[19] Paul VI, audience of September 10, 1975 ("Necessity of redemption for the salvation of man"): *L'Osservatore Romano*, no. 302 (14 September 1975).

[20] Some liberation theologians juggle with the concepts of "man" and of "non-man", like Hegel with his concepts of Being and Non-being. We prefer the view of J. Daniélou: "I regret that too much importance is attached nowadays to the originality of an idea or a work of art. What is important for me is that it makes me know the reality. . . . It is the truth which counts, not the originality or the theory" (op. cit., p. 28).

to save itself from its own fetters, from what prevents it from being what it aims to be, that is what it would seek to be, before being submerged in its own turn by the next wave of neo-theology which may reach us from Asia or Africa?

San Paulo, Brazil

VI

JOHN O'DONOHUE

SOCIALIST IDEOLOGY

I. THE EMPIRICIST TRADITION

If the word "socialism" is used to denote a practical program for freeing human beings from unnecessary obstacles to their authentic development, then every decent human being must be a socialist, and therefore every Christian. No one who accepts the Christian Gospel as the guide to the way life on earth is to be lived could agree that some individuals may use wealth, or the accident of birth, to dominate other individuals and to exclude them from such full participation in the life of their community as their talents, natural and acquired, allow.

"Socialism" as a total philosophy for man is, however, another matter, for we are dealing here, not simply with a practical program for curtailing the exploitation of man by man, but with a definition of man and of the meaning of human life. "Socialism" in this sense of an "ideology", or master-idea, holds that the construction of a materially comfortable world for all mankind is the final object, the Supreme End, of all human endeavor. It is in this latter sense of "comprehensive philosophy" that the word "socialism" is used in this article. I discuss in this first section the Empiricist tradition which has led to the socialist ideology, and in the two succeeding sections I examine the two principles on which this ideology is based, namely "All men are good" and "All men are equal".

> Presume not then thy God to scan.
> The proper study of mankind is man.

Pope's words neatly summarize the impatience with uncertainty which was a marked characteristic of seventeenth- and eighteenth-

Reprinted by permission from *The Tablet* (27 January 1979).

century Europe. Whereas medieval man, like primitive man, had been to a large extent satisfied to live in an incomprehensible universe, post-Renaissance men were not satisfied just to be: they wanted also to know. Descartes' quest for an unshakable ground of certainty reflected the general feeling that vague beliefs would not do. We must sink solid and certain foundations, and then we will be able to build a house that will endure. Men were possessed by the desire to be sure, to pluck the heart out of mysteries, to get to the bottom of things, to reduce the complex to the simple, to extract order from disorder. They wanted to have everything properly sorted out, all neatly labeled and classified. The call of the Enlightenment was above all a call to men to be realistic, to banish fantasies, to stop dreaming and start living.

This passion for understanding things, for attaining certainty, produced extraordinary developments in the field of the physical sciences. The thirst for certainty enabled men to understand, and so to some extent to control, the physical environment to an astonishing degree. The Enlightenment brought more general benefits also. The rigorous examination of the grounds of human knowledge undoubtedly sharpened men's wits and cleared away a great deal of the intellectual rubbish which had built up over the centuries. The demand for evidence made it much more difficult thenceforth for anyone to gain a hearing for mere assertion. Statements unsupported by evidence became inadmissible. It will perhaps never be possible totally to extinguish the attraction which fortunetellers and cranks and visionaries of all kinds exercise over some people. Purveyors of prophecies of imminent doom, horoscope vendors, tales of unlikely visions and marvels, claims to secret powers, whether of curing cancer or of bending spoons from a distance: human frailty is such that these things will perhaps always be with us. Nevertheless, life has been made much more difficult for the seers and marvel-mongers, which each generation of men seems to throw up, since philosophers started analyzing the grounds of human knowledge and establishing rules of evidence. The "popular" newspapers will no doubt go on printing their horoscopes, and the Loch Ness monster continue to enrich the Highlanders of Scotland; but witches and hippogriffs have probably gone for good. The Empiricist movement has succeeded in implanting in men's minds a healthy scepticism about unsupported assertions concerning the inherently improbable. Hume's sound principle, for which he has been so often reviled, that it is more likely that men are telling lies than that the unprecedented has really taken place, has undoubtedly by now been widely accepted as a working rule for assessing the worth of unlikely tales, and men have thus been liberated from false beliefs and armed against deceivers. The Empiricist principle that experience alone can furnish true knowledge has substantially reduced the sum of human foolishness. The search for certainty and the insistence on evidence which has characterized Western thought for the last three hundred years has increased men's confidence in their reasoning powers and made them less gullible and more independent and dignified. There is no difficulty in recognizing that the Empiricist movement in philosophy has made an important, indeed a massive contribution to human development.

All men's achievements, however, seem fated to have an ambiguous character. Not only can mistakes, and even wickedness, in spite of themselves, sometimes produce good fruits—for example, wars, whose object is to kill men, generate scientific developments which eventually assist peaceful progress and even help to prolong people's lives—but also attitudes and achievements good and true in themselves can bring evil in their train—for instance, zeal for truth produced the Inquisition, and the invention of the airplane led to the B-52 bomber; and even at the individual level, love, for example, seems inevitably also to generate jealousy. So it was with the Empiricist movement: good and beneficial in some respects, it has proved extremely damaging in others.

The urge to know for certain was felt, not only by scientists, but by speculative thinkers too. People wanted to be sure, not only about the physical universe, but also about man and, above all, about God. They aspired to get ultimate reality too securely taped and sewn up. It was here that the Empiricist movement went badly astray. For the refusal of uncertainty is a good thing in regard to matters in which certainty is possible; but it is an error, and must be considered a moral fault, in regard to matters which, by definition, defy certain knowledge by man. The basic question of the Empiricists, "of what can we be sure?" soon developed into the proposition, "matters about which we cannot be sure have no importance", which eventually became "matters about which certainty is unattainable have no existence". Philosophy thus underwent a fundamental curtailment. Instead of being a quest for ultimate reality, it came to be restricted to the effort to establish the grounds and limits of human knowledge.

This was a grievous impoverishment. The possible field of human knowledge was narrowed to what could be known with certainty, and, finally, to what was "verifiable in principle" by observation. Instead of "What is the ultimate nature of reality?", the central philosophical question became "What can I know with certainty?" and "What are the grounds of certainty?"

It is the Empiricists' refusal to tolerate uncertainty that has done the damage. The assumption that what cannot be proved is insignificant, that a truth which cannot be certainly known is not worth striving for, and indeed is not a truth at all, undermined the classical vision of man as a finite being striving for the infinite. Empiricism led to an impoverishment of the spiritual life of the human race in more or less direct proportion to the material prosperity which it ultimately generated. Empiricism in fact, when its principles were extended to the whole of human life, emptied that life of all possible meaning. In disposing of demons and hobgoblins, it also removed the dimension of the infinite from human life and turned it in very truth into a tale told by an idiot, signifying nothing. In restricting the "real" to the "empirically verifiable", in refusing submission to any reality which they could not fully comprehend, the Empiricists made man himself into the ultimate reality. Henceforth man became indeed the measure of all things. The human mind no longer received truth, but manufactured it, man was himself the *source* of truth. Torn out of the context of the infinite, he became his own meaning. Man-worship replaced God-worship, theology did indeed become anthropology, as Feuerbach was eventually to recommend. Ye shall be as gods.

Superficially, the Empiricist enterprise seemed to display a becoming modesty, as Pope's words suggest. To recognize man's limitations, to restrict the possibilities of human knowledge to what can be certainly known in experience, not to aspire to matters essentially beyond man's reach: all this seemed to reflect no more than an honest and realistic appraisal of man and of his situation.

There was, of course, nothing new in asserting that man is incapable of comprehending ultimate truth. It was a commonplace of medieval theology and may indeed be regarded as a simple tautology. The fatal step was taken when the Empiricists proceeded to declare that what man cannot comprehend is nonexistent, and this is not modesty but great arrogance, of a piece with the behavior of one who, at the individual level, would claim that any knowledge which he did not himself possess was not worth having, and, indeed, was not real knowledge at all. By proposing to restrict human knowledge to that which could be certainly known, by declaring that it was an abuse of reason for man to try and penetrate the ultimate background to his existence, the Empiricist movement inevitably generated the sense of the meaninglessness of life which is so marked a characteristic of twentieth-century man.

The refusal to tolerate uncertainty amounts, in fact, to a refusal of the human condition, for this seems to consist essentially in a continuous search for what always remains unattainable in its totality. The Christian explanation of human life as the progressive tending of the finite toward the infinite seems in truth to fit man's experience far better than the Empiricist's claim that the natural human condition is a state of complete rest in total certainty. No doubt, human progress consists in the progressive conquest of uncertainty, in replacing individual areas of uncertainty with certainty. What was once unknown becomes securely known. But the movement toward certainty is a never-ending process. The overcoming of one uncertainty only generates another. This seems to be the true dialectic of human life, the continual splitting of new syntheses into fresh problems. When there are no longer any problems to solve, human life loses its meaning. We can all sympathize with Alexander's complaint that there were no more worlds left to conquer. When the quest ceases, life ceases. Total certainty spells finality. It was that same Pope who also observed that it is not blessedness, but hope of blessedness, that is the true hallmark of human life.

It is not, therefore, surprising that the Empiricists' refusal of uncertainty led to the proposition, frequently heard today: human life has no meaning. If, as so many thinkers have believed, movement and change constitute the very essence of all life, to refuse uncertainty in human life is to refuse life itself. This indeed is precisely the contradiction in Marxism, for all its talk of dialectic, that it pretends to halt the onward flow of human life at a gratuitously determined point, namely, the Revolution. There must always be uncertainty in human life, because human life is essentially, not a state of being, but a process. To say, therefore, that only that which can be certainly known is "real" is to remove from human life that forward-looking dimension which seems to be its indispensable prop. When the old vision of an incomprehensible infinite had been destroyed by the Empiricist approach to truth, it had to be replaced by some other vision by which men could live.

It so happened that a new "science" was developing just in the nick of time. The kingdom of God had been laughed away, and theology declared a non-subject. But there remained the kingdom of Man. Theology was dead, but "sociology" had risen from its ashes, and it was not only able, it was positively eager, to furnish mankind with new goals which were both thoroughly intelligible and completely realizable. What man should now aim at as his ultimate goal was no infinite fantasy, but quite simply the Perfect Society, defined in terms of the only reality there was, the observable material world. What it all came down to in the end was that the final objective of all human life and human endeavor was to provide every man, woman and child with adequate, and ultimately comfortable, food and shelter. It was for this, and this alone, that men existed. To ask why they should work for this objective, and make personal sacrifices for its realization, would be as meaningless as it would have been under the old world-view to ask why men should pursue truth and goodness. It was simply self-evident, a categorical imperative, almost a tautology, something which no man in his right mind could query. For what other goal could the human race possibly have, now that all religious nonsense about the infinite had been finally disposed of, except to make as comfortable and as pleasant as possible, for as many people as possible, the only life which men would ever know?

The substitution of the kingdom of Man for the kingdom of God was the fruit of the Empiricist philosophy, and it led to a number of conclusions which dominate the modern world. At

the same time, however, Empiricism has generated contradictions which must eventually lead to its being discarded as an
adequate, total philosophy for man.

II. "ALL MEN ARE GOOD"

Belief in man's essential goodness is axiomatic for anyone who
believes in God. The doctrine of "total depravity" is incompatible with belief in a benevolent Creator. Trust in God means
trust in man, and you cannot trust what is wholly evil.

Nevertheless, men, though good, are also evil. If there is
anything that experience teaches, it is surely that. Everyone
knows, in the first place from his own experience of himself, that
men are profoundly, and apparently incurably, selfish, greedy,
lazy, and unloving. Every man who has risen above the life of
pure impulse knows that life consists to a very large extent of a
continual striving to overcome tendencies which he recognizes
as undesirable, but which are also very deep and strong. Charac-
ters as diverse as the poet Ovid ("I see, and approve, what is
better: but I do what is worse," *Met.*, VII, 20–21) and the apostle
Paul (Rom 7: 21–23) have written with exasperation of their
inability to do what they wanted to do, and conversely, of their
powerlessness to prevent themselves from doing what they did
not want to do. Such undoubtedly is every man's experience of
his own inner life, and the most charitable observer of other men
and their ways cannot fail to perceive that they too, in spite, very
often, of good will, are frequently guilty of selfish and unloving
behavior. Every child knows the truth of the old catechism
formula: men are prone to evil from their very childhood.

If we accept Schleiermacher's view that the essence of sin is
replacing God-consciousness by world-consciousness, sin may
be seen as rejection of life in its fullness, the attempt to reduce
human life to manageable proportions by denying reality to
whatever is not immediately and wholly comprehensible. Sin is
hiding from the mystery in life by pretending that the mystery
does not exist. Sin is treating the proximate as ultimate, the
relative as an absolute. If this is what sin really is, then the moral

JOHN O'DONOHUE   233

struggle can be defined as the refusal to rest in anything short of
absolute truth and absolute goodness. And since these "abso-
lutes" must always be unattainable for finite man, the moral
struggle can never cease this side of the grave. The only rest
which men can look forward to is eternal rest.

Moral evil therefore has meaning only if there is some infinite
ground to human existence. If there is no infinite, there can be no
sin, and to describe men as "evil" is meaningless. The Empiricist
philosophy is therefore driven to deny that men are sinful.

With all the good will in the world, however, even the most
ardent ideological socialist cannot deny that men do in fact very
often behave in a way that can only be called selfish, lazy and
greedy, that they are very much inclined to put selfish grati-
fication before the general welfare, and to prefer immediate
satisfaction of short-term desires to deeper, long-term and more
authentic fulfillment. There is a limit to even the zealot's capacity
for closing his eyes to the facts in order to maintain a precon-
ceived theory.

Since there is, in the Empiricist view, no ultimate context in
relation to which men's actions can be regarded as disorderly, it is
necessary to explain unfortunate tendencies to pride, covetous-
ness, lust, anger, gluttony, envy and sloth, in terms of "alienation" or "false consciousness". They are mistakes, the result of
ignorance on the part of men who have not grasped that the
ultimate reality is man, and that the truly satisfying, ultimate goal
of all human activity is the Universal Welfare State, with free
food, and free housing, and free brothels, and free medical care,
and free abortion and cremation facilities for all. That this is the
final and ultimate goal of human life, a state of affairs in which
men will experience total felicity, must be evident to the meanest
intelligence: although, as will be seen presently, it is improper to
speak of intelligences as more or less mean. The goal of human
life is no incomprehensible ultimate to be groped after in faith,
but something so obvious that it has only to be presented for it to
be immediately accepted. Anyone who does not know needs
only to be told and he will see at once. And once he has seen,
there will no longer be any problem about relating his behavior
to man's ultimate end. Thus evil is an appearance only, the
consequence of ignorance, and it will disappear once men have

been brought to understand how simple human life really is, how plain is the path to happiness.

The old notion that man's evil will is the real enemy of human progress and human development, and that the energies of the race are best employed in confronting men with their own evil, and persuading them to do something about it: such a notion only makes sense if man's fundamental vocation is to be found in the pursuit of the Infinite for its own sake. If the ultimate goal of human life is just a simple matter of constructing a universal welfare state, then every man in his right mind must be willing, nay eager, to work for its expeditious realization. If he lacks eagerness, it can only be that for some reason he is failing to perceive the obvious. This failure cannot be explained in terms of "evil" or "moral weakness", since such terms only make sense if man is rooted in some kind of infinite reality to which he is invited to reach out. There must therefore be some factors external to man which are distorting his vision and blinding him to the obvious. He is not evil, he cannot be, but he is suffering from a "blockage", and the thing to do is first to identify and then to remove this blockage. There may be purely personal causes for these unfortunate blockages, and a psychic operator may be called in to deal with them. Sometimes however such blockages are found in whole sections of a population, or even throughout a whole population. It is undoubtedly very strange, but facts must be faced, and it is unhappily a fact that there are whole societies in which hardly anyone is prepared to devote his life to constructing the socialist paradise. Ignorance on this vast scale certainly suggests a cause more generalized than a failure in mother-love or in potty-training, and demands a commensurate explanation. When a whole society has been so grievously misled about the meaning of human life, it can only be that society as such is responsible. So "social structures" are the favorite candidates for the role of these distorting and alienating factors which hide from man the truth about his nature and destiny, and lead him to pursue selfish ends. That must be it. The structures are responsible for what appears to be moral evil in man. No one seems to have attempted to explain how it could come about that men should have created structures so damaging to their own real interests. Still, wherever they came from, they are there, and man's first task is obvious: he must get rid of them. And that is the function of the Revolution.

There is, however, another task to be undertaken, though this can only be a temporary one. This is the reeducation of those whose thinking has been deformed and who have been alienated from the true end of human life, contaminated it may be in their very being, by those wicked social structures. There will therefore have to be reeducation centers, and these may have to be quite strict places, for a generation after the Revolution. They will not however be needed after that, since there will no longer be any false structures to hide from man his true nature and the real goal of his life. Once the Dictatorship of the Proletariat has been securely established, there will no longer be anything to deform men's consciousness. What looked like human evil will simply melt away in the sun of universal socialist benevolence, and man will shine forth as the good being that he really is.

Experience, that secure fount of all knowledge, has, of course, proved by now that this is all appalling nonsense, which future generations will no doubt regard with even more amazement than that with which we regard medieval witches or hobgoblins. Revolution or no revolution, men's evil obstinately refuses to go away. Not only are there at least as many thieves and murderers and adulterers and drunkards after the Revolution as before, but a new and quite unsuspected evil has made its appearance, the evil of deviationism. People who have no reason at all to be unhappy, since all those distorting social structures which are the source of all unhappiness have been torn down, still refuse to be happy, and even start running away to other countries where the evil social structures are still intact. Inexplicably, people just refuse to know what is good for them, although what is good for them is so patently obvious. It is all very bewildering, but people are actually risking death in order to get to West Berlin or Hong Kong or Malaysia. Such madness has to be stopped. People cannot be allowed to ruin themselves by returning to the source of all human evil. There can be no question of querying the theory. If mankind had some goal beyond the socialist paradise, we would have to start thinking in terms of an incomprehensible and mysterious element in human life, and of some destiny which cannot be known with certainty. This, however, is intolerable, since it is axiomatic that what cannot be known with certainty does not exist. If, then, experience seems to show that even people who live in a society where the structures have been reformed to suit man's true destiny are still as wicked as before, and even perhaps more wicked than before, so much the worse for experience. It just cannot be true.

The call of the Enlightenment was a call to men to banish illusion and futile dreaming, to live in the real world and to content themselves with the reliable. The Empiricists undoubtedly regarded themselves as hard-headed realists. Hume's immortal words may be taken as a succinct expression of eighteenth-century European thinking: "When we run over libraries, persuaded of these principles, what havoc must we make! If we take in our hand any volume, of divinity or school metaphysics for instance: let us ask, does it contain any abstract reasoning concerning quantity or number? No. Does it contain any experimental reasoning concerning matters of fact and existence? No. Commit it then to the flames: for it can contain nothing but sophistry and illusion."[1] We must base human life on the sure rock of experience, and banish, once and for all, all fantasies about "another world" beyond space and time. There must be an end to all foolish talk about God and heaven, and all those other imaginary "entities" which have their real source, not in reality, but in man's disordered imagination. We must learn to live in the real world, and refuse the name "knowledge" to anything which is not based on practical, public, demonstrable experience.

Such was the program. And yet a tradition which began in the exaltation, not to say deification, of experience, in that it made experience the ultimate test of reality, has ended up by rejecting experience in favor of a new metaphysical fantasy. By a completely unexpected circular process, the principle "experience is the sole ground of knowledge" has produced the proposition "experience must be rejected when it shows that the Revolution does not solve the problem of human evil". The stubborn fact that men remain observably and apparently incurably selfish, and that no amount of tinkering with "social structures" seems to make the slightest difference, unless, indeed, it is to make the situation worse: this plain deliverance of experience is simply ignored. It has to be. For the only alternative is to restore man to his place in an infinite context which cannot be known with

[1] *Enquiry into Human Understanding* (1784).

certainty. And there can be no such context, since what cannot be known with certainty does not exist.

III. "ALL MEN ARE EQUAL"

Belief in the essential equality of all men, like belief in their essential goodness, is entailed by belief in God. The Christian view is that all men are equal because all are children of the same Father, and all have been redeemed by the same Christ. All men have the same basic, natural dignity before God. It is offensive to humanity to classify people into "higher" and "lower" on the basis of some purely external criterion, whether this be where you live, or what language you speak, or what school you went to, or how your father earned his living, or what kind of skin you have. It is offensive because it implies that men are essentially defined, not by their sonship of God, but by some purely external, contingent circumstance.

There is, however, a distinction to be drawn between essential equality and accidental inequality. Equality does not mean identity, and here again experience must be our teacher. A child opening its eyes for the first time at once perceives that some human beings are bigger than others, or more agreeably shaped, and before long it realizes also that some human beings are kinder, cleverer, more generous, more reliable, more industrious, stronger, better singers, better football players—the list is endless—than others.

To some extent, the differences between men may be called horizontal, not making men better or worse, but just different. Thus the fabric of human society, based on the division of labor, is woven out of the different skills of the different human beings who compose it, without implying any individual superiority or inferiority. But there is more to human inequality than this. The term "good", or "better", is generally used, without qualification, of moral quality, and it may be thought that this is a proper usage, since the pursuit of moral perfection is man's fundamental vocation, and those who engage in this pursuit more wholeheartedly may be said to be absolutely "better" people than those who engage in it less whole-heartedly. In the other half of man's vocation, the pursuit of truth, some men are clearly better equipped by nature than others, as every schoolchild knows. However, since intelligence may be used for unworthy ends, like collecting money for selfish purposes, or organizing wars, the possession of superior intelligence cannot be said to make one man superior to another without qualification. Still, other things being equal, and especially the moral quality being the same, there is no objection to saying that more intelligent people are "better" human beings than less intelligent people. In the same way, there is a real sense in which it can be said to be "better" to be musical than non-musical, artistic than non-artistic, "good at math" than "bad at math". There is a vast number of ways in which people are really different from each other, and in which some must be considered superior to others.

Within the context then of the same ultimate vocation, and while sharing the same basic nature and destiny, men are not only different but unequal. When we recognize that human persons are individual expressions of the same inexhaustible, infinite reality, we can accept the observed differences between men as a given fact for which we can offer no completely satisfactory explanation. That men are not equal is no one's fault and no occasion for complaint. It is simply of a piece with the pattern observable throughout creation, and efforts to create the best possible human society must start from this fact, as from all the other given facts of creation.

If, however, there is no reality beyond man, if man is to be explained totally in terms of himself, then indeed the inequalities between men constitute a serious problem. Man is the ultimate reality of whose existence we can be certain. If we proceed from this fact to assert that man *is* the Ultimate Reality, that beyond him there is nothing, then men must be responsible for themselves and for each other, and they must indeed be convicted of injustice in producing better and worse specimens. The differences between men now generate, not a sense of wonder at the variety of creation, but a profound sense of guilt. Man himself has brought it about that some men are better and some worse. And what man has done, man can, and must, undo. Somewhere, somehow, men have generated inequalities among themselves, and the whole political and social apparatus must be called in to redress them. All men's energies must be harnessed to the great task of repairing the grievous injustice which men have inflicted on each other by creating a race composed of unequal individuals.

Here again, however, the facts seem stubbornly to resist treatment. In spite of all the welfare programs and comprehensive education and decolonization, the differences between men refuse to go away. It is all very odd, but even children brought up in exactly the same way in the same family manifest disturbing differences of intelligence and character, and it impossible to deny that some are cleverer, or just nicer, than others. A whole industry has grown up to produce explanations of these differences without obliging us to admit our ignorance and submit to the ultimate incomprehensibility of reality. Sociological and psychological manufacturers have been able to do splendid business in recent years by turning out all kinds of theories purporting to explain why men are different and unequal.

At the wider level of whole societies, it is manifestly the case that some have developed more satisfactorily than others. Again, this unequal development cannot be simply accepted as a datum which defies explanation: for that would imply an incomprehensible ground of reality. It cannot be denied that some societies contain a higher proportion of intelligent, industrious and compassionate individuals than others, although certainly there are no societies in which such individuals are completely lacking. Nor can it be denied, with all the good will in the world, that some societies have shown themselves better at handling the physical environment than others. There can, however, be no mystery about why this should be so, since mystery means uncertainty, and what is uncertain cannot be. We are thus driven to ask who is responsible for the fact that some societies are more backward than others. Colonialism comes in handy, of course, but there are societies which have known neither the slave-trade nor colonialism, but have remained very backward. For them we can only fall back on "unknown historical factors", or perhaps just "the unknown effects of a difficult climate, or soil, or perhaps cultural isolation, or just general environmental factors".

The only thing that cannot for a moment be contemplated is that perhaps it is the case that some groups of men, while sharing the same human nature and called to the same destiny as other men, are just less well-endowed by nature for coping with the environment, and need to be helped by those who are better-endowed. At all costs, someone, or some ascertainable element, must be responsible for the inequalities between men: for otherwise we shall have to go back on the fundamental Empiricist principle that what lies beyond experience cannot be true, and so find ourselves bogged down again in the medieval mysteries from which it had been hoped that the Enlightenment had emancipated mankind forever.

The patent inadequacy of the explanations of human inequalities concocted by sociological and psychological sorcerers will of course lead eventually to their being discarded. There is that within man which makes it impossible for him to tolerate nonsense forever. Urban terrorism and football hooliganism and the disaster of post-colonial Africa will force men in the end to face reality once more, and come to terms with the fact that there are apparently irreducible inequalities between men, as well as multiple forms of human malice. It is gradually becoming clear that psychological and sociological explanations of both human wickedness and human inequalities, while they may throw a certain amount of incidental light on the situation, can do very little, if anything, to remedy it. Men will no doubt return eventually to sanity, which means recognizing that there is a mystery at the heart of man, that there are problems about man which are simply insoluble by man, i.e. that there is an infinite dimension to reality which man cannot fathom. Once the notion of God, purified of expressions which belong to an early stage of human development, has again been accepted as the only possible ultimate explanation for things, men will no longer feel obliged to torment themselves by trying to produce explanations for phenomena which are simply to be accepted rather than explained, or worse, explained away. But in the meantime the damage wrought by pseudo-explanations of moral evil and human inequality is considerable. The notion of life as a moral struggle has been eroded, and the result has undoubtedly been a moral weakening of the race as men seek, not to improve and reform themselves, but scapegoats for their own stupidity and malice.

As far as societies are concerned, it should be observed that different societies prosper at different times, so that one which is "superior" in one period may be "inferior" in another. Is modern Greece as "developed", relative to other twentieth-century societies, as was ancient Greece? And how does the world-standing of modern Rome, or Spain, or Portugal, compare with its standing in earlier centuries? There can be no question of making any kind of eternally valid pronouncement on the different levels of different societies. Nevertheless, at any one time we can, and must, use present experience to determine present reality. It is their today that concerns the men of every generation.

What, we may finally ask, would David Hume make of this new metaphysic with its new fantasies of the goodness and equality of men? We can only guess, but we may hope that, honest man that he was, he would recognize it as the legitimate child of his own philosophy. Let us invite him to run over with us the psychology and sociology shelves of a modern library, convinced of the principle that experience alone can furnish true knowledge. What havoc indeed must we make, and what a conflagration must we raise. For a different image, we might turn to the Communist Manifesto, which declared that what the bourgeoisie above all produces are its own gravediggers. Perhaps the time is now at hand when the socialist ideology, the lawful child of Empiricism, will in its turn have completed the sepulcher in which it can finally be left entombed. Undoubtedly it has done more than enough harm already. Empiricism may be good physics but it is bad philosophy.

VII

JOHN PAUL II:
MESSENGER OF THE GOSPEL
IN LATIN AMERICA

Translated by Rev. James V. Schall, S.J.

It is significant that when he decided to go to Mexico to open the Third General Conference of Latin American Bishops, John Paul II chose to retrace the route followed in the past by the missionaries who went from Europe to the New World, the route which had at that time been only recently discovered by Christopher Columbus. In fact, the Pope also went to Latin America as a missionary of the Gospel, whether to instill faith in Christ among those who do not know him or who barely know him, or to vivify and solidify the faith of those who already believe, or, finally, to encourage, sustain, and confirm in faith all those who are involved in the work of evangelization on the continent—bishops, priests, religious and laity.

There is no doubt, indeed, that the Church in Latin America finds itself at a crucial moment in its history and that the basic problem that it ought to confront is that of faith and of its significance. What does it signify? And what does it mean to be a Christian today in Latin America? The presence of the Pope in that continent was meant to be a proclamation of faith in Christ, accompanied by a personal testimony of it. This character of the papal trip was manifested by the Pope's urgent insistence upon meeting the greatest number of people possible, at the cost of heavy personal sacrifice, as well as by his desire to give a word of faith to all. The number of discourses John Paul II gave during the week in Latin America was certainly impressive, but more impressive still was the insistence with which he recalled his

Originally published under the title "Giovanni Paolo II, messaggero del Vangelo nell'America Latina" in La Civiltà Cattolica, (17 February 1979) 313–22. Reprinted by permission.

hearers to faith in Christ and fidelity to his person and his teaching.

John Paul II reached the highest point of his mission of teaching and testimony in his opening discourse to the Puebla Conference. Since this discourse is reported here in full,[1] we will only touch the main themes, and above all, we will restrict ourselves to ascertaining its general sense, placing it in the context of the actual Latin American situation and showing how it responds to the grave and torturous questions that Christians on that continent today ask themselves.

It is well known that Latin America is one of the most explosive zones of the world today. In fact, the people of this continent are formed in great part of the *campesinos* (peasants), who lack land or stable employment; of Indians, who have been deprived of their land by new colonists and multinational organizations; of Afro-Americans, who live in a marginalized condition and, with the Indians, are "the poor among the poor"; of exploited women; of workers who earn a minimum wage and are always threatened by loss of work; of youth (twenty per cent of the population of Latin America is between sixteen and twenty-five years of age), who have no prospect for work and are attracted to communism or who abandon themselves to delinquency or drugs. None of these are disposed to support any longer the condition of extreme poverty, of oppression, of profiteering, in which they live. They wish to get out of such a situation by almost any means, and in the shortest possible time.

In reality, they are not wrong. Latin America is a very rich continent, but its immense riches are in the hands of a few or come to be profitable to the advantage of foreign organizations, especially from the United States, ones which are the only ones capable of disbursing the enormous capital needed for the cultivation and exportation of agricultural and mineral products. It happens, then, that there is a vast gulf between the multitude who live in extreme misery and the few rich who live in the most impudent luxury. The same industrialization that has occurred in many countries of Latin America has brought benefits more to

---

[1] See below, Document 1.

the comfortable classes than to the poor. Almost all of these countries are struck by the whip of inflation. Thus—as the Working Document prepared for the Puebla Conference said— "a great percentage of our population cannot be supplied with the basic necessities of housing, food, health, education and provisions for their future."[2]

Unfortunately, the structural changes needed to eliminate such a grave and evident situation of injustice and to inaugurate a new social justice either come with extreme slowness, or are ineffectual, or are counteracted by regimes of force which are imposed on most of the Latin American countries, making the situation worse. In fact, to the denial of the most elementary human rights in the social and economic fields, there is added the denial of human rights in the political and juridical areas.

The Working Document said:

> In these last years, we see a deterioration in the political situation in our countries. The proliferation of military regimes implies a grave deterioration in the participation of the citizens in the conduct of their own proper destiny. Frequently there occurs an abuse of power, typical of such regimes, in violating basic human rights. The repression is accompanied by delay, by violations of private affairs, by torture, exile, disappearance of persons, about which not even parents have any notification, detentions without juridical process and an attenuated or impeded justice.[3]

In this situation, which is a situation of "social sin",[4] in which "the sin, properly of persons, is manifested in structures and ideologies which consolidate the injustice and proclaim the violence",[5] what ought the Church to do? What are its functions and competencies?

To these questions, the Second Conference of Latin American Bishops at Medellín, in 1968, gave an initial response, proposing a Church at the service of all men, especially of the most needful, a Church poor, and, as an agent of ferment and change, directed in the cause of social justice which would liberate the people of Latin America from the situation of sin and oppression that

---

[2] Puebla Conference, Working Document no. 85.
[3] Ibid., no. 96.   [4] Ibid., no. 80.   [5] Ibid., no. 145.

breaks their integral development. In fact, in the decade after Medellín, the Church has strongly committed itself to the cause of social justice both in the defense and promotion of fundamental human rights in all the continent, and to reveal the most efficacious force for a nonviolent change of situation. This has incited a strong opposition to it—which has sometimes broken out into open persecution against bishops, priests, religious and laity, imprisoning, exiling, torturing, killing, or otherwise causing their disappearance—from the repressive regimes and those political and social forces which are contrary to every change.

None the less, some—be they theologians or those in political or social fields—have held that we cannot limit ourselves to Medellín, but must go beyond. Thus, as regards the analysis of the causes of underdevelopment, of the theory of "marginality"— which supposedly explains the phenomenon of underdevelopment by the absence of active and passive participation of the people—it was formerly argued that to remedy the situation it is enough that the developing countries take the means necessary, make sacrifices and initiate a process of asceticism that will carry them to the level of the developed countries. Now some have passed on to a theory of "dependence", which sees in underdevelopment the consequence of the dependence on the developed countries, especially Europe and North America, on which Latin America depends economically and culturally. In substance, then, Latin American development, in this view, comes to be promoted or limited in the measure in which it serves the development of these wealthy countries. From such an analysis of the situation, then, which puts in relief a conflict of interest inside the capitalist system between the "center" (North America and Europe) and the "periphery" (Latin America), there follows the idea that the development of these latter countries is only able to occur in the measure in which they free themselves by revolution from the lands that hold them in the vise of underdevelopment and from the regimes that represent them.

In this context, there has developed a new theological movement: the "theology of liberation". In reality, it is not a unitary movement because there coexist within it extreme tendencies, such as those represented by H. Assmann or P. Richard, and more moderate tendencies, such as those represented by G.

Gutíerrez and S. Galilea. According to these diverse tendencies, the same basic concepts of this theology are interpreted in different ways. Thus, the central concept of "liberation" for some comprehends, in the first place, the liberation from sin and then the liberation from social evils or economic exploitation. For others, it is reduced only to social and political liberation, to be realized by a revolution, violent, if necessary. We ought, then, to speak, not of a "theology", but of "theologies" of liberation; and our judgment of them ought to take account of the differences, so that the evaluation, sometimes gravely negative, of some of these does not signify a condemnation of the whole movement.

There are, however, some risks which all the theologies of liberation encounter, though in different measure. These seem to be: the recourse to Marxist analysis and revolutionary "practice" as a point of departure for the theology; the excessive politicization of the faith and the tendency to reduce the Christian commitment almost solely to a political and social one; the presentation of Christ principally as a political liberator, if not as a revolutionary and a "subversive"; the reduction of Christianity to a message and practice of liberation from oppression and exploitation, obscuring or even eliminating its transcendent and religious character.

It is in this way that the theology of liberation has posed the problem of the meaning of Christianity and the mission of the Church in a new and radical manner to the conscience of the Latin American Church. The competency of the Church is, certainly, evangelization. But what does this evangelization mean in the present situation of Latin America?

To such a question, John Paul II responded with his discourse at Puebla.[6] He did not, certainly, respond only with this address, for we would gravely limit the message that the Pope intended to deliver to the Latin American Christians if we reduced it to only this opening discourse to the Episcopal Conference without integrating it with other important discourses, for example, those given to the Indians of Cuilapan and to the workers of

---

[6] See below, Document 1.

Guadalajara and of Monterrey.[7] There is no doubt, none the less, that the discourse at Puebla constituted the heart of his message.

This message concentrated on *truth*. The Pope did not begin, therefore, from "liberation" or "practice", but from "the truth that comes from God". This "bears with it the principle of the authentic liberation of man" and "the only one to offer a solid base for an adequate 'practice'." Evangelization is, therefore, essentially the proclamation of the truth of Jesus Christ about the mission of the Church and about man. *The truth of Jesus Christ*—which constitutes the center and "the essential context" of evangelization—is contained in the profession of faith of Peter: "You are the Christ, the Son of the Living God" (Mt 16:16). The Pope, therefore, rejected that "rereading" of the Gospels which either denies that Jesus is the Son of God, making of him only a "prophet", an "announcer of the kingdom and of the love of God", or presenting Jesus as a politician or a revolutionary and his death as "the solution of a political conflict". Before such "rereadings", evangelization—John Paul II affirmed with some vigor—"cannot cease to affirm the faith of the Church: Jesus Christ, the Word and Son of God, became man to draw near to man and offer him, with the force of his mystery, salvation, the great gift of God." Only this faith, he added, can bear the "capacity to serve man, to transform hearts, to humanize systems and structures". Therefore, "any silence, forgetfulness, mutilation or inadequate accentuation of the integrity of the mystery of Jesus Christ which distances itself from the faith of the Church cannot constitute a valid content of evangelization."

This insistence of the Pope on a Christology in conformity with the faith of the Church is not explained only by the fact that the mystery of Jesus—Son of God, made man, crucified and risen for the salvation of men—is the center of the Christian message, but also by the fact that the significance of the person of Jesus, of his evangelizing work and of his death, is the very object of a burning debate in Latin America. In reality, in the Christology

[7] All the Pope's Puebla and Mexican addresses can be found in *Puebla: A Pilgrimage of Faith* (Boston: Daughters of St. Paul, 1979).

of a Latin American style, sometimes, as the Working Document of Puebla observed,

> certain aspects of the life and message of Jesus are emphasized, forgetting or excluding others; there is insistence on the man Jesus, without affirming clearly his divinity; christology is reduced practically to a following of Jesus as a revolutionary and simply political practice, without a confession of faith. The life and works of Jesus are interpreted by means of a schema of class struggle, proper to Marxist ideology. The faith of the Church in Jesus is opposed, drawing it in theory from the need of political practice. Data as important in the Gospels as the virginal conception, the messianic and filial conscience of Jesus, his pre-existence, his salvific death for all men, his resurrection, the foundation of the Church, his priesthood, the ethical, social and political dimension of his message are either denied or passed over in silence.[8]

The second truth which evangelization ought to proclaim is that of the Church: "There is no guarantee of a serious or vigorous evangelization," the Pope said, "if there is lacking a well-founded ecclesiology, . . . a correct vision of the Church." Therefore he recalled some essential points of Catholic ecclesiology: the Church was founded by Christ as a community of life, charity, truth, and as a body, a fullness and sacrament of Christ, in which dwells the fullness of the divinity. The Church was born in the response of faith, which we are given by Christ and therefore is composed of those who believe in Jesus. The Church is our Mother and we are her children. Thus we ought to respect it, serve it, love it. "The love of the Church ought to be an act of fidelity and of confidence," the Pope suggested, and ought to generate "a prompt and sincere adherence to the Sacred Magisterium", by taking into account its "objective" importance.

Why are these points recalled? John Paul II has remarked that in the preparatory documents for the Puebla Conference, "there was sometimes the suggestion of a certain feeling of hostility with respect to the very interpretation of the nature and mission of the Church." Thus, some establish a separation between the Church and the kingdom of God, intending this in a sufficiently

[8] Puebla Conference, Working Document no. 87.

secularized sense, so that one might arrive at the kingdom of God without the mediation of the faith or belonging to the Church, but simply by means of a mere structural change and a socio-political intervention. Thus, it was implied, the kingdom of God would be present there where works for justice exist. Opportunely, therefore, John Paul II has recalled the conciliar affirmation according to which "the Church receives the mission of announcing and inaugurating among all peoples the kingdom of Christ and God, and this kingdom constitutes on earth the germ and beginning."[9] He also recalled the statement of John Paul I according to which "it would be an error to affirm that political, economic, and social liberation coincides with salvation in Jesus Christ."

The Pope then recalled that "there is generated, in certain cases, an attitude of distrust towards the 'institutional' and 'official' Church, qualified as alienating, and to which there ought to be opposed another 'popular' Church, which is rooted in the people", especially concretized in the poor. These positions could be implied in different grades of clarity, not always easy to make precise, but from notably ideological suppositions. In reality, it is on this point that the harshest controversy in Latin America arises, between the "continuing" ecclesiology and the "newer, non-continuing" theories of the Church. This latter proposes the construction of a so-called "popular" Church:

> Inhabited and constructed by the poor, a "class" Church, in the sense of a Church which is situated with clarity and in a decisive and definitive manner in favor of the popular classes in their struggle against the oppression and repression of the system. The visible organization of this Church is to be constituted fundamentally of ecclesial "base" communities, born from a process of the regrouping of dispersed Christians who have made a conscious political option. In this community, the political work of the struggle for justice is not any sort of supplementary or marginal affair, but the very nucleus of evangelization. The struggle is carried out in the privileged place of the meeting with God, the struggle is the very place of meeting. The opting for the poor and for justice does not

[9] *Lumen Gentium*, no. 5.

appear as an "important" or "privileged" option, but as a constitutive option of the very Church itself. In the popular Church, the
axis of the organization of the Church is not defined by the
dichotomy "faith-atheism", but that of "domination-liberation".[10]

The third truth that evangelization ought to announce is the
truth of man: the essential proclamation, in an age like ours, which
is certainly "the epoch of humanisms", but "is also the epoch of a
profound anxiety of man about his proper identity and destiny."
Now, "the Church possesses, thanks to the Gospel, the truth
about man" and has the duty to proclaim it "before all other
humanisms, especially those enclosed in a vision of man strictly
economic, biological or psychological", such as are the Marxist
and Freudian humanisms. There is "the better service", which
the Church can set before men. "This complete truth about the
human being", John Paul II continued, "constitutes the basis for
the social doctrine of the Church, and so also the basis of a true
liberation. In the light of such truth, man is not a being submerged in economic and political processes but these processes
are ordained to man and ordered by him."

In this way, the Pope has derived from Christian anthropology
—which sees man "as the image of God, irreducible to a simple
particle of nature or to an anonymous element of the human
city"—the duty of the Church for the liberation of man, and that
"rich and complex patrimony of principles and norms of action
which go by the name of the social doctrine and teaching of the
Church." In other words, to love and defend man and to collaborate in his liberation, the Church does not need to have
recourse to other systems and ideologies. "There is at the center
of the message, of which it is the depository and bearer, an
inspiration for working for fraternity, justice and peace, against
all the domination, slavery, discrimination, violence, attacks on
religious liberty, aggressions against man and attacks on life."

John Paul II thus has responded to the most lively problem that
agitates and divides the people of Latin America, the problem of
Marxism. On the basis of the principle that the fount of all evils

[10] P. Richard, "La Chiesa nasce della lotte del popolo", in *IDOC*, nos. 6–7
(1978) 110–11.

in Latin America is capitalism (which in Latin America is a "dependent" capitalism), many Christians of that continent insist that the essential obligation of the Church, if it truly wishes to work for the liberation of the Latin American people, is the struggle against capitalism and the capitalist regimes, and for the inauguration of a non-capitalist system. But this position poses two problems: what system to install in its place, and with what ideological and practical tools? The Church, in its social teaching, has criticized both liberal capitalism and Marxist collectivism and has proposed a "third way", understood not as a third economic system, but as a complexus of principles—personalism, solidarism, participation—which ought to inspire economic activity.

Many Christians in Latin America, however, have rejected this "third way"—which they call *"tercerismo"*—because it would only be an effort to "reform" capitalism, not to overcome it. For these, socialism alone represents the way out of capitalism. Further, to pass from capitalism to socialism, the ideological and practical instruments cannot be the social doctrine of the Church, which remains within the capitalist logic, but a Marxist analysis of society, as the ideological instrument, and the practice of class struggle and revolution as the practical instrument. This leads to the acceptance of Marxism, with grave danger for the faith and Christian practice.

This explains why John Paul II insisted with some vigor on the permanent validity of the social doctrine of the Church— opportunely reformulated in norms of action and practical directives with the collaboration of all the members of the Church, an emphasis already in Paul VI's *Octagesima Adveniens* (no. 4)— asking Christians to trust responsibly in it, to study it seriously, to be faithful to it. Thus, he added, "these qualities in a son of the Church are a guarantee of the authenticity of his duty in the delicate and demanding social doctrine, and of his effort in favor of the liberation and promotion of his brother."

The duty of the defense and promotion of the dignity of man, considered in his integral being, is part of the mission of the Church, because if the mission of the Church is evangelization, an "indispensable part" of this is the directives of justice and the work of promoting man, so that evangelization would not "be

252&

LIBERATION THEOLOGY

complete if the Church did not commit herself to justice". It is not, then, because of opportunism or the desire of novelty that this Church engages itself in defending human rights, the Pope has said, but "for an authentic evangelical duty, which, as with Christ, regards those in greater need." The Church engages in this defense of man "not by violent means, or by power plays, or political systems, but through the means of the truth of man, as the way to a better future." In other words, the Church arrives at man, at justice, "through the mediation of evangelization".

Saying that, John Paul II did not intend to deny the validity of political action, but, speaking to an episcopal assembly, stressed that, while concrete political action ought to be left to the laity, as their proper competency; to bishops and to priests belongs the mission of evangelizing justice, that is, of announcing the will of God in the field of justice and the promotion of human dignity and of the rights of man. The Pope himself gave an example of evangelizing for justice, when he recalled that, according to the teaching of the Church, "in all private property there is a social context", and when he affirmed that "the indispensable sign that an economic system is just is that it favors the development and diffusion of public instruction and culture." In fact, it is especially the problems of private property and of public instruction which are the most dramatic on a continent where, precisely because the property in land is in the hands of a few, "to the increasing riches of the few corresponds the parallel misery of the masses", and where the rate of illiteracy is so high that it renders social and economic development impossible.

Always with his thought centered on the problems of Latin America, the Pope recalled "the mechanisms which are not impregnated with an authentic humanism but with materialism", products at the international level that result in the "rich always getting richer beside the poor always getting poorer", especially in international commerce. To those who would change such mechanisms with only political and economic instruments, he said:

> There does not exist an economic rule capable of changing by itself such mechanisms. We must have recourse to an appeal in international life to the principles of ethics, to the demands of justice, to

the first of the commandments, that of love. It is necessary to give
the primacy to morality, to the spiritual, to that which is born of the
fullness of the truth of man.

Further, he reflected, "the sometimes massive increase of violations of human rights in every part of the society and of the
world" is evident. This is a phenomenon which is also verified
in Latin America, where the proliferation of authoritarian and
dictatorial regimes is common, in which the violation of human
rights is not only habitual, but also justified with the doctrine of
national security. Against such violence he has said: "Yet one
more time we must cry strongly: Respect man. He is the image
of God."

Finally, John Paul II underscored the central theme of liberation in Latin American theological reflection by recalling that
"the proper mission of Christ cannot be reduced to a pure and
simple economic, political, social or cultural dimension." There
are "signs which help to decide if there is a Christian liberation
under discussion" or rather only ideology not conformed to the
Gospel. These are fidelity to the Word of God, to the living
tradition of the Church, to the magisterium, to the sense of
communion with the bishops and with all the people of God, to
the real establishment of community, to the love of the poor and
the oppressed, because we see in them the image of Christ.

It would take too long to report the judgment of the press on
this discourse of John Paul II.[11] It will only be noted here that
the first quick judgments, which spoke of a "conservative"
discourse, one practically favorable to the maintenance of the
present situation—the judgment of Don G. Baget Bozzo, who
defined the Puebla discourse of the Pope as a "spiritual disaster",
appears especially sharp and unjust to us[12]—were followed by
other more equitable and analytical ones.

It seems to us then that an attentive study of the basic papal
discourse of Puebla—which we have endeavored to do here—
shows that with such a call to fidelity in the Gospel and to the
tradition of the Church, the Pope did not intend absolutely to

[11] See chap. 5.
[12] *La Republica* (30 January 1979).

limit or break the aspirations and tendencies of Latin American Christians for a greater justice in their continent, but rather he wished to give to them a more solid basis for it. Above all, he wished to indicate the road which Christians ought to take in order that their duties of justice and the humane promotion of the poor and oppressed of Latin America be not converted into a new form of injustice, oppression, and slavery. Now, this road is precisely that indicated in the Bible and the social teaching of the Church drawn from it by reading it in the light of the "signs of the times". Therefore, by giving the message of the Gospel in Latin America, John Paul II has rendered a service of great value to the poor and oppressed of that continent.

But he has not just given service to them, but to all the Church and to all Christians. In fact, many of the problems confronted by the Pope at Puebla are common not only to Christians of Africa and of Asia, but also to Christians of Europe and North America. The three great *truths*—of Christ, of the Church, of man—which John Paul II has recalled at Puebla, serve to remind all Christians that, in every part of the Catholic world today, they have more or less become the object of contention and doubt. Certainly, the problems which are posed about the underdevelopment of Latin America are not those posed by consumerism in Europe and North America. But everywhere in the world of today, we must ask ourselves about the sense of Christianity and about the nature of the Christian presence in history. Thus, the discourse at Puebla has a universal import and it ought to be read with such a background.

VIII

DALE VREE

POLITICAL TRANSUBSTANTIATION

A serious dialogue between Marxists and Christians has been going on in Europe and North America for almost a decade and a half. This dialogue, which has frequently led to theoretical attempts to synthesize Marxism and Christianity, has certainly been intellectually innovative and stimulating. Collaborative political action between Marxists and Christians has been an important political factor in the politics of Italy, France, Spain, Czechoslovakia, and Yugoslavia, but in terms of depth of commitment and readiness to resort to violence, such action has not yet been matched by what can be found in Latin America. There, important segments of the Catholic priesthood and hierarchy have been dramatically radicalized. It is not unusual to see bishops issue statements generally critical of the domestic and inter-American status quo and supportive of socialist and nationalist alternatives. Nor is it unusual to see priests—such as the late, "martyred" Camilo Torres—throw off their cassocks, pick up rifles, and run off with a band of guerilla warriors. But in terms of political theory, the Latin Americans have been well behind the Europeans and North Americans who, having felt less urgency to act, have enjoyed more time for scholarship and reflection.

The "Liberation Theology"

A Theology of Liberation[1] by the Peruvian theologian and activist, Gustavo Gutíerrez, is an important attempt to begin to redress the imbalance in theoretical output. Although the thought of Gutíerrez is not as original or complex as that of

Reprinted by permission from *Freedom at Issue* (May–June 1976); copyright 1976 by Freedom House, Inc.

[1] Gustavo Gutíerrez, *A Theology of Liberation* (Maryknoll, New York: Orbis Books, 1973).

European dialogue-makers such as Jürgen Moltmann, Ernst Bloch, Johannes Metz, Roger Garaudy, and others, his book is generally recognized as a unique intellectual breakthrough; indeed, as perhaps the most sophisticated voice of Marxist-Christian dialogue in Latin America to date. Contrary to most books of this genre, its significance seems to grow with each passing year. Gutiérrez has emerged as the intellectual spokesman for a new worldwide current in Christian social ethics known as "liberation theology". In the United States, liberation theology has served as the idiom for Christians anxious to promote their favorite liberation movements—particularly for blacks and for women.

More recently, liberation consciousness has been expanding to encompass the entire Third World. Just last August, the Latin American Secretariat of the U.S. Catholic Conference and the Latin American Working Group of the National Council of Churches sponsored a week-long conference on liberation theology in Detroit—the significance of which was noted and celebrated in *Time* magazine (September 1, 1975) with a full-page story. An appearance by Gustavo Gutiérrez was the main attraction of the conference. Beyond the United States, the World Council of Churches—much like the United Nations—effectively functions as a forum for Third World causes and interests. The World Council has already committed its prestige and its money to the liberation movements directed against the white governments of southern Africa. Indeed, the "pervasive philosophy" of the World Council has become a " 'solidarity with the oppressed' liberation theology which recognizes no challengers".[2] Israel is not much more popular with the Council than South Africa, and one wonders when Israel too will feel the lash of the Council. Because of the popularity of liberation theology in World Council circles, it would be well to have a closer look at Gutiérrez' *A Theology of Liberation*, the basic guide-book of liberation theology.

Although Gutiérrez borrows frequently from European thinkers, his politico-theological thought is unparalleled by Europeans

---

[2] Elliot Wright, "The Good Ship *Oikoumene*", *Worldview* (November 1975) 18.

because he is responding to the Latin American experience. Gutiérrez is not primarily reacting to other people's ideas, but rather to his own existential condition as an inhabitant of the Third World. The difference between the Third World and the developed world is not only geographical; it is also psychological. For the theologian, the situation of the developed world is as Dietrich Bonhoeffer described it: the *mündige Welt* (the world come of age) where technologically competent people no longer feel a need for God. In Latin America, on the other hand, the theologian must respond to quite another situation, a situation where people feel incompetent and helpless, and where suffering is a way of life with no end in sight. Here people *do* feel a need for God, but are at pains to understand how a loving God could have created such an unlovely world.

Inasmuch as the Church is now widely regarded as the most "progressive" institution in Latin America, and insofar as much of Latin America is in a potentially revolutionary situation, we have further reason to examine Gutiérrez' *magnum opus* with some care. It is easy enough to applaud Gutiérrez' book as a reflection of the Latin Catholic Church's turning from corruption and concubinage, and toward commitment and change. Be that as it may, "progressive" Latin American Catholic thought (or liberation theology, as it is now called) need no longer be patronized in that way. Liberation theology is ready to stand on its own feet, to stand up to normal intellectual scrutiny.

Eschatology and Marxism

A central motif in the international Marxist-Christian dialogue is eschatology, or the doctrine of the Last Things. The theological locution most often associated with eschatology is the "kingdom of God". Christians have traditionally equated the fullness of the kingdom of God with the experience of heaven after death. The kingdom has also been thought to be embryonically present in the heart of the believer as a kind of foretaste of heaven. But rarely has the kingdom been thought to have any bearing on political matters. However, those Christians who have engaged in dialogue with Marxists have tried to expand the notion of the kingdom into the hope for an earthly millennial society built—in part at least—by human political action. If this notion of the kingdom is accepted, and if the full-blown communism of which Marxist-Leninists speak can be understood as a secular version of millennialism, then it is obvious that Christians and Marxists have much in common and every reason to engage in dialogue.

Making eschatology a central motif allows for a much more interesting dialogue than if, say, ethics is made a central motif. A generation ago, such "First World" Christians as Hewlett Johnson (the "Red" Dean of Canterbury) and Harry F. Ward of Union Theological Seminary, tended to focus on the ethics of Jesus as the basis for cooperation with Marxists (in particular, with Stalinists). The problem with that approach is twofold: first, Christianity has clearly been more than an ethical system; it has been a *theo*logical system which presumes to talk of God, the mystery of the kingdom, the meaning of history, and the life of the world to come. To stress ethics is to seem to be too rationalistic and too neglectful of the mystical dimensions of the faith. It is to reduce the kingdom to an ethical metaphor. Those Christians who get themselves fixated on ethics are too easily suspected of being nothing but ethical humanists—eccentric ones, to be sure. Second, Marxist-Leninists are not really interested in ethics. They are interested in the laws of history and the economy, of which ethics is only an epiphenomenon. A concern with ethics is the hallmark of utopian, not scientific, socialism. Hence, it is very difficult to achieve a sustained intellectual interchange between Christians and Marxists when attention is limited to ethics.

Because of their eschatological focus, present-day Christian dialogue-makers are in a better situation. Yes, they do talk about ethics. But they are really interested in the *dynamics* of historical, economic, and political change—just as the Marxists are. Furthermore, they do not *seem* to be ethical humanists because they are very anxious to talk about God, salvation, providence, prophecy, the kingdom, etc.—almost all of the paraphernalia of traditional Christianity—in the same breath with which they talk of the dynamics of change. Finally, by going beyond ethics they are better able to sidestep embarrassing questions about the alleged pacifism of Jesus.

This brings us directly to Gustavo Gutiérrez and his *Theology of Liberation*. Without doubt, Gutíerrez is interested in salvation, and his interest in political liberation for Latin America (namely, "liberation" from American hegemony and domestic capitalism) is an integral part of his interest in salvation; indeed, liberation is part of a "single salvific process".[3] This is where matters become intriguing—and sticky. Since the Second Vatican Council, the Catholic Church has been willing to say that political action (or "liberation") has something to do with the kingdom of God, although it has refused to specify exactly what the relationship is, and has insisted that political goals cannot be identified or equated with the kingdom.

Were one to say that the kingdom is political liberation and that liberation is the product of human action, one would all too easily fall into the classical *Pelagian* heresy—that is, one would be saying that man is saved by good works, not grace. To say that is to deny the salvific significance of Christ's atoning sacrifice on the Cross and his Second Coming. It is to deny that God in Christ is the source of salvation. Without Christ, there is no authentic Christianity. Hence, it is impossible for a *Christian* to equate liberation with salvation.

But Gutíerrez is unhappy with the recent Catholic position that political action has some (unspecified) relation to the kingdom. Says he: "It is not enough to say that Christians should not 'shirk' their earthly responsibilities or that these have a 'certain relationship' to salvation."[4]

Although Gutíerrez wants to relate eschatology to politics by uniting liberation and salvation into a single process, he also wants to keep liberation and salvation separate—for fear of sliding into Pelagianism. Traditionally, both Catholics and Protestants have said that salvation—or the kingdom—is an act, a gift, of God. After all, God saves man, man does not save himself: "For by grace are ye saved through faith, and that not of yourselves, it is the gift of God: not of works, lest any man should boast" (Eph 2:8–9). According to official Catholic theology, the kingdom "will be the effect solely of divine intervention."[5] The

---

[3] Gutíerrez, op. cit., x.   [4] Ibid., 46.
[5] *New Catholic Encyclopedia* (1967), s.v., "Kingdom of God", by M. J. Cantley.

problem for any *theology* of liberation is to talk of salvation as a gift without inducing passivity and indifference to politics— which is frequently what happens. So Gutíerrez' problem is twofold: How can man's political liberation be seen to be a part of a salvific process which finds fulfillment in God's kingdom— without opening the door to Pelagianism? And how can one talk like a Christian out of one side of one's mouth, and like a Pelagian out of the other, without choking on the law of non-contradiction?

Let us hear what Gutíerrez has to say: He sees man "assuming *conscious responsibility* for his own destiny." The result will be "the creation of a new man and a qualitatively different society."[6] And yet Gutíerrez also says that, "The Bible presents liberation— salvation—in Christ as a *total gift*. . . ."[7]

But how can the integral "salvific process" be a product of both men's "conscious responsibility" as well as a "total gift" from Christ? Is liberation-*cum*-salvation something humans must go out and earn for themselves or not? If so, then it cannot be a "total gift". If not, then it is something humans are not fully responsible for. Gutíerrez does not seem to know whether he wants to be a Christian, a Pelagian, or both. If it is possible to grant that Gutíerrez avoids complete capitulation to Pelagianism, it is not possible to grant that he escapes logical contradiction.

But perhaps what Gutíerrez wants to say is that man must initiate his liberation while God will have to finish it by turning liberation into salvation. This is the most generous interpretation I can come up with. Says Gutíerrez: "*Without liberating historical events, there would be no growth of the Kingdom. But the process of liberation will not have conquered the very roots of oppression and the exploitation of man by man without the coming King-dom, which is above all a gift.*"[8] Gutíerrez is trying to protect man's autonomy and free creativity as well as God's sovereignty. But Gutíerrez actually succeeds both in truncating man's autonomy (because man cannot finish what he has started) and compromising God's omnipotence (because God cannot start what he alone can finish). For Gutíerrez, salvation is obviously *contingent* on man's *prior* action. Gutíerrez *wants* to affirm that the

[6] Gutíerrez, op. cit., 36–37; italics added.
[7] Ibid., x; italics added.   [8] Ibid., 177; italics added.

coming kingdom is above all a gift, but one must conclude from what he has said that the coming kingdom (which he described as the "complete encounter with the Lord" which will "mark an end to history"[9]) is first and foremost a product of human action. Enter Pelagius! Enter Thomas Müntzer and a whole host of heretical chiliasts whom Friedrich Engels correctly identified as forerunners of Marxism.

Marxists Doing God's Work?

At the root of Gutiérrez' tortuous theologizing is his attempt to blend Marxism with Christianity. By making political liberation a necessary part of the salvific process, Gutiérrez is able to bring Marxism into the drama of Christian salvation. As a result, it is obvious that Marxists are *really* doing God's work. Furthermore, by liberating man, Marxists are *quite literally* freeing God's hands so he can usher in the kingdom. Hence, Marxists are really Christians incognito.

Gutiérrez says he believes in salvation for everyone—believers and nonbelievers alike. There is no doubt in Gutiérrez' mind that God will grant salvation to Marxists, but curiously, there seems to be some doubt that all Christians will be saved. Lest one think Gutiérrez to be a modern ethical humanist, he reminds us that he *does* believe in divine judgment: "we will be definitively judged by our love for men, by our capacity to create brotherly conditions of life."[10] And there is no doubt in Gutiérrez' mind that many, perhaps most, Christians are not measuring up to that standard. So his best pastoral advice to Christians would be to join with Marxists, who are presumed to be actively creating brotherly conditions of life. This is the safest bet—Gutiérrez' version of Pascal's wager! Such counsel sounds bizarre coming from a Catholic priest, but Gutiérrez does not seem to be kidding. Liberation is a precondition for salvation, and, as Gutiérrez repeatedly makes clear, liberation is another term for revolutionary (not social democratic) socialism. And for revolutionary socialism to be efficacious it must be a "scientific" socialism, Gutiérrez tells us. Finally, he leaves no doubt in the reader's mind

[9] Ibid., 168.   [10] Ibid., 198–99.

that he considers Marxian socialism to be scientific (although not necessarily atheistic).

Not only do the Marxists—unknowingly—hold the keys to the kingdom of God, but they are undoubtedly spiritually gifted. Since Marxists are very adept at loving mankind, and since loving mankind is the "only way" to have a "true encounter with God",[11] and since a "knowledge of God" is actually a "necessary consequence" of loving mankind,[12] one is forced to conclude that Marxists are remarkably religious people. Never mind the fact that Marxists do not seem to be aware of their spiritual gifts; Father Gutíerrez is aware of them and that seems to be what counts. The good Father is empowered to turn bread and wine into Christ's body and blood. Now he presumes to turn Marxists into Christians.

But sometimes I wonder what all this has to do with helping the poor and the powerless. Priests have been notorious for sprinkling holy water on whatever political organization seemed to be the going concern at the time—or the coming concern (in the case of far-sighted priests). Perhaps Marxists should allow themselves to be amused—and tickled—by this sacerdotal sprinkle. Perhaps the water is a good omen for them, signifying that Marxism holds the winning ticket in the race for power in Latin America. (Indeed, Gutíerrez says again and again that he bases his thought on a reading of the "signs of the times" in Latin America.)

But Marxists would do well to bear in mind that the good *padre*, despite his frequent genuflections at the altar of scientific socialism, is no scientific socialist himself. He has *his own— utopian*—reasons for blessing Marxism. For him, "utopian thought" is the basis of scientific knowledge; indeed, it is the source of political action and a "driving force of history".[13] Marxists will perhaps not be surprised that behind this socialist priest there lurks a visionary dreamer. Neither perhaps will more orthodox Catholics (not to mention Protestants and Jews) be surprised that one who places Marxists at the head of God's Elect is nothing but a fanciful utopian.

---

[11] Ibid., 202.　　　　[12] Ibid., 206.　　　　[13] Ibid., 232–34.

But let us not forget the prerogatives of priestcraft. In the old pre-Vatican Council days, priests used to stand at the altar with their backs to the people mumbling Latin words through a cloud of incense faster than the speed of sound. "Mumbo-jumbo", the irreverent were wont to call it. Now the priests stand in back of the altar, face the people, and—with the help of microphones—clearly enunciate the words of the Mass in the vernacular of the people. No more mumbo-jumbo. That they save for their books on politics—where Marxists are transformed into Christians by transforming Christians into Marxists.

IX

RAFAEL BELDA

CHRISTIAN REFLECTION ON MARXIST ETHIC

Marxism, proud of its "scientific" base, labels religious ethics "pre-scientific" or "idealist". Such "transcendent" ethics center human conduct on an ideal outside or above man himself—divine commandments. This dilutes reasonableness and human responsibility. The laws of the gods, says Bertold Brecht, do not help in constructing the world of men.

Critique of Religious Ethic

True, many believers with no care for their authenticity see and live God's commands as something alien and thrust upon their freedom.

Man's moral task does have a radical religious meaning, for human action concurs with God's plan of liberation. But fulfilling moral "law" does not mean surrendering human creativity to the caprice of a despot. It rather means fidelity to the ethical exigencies which build the human person in human community. Man, a social and historical being, discovers, by trial and error, the law which channels his human growth. Thus natural moral "law" is immanent (to individual and social structures) *and* transcendent (expressing God's creative and liberating plan).

Marxism reacts against glorifying the transcendence of moral values. Such "dualism" appears in the traditional conception of sin as rebelling against God's will (moral laws), while ignoring sin's human and earthly dimension. In reality, sin offends God *because* it offends human dignity (our own and others') and aims at derailing the advance of world structures.

Reprinted by permission from *Theology Digest* (Spring 1979) 25–29. This is an abstract from an article originally published under the title "Reflexión cristiana sobre ética marxista" in *Pentecostés* 16:52 (January–March 1978) 19–29.

Moral law's obligation stems from its reasonableness, its agreement with the principles of development immanent to human being. Violating moral values dehumanizes man, prevents building the human family, impedes world growth and—so!—wages war on God's project of liberation.

The Christian's moral task is realizing the new man and the new earth, by assimilating Gospel values and life-style. Christian ethics synthesizes redemption (divine gift) and creative acceptance (free, responsible flowering of our humanness). The divine gift meshes with man's inner hopes and, without making men puppets, transcends and fulfills.

Structure and Moral Task

Marxism has accused Christian ethics of imprisoning men in their individualness, disdaining the earthly city. The moral task is reduced to rectifying abuses of personal freedom and to patching up private relationships. "In an immoral world," says A. Gisselbrecht, "true morals do not consist in keeping divine precepts, but in building a good world."

A grasp of Christian ethics that is faithful to the Gospel shows that a right pursuit of God's command must issue in commitment to changing the world. Christian love has a social-political dimension.

Nevertheless, Catholic moral teaching has often fallen prey to *moralism*: The Church has tended to individualize guilt and responsibility, neglecting the dynamic within structures (the established system) that can determine human conduct.

The question comes down to the relation between ethics and anthropology: Traditional Christian ethics has tended to reduce the person's radical reality to the individual, and to devalue the communal and earthly aspect: Marxist ethics has tended to blend the individual into his class and into a web of social relationships. These anthropologies entail two conceptions of the moral task: one *solely* private and one *solely* public and structural (fulfilling one's class mission and changing structures).

Biblical sources give a more integrated picture. Christ is the first-born of the human family and sums up the whole universe. The Resurrection of Jesus of Nazareth means that all mankind and the material world are freed, in principle, from sin and death—in their personal and social dimensions. This beginning liberation must move forward, in history, by men's free commitment. The Resurrection means that Jesus lives on in each of us and in human history as a seed requiring resurrection and liberation. Here is "the moral task".

Claude Tresmontant has shown that the prophets of Israel came to an analysis of sin (moral disorder) which unveiled its political dimension: The sins of a *polis* are a community reality because they are expressed in social structures, value systems, ideologies, traditions, group conduct, common attitudes. And the individual born into this polity, because of his milieu, education, mimetic instinct, gregariousness, his personal and class interests, is impelled to perpetuate this state of sin, this enforced disorder and oppressive system.

The Christian's commitment to justice in the world—inspired by returning to biblical sources and spurred by Marxist critique—should result not from opportunism, but rather from the effort to keep the truth in our tradition, while inserting it into a new context. L. L. Radice (a militant Marxist) puts it thus:

> The *mark* of Christianity is its faith in the absolute value of each man for what he is. . . . The specifically Christian consists . . . in loving one's . . . neighbor . . . apart from any collective perspective on the ladder of world history. . . .
>
> This principle cannot derive from Marxism—a historical doctrine of man's collective and revolutionary liberation. . . .
>
> Christian reflection on the value of the individual for what he is supposes an enrichment of Marxist thought.

Marxist Historicism

Ethics' historicity (not open to serious discussion) is a thing apart from Marxism's moral historicism: refusing anything absolute to moral values. Must we maintain that moral values are *wholly* dependent in origin and evolution on determined relations of production and society's division into classes? that no human actions are inherently good or evil? Marxism has seen that the mode of producing goods deeply affects human relations, institutional functioning, and the contents of individual conscience. Hence Marxism has been skillful in showing a connection between class membership and supposedly universal values.

But the fact that, chronologically, human survival demands that we begin by subduing nature through productive labor cannot be erected into a value judgment covering all human activity. Nor can class-mentality's conditioning effect on individual conscience authorize the statement that ethics is a class product, a justification of class interests.

Marxist tradition, in my thinking, absolutizes historical fact and defines man in light of this contingency. True, individuals tend to read moral values in accord with their class interests. But such class conditioning is not total. People of bourgeois origin have fought against bourgeois values: and laborers can share bourgeois attitudes. If one answers that this means a break with one's own (true) class, then Marxism's claim that conscience is determined by social existence becomes rhetoric.

To return to our question: Are there moral values that stand above historical eras with their particular mode of production and societal class structure?

Some Marxists assert that communist ethics will inherit and develop the positive moral values of all times. A. Sánchez-Vásquez writes:

> The ethic of every society and class is relative, but insofar as it has
> . . . living elements, such particulars are integrated into . . . the
> conquest of a truly human and universal ethic. Proletarian ethics is
> that of a class historically destined to disappear . . . to give way to a
> truly human society. Hence it paves the way for a universally
> human morality.

By reacting against the idea (not unknown to Christian tradition) of values as *fixated*, Marxism has unhappily locked itself into an unneeded dilemma: either absoluteness (read, *fixation*) of moral values or materialistic historicism.

But *historicity* and *absoluteness* need not be contradictories. Moral values are discovered through the evolutionary process of man's historical experience. But through such experience there is also revealed the absolute character of moral value, whose final interpretation is with reason grounded in a meta-historical being which, though distinct from men, is more present to men than they are to themselves.

Man is a created being, embodied spirit, lord of the material world, agent and goal of socio-economic, political and cultural life. We cannot speak of realization as persons (the moral task) unless we remain faithful to these referents that give meaning to man's historical unfolding. If some Marxists admit a continuity-in-discontinuity in man's moral realization, does this not imply a human structure that transcends modes of production and social classes and alone gives meaning to talk about progress?

Marxist Utilitarianism

Accepting a meaning of history ontically superior to the destiny of individual existence pushes Marxism (especially Leninism) into a moral utilitarianism: Means become licit by reason of their promoting this "meaning". He who desires mankind's liberation must desire the proletarian revolution and the praxis of class struggle.

At stake are two theses: 1) the priority of the species over individuals. Must the cost of mankind's liberation be met by trampling on the dignity and the rights of individuals? 2) What is the content of this liberation? This "content" will obviously affect the means used to promote it.

Granted the structural and public dimension of the Christian moral task, then the institutional Church and individual Christians (as citizens) must engage in the struggle for integral liberation, in the fight for justice and human rights, gradually suppressing all situations of injustice and structural a-solidarity.

But the Christian, faithful to the Gospel, must reject means of struggle that cannot protect or restore those values for which he struggles. The Christian opposes such means as vilifying adversaries, the physical liquidation of defenseless or innocent people—not out of scruples about "moral taboos", but for the sake of the persons themselves he hopes to set free.

Political and historical experience should teach us: 1) Truly liberating means must contain—at least in germ—the goals we seek to attain. We have no human guarantee that we can eliminate injustice if our means introduce fresh injustices. There should be a proportion between our means and the situation we hope will eventuate: we must be sure that means are politically acceptable and coherent with our Christian world vision.

2) Some means capable of overthrowing power need not be liberating–promotive of morally superior human relations. Man's liberation does not primarily consist in cashiering today's functionaries and putting in new, but rather in replacing unjust human relations with those that better fit with the ethical demands of our human condition.

Two errors should be avoided: *Defending a double standard*: The oppressor's "crime" becomes the oppressed's "political error". *Defending a pre- and a post-revolutionary ethics*: Having inaugurated a new mode of production and the abolition of classes, actions that were justified for their role in achieving victory would now alter their ethical nature.

As a result we have become entangled in such inconsequentialities as saying *No* to the death penalty and *Yes* to executing political enemies: *No* to special tribunals (lack of due process) and *Yes* to revolutionary tribunals which summarily impose guilt and execution.

We must defend the moral values inherent in the dignity of each and every person and respect them in each and every situation. Immediate results are not a moral norm; and they lose their meaning if they exclude respect for rights and freedoms, for these have a value superior to a class struggle conducted by an interested party that unilaterally defines truth and moral good.

X

ROGER HECKEL, S.J.

ON THE RELEVANCE OF THE CHURCH'S SOCIAL DOCTRINE AND PRACTICE

As it has been rightly observed, those who intend to disregard history, those who do not appropriate their own history—in the false hope that in this way they are more free to attend to immediate things and to hasten their entry into the future—are in fact doomed to lag behind in indefinite repetitions of history. With no roots in a tradition, they are tossed about and swept along by the fashions of the moment towards a future of illusions and fantasies, on the fringe of real life.

Besides, serious concentration on immediate tasks, even as it makes us increasingly aware of the complexity and breadth of those tasks, prompts us by its very nature to explore our living tradition more deeply. To make my meaning clear, I ask you to consider the following three points:

1. In the midst of the most relevant and ambitious quests— and the most promising for a New International Order—our contemporaries increasingly tend to stress that the *future* of mankind must spring from the *living traditions* of its diverse peoples: this is expressed by the very topical word *self-reliance*.

2. After a period of groping and hesitation, men are rediscovering —especially in those countries where the freedoms are more radically denied to individuals and peoples—the importance of *the Church's social teaching and practice*, which aim to serve humanity.

3. Finally, this more intimate presence of the Church in the world calls for a keener awareness of the indomitable originality of its *evangelizing mission*.

Reprinted by permission from *Lumen Vitae* 33, English ed., no. 1 (1978) 57–65.

I

I find it very significant that at a time when humanity is becoming more keenly aware of its *solidarity* on board the spaceship-earth, and, correlatively, of the need to give that solidarity organic expression on a worldwide scale, the emphasis is being more and more firmly laid on *self-reliance*.

In its intuition, if not in all the modalities proposed for its implementation, the concept of self-reliance ties up with what John XXIII in *Mater et Magistra*, then Paul VI in *Populorum Progressio*, have sought to convey to us by emphasizing that peoples must be the agents and artisans of their own development. Here time prevents me from making a detailed analysis of this concept, but an image might adequately suggest what self-reliance is all about: the image of a living organism which carries within it its own vital principle; an internal principle of *dynamism*; an internal principle of *regulation*, a law of growth which makes possible the harmonious integration of external contributions; an internal principle of *openness* to others. *Mutatis mutandis*, a people may be likened to such a living organism:

—it can, of course, and indeed must be helped by external dynamic forces, but all such assistance must aim, not to stifle the people's internal dynamism, but to liberate it—to liberate the living tradition which it has created and from which it draws its nourishment;

—the necessary economic, cultural and political changes must enable each people to incorporate the external contributions in accordance with its own law of growth; failing this, growth becomes cancerous; it destroys life and, in any case, creates an imbalance which makes the life of a people vulnerable and over-dependent on external decision-making centers;

—openness to others, in extensive and effective solidarity, can be aided by external constraints; but it, too, finds its real strength and health in the liberation of the internal impulse that prompts a people to cooperate freely in the common tasks.

Openness to the *universal*, the building of a *world* order, the creativity from which *new* things are born, depend on each people's now acknowledged possibility of liberating its own vital principle, of tying up with its deep *tradition*, so that in this same impulse it may be freely involved in the common adventure and thus shed its outmoded and atrophied elements. This vital principle has to be freed of both the pressures unjustly imposed from without and the obstacles that hinder it internally.

There is a vocabulary now current in Christian circles which implies that freedom can be assured by rejecting all constraint as "domination". In reality, human freedom among individuals and peoples must be achieved by acknowledging, by coming to terms with and humanizing, life's inevitable constraints: to deny them is both unrealistic and useless. The interdependent growth of freedoms cannot do without organized solidarity, which implies institutional constraints and powers.

II

The more tasks become difficult and novel, the more individuals and peoples are thrown back on the sources of their personality and living tradition to cope with those tasks effectively. Within each nation, this is also true of Christians: it is not by rejecting their tradition, by which they have forged their identity, but rather by appropriating their tradition, that Christians will more distinctively become men among their fellow men.

As far as the social thinking and practice of the Church is concerned, the Vatican Council was undoubtedly followed by a moment of hesitation and even of rejection. This obliges us to seek the causes of such a reaction. To some extent, they are connected with a misreading of the Church's social teaching and practice. But there are clear signs that the situation is now changing.

1. Wherever dictatorships or brutal authoritarian regimes reign —and they are common today, whatever ideology they may adduce to justify their action—one is struck by the fact that the episcopates make remarkably forceful and relevant pronouncements by quoting the social encyclicals, starting with the earliest,

Rerum Novarum. We thus find that even in the absence of an efficacious policy—for in the cases I have in mind, the Church has no chance of developing on its own an "alternative" policy—the courageous reminder of *the simple and profound intuitions* of the magisterium's teaching already has a real power to protect what could become a more Christian policy, to rescue men from discouragement, and patiently to prepare the conditions whereby peoples can once again be the masters of their own destiny. The Church's teaching cannot be reduced to these general principles, but by reminding men of them in a context where they may be ignored and sometimes distorted, it renders an immediate and most valuable service.

2. In these situations where religious freedom, together with the other freedoms with which it is intimately connected, is disregarded or, at any rate, checked and hindered, men also rediscover the considerable strength that springs from the possibility of relying on the authorized magisterium of the universal Church, and particularly of the pope. In this, the local church finds a hope that rescues it from its isolation, and quite frequently the political powers are more impressed than they care to admit. Thus men rediscover *the importance of the magisterium* in the Church's effort to reflect and to act.

3. To master the new and complex problems which confront mankind, we need innovating solutions which require much courage on everyone's part. Even today, Christians all too often cling to a social doctrine of the Church which they interpret merely as an endorsement of the status quo. Others, while criticizing that doctrine as being influenced by the dominant conservative forces, do not hesitate to take some of its elements out of context in order to justify their own options. Clearly, there is now a growing need for clarification by which men can rediscover not an impossible and unproductive uniformity, but *the common demands of the Gospel* and of the Christian faith, as well as an authoritative expression of those demands.

4. John XXIII and the Council had awakened in the Church a powerful feeling of liberation because they did not condemn but directed all their efforts toward a positive proposition of the faith and its social requirements. This is not to say that they entertained

the illusion that the Church could avoid being a sign of contradiction or firmly saying "No" when necessary; but they had to
react against the all too frequent obsession with the *denunciation of
evil* and to be mainly concerned with *sustaining the positive efforts* of
men grappling with difficult situations, with helping those men
to advance starting from realities in which they were personally
involved (and not from some abstract zero point), and which
could thus be the beginning of a realistic path toward social
progress. But very soon—and this time not so much among
the hierarchy as among the laity—the one-sided tendency to
denounce was reborn. Here too a bit of historical sense will help
us to locate the necessary denunciations in the more difficult
positive effort to educate, to propose and to encourage, which
characterizes God's love, and the Church's love, for mankind.
Denunciation is not always and automatically "prophetic" or
inspired by the Spirit of God; moreover, prophecy also, and
mainly, entails the proclamation of hope: Isaiah's book of consolation is also of the prophetic genre.

5. One of the most enduring sources of aggression against the
Church's social teaching lies in the presentation of this teaching as
a *"prefabricated" social model*, too facilely deduced from the Gospel
or from certain conceptions of the natural law. In reality, this
teaching (without confining itself to the proclamation of a few
general principles, however useful this may be) enables us to
bring out and strengthen the basic elements of an anthropology.
It is up to Christians to link up those convictions with the realities
of their daily life and, through trial and error, to seek in them,
together with all their fellow men, what the conduct and structures of a genuine human progress ought to be: faith and the
social teaching which the Church develops in the light of faith
do not dispense Christians from running the risks of human
existence.

6. It is not the fact of being too familiar with the magisterium's
social teaching which deprives the Christian of his freedom and
creative sense, but rather the fact of knowing it superficially,
without assimilating it. In such circumstances, Christians are
liable to repeat a few quotations out of context and foolishly to
apply them to a wholly inapplicable situation. Here as in other
spheres (art, professional life, etc.), it is *the knowledge he has*

assimilated and integrated into his culture which makes man free to cope serenely with often unforeseeable situations.

III

In these resolute efforts toward development, liberation, human advancement, or the New International Order (words rapidly change from year to year and from one country to the next), *the unshakeable originality of the Church's mission* is put to the test: it might emerge from the latter strengthened and purified, or, on the contrary, watered down and insipid. Past and recent history shows that the Church must ceaselessly steer a course between two opposite dangers: 1) that of a *dissociation* between the advance of God's Kingdom and involvement in the tasks of the city; and 2) that of *confusing* levels, so that in practice the building of the city *absorbs and reduces* the Kingdom.

1. The Church has vigorously reacted against the temptation to *dissociate*, which philosophical, then political and economic, liberalism fosters. Without disregarding the specific consistency of the secular domains (economics, politics, culture, etc.), it has constantly reminded us that all those realities are the responsibility of man and, by that very fact, dependent on the basic moral drives which direct man in all his undertakings, thus giving them their human and humanizing value. This dissociation is now tempting man far beyond the frontiers of liberalism.

Clearly, it contradicts the Gospel. When Jesus, in the few years of his public ministry, devoted valuable days to healing the sick, his deeds were *an integral part of the Gospel* and manifested the coming of the Kingdom. They were not just "means" of preparing the way for evangelization; they were acts inseparable from the Gospel. This equally applies to the miracle of the loaves, in which the Church has always seen an invitation, through fidelity to Christ, to be as concerned as one possibly can with all mankind's needs.

2. The temptation most frequently encountered today (although the preceding one constantly finds new sustenance) is probably the temptation to *confuse* different levels of existence. Unity must, of course, be achieved, but not in the simplistic and headlong

way that some often have in mind when, for example, they thoughtlessly adduce an isolated pronouncement of the 1971 Synod. The way in which man's necessary effort to create more justice becomes incorporated into the growth of the Kingdom (as it undoubtedly does) is more complex. Today we understand better that the pure and simple "transferring of technologies", however beneficial these may be in themselves, does not necessarily signify progress when the techniques in question are not assimilated by the culture at the receiving end. The unity between all man's socio-cultural efforts and the progress of God's Kingdom in persons and nations is achieved by a far more demanding process. In other words, the social fruitfulness of the Gospel is indeed an integral part of the Good News, but according to a relationship which implies far more than acquiring and accumulating: it is a *sign* of the Kingdom, certainly, and inseparable from the Kingdom, obviously; but it is not a wholly expressive and transparent sign of the transcendental treasures of the Kingdom. *Nor is there in the first place a human unity* which can be achieved simply by the efforts of men *and which already represents the full substance of the Kingdom*; for the Kingdom and its powers are precisely what enable man and humanity to discover their real unity; they are the preconditions of that discovery. In short, there is no *common measure* between the advance of human justice and the advance of the Kingdom.

In the Old Testament, the sacred history of God coming to reconquer mankind's friendship is clearly woven into the concrete social and political history of the Jewish people. But this does not mean that there is a parallelism between the people's social advance and the progress of the Kingdom: the spiritual summits of Israel's history do not coincide with the peaks of its temporal achievements; rather they are to be found in the desert and the exile.

Another example. The miracle of the loaves aroused in the beneficiaries the messianic expectation of a temporal liberation ("they wished to make him king"), which, though legitimate in itself and having profoundly religious overtones, prevented the crowd from grasping the deepest dimension of Gospel liberation. In order to awaken in them a more profound thirst and hunger, Jesus had to "break the spell" by teaching them that they must break away from their purely material desires (see Jn 6) and, as we know, this teaching profoundly disappointed them ("many of his disciples drew back and no longer went about with him"). All too often we dream of a kind of linear progress which would lead effortlessly from the advance of social justice straight to the Kingdom. Once again, we must seek unity, by all means, but it cannot be achieved in the simplistic and headlong fashion that we spontaneously have in mind.

Catholic organizations, through the diversity of their statutes and objectives, share in the one evangelizing mission of the Church. *Evangelii Nuntiandi* has vigorously underlined the central element of this mission: to know, to love and to worship Jesus Christ; to get others to know him. At this moment and not *after* humanity has fully achieved its economic, social and political liberation—besides, the work of liberation is never completed. At this very moment men, and especially the poorest of them, have the right to know God's love, which he offers them. Blessed are you, the poor, because in the very heart of your poverty God's love already comes to you and liberates you. Witness all those generations of Christians who have found the liberating faith in the very heart of their insignificance and wretched social status ("not many of you were of noble birth," said St. Paul to the Corinthians). Witness all those who, in our time, exhibit an exceptional Christian vitality in persecution and in situations where they are denied all human rights.

But from this source directly springs the enlightenment and energy which, like leaven, must penetrate the whole of life and oblige Christians and the Churches to make use of all their resources so that liberation may reach all the spheres of existence. To return constantly to the center, Jesus Christ, is not a detour or an escape from reality: he is the fruitful path that nourishes hope, even when all hope has been abandoned, and which leads to the demanding service of men, our brothers, wherever their destiny is involved.

XI

MICHAEL NOVAK

LIBERATION THEOLOGY AND THE POPE

On his highly publicized voyage to Mexico late in January 1979, Karol Wojtyla, only recently become Pope John Paul II, faced two systems of authoritarianism. He faced Latin American feudal regimes of cruelty well known to the bishops he was about to address, some of whom had experienced prison themselves. And he faced a rising enthusiasm, particularly on the part of foreign-trained Latin American clergymen, for "Marxist liberation".

The Pope addressed the Conference of Latin American Bishops (CELAM) at Puebla on January 28. At first his eight thousand word sermon drew words of disappointment and sarcasm from many of the "liberation theologians" he was taken to be attacking. Then began a process by which the Pope's straight sentences were gradually softened and transmuted until, we were told by the New York *Times* (February 18), the theologians in question celebrated the end of the conference by drinking beer, singing "folk songs from all over the continent", so that "well past midnight their songs echoed through the streets . . . sounding suspiciously like a victory celebration." What had actually happened? Had the Pope attacked "liberation theology" or had he given it official sanction?

The meeting at Puebla was the third major meeting of CELAM in twenty-five years. At the first one in Rio de Janeiro, the bishops of Latin America had established a continent-wide organization. Over the years, they formulated some fairly clear views about their own special needs and the general need for a reorganization of the international Church. Thus, at the Second Vatican Council (1961-65), their regional unity was already conspicuous, and their interventions helped the "progressive" forces at the Council do much more than expected. Then in 1968—the

Reprinted by permission from *Commentary* (June 1979); all rights reserved.

year of vast student unrest in the United States, Mexico, France, and elsewhere—the bishops met for the second time, at Medellín, Columbia, and produced a document that addressed the public-policy needs of the continent. Tinged with Marxist rhetoric, that document gave rise, two years later, to the first writings self-described as "liberation theology", that is, formal attempts to translate Christianity into Marxist categories. Works in this genre have multiplied since.

Pope John Paul II went straight to the heart of all this in the opening paragraphs of his address at Puebla. He said immediately that his "point of departure" was "the conclusions of Medellín" as well as the sympathetic support of those conclusions by Pope Paul VI in *Evangelii Nuntiandi*. But he did not hesitate to qualify his praise of "all the positive elements" that the Medellín conclusions contained, with the warning that he was not about to ignore the "incorrect interpretations at times made and which call for calm discernment, opportune criticism, and clear choices of position."

The misconception, the confusion which the Pope wished to sweep away was that Christianity is reducible to Marxist categories. He opposed those "rereadings" of the Gospel that "cause confusion by diverging from the central criteria of the faith of the Church." He opposed those for whom "the Kingdom of God is emptied of its full content and is understood in a rather secularist sense," as if it were to be reached "by mere changing of structures and social and political involvement, and as being present wherever there is a certain type of involvement and activity for justice." And he particularly opposed those who "claim to show Jesus as politically committed, as one who fought against Roman oppression and the authorities, and also as one involved in the class struggle. This idea of Christ as a political figure, a revolutionary, as the subversive man from Nazareth, does not tally with the Church's catechesis."

The Pope observed that "our age is the one in which man has been most written and spoken of," yet it is also "the age of man's abasement to previously unsuspected levels, the age of human values trampled on as never before." Like Solzhenitsyn in his commencement address at Harvard last year, Pope John Paul II attributed this to "the inexorable paradox of atheistic humanism". By contrast, "the primordial affirmation of [Catholic] anthropology is that man is God's image and cannot be reduced to a mere portion of nature or a nameless element in the human city." He rejected a "strictly economic, biological, or psychological view of man", insisting instead that "the complete truth about the human being constitutes the foundation of the Church's social teaching and the basis of true liberation. In the light of this truth, man is not a being subjected to economic or political processes; these processes are instead directed to man and subjected to him." It is necessary, in short, to reject a materialist interpretation of history and to defend the primacy of the spiritual.

At this point, Pope John Paul II showed himself in consonance with the traditional political philosophies of Western civilization. Tocqueville, for example, had made a similar observation; "There is no religion which does not place the object of man's desire above and beyond the treasures of the earth, and which does not naturally raise his soul to regions far above those of the senses. Nor is there any which does not impose on man some sort of duties to his mind, and thus draws him at times from the contemplation of himself." Correspondingly, the Pope discerned in "human dignity a Gospel value that cannot be despised without greatly offending the Creator," and then launched one of his two explicit condemnations of Latin American practices:

> This dignity is infringed on the individual level when due regard is not had for values such as freedom, the right to essential goods, to life ... it is infringed on the social and political level when man cannot exercise his right of participation, or when he is subjected to unjust and unlawful coercion, or submitted to physical or mental torture, etc. I am not unaware of how many questions are being posed in this sphere today in Latin America.

The Pope then turned to problems of action. The mission of the Church, he said, "although it is religious and not social or political, cannot fail to consider man in the entirety of his being." This mission "has as an essential part action for justice and the tasks of the advancement of man." But the Church "does not need to have recourse to ideological systems in order to love, defend, and collaborate in the liberation of man ... acting in

favor of brotherhood, justice, and peace, and against all foes
of domination, slavery, discrimination, violence, attacks against
religious liberty, and aggression against man, and whatever
attacks life." The Church has a commitment, like Christ's,
"to the most needy. In fidelity to this commitment, the Church
wishes to stay free with regard to the competing systems, in order
to opt only for man."

The Pope then went on to define liberation in a Christian way,
first positively, and then with this negative: "Liberation . . . in
the framework of the Church's proper mission is not reduced to
the simple and narrow economic, political, social, or cultural
dimension, and is not sacrificed to the demands of any strategy,
practice, or short-term solution." The important thing is "to
safeguard the originality of Christian liberation", and "to avoid
any form of curtailment or ambiguity" which would cause the
Church to "lose her fundamental meaning" and leave her open to
"manipulation by ideological systems and political parties."

What is the liberation theology to which the Pope so clearly
addressed himself? The headquarters for liberation theology in
the United States, and perhaps in the entire world, are located
near the Hudson River at Maryknoll, New York, international
center of America's most active missionary order, the Maryknoll
Fathers and Sisters. In a recent bibliography of Third World
theologies, thirty-two of eighty-two titles were published by
Maryknoll's Orbis Press. Founded in 1970, Orbis announced
that it

 draws its imperatives from and orders its priorities on the fact
 that the majority of Christians live in the affluent countries of the
 North Atlantic community, which controls almost 80 per cent of
 the world's resources but accounts for only 20 per cent of the
 world's population. . . . Christians bear a heavy responsibility for
 a world that can annually "afford" to spend $150 billion on arms,
 but can scarcely scrape together $10 billion for economic and social
 development.

At the heart of the matter, according to the initial Orbis release,
was the need for a change in intellectual focus:

Total development will demand the restructuring of oppressive political and social orders wherever they exist, in Calcutta or Chicago, New York or Recife. For this reason, the word *development* should be replaced by *liberation*.

It is quite remarkable that the list of cities requiring liberation did not include Cracow or Leningrad, Havana or Peking, Hanoi or Prague. The complete Orbis catalog of 141 titles, as of the end of 1978, maintains this distinction intact.[1] Thirty-nine titles are concentrated on Latin America, a few on Africa and other places, none on communist lands, even though such lands were once the target of intensive missionary effort.

The focus on Latin America is not accidental. Liberation theology is mainly, although not entirely, a product of the Spanish-speaking world. Father Sergio Torres of Chile, lecturer at Maryknoll, describes his world view and that of his fellow Latin American theologians in this way:

> What we understand is that we are at the end of a stage in the history of the world. Europe and Western society is no longer making the history of the world as it has been since the Roman empire. We understand that history is now being made by the peoples of the Third World. The oil crisis is getting that through here in the United States. . . . We in Latin America are the only continent that is both Christian and underdeveloped, so we are in a special place. We will start a new understanding of the faith because we belong to the churches, Catholic and Protestant, and are living in a situation which makes them functional to the system. . . . The process of colonization, liberation, and organization is best understood in Marxist terms.

Father Miguel D'Escoto, a Nicaraguan, the director of communications at Maryknoll, adds:

> As Latin Americans, we know capitalism in a way young people here don't know it. We had no New Deal, no Roosevelt to come

---

[1] Incidentally, in a recent collection of essays about liberation theology and oppressed groups, not a word is said about Catholics from Eastern Europe, or Lebanon or Ireland or Armenia. See *Mission Trends* no. 4, edited by Thomas S. Stransky and Gerald H. Andersen (Paulist Press, 1979).

along and soften it up. Capitalism is intrinsically wrong at its base. The basic concept is that man is selfish, and being realistic, we should accept this and cater to it rather than change it.

The chief systematizer of liberation theology, Father Juan Luis Segundo, whose five-volume treatise, *Theology for Artisans of a New Humanity*, has sold sixty-four thousand copies, recently told a group of American Jesuits:

> There is no perfect solution. The only way is for us to choose between two oppressions. And the history of Marxism, even oppressive, offers right now more hope than the history of existing capitalism. . . . Marx did not create the class struggle, international capitalism did.

The most widely read of all the liberation theologians is Father Gustavo Gutiérrez of Peru whose *A Theology of Liberation* (Orbis) has sold forty-five thousand copies. He writes:

> It is undeniable that the class struggle plants problems for the universality of Christian love and church unity. But every consideration on this matter ought to begin with two elemental attestations: class struggle is a fact and neutrality in this matter is impossible.

But it is not merely the theologians and the priests of Latin America who have looked upon Marxism with favor. Distinguished bishops, like the Bishop of Cuernavaca, Arceo Mendez, and the Archbishop of Recife, Dom Helder Camara, have been unambiguous in their preference for Marxism. Archbishop Camara, for example, addressed the University of Chicago's celebration of the seventh centenary of St. Thomas Aquinas in these terms:

> When a man, whether philosopher or not, attracts irresistibly millions of human beings, especially young people; when a man becomes the inspiration for life and for death of a great part of humanity, and makes the powerful of the earth tremble with hate and fear, this man deserves to be studied. . . . As the University of Chicago chose to take upon herself the responsibility of celebrating St. Thomas Aquinas's Seventh Centenary, we have the right to

suggest that the best way to honor the centenary . . . should be for the University of Chicago to try, today, to do with Karl Marx what St. Thomas, in his day, did with Aristotle.

The social and intellectual background of the liberation theologians is germane to their views. When I was studying theology in Rome at the Gregorian University in 1956–1958, I became familiar with some of the Latin American and Spanish seminarians, and several clear impressions about their political-theological culture fixed themselves in my mind. First, it was obvious that they chafed under the image of Latin cultures which prevailed in the English-speaking world. They were, they felt, the victims of an Anglo-Saxon ethnocentric bias, a Protestant bias to boot, and a bias informed by the sort of individualism, pragmatism, and materialism they found especially abhorrent. Some seemed, in effect, to be still carrying in mind the long-ago defeat of the Spanish Armada in much the same way some Southerners recall the humiliation of defeat in the Civil War.

Many of these bright young men studied not only in Rome but in Belgium, and France, and Germany as well. There they shared in what was then known as *nouvelle theologie*—that contemporary reaction against Thomism, strong on Scriptural studies and "salvation history", intensely preoccupied with the renewal of the Church from biblical and patristic sources (and hostile to the theory of Christian democracy developed by Thomists like Jacques Maritain). On their return to Latin America, many of them became involved in the movements organizing peasants in credit unions and agrarian cooperatives. Much of their earlier training seemed far too theological, and they reacted with a veritably Oedipal vehemence against their European teachers.

Yet in their work among the peasants, many found themselves already upstaged by Marxist organizers; as for the sophisticated French and German theology they brought to the peasants, it served little useful purpose. So the younger clergy began to attend more intently to the indigenous piety of the people. They discovered the power of popular religion. In its quiet endurance and strength, they found new theological resources—resources, moreover, which served to differentiate them from the despised Yankee experts and technicians who imported into Latin America the strange and threatening concepts of "development", capitalist-style. In expressing their resentment of the Northern experts, such activists have had no better spokesman than the brilliant but erratic Ivan Illich of Cuernavaca, whose anti-institutional reflections have become so popular in radical circles in North America.

When the Latin American liberation theologians speak of "class struggle", they are thinking primarily of the struggle within feudalism of landholders and peasants, hardly at all of the classic Marxist picture of an industrial proletariat. (What Latin Americans persist in calling "capitalism" is, in Latin America, largely a form of syndicalism or corporatism, which descends from the rights given by the Spanish or Portuguese crown to certain large landholders or adventurers and constitutes virtual monopoly or state mercantilism.) Both the Industrial Revolution and the social revolution that would have broken the power of the traditional landholders, as the Glorious Revolution did in Great Britain, have hardly been known among them. In most of Latin America, the middle class is quite small, and "bourgeois values", of the sort well-established in the North Atlantic world, scarcely exist.

The full effect of the Protestant spirit of dissent and individual conscience has thus not been felt in Latin cultures. By the same token, the compensating social forces of pragmatic compromise, voluntary association, and cooperative fellow-feeling that characterize Anglo-American individualism are equally missing in Latin American politics. Latin forms of idealism and romanticism make for acute political fractionalization. There is in Latin America little scope for the entrepreneur, for invention, for enterprise. There are few Horatio Algers. The virtues most celebrated—honor, nobility, dignity—are the opposite of bourgeois.

The system confronted by Latin American Catholics is one of entrenched inequality, in which powerful landholders (often of early Spanish stock) have power and privileges far removed from those of peasants and workers (often of Indian stock). The Latin American elites lack those traditions of service, stewardship, and public-spiritedness that within the United States have softened the impact of economic elites upon political life. The lower

classes in Latin America have had little opportunity to develop
the political consciousness which has characterized the Anglo-
Saxon yeoman for several centuries, and have scarcely shared in
the traditions of "the rights of Englishmen" which have affected
Anglo-Saxon consciousness.

The picture is further clouded by the powerful traditions of a
strong, authoritarian military. In many Latin American countries, a military career has offered ambitious youngsters more
opportunities for higher education and advancement than any
other profession. Not infrequently, the military provides leaders
of idealistic tendencies both on the socialist and on the democratic
side. In recent years, however, military regimes have grown
more "modern" in precisely the least humane ways: in the
techniques of cruel repression.

All this, moreover, takes place in an environment in which
European ideologies—both the fascism of the World War II era,
and the Marxism of Stalin's time—exist not merely as abstract
theories, but as embodied political forces. In such an environment, the theological idealist is often forced to take sides, to
throw in his lot with one or another active organization. In many
places, there are few organized alternatives of the middle, liberal,
democratic way.

Thus it was that in 1968, the second Conference of Latin
American Bishops at Medellín legitimized not only the normal
preaching of the Church about social conscience ("the formation
of Christian conscience") and not only the classical, peaceful
tactics of social reform (labor unions, credit unions, cooperatives,
and the like), but also the bald use of Marxist categories. It
did so in a context in which instances of armed insurrection
by a few "guerrilla priests"—not simply as chaplains but as
active combatants—were occurring, and in which the public-
policy elites of the continent, especially the university intelligentsia, were already deeply immersed in Marxist thought.

But in what sense are the liberation theologians Marxist? None
of them shows evidence that he has actually studied Marx, the
social systems derived from Marxist thought, or the literature
assessing socialist experiments. They do not, apparently, believe

in the total abolition of private property (the principle Marx offered as a pithy summary of his theory). They claim not to be materialists. They are not atheists. They say that they are not totalitarians, as Castro is. They surely do not hold—since few Marxists today do—that economic gains for the poor are empirically to be achieved through the nationalization of major industries. It is doubtful whether they believe in the humane quality of the authoritarian, bureaucratic state which is the natural outgrowth of socialism. It is not clear that they are ready to impose equality, to command choices of what society and individuals "need", to insist upon planning by technical experts, or to repress private initiatives.

Nevertheless, there do seem to be two senses in which they are Marxists. Repeatedly, liberation theologians insist that they are Marxists "because the people are". By this they do not mean that "the people" have ever read Marx or know much about him but a few slogans. But the slogans are the point. If it is difficult to take liberation theologians seriously as theoreticians of Marxism, one can grant that they are "populist Marxists", using Marxist slogans to ventilate some of the frustrations and aggressions of people whose aspirations have long been colored by external propaganda.

There is a second sense in which they are Marxists. Marxism in Latin America is not just a theory. It is a well-financed, well-organized political institution, with parties, officials, printing presses, secret agents, operatives, intellectual sympathizers, international connections, and designated politicians. To be a Marxist, as the liberation theologians say, is not merely to hold a theory but to be committed to a praxis. Yet the innocence with which the liberation theologians are committed to the Marxist praxis speaks volumes.

Marxist praxis is something of which the world has had some experience—but one would not know it from the writings of the liberation theologians. The literature of liberation theology, which is rich in general allegations about "capitalist" practice, is silent when it comes to the empirical evidence of how Marxist regimes operate. Since almost three-quarters of the world's nations are, officially, Marxist in design, and since most have had upward of thirty years to prove themselves, it should not have been beyond the capacity of theologians to work out an assessment, even a theological assessment, of their actual daily praxis, and judge these in the light of the Gospels. But this the liberation theologians have conspicuously not done.

In recounting the experience of the "poor and the oppressed" of the Third World, strange gaps appear in the empirical reasoning of liberation theologians. No notice is taken of those Third World nations whose annual rate of economic growth borders on ten per cent—nations like Taiwan, Hong Kong, South Korea, Singapore, whose secrets in overcoming poverty are open to inspection. No empirical survey of the comparative inequalities between elites and the poor is made as between socialist and capitalist regimes. Little attention is paid to measurements of institutional respect for human dignity and liberties, as, for example, between South Korea and North Korea.

There are other strange gaps in empirical knowledge. Bishop Helder Camara, in his youth a fascist as in his maturity a Marxist, is constant in his criticism of liberal democracies. He is especially fond of the suggestion that a small fraction of mankind uses a large fraction of the earth's resources, and that poverty results for millions. Is this in fact true? A special kind of human culture is required for the production of wealth. Not every organization of society or culture is suited to such production. Indeed, only a small fraction of the earth's population *produces* the larger part of the world's wealth. Besides, many of the earth's resources were unknown even a century ago, or no use for them—hence no value—had yet been found. In fact, Latin America is immensely rich in resources, now that other cultures have discovered their secrets and learned their uses.

It is not empirically true, either, that "the poor are getting poorer". In longevity, medical care, and nutrition, the modern production of wealth has raised the levels of the entire population of the world by unprecedented annual increments over the last fifty years. Average personal incomes have also risen annually, in Latin America even more than in Asia or Africa. If the present organization of the production of wealth is "sinful", what shall we say of rival Marxist systems, which are not raising the levels of the poor by so much?

Catholic theologians, especially those who claim to speak for "liberation", have a duty to study how liberation has, in fact, been attained in human history, and by what empirical and practical means its scope can be extended. If such a study were undertaken dispassionately and in good faith, I believe it would show that the greatest chances for improving the concrete daily life of human beings everywhere lie with the forces not of Marxist "liberation" but with the forces of democratic capitalism. Others may disagree; but that Catholic social theory has so far failed even to raise the necessary intellectual questions is a sign of its bankruptcy in this area, and of the extent to which too much of it has, in fact, already fallen hostage to Marxist categories of thought.

In the writings of liberation theologians, the contradictions of Marxist theory and practice go unnoted. And this tells us something about the liberation theologians: they are Marxists not by reason or by experience, but by faith. As Leszek Kolakowski, who (like Pope John Paul II) has lived through the Marxist phenomenon in Poland, has observed:

> Almost all the prophecies of Marx and his followers have already proved to be false, but this does not disturb the spiritual certainty of the faithful, any more than it did in the case of chiliastic sects: for it is a certainty not based on any empirical premises or supposed "historical laws", but simply on the psychological need for certainty. In this sense Marxism performs the function of a religion, and its efficacy is of a religious character.

In the real world, Marxism has been immobilized for decades as the ideological superstructure of totalitarian states and of parties aspiring to that status. As an explanatory system, Marxism "explains" little. There is nothing in the Latin American system, to which the liberation theologians point, for which Marxism affords the only or the best explanation. It offers no "method" either of inquiry or of action by which modern life is to be better understood, its future predicted, or its utopian hopes realized. Contemporary Marxist literature, as Kolakowski shows, is dogmatic, sterile, helpless, out of touch both with modern economics and with cultural life. But what Marxism does do very well today is to inspire with fantasies of utopian fulfillment, and to license the identification of some malevolent enemy as the only roadblock to that fulfillment. In a quite literal sense, the works of liberation theologians are innocent both of empirical verification and of sophistication about Marxist theory. Their originality lies chiefly in their openness to fantasy.

It is thus hardly surprising that Pope John Paul II's clear-eyed account of Marxism in Puebla proved to have a stronger bite than many Catholics could accept. He attempted to staunch the unthinking fantasies of theologians bent on the creation of totalitarian processes whose consequences they do not allow themselves to foresee and whose dynamics they cannot control. As against this, the Pope maintained the independence and integrity of the Church. He based himself on sound political philosophy. He spoke for the authentic interests of the poor and the oppressed, against those who would transmute their sufferings into envy, hatred, and coercion. He refused to adopt the role of Dostoyevsky's Grand Inquisitor, offering bread in exchange for liberty. For this, even those who are secular have reason to be grateful.

XII

MICHAEL E. SMITH

IS FIGHTING SOCIAL INJUSTICE THE MAIN BUSINESS OF THE CHURCH?

Responding to criticism within the Episcopal Church concerning the ordination of women and the revised Book of Common Prayer, the Episcopal Bishop of California declared: "It is tragic that our church must expend massive amounts of psychic energy bickering over forms of worship and sexuality in the priesthood, while the world is burning down. The problems of martyrdom in Uganda and elsewhere, of poverty and world hunger, racism, sexism, repressive governments, violations of human rights, and the raping of the world's environmental system—all these challenges for human relationship with the transcendent God and Jesus of Nazareth are the issues with which the church should be grappling."[1]

As most readers of the *New Oxford Review* know all too well, the debate over the ordination of women involved nothing less than the question, what is God's will for the administering of his sacraments?—while revision of the Book of Common Prayer unavoidably raised the question, what are the liturgical essentials of the Christian faith? Thus the Bishop's statement conveyed to his audience that pursuing God's will and truth in the realm of worship is of relatively little importance; the main duty of the Church is to fight social injustice.

This point of view has been expressed increasingly during the past fifteen years. It is now apt to be heard whenever certain matters are under discussion within the Christian Church: Should the Church revise its traditional doctrines and practices? How should the income and property of the Church be used?

Reprinted by permission from the *New Oxford Review*, Oakland, California (July–August 1979) 4–9; copyright 1979. The author has made minor changes in the article as it originally appeared.

[1] *The Living Church* (May 8, 1977) 7.

Should the Church espouse specified political causes? And twice recently, who should lead the Church? Nor is the viewpoint confined to peripheral adherents of the Church, as the Bishop's example demonstrates; indeed, only six years ago he was a major candidate for Presiding Bishop of the Episcopal Church. Clearly this is a point of view with which serious Christians must come to grips.

My way of coming to grips with it has been to determine, as best I can, whether the Bishop's attitude is in accord with Jesus' acts and teachings as recorded in the Gospels. In doing so, I would gladly have relied on the findings of discerning scriptural experts. In my limited experience, however, I have not come across any discussion of the whole gospel record on this issue. There are, to be sure, abundant commentaries on particularly favored gospel passages. The apparent purpose of many of these, however, is to promote prior social commitments. My purpose, on the other hand, has been to help myself to transcend my one-sided desires and understanding. For this purpose, only the whole gospel record suffices.

Before describing what I found in the Gospels, I ought nevertheless to disclose my social commitments. I used to be a conventional left-liberal, but apart from certain residual attachments, I no longer regard myself as one. I now have a strong penchant for moderate, compromise solutions to social problems.

THE BISHOP'S CASE

I think it useful to start my account by putting the case for the Bishop's statement as cogently as I can. In some instances I have objections, or partial reservations, to these arguments, but I will postpone most of them to a later section.

Of all the "oughts" in the Gospels, the command that we love each other is perhaps the most frequently asserted. Stated in many different ways in the synoptic Gospels, it is most commonly quoted as the second commandment, "You shall love your neighbor as yourself" (Mk 12:31).[2] John also records the point

[2] All scriptural quotations are from the Revised Standard Version.

repeatedly, as in this familiar text: "A new commandment I give to you, that you love one another; even as I have loved you, that you also love one another. By this all men will know that you are my disciples, if you have love for one another" (Jn 13:34–35).

General as it is, this command might possibly be interpreted as referring only to predominantly personal relations, such as those within a family or parish. In many other passages, however, Jesus gave the command a distinctly social point.

First, Jesus was anxious to comfort the poor and oppressed for their sufferings in this life. According to Matthew and Luke, in response to John the Baptist's inquiry, "Are you he who is to come, or shall we look for another?" Jesus represented consolation of the poor as half of his earthly mission: "Go and tell John what you hear and see: [the disabled are healed] and the poor have good news preached to them" (Mt 11:2–5). Luke gives an example of such preaching in his version of the Beatitudes: "Blessed are you poor, for yours is the Kingdom of God. Blessed are you that hunger now, for you shall be satisfied" (6:20–21).

Jesus did not limit himself simply to consoling the poor and oppressed; he repeatedly exhorted those who are well-off to care for the less fortunate. One of the best-known passages, found in all of the synoptic Gospels, is Jesus' response to the man of "great possessions" who asked what he should do to inherit eternal life: "Sell all that you have, and give it to the poor, and you will have treasure in heaven" (Mk 10:17–22). Another famed saying, from Matthew, is this: "Come, O blessed of my Father, inherit the Kingdom prepared for you from the foundation of the world; I was hungry and you gave me food, I was thirsty and you gave me drink. . . . I was naked and you clothed me. . . . I was in prison and you came to me. . . . Truly, I say to you, as you did it to one of the least of these my brethren, you did it to me" (25:34–40). There are many other Gospel passages to the same point.

Jesus went further, warning not only against lack of generosity or other misuse of wealth but against wealth itself. After the man of "great possessions" found himself unable to obey the command to "sell all that you have", Jesus explained to his disciples, "How hard it will be for those who have riches to enter the Kingdom of God! . . . It is easier for a camel to go through the eye of a needle than for a rich man to enter the Kingdom of God"

(Mk 10:23–25). The same message, stated even more caustically, is in Luke's parable of the rich man (12:16–21) and in his version of the Sermon on the Mount: "But woe to you that are rich, for you have received your consolation. Woe to you that are full now, for you shall hunger" (6:24–25). The reason behind these warnings is debatable; the warnings themselves are inescapable and tend toward a redistribution of wealth.

In a variety of settings, Jesus also condemned social privilege. One familiar passage, found in all of the synoptic Gospels, has the disciples disputing over their rank, to which Jesus objected, "You know that those who are supposed to rule over the Gentiles lord it over them, and their great men exercise authority over them. But it shall not be so among you; but whoever would be great among you must be your servant, and whoever would be first among you must be slave of all" (Mk 10:41–44). Equally powerful is Jesus' denunciation of the scribes, also recorded in all of the synoptic Gospels: "They love the place of honor at feasts and the best seats in the synagogues, and salutations in the market place, and being called rabbi by men. But you are not to be called rabbi, for you have one teacher, and you are all brethren" (Mt 23:6–8).

Though the evidence is more debatable, it appears that Jesus likewise sought to protect the socially vulnerable against *moral* oppression by the powerful. The primary text is John's account of the woman caught in adultery whom Jesus saved from stoning (8:3–11). It cannot be said that Jesus regarded the prohibition against adultery itself as an oppressive taboo; on the contrary, he took adultery seriously enough, here as elsewhere in the Gospels, to send the woman away with the words, "Do not sin again." But it is arguable that he was offended by the fact that this violent outrage was directed at such a vulnerable social target, a sexually offending woman.

By his acts, also, Jesus disparaged established social prejudices. Women were prominent among his intimates, for example, and he repeatedly ministered to non-Jews. Yet this particular point ought not to be overstated, as liberationists may be apt to do. It is inescapable that Jesus chose only men as his primary disciples, and according to Matthew and Mark he healed the daughter of the Gentile woman only after rebuking the latter in a manner unaccountable by modern standards: "I was sent only to the lost sheep of the house of Israel. . . . It is not fair to take the children's bread and throw it to the dogs" (Mt 15:24, 26).

To summarize, it seems to be indisputable that a significant part of Jesus' mission on earth was to console the poor and oppressed; to persuade the comfortable to care for those less fortunate; to discourage undue wealth and social rank; and partially to break down ethnic and sexual bounds. This is a substantial social commitment. The question remains, does espousing it constitute the main duty of the Church?

GENERAL OBSERVATIONS

Before responding directly to this question, I think it useful to throw certain sidelights on it. Probably most people, speaking as did the Bishop, would formulate their aim as vindication of the rights of the poor and oppressed and would expect to achieve it primarily by organized social action. Yet at no point in the Gospels did Jesus urge collective action. His whole emphasis was on individual acts of decency and generosity. Moreover, he nowhere spoke of the "rights" or even the material interests of the poor and oppressed. In every passage advocating social action, it was the soul of the giver, not the material advantage of the receiver, that was his explicit concern. He consoled the poor and oppressed solely with spiritual assurances. In short, Jesus' mission on earth was the spiritual salvation of humanity, to be attained by each person individually.

Consider those Gospel passages in which wealth and poverty are most clearly juxtaposed. One is the well-known incident of the "widow's mite" reported in Mark (12:41–44) and Luke. Readers will recall that Jesus observed rich folks putting large sums into the temple treasury, and then a poor widow contributing a penny. What was his reaction? Not that a more progressive temple tax would produce greater revenues from those most able to pay. Not even that in all fairness there ought to be a total tax exemption for the poor. No, he instead lauded the poor widow for her self-sacrifice. His concern was for her soul— and those of the rich contributors—rather than for material fairness to the poor.

Another text, equally famed, is the parable of Lazarus and the rich man in Luke (16:19–31), in which Jesus portrayed the extremes of wealth and poverty. Here, if anywhere, we would expect him to insist on the material interests of the poor, but he made no such point. His teaching was that Lazarus would be amply compensated in the next world, while the rich man would suffer eternal torment because of his lack of personal generosity. Coming from the same Evangelist who quoted Jesus as consoling the poor and warning the rich, this parable provides a persuasive interpretation of that message. What matters most is the spiritual condition of each person.

These themes are carried to a remarkable extreme in two passages in John (9:1–3; 11:1–4). There Jesus suggested to his disciples that they not be distressed on account of the sick and disabled, including a man blind from birth, for belated cures would redound to God's glory. Jesus could hardly have expressed greater indifference to the purely material interests of his beneficiaries or more complete concentration on the spiritual consequences of his acts.

It is not my intention to diminish the force of Jesus' admonitions to those of us who are well-off. It ought not to salve our consciences that God has nonmaterial ways of caring for those we victimize by our social indifference. Indeed, the message is arguably even more terrible than it might otherwise be—we are free to gain and keep the whole world, but at the expense of our most precious possession, our souls. My intention, rather, is to root Jesus' message of social concern in the soil of authentic Christian belief.

I have another preliminary observation on the Bishop's statement. If one had to designate the foibles most characteristic of social activists, one might well choose animosity toward their social adversaries and pride in their own purity of heart. Yet these traits, particularly the latter, were emphatically condemned by Jesus. The Gospels are full of passages advocating charity toward our adversaries, social or otherwise. The most forceful is in Luke's version of the Sermon on the Mount: "Love your enemies, do good to those who hate you, bless those who curse you, pray for those who abuse you" (6:27). I recognize that the implications of these commands are highly problematic. They were apparently not meant to prevent us from condemning our neighbors' misconduct, for both Luke and Matthew subsequently quote Jesus as saying, "If your brother sins, rebuke him . . ." (Lk 17:3). If the commands mean anything, however, they forbid the rankling bitterness that often characterizes social activism.

Jesus was even harsher on the self-righteous. In my view one of the most telling passages in the entire Gospels is the parable in Luke of the Pharisee and the tax collector: "Two men went up into the temple to pray, one a Pharisee and the other a tax collector. The Pharisee stood and prayed thus with himself, 'God, I thank thee that I am not like other men, extortioners, unjust, adulterers, or even like this tax collector. I fast twice a week, I give tithes of all that I get.' But the tax collector, standing far off, would not even lift up his eyes to heaven, but beat his breast, saying, 'God, be merciful to me a sinner!' I tell you, this man went down to his house justified rather than the other; for every one who exalts himself will be humbled, but he who humbles himself will be exalted" (18:10–14). In my experience, social activists are more often reminiscent of the Pharisee than of the tax collector.

I do not mean to suggest that proponents of the Bishop's statement have a monopoly on ire or pride about social matters. I find an abundance of these traits in myself, and in some others who might be called "counter-revolutionary"; we have no more reason to feel morally superior to the social activists than they to us. My point is only that social activism, like every other earthly virtue, has its accompanying serious vices, of which its practitioners seem to be mostly unaware.

THE OPPOSING CASE

I am now prepared to comment directly on the Bishop's statement suggesting that to fight social injustice is the main duty of the Church. Even if one takes the Gospels as addressed primarily to our relations with the needy, it cannot be maintained that our only "needy" neighbors are the poor and oppressed.

Proponents of the Bishop's statement may find it supported by Luke's parable of the good Samaritan (10:29–37) and by the ubiquitous miracle of the loaves and fishes whereby Jesus fed the hungry multitudes (e.g., Mk 6:35–44). Yet the only relevant evidence in either of these accounts contradicts the notion that the beneficiaries were poor people. Rather, they were people in physical need quite without regard to their economic condition. Thus these passages tend instead to controvert the Bishop's statement; they stand for an obligation to aid all who are in need, rich or poor.

This point is made far more frequently and forcefully by the Gospel accounts of healing. Jesus' healing acts greatly outnumbered any of his other acts of material welfare, and they are described by Matthew (e.g., 9:35) and Mark, along with preaching the good news, as half of his entire mission prior to his passion and death. What is perhaps even more relevant to the duty of the Church, when Jesus sent his disciples out, healing was half of their assignment as well. According to each of the synoptic Gospels, "He called the twelve together . . . and he sent them out to preach the Kingdom of God and to heal. . . . And they departed and went through the villages, preaching the gospel and healing everywhere" (Lk 9:1–6). It is probably unnecessary to add that as far as the Gospels reveal, Jesus and his disciples ministered to the sick and disabled without regard to their economic condition.

Even in Luke's version of the Beatitudes, partly quoted above in support of the Bishop's statement, Jesus made it clear that his concern for human suffering extended beyond the poor and oppressed. He went on to preach, "Blessed are you that weep now, for you shall laugh" (6:21), or in Matthew's more familiar words, "Blessed are those who mourn, for they shall be comforted" (5:4). The same comment applies to the familiar passage in Matthew, also partly quoted above, in which Jesus addressed the inheritors of the Kingdom. There he added, "I was a stranger and you welcomed me. . . . I was sick and you visited me . . ." (25:35–36).

Jesus likewise enlarged his concern for the victims of moral outrage to embrace, not only the oppressed, but also their oppressors. In addition to a number of general texts, each of the

synoptic Gospels gives the story of Jesus dining with tax collectors, in explicit defiance of his "righteous" critics (e.g.,
Mk 2:15–17). Now tax collectors were despised in large part
because they made a great deal of money out of bullying and
cheating the people (cf. Lk 19:8)—just the sort of oppressive
conduct that the Bishop's statement would properly deplore.
In this story, therefore, Jesus disparaged outrage even though
socially enlightened; his message of moral humility transcends
class and ideological lines. The parable of the Pharisee and the tax
collector, which I recited previously, makes the same point.

My next observation carries these comments on the Bishop's
statement a step further. Jesus' concern for our relations with our
neighbors did not pertain only to the needy and despised. He
also cared greatly about social conduct of other kinds. In each
of the synoptic Gospels Jesus espoused the traditional Hebrew
commandments as ways to inherit eternal life: "Do not kill. . . .
Do not steal. Do not bear false witness. Do not defraud . . ." (Mk
10:19). He made the same point with his teaching, reported in
Mark and Matthew, that sin consists of what a person does rather
than what he eats: "For out of the heart come evil thoughts,
murder . . . theft, false witness, slander. These are what defile a
man" (Mt 15:19–20). In this category also belongs Jesus' repeated
teaching, referred to previously, that we should act charitably
toward all with whom we are in conflict.

Jesus was also much concerned with human relations of a
peculiarly personal nature. In each of the synoptic Gospels he
discoursed at length on marriage and adultery (e.g., Mk 10:2–12);
his teachings, very strict by modern standards, cannot possibly
be squared with the ordinary liberationist program. In Mark
(7:10–13) and Matthew he pointed out certain implications of the
command to honor one's parents. In John he repeatedly preached
loving service *within* his small band of disciples, most familiarly
in his observation, "Greater love has no man than this, that a man
lay down his life for his friends" (15:13). Indeed Jesus' first
miracle, recorded by John, was to provide wine for the enjoy-
ment of friends at the wedding party at Cana (2:1–11).

Thus far I have assumed the contention basic to the Bishop's
statement, that our main duty as followers of Jesus is to serve
other people. Yet there is much in the Gospels to suggest that our

first duty, rather, is the worship of God. The primary text is Jesus' familiar response in all of the synoptic Gospels to the scribe's question, "Which commandment is the first of all?": "The first is, 'Hear, O Israel: The Lord our God, the Lord is one; and you shall love the Lord your God with all your heart, and with all your soul, and with all your mind, and with all your strength'" (Mk 12:28–30). The second commandment, love of our neighbors, is "like" the first, but it was not said to be the same.

More than the other Evangelists, John recorded this teaching in a specifically Christian way. In reply to the inquiry, "What must we do, to be doing the work of God?" Jesus commanded, "This is the work of God, that you believe in him whom he has sent" (6:28–29). There are numerous other passages in John to the same effect; two texts of unusual familiarity and beauty are these: "For God so loved the world that he gave his only Son, that whoever believes in him should not perish but have eternal life" (3:16). "I am the resurrection and the life; he who believes in me, though he die, yet shall he live, and whoever lives and believes in me shall never die" (11:25–26).

Luke gives an extremely vivid description of what belief in Jesus is like: "Behold, a woman of the city, who was a sinner, when she learned that he was sitting at table in the Pharisee's house, brought an alabaster flask of ointment, and standing behind him at his feet, weeping, she began to wet his feet with her tears, and anointed them with the ointment." Jesus' subsequent teaching made the point inescapable: "I tell you, her sins, which are many, are forgiven, for she loved much" (7:36–50). Such adoration is in a realm quite beyond that of the social gospel.

Jesus also preached, above other virtues, respect for the third Person of the Trinity. In each of the synoptic Gospels he warned, "Truly I say to you, all sins will be forgiven the sons of men, and whatever blasphemies they utter; but whoever blasphemes against the Holy Spirit never has forgiveness, but is guilty of an eternal sin" (Mk 3:28–29).

The primacy of worship in the work of the Church encompasses not only encouragement of personal devotion but also performance of the sacraments and other observances. At the close of Matthew's Gospel, Jesus gave his disciples a twofold mission, the first of which was sacramental: "Go therefore and make disciples of all nations, baptizing them in the name of the Father and of the Son and of the Holy Spirit [and teaching them my commands]" (28:19–20). And in John's Gospel, immediately after bestowing the Holy Spirit on the disciples, he sent them forth to administer the Sacrament of forgiveness (20:21–23). The end of Luke's Gospel (24:47) may be read as making the same point. These final words of Jesus to his disciples collectively are bound to be of special relevance to the Church's main duty.

As far as we know, Jesus used physical force against other people only once in his life on earth. The occasion for this ought also to be of special significance, particularly to proponents of liberation theology. In fact it was the cleansing of the temple, described in every one of the Gospels, and Jesus' words of explanation were these: "Is it not written, 'My house shall be called a house of prayer for all the nations'? But you have made it a den of robbers" (Mk 11:15–17). What stirred Jesus to singular wrath was the desecration of the place set aside above all others for the corporate worship of God.

Even in his mission of succoring the needy, Jesus asserted the greater importance of devotion to God. Thus after feeding the hungry multitude, according to John, he preached to them, "Do not labor for the food which perishes, but for the food which endures to eternal life, which the Son of man will give to you" (6:27), and then follows Jesus' magnificent discourse on the theme, "I am the bread of life."

Likewise in Jesus' warnings against wealth his primary concern was the effect of all worldliness on proper devotion to God. Perhaps the most challenging of all of Jesus' social sayings is his message, previously quoted, to "sell all that you have, and give it to the poor. . . ." Yet the culmination of Jesus' command is strongly spiritual: "Come follow me." This teaching is further explained in his subsequent discourse with the disciples: "Truly, I say to you, there is no man who has left house or wife or brothers or parents or children, for the sake of the Kingdom of God, who will not receive manifold more in this time, and in the age to come eternal life" (Lk 18:22, 29–30). There are many other Gospel texts that make the same point. Now if in some sense we are meant to renounce loved ones as well as wealth, we are plainly dealing primarily with a God-centered rather than a human-centered program.

For me the most complete expression of this view is the familiar passage in the synoptic Gospels, "If any man would come after me, let him deny himself and take up his cross and follow me. For whoever would save his life will lose it; and whoever loses his life for my sake and the gospel's will save it. For what does it profit a man, to gain the whole world and forfeit his life?" (Mk 8:34–36). Neither Jesus' words nor the context limit the point to relinquishment of property and worldly status. Denying ourselves, losing our lives, disavowing the world—these comprehend every worldly connection or aim that causes us to place our will ahead of God's. We are as much called upon to give up our favorite social program, in order to follow Christ, as we are to give up our material aspirations.

It is terribly important, however, that these texts not be made an excuse for ritualism at the expense of our neighbors. The Gospels abound with warnings against this tendency. For example, Matthew and Luke record the saying, "Woe to you, scribes and Pharisees, hypocrites! for you tithe mint and dill and cummin, and have neglected the weightier matters of the law, justice and mercy and faith; these you ought to have done, without neglecting the others" (Mt 23:23–24). Similarly, all of the synoptic Gospels report Jesus' dismay at the "hardness of heart" of the Pharisees who would denounce him for healing a crippled man on the sabbath (e.g., Mk 3:1–6).

Thus far I have neglected two texts that are apt to be particularly familiar to those who disagree with the Bishop's statement. I assume that in these days of the semi-welfare state, conservatives have ceased cherishing Jesus' advice in each of the synoptic Gospels about paying taxes to Caesar (e.g., Mk 12:13–17). On the other hand, some may still cling to Jesus' remark, "You always have the poor with you," found in all of the Gospels but Luke, as ground for abstaining from social justice. I have disregarded this text for two reasons: First, the context limits its scope sharply. Readers will recall that Jesus was responding to those of his disciples who reproved the woman of Bethany for anointing Jesus instead of giving the price of the ointment to the poor. His full teaching was, "You always have the poor with you, and whenever you will, you can do good to them, but you will not always have me" (Mk 14:3–9). Thus he disparaged the use of wealth to succor the poor only by contrast to extreme devotion to his person. Second, even taken out of context the saying cannot be made to support an asocial attitude, for Jesus never treated the inevitability of a deplorable situation as reason to condone it. The most dramatic text, found in the synoptic Gospels, is Jesus' remark about Judas Iscariot at the Last Supper: "The Son of man goes, as it is written of him, but woe to that man by whom the Son of man is betrayed! It would have been better for that man if he had not been born" (Mk 14:18–21).

To summarize: We are to aid, not just the poor, but all in need; we are to avoid intolerance, not just of offenders who are oppressed, but of all who misbehave. We also have major duties to neighbors other than the needy and despised; these duties may run preeminently to family and friends. Most important of all, we are bound to worship God. The Christian Church's business is to nurture all of these actions, for they relate alike to our personal salvation, which is the true main business of the Church.

Thus I object to the Bishop's viewpoint, but not because it is totally fallacious; on the contrary, in its affirmative aspect it asserts the truth. My objection is that the statement proclaims only part of the truth, at the expense of the rest. Now over-emphasis on a part of the truth may be warranted when that part is otherwise falling into neglect. In my view, however, such is not the case here. On the contrary, the center of gravity in many of the establishment churches of the affluent West seems to me already to have shifted toward social action at the expense of more personal and spiritual virtues. The Bishop's viewpoint, like that of many other Church leaders, increases the imbalance.

XIII

JOHN M. FINNIS

CATHOLIC SOCIAL TEACHING SINCE "POPULORUM PROGRESSIO"

The purpose of *Populorum Progressio* [Pope Paul's encyclical *On the Development of Peoples*] was to create a new imaginative horizon, in which "the social question" will be *seen* and *felt* to have become "world-wide" (*Populorum Progressio*, 3)—"to help everybody *grasp* this serious problem in all its dimensions, and to *convince* them that solidarity *in action* at this turning point in human history is a matter of *urgency*" (1, emphasis added). Where the papal and conciliar documents of the early and mid-sixties have, on the whole, the form and tone of treatises, *Populorum Progressio* has the form and tone of an appeal—"an appeal for concrete action toward man's complete development and the development of all mankind" (5).

Lack of Brotherhood

The last quoted phrase sums up both the structure and the content of this carefully composed encyclical. The "sickness of the world" is diagnosed as "lack of brotherhood" (66, 87). Correspondingly, the basic appeal is to our duty of solidarity (17, 43, 44, 48), a duty distinct from but reinforcing our duties of social justice and charity (44, 56–65, 66–75). For the duty of solidarity is the duty to aid the complete development of *all* mankind (5, 13, 42, 44, 84).

Hence, for example, the duties of propertyholders (e.g., their duty to place their "superfluous wealth" at the service of the poor) now extend to the whole world (22, 49), and governments have a duty to impose on their citizens taxes on their luxuries, to

Reprinted by permission from *Social Survey*, Australia (August 1978) 213–20, (September 1978) 250–54.

foster the development of all mankind (84; on property see also *The Universal Purpose of Created Things: On the Conference on the Law of the Sea*, Working Paper No. 2, Pontifical Commission on Justice and Peace, Vatican 1977, pp. 6–10; note that the Commission is not a source of doctrinal authority in the proper sense, but serves the Church's magisterium by studying its social doctrine and disseminating it). *Populorum Progressio* also states that there ought to be a World Development Fund (51–53); indeed, there ought to be a move by degrees toward an effective "world authority capable of acting effectively on the juridical and political plane" (78, 64). Solidarity joins with social justice in the strict sense, in demanding more equitably regulated arrangements between trading partners of such disparate economic strength as the developed and the underdeveloped nations (57–61).

None of the foregoing concepts, principles and recommendations was at all new: all can be found in papal and conciliar documents of the early and mid-sixties, if not earlier. What is new is the explicit insistence that "development demands bold transformations, innovations that go deep" (32), the directness of the appeal to the conscience of the rich, the vigor of the attempt to increase a sense of obligation that could break through their selfishness, shortsightedness and materialism (cf. 41, 49). The ambition of the encyclical is to hold in tension two poles while charging each pole with the maximum moral force: the one pole is extensive, the horizon of *all men*, the whole of *humanity*, all become our neighbors and brothers; the other pole is intensive, the *fully-rounded* development of the *whole man* (42, 5, 13, 16–18, 44, 84).

Subsidiarity

Understood in this double sense, "human fulfillment constitutes, as it were, a summary of our duties" (16). Around the second pole cluster a number of long-standing principles of Catholic social thought. Consider, for example, the famous remark that men now aspire, rightly, "to do more, *know* more and have more in order to *be* more" (6): the order, in which "do more" has priority, is significant. For a constant theme throughout the encyclical is that a man is only man when he is author of his own advancement (34, 15); that a basic human need is to *act*, responsibly and on one's own initiative (9, 28, 30, 34, 35, 55; also *Message of Cardinal Roy*, 15); and that public planners should be careful "to associate private initiative and intermediary bodies with their work" (33). The fundamental intermediary body is the family, whose well-being is essential if man is to find his true identity (*Message of Cardinal Roy*, 36; *Humanae Vitae*, 9; *Octogesima Adveniens*, 18; *Evangelii Nuntiandi*, 29).

Thus the old principle of subsidiarity and participation makes its presence strongly felt, though without explicit mention (see also *Communio et Progressio*, 85–86; *Octogesima Adveniens*, 47). And at the same time, the principle that human fulfillment is not attained by passive reception of goods develops in this encyclical toward the concept of liberation: "the struggle against destitution, though urgent and necessary, is not enough. It is a question, rather, of building a world where every man . . . can live a fully human life, *freed* from servitude imposed on him by other men or by natural forces over which he has not sufficient control; a world where freedom is not an empty word and where the poor man Lazarus can sit down at the same table with the rich man" (*Populorum Progressio*, 47).

Population Control

If we are looking for a distinct development of doctrine in *Populorum Progressio*, perhaps we can find it in the affirmation that "it is certain that public authorities can intervene, within the limit of their competence, (to check population growth) by favoring the availability of appropriate information and by adopting suitable measures, provided that these be in conformity with the moral law and that they respect the rightful freedom of married couples," and that in deciding on the number of their children, parents must take into account their responsibility to, amongst others, their community (37). The insistence of *Populorum Progressio* that the development of all peoples must be guided by a global vision not only of all men but also of the whole man (13, 42), is explicitly echoed in the encyclical *Humanae Vitae* of 1968 (7).

A Warning

There is in that document a clarification of the moral law; so far as concerns Catholic social teaching, suffice it to notice two relatively peripheral points. First there is the warning, so soon to be verified, that if individuals are themselves unwilling to contemplate the self-mastery of abstinence (periodically) from sexual intercourse as the means of regulating their own fertility, they should not be surprised if governments become their masters by intervening, to impose temporary or permanent sterilization upon them (17, 21; see also *Justice in the World*, p. 11, against the imposition of contraceptives). Secondly, pornography is condemned as inimical to human civilization, a theme that variously recurs throughout our period (*Humanae Vitae*, 22; *Evangelii Nuntiandi*, 80; cf. *Octogesima Adveniens*, 20; *Justice in the World*, p. 1; *Persona Humana*, 1, 2, 13); it is not, however, stressed in *Communio et Progressio*.

It is now time to ask, what (if not the mere occasion of an anniversary) called for *Octogesima Adveniens*? The answer seems to be this: just as *Populorum Progressio* was needed to widen the imaginative horizon of the faithful and, indeed, of all advantaged peoples, so *Octogesima Adveniens* was needed to deepen their understanding of "the social problem". The encyclical of 1967 concerns the plight of the underdeveloped peoples and the consequent duties of the developed. The apostolic letter of 1971 concerns the problems that spring from development itself, in its contemporary forms.

Urbanization

Primary among these problems is urbanization, the flight from the land and the birth of new proletariats and belts of misery in the disordered growth of cities (*Octogesima Adveniens*, 8–12). The encyclical sets aside bucolic illusions by taking it for granted that "urbanization is undoubtedly an irreversible stage in the development of human societies" (*Octogesima Adveniens*, 10). As late as *Mater et Magistra* (1961), Catholic social thought had given a certain priority of attention to the rural sector (*Mater et Magistra*, 122–156); *Octogesima Adveniens* forcibly redirects attention to new, particularly urban, problems of dehumanization, demoralization, "a new loneliness", a new division between youth and its elders, a new doubt about the meaning and value of progress (10, 13, 14).

Meanwhile, many problems emphasized in earlier papal teaching remain: discrimination against women, problems of trade union freedom and of abuse of trade union power, racial discrimination, migration, unemployment, overpopulation, the mass media (*Octogesima Adveniens*, 13–20). To them can now be added the newly perceived problem of ill-considered exploitation of nature which degrades the environment and threatens the human future (21; on the basic legitimacy of exploiting nature, see *Gaudium et Spes*, 64; *Populorum Progressio*, 22, 25).

Unlike so many discussions of the problems of urbanization, population growth and exploitation of the environment, *Octogesima Adveniens* refuses to ignore the human context in which those problems have to be faced: the context of actual human aspirations and currents of ideas. When the Christian takes on responsibility for "a destiny which from now on is shared by all" (21), he does so in a world in which men are aspiring to equality of rights and participation both in particular groupings and in the political community (22–25). (As one would expect, the apostolic letter strongly favors both of these aspirations: 46–47.)

Marxism

At the same time, the Christian has to deal with men who are in danger of being alienated from themselves (27) because they are involved with ideologies, ideologies which moreover "radically or substantially go against his faith and his concept of man" and thus against many of his ideas for solving the common problems (26). The Christian "cannot adhere to the Marxist ideology, to its atheistic materialism, to its dialectic of violence and to the way it absorbs individual freedom in the collectivity, at the same time denying all transcendence to man and his personal and collective history, nor can he adhere to the liberal ideology which believes it exalts human freedom by withdrawing it from every limitation, by stimulating it through exclusive seeking of interest and power, and by considering social solidarities as more or less automatic consequences of individual initiatives, not as an aim and major criterion of the value of the social organization" (26).

Liberty

The apostolic letter then offers some nuanced pages on socialist currents and movements, with which Christians can only co-operate to the extent that values such as liberty, responsibility and openness to the spiritual are safeguarded (31, 49); on the historical developments and splintering of Marxism itself (32, 34); on the danger of idealizing liberalism (35); on "a new positivism: uni-versalized technology as the dominant form of activity, as the overwhelming pattern of existence, even as a language, without the question of its meaning really being asked" (29, also 37–40 on science and scientism); and on the rebirth of utopias, often an alibi for rejecting immediate responsibilities, but also often a useful source of perceptive criticism, social dynamism, and openness to the "mystery of man" which lies beyond every system and every ideology (37). "At the heart of the world there dwells the mystery of man discovering himself to be God's son in the course of a historical and psychological process in which constraint and freedom as well as the weight of sin and the breath of the Spirit alternate and struggle for the upper hand" (37). *Octogesima Adveniens* concludes:

—by renewing the appeal of *Populorum Progressio* for inter-national justice and solidarity, adding a warning about multi-national corporations (*Octogesima Adveniens*, 43–44);

—by reminding Christians that "liberation (from need and de-pendence) starts with the interior freedom that men must find again with regard to their goods and their powers; men will never reach it except through a transcendent love for man, and, in consequence, through a genuine readiness to serve", and not through "revolutionary ideologies, leading only to a change of masters" (45; cf. *Populorum Progressio*, 11, 31);

—by recalling the teachings of Pius XI and John XXIII on

subsidiarity and participation (*Octogesima Adveniens* 46–47); and
—by noting that Christians have a legitimate variety of options
in the effort (which must usually be a political effort: 46) to
remedy the problems of the age, since the social teaching of
the Church, "in the face of widely varying situations," "does
not intervene to authenticate a given structure or to propose a
ready-made model" or to "put forward a solution which has
universal validity" (4, 42, 49, 50). On the other hand, that social
teaching "does not limit itself to recalling general principles. It
develops through reflection applied to the changing situations of
this world, under the driving force of the Gospel, as the source of
renewal when its message is accepted in its totality and with all its
demands" (42).

Liberation

Octogesima Adveniens expressly looked forward to the then
forthcoming Second General Assembly of the Synod of Bishops
"to study more closely and to examine in greater detail the
Church's mission in the face of grave issues raised today by the
question of justice in the world" (6).

The resulting document, *Justice in the World*, notes that the
world is marked by the grave sin of injustice (p.13); but it is less
concerned to stress the duties in conscience of the rich than
to affirm (in rather unclear terms), that the Church's mission
includes the "liberation (of the human race) from every oppressive situation" (p. 6; cf. *Evangelii Nuntiandi*, 9), and that those
who are oppressed by unjust systems and structures (*Justice in the
World*, p. 5) have "the right to develop . . . a dynamic inter-
penetration of all those fundamental human rights upon which
the aspirations of individuals and nations are based . . . a right
to hope according to the concrete measure of contemporary
humanity" (p. 9; cf. Paul VI, "human fulfillment constitutes a
summary of our duties," *Octogesima Adveniens*, 16).

What the concrete duties of others are, that correspond to this
right of the underdeveloped, is largely left to be gathered from
the earlier papal and conciliar social teachings to which the
document compendiously refers (*Justice in the World*, p. 20; note
that the Synod, as a counsel to the Pope, does not have a conciliar
type of authority).

The Church's Task

"Many, even generous Christians who are sensitive to the dramatic questions involved in the problem of liberation, in their wish to commit the Church to the liberation effort, are frequently tempted to reduce her mission to the dimensions of a simply temporal project . . . a man-centered goal . . . material well being . . . initiatives of the political or social order" (*Evangelii Nuntiandi*, 32). In the face of this, the apostolic letter *Evangelii Nuntiandi* (1975) stresses that the salvation in Jesus Christ which is the foundation, center, and summit of the Church's proclamation, is not immanent but transcendent and eschatological, having its beginning in this life but fulfilled in eternity (27); and that Christian hope is "hope in the promises made by God in the new Covenant in Jesus Christ" (28; contrast *Justice in the World*, p. 25), promises which, one may add, do not appear to include the liberation of any of us, in "this life", from "famine", chronic disease, illiteracy, poverty, injustices in international relations and especially in commercial exchanges, situations of economic and cultural neocolonialism sometimes as *cruel* as the old political colonialism, in short from the state of being condemned to remain on the margin of life (*Evangelii Nuntiandi*, 30; on "marginality", see first the *Message of Cardinal Roy*, 12, 16 iii).

Death

As *Octogesima Adveniens*, 41, points out, all "progress necessarily comes up against the eschatological mystery of death," and "the only hope which does not deceive" is our hope of sharing the glory of God (Rom 5:2, 5). None the less, predicated upon the brotherly love that springs from the love of God and is the kernel of the Gospel (*Evangelii Nuntiandi*, 28), it is the Church's duty to assist the birth of liberation from marginality, to give witness to this liberation, and to ensure that it is complete: "this is not foreign to evangelization" (30; cf. 14). There follow nuanced pages seeking to "remove the ambiguity which the word 'liberation' very often takes on in ideologies, political systems or groups," while the Church is striving to "insert the Christian struggle for liberation into the universal plan of salvation which it proclaims" (38).

312

Special Themes[1]

Peace

In a message of December 8, 1967, the Pope inaugurated a World Day of Peace, observed on New Year's Day since 1968, to emphasize the Church's concern for peace, and accompanied by an annual papal message on a special theme: e.g., "The Promotion of Human Rights, the Way to Peace" (1969); "If You Want Peace, Defend Life" (1977). The theology of peace presupposed in all this is to be found in *Gaudium et Spes*, 78.

Disarmament

The very frequent calls for an end to the arms race, "a machine that has gone crazy", are collected in a document, submitted to the disarmament committee of the United Nations, and republished by the Justice and Peace Commission as *The Holy See and Disarmament*. The rhetoric of the opening pages of that document (and of *Reflections of Cardinal Roy*, pp. 53–54) cannot, however, gloss over the awkward fact that, though disarmament is and is said to be required by reason, the Church continues to admit that nations are entitled in reason to defend themselves and to arm themselves for that purpose (*The Holy See and Disarmament*, p. 8).

Deterrence

The only development of doctrine in this area—and it could rank as one of the most important developments in Catholic social teaching—is to be found in the U.S. Bishops' pastoral letter of November 11, 1976; "not only is it wrong to attack civilian populations *but it is also wrong to threaten to attack them as part of a strategy of deterrence*" (*To Live in Christ Jesus: A Pastoral Reflection on the Moral Life*, National Conference of Catholic Bishops, U.S.A., 1976, p. 34; *L'Osservatore Romano*, 13 January 1977, p. 7, col. 4; emphasis added). In citing this, I make an exception to my decision to refer to only those currents of Catholic social thought

[1] This section refers frequently to documents of the Pontifical Commission of Justice and Peace. These are used in the sense explained in the second paragraph of this article.

which find expression in documents of the Roman magisterium. The importance of the American Bishops' pronouncement is that it is a measured condemnation of the fundamental element in the contemporary strategy of war and deterrence (of the great powers) and of armed struggle (by "freedom fighters"). It offers thus to resolve issues left dangling by the Council (*Gaudium et Spes*, 80).

Confusion

Human rights

The Justice and Peace working paper *The Church and Human Rights* allows us to see the prominent role of the concept of human rights, and of specifications of such rights, in the social teaching of the Church since, at latest, *Pacem in Terris*. A few critical observations may, therefore, be in place.

Firstly, theological handling of this juridical concept often displays a poor understanding of its logic. For instance, it is said that a right has "two aspects . . . *facultas and obligatio*, existence of right and its consequent responsibility, meaning the responsibility of the right-holder himself" (*The Church and Human Rights*, p.4). But in fact, *facultas*, i.e., moral liberty or power to *act* in a certain way, is only one of three fundamental types of moral rights. The other two types, which are at least as prominent in ecclesiastical and other declarations of rights are: 1) the right to be given something, or assisted in a certain way, by someone (who has the strictly correlative duty so to give or assist); 2) the right *not* to be treated in a certain way by someone (who has the strictly correlative duty to abstain from acting in such a way)—this latter right is often, but not always, ancillary to a *facultas* of acting which it protects by guaranteeing non-interference with the exercise of the *facultas*.

Oversight

Secondly, the foregoing local distinctions assist in clarifying a much more important oversight or omission in many theological pronouncements on human rights: omission to notice that while, in a sense, all human rights are "inviolable, inalienable and universal" (*The Church and Human Rights*, p. 37), some human rights are absolute, while others are relative or conditional. Virtually all faculty-rights, even rights of primary importance (*Evangelii Nuntiandi*, p. 39; *The Church and Human Rights*, p. 115) such as liberty of religious practice, are subject in their exercise to the exigencies of public order, public morality and certain other aspects of the common good (*Dignitatis Humanae*, 7). But there are many rights, especially rights not-to-be-treated-in-a-certain-way, which are absolute, i.e., which prevail over all other considerations whatsoever: e.g., the right of bystanders or civilian populations not to be taken and killed as hostages, or the right not to be directly aborted (*Declaration on Procured Abortion*, p. 14). The Church's teaching that evil may not be done for the sake of good (*Humanae Vitae*, p. 14) will be prejudiced if this distinction is not kept clearly in sight; indeed, human rights will obviously suffer if *all* human rights are treated as subject to other exigencies.

Human Dignity

Thirdly, the notion that human aspirations are based on human rights (e.g., *Justice in the World*, p. 9), though it can be interpreted so as to be acceptable, tends to invert the true order of explanatory priority. Basic human aspirations are based, not on juridically conceived relations with other men, but on our created nature, the "set of aptitudes and qualities granted to each man at birth, in the design of God, for him to bring to fruition" (*Populorum Progressio*, 15). These aptitudes include friendship (at its lowest, solidarity), of which one aspect is justice (cf. *Populorum Progressio*, 17, 19, 20, 43, 44, 75). The fundamental category of Catholic social thought remains the "*goods* of human dignity, brotherhood and freedom, that is to say, all the *good fruits of our nature* and our work," goods which "we shall find, but freed of stain, burnished and transfigured, when Christ hands over to the Father 'a Kingdom . . . of truth and life . . . of justice, love and peace' . . . that will be brought into full flower when the Lord returns" (*Gaudium et Spes*, 39; cf. the truncations in *Justice in the World*, p. 25). In short, fourthly, the term "rights", like the term "violence", can become devalued and emptied of meaning by inflationary use (for a devalued use of "violence", see *Reflections of Cardinal Roy*, p. 47).

Foundation of Rights

Natural Law

People often ask whether the natural law has been replaced, perhaps by "something more phenomenological or existential", in contemporary Catholic social teaching. The remarks in the preceding paragraph suggest an answer to this question. Certainly the terms "natural law", "natural right", "natural reason", are not much used in recent documents. (There is an unfortunate tendency to retain them *only* in relation to absolute negative duties, which on any view are only one aspect of the natural law: e.g., *Gaudium et Spes*, 79; *Humanae Vitae*, 11; *Declaration on Procured Abortion*, 14; *Persona Humana*, 4, 5.) But, on the one hand, no foundation can be found in Catholic theology for the "fundamental human rights" to which such constant appeal is nowadays made, other than the foundation affirmed in the first pages of *Pacem in Terris*, viz., the principles of order divinely inscribed in the inclinations and capacities of our created nature, discernible more or less clearly by our practical intelligence, and crystallized with moral force in our conscience (see also *Reflections of Cardinal Roy*, pp. 19, 20, 64–70, 74; *The Church and Human Rights*, pp. 6, 32, 36, 37).

Now for some methodological reflections. In an earlier paragraph, I referred to the ambition of the magisterium to hold in tension two poles, while charging each pole with maximum moral force. And this is the ambition not only of *Populorum Progressio*, to which I was there referring, but also of the whole period. Along with this goes, secondly (but not wholly independently), an old Christian ambition: to baptize certain profane concepts, to despoil (plunder) the Egyptians, to overcome that "fear and nostalgia" noticeable in the period before *Rerum Novarum*, but which continued in respect of certain established patterns of language (systems of concepts) right up to the beginning of my period—not altogether without reason. I want to illustrate these two methodological ambitions, which characterize my period, by reference to the adoption in magisterial documents of the language of "liberation" and "struggle".

Liberation

It is sometimes said (for example by Fr. Alfaro, the principal theologian to the drafting committee for the synodal document *Justice in the World*)[2] that "the first time that the biblical concept of liberation appears in the Magisterium of the Church" was in that document, in 1971. This seems to me misleading: in no less than ten documents of Vatican II, the notion of liberation appears (with a biblical sense) in the verbal and adjectival forms, *liberare*, *liberans*, and as *liberator* and *liberatus*; in all, twenty-five times. Still, it is true that the abstract noun *liberatio* was used by the Council only to describe Buddhist and Marxist ideas. And this restriction is overcome, not indeed only in *Justice in the World*, but earlier, in *Octogesima Adveniens* (45). Still, it would be foolish to deny that when we read in *Evangelii Nuntiandi* that "evangelization involves . . . a message especially energetic today about liberation" (*Evangelii Nuntiandi*, 29), we are hearing a new accent, a new tone of voice.

This picking-out of a word from the great babble of human intercourse involves risks that Christianity has, from the very beginning, been willing to run—but not to run unconditionally. In the present case, the risks are particularly obvious: the word "liberation" is used with an enormous range of varying meanings and resonances: at one extreme, as the pragmatic symbol of rather commonplace politico-military projects for replacing one ruler with another or others; at the other extreme, as the symbol for a passionately desired but vaguely conceived transformation of human nature, as in the Marxian "realm of freedom" which is supposed (quite without credible reasons) to be produced by "the revolution" against "capitalism" and the bourgeois stage of history (or should I say, "pre-history"). Still, it seems to be right to take a relaxed attitude to the concept, provided one is clear about the conditions on which one is using it.

[2] See p. 11 of *Theology of Justice in the World* (Rome: Justice and Peace Commission, 1973).

Six Conditions

In the present case, one can list at least *six* conditions which bracket the meaning of "liberation" in Catholic theology as expounded by the Roman magisterium. These six conditions do not weaken the meaning of the word itself, which remains: the freeing of men from all forms of fear, distress, oppression and "everything that condemns them to remain on the margin of life: famine, chronic disease, illiteracy, poverty", etc. (*Evangelii Nuntiandi*). That pole of meaning, demanding strenuous efforts and deep innovations on the part of both rich and poor, or exploiter and exploited (the two pairs of terms are not equivalent!), remains charged to the maximum. But there remains the other pole or poles which can be identified by some or all of the following six partly overlapping features, conditions and provisos.

The Goal of Liberation

Firstly, liberation is to have as its final goal salvation, with which it is linked but never to be identified (*Evangelii Nuntiandi*, 35). The magisterium is not inhibited from repeating the common teaching of centuries, in which salvation is proclaimed (as *Evangelii Nuntiandi*, 9, puts it) as "liberation from everything that oppresses men, above all liberation from sin and the Evil One, *in* the joy of knowing God and being known by him, and of being given over to him" (to which one might add, rather overlooked in *Evangelii Nuntiandi*, "in the company of many brothers and sisters"). To this, paragraphs 27 and 28 add the essential precision (to which I return in my remarks about hope and the Kingdom below); this liberating salvation is "not an immanent salvation, meeting material or even spiritual needs, restricted to the framework of temporal existence . . . but one that exceeds all temporal desires, hopes, affairs and struggles, all these limits . . . a transcendent and eschatalogical salvation which indeed has its beginning in this life but which is fulfilled in eternity," since "man's profound and definitive calling [is] to a hereafter, in both continuity and discontinuity with the present situation: beyond time and history, beyond the transient reality of this world—beyond man himself."

Secondly, the liberation proclaimed by the Church requires "a conversion of heart and of outlook", the "total interior renewal, which the Gospel calls *metanoia*" (*Evangelii Nuntiandi*, 36, 10). The Kingdom and a liberating salvation "are available as grace and mercy, and yet each must gain them by force; through toil and suffering . . . abnegation and the Cross . . . the spirit of the Beatitudes" (10).

Thirdly, a theology of liberation is not to subordinate theology, a reflection on the divine Word once spoken, to that mysticism of praxis which Marx has announced in his *Theses on Feuerbach*, or to that prohibition of contemplation of the mysteries of existence (God, Creation, salvation through grace in death), the prohibition of which he proposes in his *Paris Manuscripts* of 1844 (see the central section, "Private Property and Communism"). For the Gospel is, *inter alia*, an answer to human *questions*, pure questions (cf. *Gaudium et Spes*, 18–21; *Evangelii Nuntiandi*, 3, 78).

Social Teaching

Fourthly, a theology and a program of liberation must alike respect, not replace, the "social teaching (of the Church) which the true Christian cannot ignore . . ." (*Evangelii Nuntiandi*, 38), for example, about the role of the family, about the liberating function (under certain conditions) of private property, about not killing the innocent, or other such teachings which bring a blush to the ears of many Christian liberators today. Liberation does not abolish the problematic of justice: it remains necessary to tackle countless embarrassing issues, of which I select one, summed up in the slogan of St. Paul (2 Th 3:10), *Populorum Progressio* (18) and the 1975 *Constitution of the Chinese Peoples' Republic* (Art. 9): "If anyone will not work, let him not eat".

Fifthly, and related to the preceding point, the concept of liberation is not to suppress the concept of development. Gutíerrez offered an understandable but quite inadequate reason for simply replacing the one concept with the other: briefly, "the deficiencies of the development policies proposed to the poor countries . . . and also the lack of concrete achievements of the interested governments", mere "reformism and modernization", timidity, and so on (*Theology of Liberation*, p. 25). But these admitted deficiencies of certain policies adopted or advertised in certain times and places provide no good reason for abandoning a fundamental concept with which those policies had only contingent links. Even the revolution and realm of freedom dreamed of by Marx is based upon the development of the industrial system and the developing reduction of working hours that system makes possible, which in turn frees man for a many-sided development of his potentialities.

In short, any fundamental social thought needs a concept to express the positive aspect of that state of affairs of which liberation is, so to say, the negative aspect. That state of affairs is compendiously called, in recent magisterial pronouncements, "human advancement" (e.g. *Evangelii Nuntiandi*, 31), and it involves both liberation *from* evils and development *of* potentialities, economy, community, etc. So liberation and development are to be paired.

Violence

Sixthly, the theology and program of liberation are not to glamorize violence, not to treat it as a matter of honor, as in some pagan and half-Christian cultures; not to accept it fatalistically, as in some other cultures, not to glamorize it as the occasion of a transformation of human nature, as in more than one modern ideology. Theologians today make heavy weather of the question of violence, by which I mean the use of armed force, i.e., the threat and employment of killing and wounding to overcome human opponents. I see no reason for developing a new theology either for or against violence. What needs to be said has been said in the classical teaching, initiated at the latest by St. Augustine, on the just war, and on tyrannicide, and on the *counsel* of non-resistance; in its essentials, that teaching is in perfectly good shape. This statement will evidently be shocking to some people; but are there reasons (not feelings) against it?

Political Theology

By the way of a digression, let us reflect on a remark made more than once: that political theology, or the involvement of Christians in political action, will divide the Church, not just in the obvious, matter-of-fact way, but in such a way as to create an ecclesiological problem and a search for the true Church within the Church. I must say I doubt it. Once we leave behind the medieval perspective of a sacral Christendom, in which temporal rulers or activists are subjected directly to tests of their ecclesiastical obedience, do we confront anything beyond the matter-of-fact problem of the Christian policeman who has to track down and overcome the Mafia boss who is both a murderer and a devout communicant and family-man?

Psychologically, the problems of a Church whose members are divided between, say, the political left and the political right are no doubt more vexing—but ecclesiologically? It is asked: How can oppressors and oppressed be united in one Church? Well, no one's humanity is exhausted by his membership of a class such as "oppressors" or "oppressed"; the wheat and the tares have always coexisted in the heart of the baptized, whether rich or poor, and they coexist in the garden of the Lord, and will do so till Kingdom come.

A Vision of Faith

These last words ("thy Kingdom come") can serve to introduce my second concern in this part, which is to deal with some matters raised in the SODEPAX documents leading up to the Colloquium. The SODEPAX Program *In Search of a New Society*, set out in *Church Alert No. 8*, proposes that "the churches and ecumenical groups should concentrate their thinking on how to arrive at a basic vision of faith rather than in particular theological interpretations" (p. 14)—and of course it is impossible to disagree with that. To this end, the document goes on to suggest three areas of theological concern around which we may be able to unite, as aspects of a basic vision of faith rather than mere theological interpretations. These are "the struggle of the poor", "the power of Jesus Christ", and thirdly, "a new creation: the Kingdom of God". I want to comment on the third and the first.

Hope

"Most important of all", the document says (p. 17), "the vision of 'the Kingdom of God underway' gives humanity hope that an alternative pattern will emerge." And here it quotes not only the ambiguous final pages of *Justice in the World* (1971) but also a passage from the World Council of Churches' *Nairobi Assembly* (1975): "Christians must be prepared to help transform despair into hope, and uncertainties into positive certainty", (this is in the context of "moves toward a more just order and conditions for a more helpful development process")—and the passage concludes with Hebrews (11:1): "Faith gives the assurance of things hoped for, the conviction of things not seen." I want to suggest to SODEPAX that it may be a mistake to suppose that this is part of the basic vision of faith around which Christians can unite.

Love

It seems to me that the intelligible center of gravity of Catholic social teaching remains love, and the consequent duty, command or, if you prefer, call or summons, to foster the liberation and development of my neighbor, who is now to be found, in some measure, throughout the world.

The center of gravity is not hope *relative to some vision*, however vague, *of what the human future in this world will be*. And I am suggesting that as soon as some such "vision of the coming Kingdom or of the Kingdom of God underway" moves into the foreground or center of our attention, then a cause not of unity, but of division and doubt is introduced, both as between Christians themselves and as between Christians and other men of goodwill.

The same eschatalogical discourse that in Matthew 25:31–46 teaches the basic duty to feed the hungry, clothe the naked, visit (not necessarily to release!) the prisoner, also teaches in Matthew 24:12 ff. that wickedness abounds, that the love of many will grow cold, and, in short, that there is no reason to believe that humanity as a whole will be in fit shape to greet the Lord when he comes to end the course of human history.

XIV

ROGER HECKEL, S.J.

GENERAL REFLECTION ON THE USE OF THE WORD *LIBERATION* BY JOHN PAUL II

Considering what we already know about the Pope's outlook, we could easily suggest one reason for his prudent and discreet use of the word *liberation*: he is not the type of person prone to follow changing currents. This does not make it impossible for him to discern the deep truths present in those currents, but rightly he does so by reflecting upon them on the basis of his own thought rooted in tradition and marked by his own personality.

In a much deeper sense, the Pope's attitude can be explained by his evident concern to avoid the ambiguities which, he is aware, have marked the use of the word *liberation*. Therefore, he is careful to qualify the word properly whenever he uses it. His attitude is usually critical.

The principal ambiguity would seem to be the following: the theologians of liberation invoke the religious and biblical resonance of the word but give it a more immediate meaning in terms of the various social, economic, political and cultural liberations pursued by contemporary persons and peoples. The ambiguous point is therefore in the bond which people too quickly establish between these political expressions of *liberation* and *liberation by Jesus Christ*. This bond does exist, but it must be discerned and qualified in a very clear way in order to avoid all sorts of false conclusions and confusion. This represents an even more serious problem since the most radical currents usually dominate the scene and sweep along others in their wake whether they like it or not.

John Paul II sidesteps these ambiguities through an approach which it seems to me can be expressed in three points:

—he uses the word with discretion, and when he does so almost always explains its meaning;

Reprinted by permission from *The Theme of Liberation* (Rome: Pontifical Commission on Justice and Peace, 1980) 21–24.

—he systematically gives greater emphasis to the specifically religious sense of the word;

—in his perspective of evangelization (which he would like to see shared by the entire Church), the Pope considers political liberation (economic, social, cultural) as dependent upon religious liberation by Jesus Christ.

The first point has already been dealt with at length and it will suffice to make a few remarks on the other two.

When talking about theologies of liberation, some people stress the theological dimension and use this religious resonance (warranty, fervor) for the different forms of liberation. When John Paul II uses the word, he strives to give it its full theological and religious meaning enriched by tradition, and make it cover a reality which is really a *reality of faith*.

In the truly Christian sense (biblical, theological), liberation is the work of God, the work of Jesus Christ (Gal 5:1 and Jn 8:32 are of prime importance in the Pope's catechesis on this subject and it is only in reference to these quotes from Scripture that the word *liberation* appears in *Redemptor Hominis* (12, pars. 3 and 4). The word is therefore normally linked in an explicit way to the more common words of *salvation* and *Redemption* in Christian and biblical theology. They represent, and this can bear repetition, the ordinary terminology used by the Pope. The title and the language of *Redemptor Hominis* bear eloquent witness to this point.

This liberation is beyond human strength and is the forgiveness and the gift of God. It delivers us from sin, which is something only God can do. It leads us to a new life, the very life of God, and raises us beyond our own inherent limits.

The Pope frequently stresses—another common feature of his catechesis—the fact that this liberation affects the interior person, the very center, the heart, the very source of one's being, and that each person experiences this liberation (the theological virtues of faith, hope and charity) from that moment on, even before other expressions of liberation have become tangible. From that moment on, each of us *is* free in Christ.

There are also other frequent developments on the effects and qualities of this liberation in each of us: integrality (undoubtedly in the sense of the ultimate ground of being which *integrates* everything else), universality, interpersonal communion. There is a distinct concern in the same sense to indicate the basic criteria for such a liberation: criteria as to the *content* (Christocentricity, fidelity to what is taught in this regard by tradition and the magisterium) and *attitude* (communion with the bishops and with all those who make up the People of God, a positive contribution to the building up of ecclesial communion and not to its destruction). Once again in the same sense, we note the use of this language in its traditional spiritual and ascetic meaning (liberating oneself through sacrifice and penitence).

By the force of its own momentum, this personal and interpersonal liberation received from God tends to penetrate all the concrete aspects of social existence (political, economic, cultural), where the history of the individual and of humankind unfolds.

Liberation generally proceeds from the interior to the exterior (concrete reality). This interior is constantly united to God in whom everything has its source. Here again, we have a basic characteristic of John Paul II's teaching.

The Pope is fully aware of the nature of social structures and the importance of sound social structures for personal development. However, in the context of the Church's specific contribution to human efforts, he constantly refers to the divine and gratuitous sources of that contribution.

He issues a warning against the dangers of confusion and reductionism. Human works (the liberations pursued by women and men) are never the fully adequate sign in themselves, nor even less are they the specific source of the growth of the Kingdom of God.

Finally, within the realm of their real but relative independence, in order to be authentic, the various concrete expressions of liberation cannot be guaranteed by ideologies which do not fully respect all the constituent dimensions of the human person. To an even lesser extent can they claim to liberate us when they subject us to any type of structure, make truth dependent upon praxis, or ultimately claim to free us from faith in God.

The Pope's reservation in using the vocabulary of liberation does not mean that others are prevented from using it more frequently. This fact is clearly confirmed by the very clear and profound communion at Puebla between John Paul II and the Latin American episcopacy which itself uses the word much more often. Also noteworthy is the fact, that while using the word extensively, the Puebla Assembly rejected, by more than a two-thirds vote, a veiled reference to the theologies of liberation in one of the chapters of the final document. It is surely part of the Pope's mission to induce the local churches to bring their language and theological and pastoral developments back within the context of the tradition of the Church, to *test* them by living contact with the whole tradition, and to free them from their narrowness and any possible inadequacies. This is a basic condition for these experiences to be able to reach their full development and benefit the entire Church.

III

DOCUMENTS

INTRODUCTION

In addition to the fourteen essays on liberation thought, it is also of great value to gather together certain official or semi-official statements that assess this movement. The addresses of John Paul II to the Puebla Episcopal Conference and later to a General Audience in Rome on liberation thought are, of course, of central importance. (All of the Holy Father's Mexican-Puebla addresses can conveniently be found in *Puebla: A Pilgrimage of Faith*, Boston: St. Paul, 1979.) The two papal addresses are Documents no. 1 and no. 7. The final statement of the Latin American Bishops themselves is included to reflect how they have heard and analyzed both the Pope's presentation and the situation as they see it (no. 2). The International Theological Commission also presented a detailed analysis of the implications of liberation thought which shows why many of its interpretations cause some difficulty with the structure of the Christian faith (no. 3). The two brief but well-known statements from Chicago (no. 4) and Hartford (no. 5) appeared earlier and from a somewhat different context, but they do serve to emphasize problems that exist in the Latin American movement. Finally, there are included three brief Letters to the Editor of the *New York Times*, critical of the *Times'* very negative Editorial (January 30, 1979) on John Paul II's main Puebla Address.

POPE JOHN PAUL II

TRUTH, UNITY AND HUMAN DIGNITY

INTRODUCTION

Dear brother bishops: This moment which it is my happiness to experience with you is certainly a historic one for the Church in Latin America. World opinion is aware of this. The faithful of your local churches are aware of it. Above all, you yourselves are aware of it, for you play the leading part in it and will be accountable for it.

It is also a moment of grace, for the Lord is passing among us and the Spirit of God is present and active in a special way. For this reason we have confidently invoked the Spirit at the beginning of our labors. For this reason, too, I now want to beg you, as a brother to his very dear brothers: let yourselves be led by the Spirit, open yourselves to his inspiration and influence. Let him, and no other spirit, lead you and be your source of strength.

Under the guidance of this Spirit you, bishops from all the countries, representatives of the episcopate of the entire Latin American continent, are gathering for the third time in twenty-five years to explore together the meaning of your mission as seen in the light of new needs among your peoples.

The conference that is now beginning was convoked by the revered Paul VI, confirmed by my unforgettable predecessor John Paul I and reconfirmed by me in one of the first acts of my pontificate. It is linked to the now long past conference at Rio de Janeiro that had as its most notable result the formation of the Latin American Episcopal Conference (CELAM). It is even more closely linked to the second conference, at Medellín, and marks the tenth anniversary of this latter.

Address of Pope John Paul II at the opening of the third General Conference of the Latin American Episcopate (January 28, 1979). Reprinted by permission from *The Pope Speaks* 24, no. 1 (Spring 1979) 49–67.

What a distance mankind has traveled in these ten years and what a distance the Church has traveled with mankind and in its service! This is a fact which the third conference cannot leave out of consideration. The conference will, therefore, have to take as its point of departure the conclusions reached at Medellín, with all that is positive in them, but without overlooking the erroneous interpretations that have sometimes been given of those conclusions and that require calm discernment, timely criticism and the adoption of clear positions.

The working paper so carefully prepared as a constant point of reference will serve as a guide for your discussions.

You should also have in hand the apostolic exhortation *Evangelii Nuntiandi* of Paul VI. How pleased that great pontiff was to approve the theme of this conference: "The Present and the Future of Evangelization in Latin America"!

You have assurance of this from the people close to him during the months of preparation for the present meeting. They can also testify to the gratitude he felt on learning that the basis for the whole conference was to be this text into which, in the evening of his life, he poured his entire pastoral soul.

Now that he has "closed his eyes to the sights and sounds of this world",[1] the document has become a spiritual testament which the conference will have to study with loving care so as to make it a necessary point of departure and to see how it can be put into practice. The entire Church will be grateful to you for the example you are giving and for what you are doing and what the other local churches will, perhaps, do in their turn.

The pope wishes to be with you as you start your work and he is grateful to "the Father of lights from whom every perfect gift comes"[2] that he could join you in yesterday's solemn Mass under the gaze of the Virgin of Guadalupe, as well as in this morning's Mass. I would greatly like to remain with you during your prayer, reflection and work. Be assured that I will be with you in spirit, even while the "anxiety for all the churches"[3] calls me elsewhere.

[1] Testament of Pope Paul VI, *L'Osservatore Romano* (12 August 1978).
[2] James 1:17.
[3] 2 Cor 11:28.

But before continuing my pastoral visit through Mexico and returning to Rome, I want to leave with you, as a pledge of my presence in spirit, some remarks that express a pastor's solicitude and a father's affection and that reflect my principal concerns in regard to the theme you are to discuss and to the life of the Church in these cherished countries.

TEACHERS OF THE TRUTH

It is a great consolation to the universal pastor to know that you are gathered here not for a symposium of experts or a parliament of politicians or a congress of scientists or technologists, however important these kinds of meetings can be, but for a fraternal meeting of pastors of the Church. As pastors you are keenly aware that your primary duty is to be teachers of the truth, not a human, rational truth but the truth that comes from God and contains within itself the key to man's authentic liberation: "You will know the truth, and the truth will set you free."[4] This is the truth that alone provides a solid basis for an adequate "practice".

I, 1. To watch over the purity of doctrine, the basis for building the Christian community, is, then, together with the preaching of the Gospel, the first duty of the pastor, the teacher of the faith, and nothing can take its place. How often St. Paul emphasized this point, for he was convinced that the fulfillment of this duty was a serious matter.[5]

Unity not in love alone but in truth as well is always a pressing obligation for us. The beloved Pope Paul VI said as much in his apostolic exhortation *Evangelii Nuntiandi*: "The Gospel entrusted to us is also the word of truth. The truth liberates and it alone brings peace of soul. That is the truth men want from us when we proclaim the Good News to them: the truth about God, the truth about man and his hidden destiny, the truth about the world. . . ."

The preacher of the Gospel, then, must be a man who, in complete self-forgetfulness and at whatever cost to himself, is

---

[4] Jn 8:32.
[5] See 1 Tim 1:3–7, 18–20; 4:16; 2 Tim 1:4–14.

always looking for the truth he is to share with others. He never waters down the truth, never hides it, out of a desire to please men or win admiration or rouse astonishment, or in order to be original or call attention to himself. Because we are the shepherds of a believing people, our ministry makes it a duty to guard, defend and communicate the truth without thought to any loss we may suffer or any cost to ourselves."[6]

The Truth about Jesus Christ

I, 2. From you as pastors the faithful of your dioceses expect and ask above all that you vigilantly and zealously transmit to them the truth about Jesus Christ. This truth is at the center of evangelization and provides its essential content: "There is no authentic evangelization unless the name and teaching, the life and promises, the Kingdom and mystery of Jesus the Nazarene, Son of God, are preached."[7]

On the living knowledge of this truth millions of people will depend for the vigor of their faith. Dependent on it, too, will be the strength of their commitment to the Church and their active Christian presence in the world. From this knowledge will flow choices, values, attitudes and modes of behavior that are capable of directing and defining our Christian life and of creating new human beings and, thus, a new human race through the conversion of the individual conscience and the conscience of society.[8]

It is from solid teaching about Christ that light must come on the many doctrinal and pastoral themes and questions you are proposing to study during these days.

No other Gospel

I,3. We must, therefore, confess Christ before the bar of history and before the world and do it with a deep and vividly felt conviction that, as Peter confessed, "You are the Messiah, the Son of the living God."[9]

---

[6] Apostolic exhortation *Evangelii Nuntiandi* (8 December 1975) no. 78.

[7] *Evangelii Nuntiandi*, no. 22.

[8] See ibid., no. 18.   [9] Mt 16:16.

This is the Good News and, in a sense, it is unique: the Church lives by and for it; from it derives all that the Church has to offer to mankind without distinction of nation, culture, race, period of history, age or condition. Consequently, "since that confession of faith [by Peter], the sacred history of salvation has inevitably taken on a new dimension."[10]

This is the sole Gospel and "even if we, or an angel from heaven, should preach to you a Gospel not in accord with the one we delivered to you, let a curse be upon him!" as the Apostle wrote in unmistakable terms.[11]

I, 4. Yet, today, in many places—the phenomenon is not a new one—there are to be found "rereadings" of the Gospel that are the fruit of theoretical speculation rather than of genuine meditation on the word of God and an authentic commitment to the Gospel. They are causing confusion by departing from the essential criteria provided by the faith of the Church. Yet, people are rash enough to hand these rereadings on to Christian communities in the guise of catechesis.

Christ simply a prophet

In some cases the divinity of Christ is passed over in silence or interpretations are given of it which, in fact, are at odds with the Church's faith. Thus, Christ is presented simply as a "prophet" or proclaimer of the Kingdom and the love of God but not as the true Son of God. Consequently, he is not the center and object of the Gospel message.

In other instances people try to show that Jesus played a political role in the struggle against Roman domination and against the powers that be and that he was even involved in a class struggle. This view of Christ as a political agitator or revolutionary, as the subversive from Nazareth, is incompatible with the way he is presented in the Church's catechesis.

The duplicitous claim of those who accused Jesus is taken as representing the real attitude of Jesus himself (though his attitude

---

[10] Homily of Pope John Paul II at the solemn beginning of his pontifical ministry (22 October 1978); *L'Osservatore Romano* (23–24 October 1978).
[11] Gal 1:8.

was in fact quite different), and it is claimed that his death resulted
from a political conflict. Nothing is said of the Lord's deliberate
surrender of himself and of his consciousness of his redemptive
mission.

The Gospels make it clear that in Jesus' eyes anything that
would distort his mission as Servant of the Lord was a temptation.[12] He does not accept the view of those who confuse the
things of God with attitudes that are purely political.[13] He rejects
unequivocally any recourse to violence. He offers his message of
conversion to all, not excluding even the tax collectors. The
purpose of his mission embraces far more than the political order.
It embraces the salvation of the entire person through transforming and peace-giving love, through love that brings forgiveness
and reconciliation.

On the other hand, there is no doubt that all this makes great
demands in regard to the attitude of Christians who want truly to
serve the least of their brethren, the poor, the needy, the outcast
or, in brief, all those in whose lives the suffering face of the Lord
is reflected.[14]

Evangelization and true faith

I, 5. Over against such "rereadings", then, and their perhaps brilliant but none the less fragile and incoherent hypotheses,
"evangelization in present and future Latin America" must continue to assert the faith of the Church, the faith, namely, that Jesus
Christ, Word of God and Son of God, became man in order to
draw near to men and, by the power inherent in his mystery, to
offer them salvation, that great gift of God.[15]

This is the faith that has shaped your history and formed the
highest values of your peoples. This is the faith that must, with all
its energies, continue to vitalize your peoples in their future
activity. This is the faith that makes known to men their call to a
unity and harmony that will banish the dangers of war from this
continent of hope where the Church has been such a powerful
integrating force.

This, finally, is the faith that the faithful of Latin America

12 See Mt 4:8; Lk 4:5.
13 See Mt 22:21; Mk 12:17; Jn 18:36.
14 See the *Dogmatic Constitution on the Church*, no. 8.
15 See *Evangelii Nuntiandi*, nos. 19, 27.

express with such vitality and variety in their popular religious or pious practices.

From this faith in Christ and from the bosom of the Church we draw the power to serve men and our peoples and to make the Gospel permeate their culture, transform hearts and humanize systems and structures.

Any silence, forgetfulness, mutilation or inadequate presentation of the mystery of Jesus Christ in its integrity, any presentation that thus departs from the faith of the Church, cannot validly provide the substance of evangelization.

Amid the harsh crises of the fourth century a great bishop wrote: "Under the cover of a false piety, under the illusory appearance of preaching the Gospel, an attempt is being made these days to deny the Lord Jesus." He added: "I am speaking the truth so that all may realize the cause of the confusion from which we are suffering. I cannot remain silent."[16]

Neither can you, the bishops of our day, remain silent when this kind of confusion is abroad.

That is precisely what Paul VI urged in his opening address to the Medellín conference: "Talk, speak out, preach, write. United in purpose and in program, defend and explain the truths of the faith by taking a position on the present validity of the Gospel, on questions dealing with the life of the faithful and the defense of Christian conduct."[17]

In carrying out my duty of evangelizing all mankind I myself shall not weary of repeating: "Do not be afraid! Open the doors to Christ, open them wide! Open the doors of states to his saving power, open the economic systems and the political systems, the vast realms of culture, civilization and development!"[18]

The Truth about the Church's Mission

I, 6. Teachers of the truth, men expect you to proclaim ceaselessly the truth about the Church's mission and to do it with special fervor in the present situation, for the Church is the

[16] St. Hilary of Poitiers, *Ad Ausentium*, 1–4.

[17] Address of Pope Paul VI at the opening of the Second General Conference of CELAM (24 August 1968), sect. 2.

[18] Pope John Paul II, homily at the solemn beginning of his pontifical ministry (22 October 1978).

subject of an article in the Creed we profess and provides the basic and indispensable context for our fidelity. The Lord established the Church as a fellowship in life, love and truth[19] and as the body, "fullness" (pleroma), and sacrament of Christ in whom the entire fullness of the godhead dwells.[20]

The Church is born from the response of faith that we give to Christ for it is, in fact, by sincere acceptance of the Good News that we, the faithful, gather in the name of Jesus in order that together we may seek and build the Kingdom of God and translate it into our lives.[21] The Church is "the assembly of those who, in faith, look on Jesus as the author of salvation and the source of unity and peace."[22]

On the other hand, we in turn are born of the Church: the Church passes on to us the riches of life and grace of which it is the depositary; it brings us to birth through baptism; it feeds us with the sacraments and the word of God, prepares us for mission and leads us to fulfill God's plan, which is the reason for our existence as Christians. We are the children of the Church and with legitimate pride we call it our Mother, thus repeating a title that comes down to us through the centuries from the earliest times.[23]

The Church our Mother

We must, therefore, invoke the Church, respect it and serve it for "no one can have God for Father who does not have the Church for Mother."[24] "How can anyone say he wants to love Christ but not the Church?"[25] "In the measure that a man loves the Church of Christ he possesses the Holy Spirit."[26]

Love for the Church must include fidelity and trust. In the first address of my pontificate I emphasized my determination to be faithful to the Second Vatican Council and my intention of focusing my major concern on the area of the Church. There I

[19] See the Dogmatic Constitution on the Church, no. 6.

[20] See ibid, no. 7.

[21] See Evangelii Nuntiandi, no. 13.

[22] Dogmatic Constitution on the Church, no. 9.

[23] See Henri de Lubac, The Splendor of the Church (New York: Sheed and Ward, 1956), chap. 7: "Ecclesia Mater".

[24] St. Cyprian, De ecclesiae catholicae unitate, 6.

[25] Evangelii Nuntiandi, no. 16.

[26] St. Augustine, In evangelium Joannis, tractatus 32, 8 (CCL 36:304).

urged my hearers to take in hand once again the dogmatic constitution *Lumen Gentium* and to meditate "with a renewed and invigorating zeal . . . on the nature and function of the Church, its manner of being and acting," in order "not simply to make real the life-giving communion in Christ of all who believe and hope in him but also to work for the closer and more inclusive unity of the entire human family."[27]

I repeat that invitation now, at this moment, that is so extremely important for evangelization in Latin America: "Fidelity to this conciliar document, as understood in the light of tradition and as integrated with the dogmatic formulas enunciated a century ago by the First Vatican Council, will be a sure guide for all of us, pastors and faithful alike, and an incentive—let Us repeat—to walk the ways of life and history."[28]

A solid ecclesiology required

I, 7. There is no assurance of serious and fervent action for evangelization without a solidly grounded ecclesiology.

This is true, first of all, because evangelization is the essential mission, the distinctive vocation and the deepest identity of the Church, which, in turn, has already been evangelized.[29] The Church is sent by the Lord and in turn sends evangelizers to preach "not themselves or their own ideas, but the Gospel, of which neither they nor she are absolute masters with power to use as they wish."[30]

The statement is true, secondly, because "evangelization is not the act of the solitary individual but is wholly ecclesial"[31] and is not to be carried on as the individual thinks best and sees fit but in communion with the Church and its pastors.[32]

For these reasons a correct understanding of the Church is the indispensable prerequisite for a proper understanding of evangelization.

[27] Pope John Paul II, radio message *Urbi et Orbi* after his election as supreme Pontiff (17 October 1978): *L'Osservatore Romano* (18 October 1978).
[28] Ibid.
[29] See *Evangelii Nuntiandi*, nos. 14–15; *Dogmatic Constitution on the Church*, no. 5.
[30] *Evangelii Nuntiandi*, no. 15.
[31] Ibid., no. 60.   [32] See ibid.

How can there be an authentic evangelization if there is lacking a prompt and sincere reverence for the sacred teaching authority of the Church and a clear consciousness that in submitting to it, the people of God are not accepting the word of men but the true word of God?[33] "The 'objective' importance of that authority must always be borne in mind and defended, seeing that crafty attacks are today being made from various sides against certain sure truths of our Catholic faith."[34]

I am well aware of your loyalty to the See of Peter, your readiness to serve it and the love you have always shown it. I thank you from my heart in the name of the Lord for the deeply ecclesial attitude these responses imply and I desire for you the consolation of being able to count on the same loyal attachment from your faithful.

I, 8. In the extensive documentation by which you have prepared for this conference, and especially in the contributions made by many churches, there is perceptible at times a kind of uneasiness regarding the interpretation of the Church's nature and mission. I refer, for example, to the separation some make between the Church and the Kingdom of God.

The latter concept is completely emptied of its proper content and given a quite secularized meaning: The Kingdom is to be reached not through faith and membership in the Church but simply through structural change and sociopolitical involvement. Where there is a certain kind of involvement with and practice in behalf of justice, there the Kingdom is already present.

This is to forget that "the Church . . . receives the mission to preach the Kingdom of Christ and of God and to establish it among all nations" and "is constituted as the seed, the first bud, of this Kingdom on earth."[35]

In one of his beautiful instructions Pope John Paul I spoke of the virtue of hope and commented: "It is a mistake to claim that political, economic and social liberation are identical with salvation in Jesus Christ; that the Kingdom of God is one with the Kingdom of man."[36]

[33] See 1 Th 2:13; *Dogmatic Constitution on the Church*, no. 12.

[34] Pope John Paul II, radio message *Urbi et Orbi* after his election as supreme Pontiff (17 October 1978).

[35] *Dogmatic Constitution on the Church*, no. 5.

[36] Pope John Paul I, address to a general audience (September 20, 1978).

In some instances people have developed an attitude of distrust toward the "institutional" and "official" Church, which is described as an alienating force and contrasted with another, "popular" Church or Church "born of the people" and concretized in the poor. In varying degrees that are not always easy to determine, these positions can imply familiar ideological presuppositions.

The Council, however, has made clear the real nature and mission of the Church, as well as the ways in which a contribution is to be made to its deeper unity and permanent upbuilding by those who have been assigned the ministries of the community and must count on the cooperation of the entire people of God.

In fact, "if the Gospel we proclaim seems divided by disputes over doctrine, opposing views and mutual recriminations among Christians because they differ on Christ and the Church or hold contradictory opinions about society and human institutions, will not those to whom our preaching is directed be confused, led astray and even scandalized?"[37]

The Truth about Man

I, 9. The truth we owe man is above all the truth about himself. As witnesses of Jesus Christ we are heralds, spokesmen, servants of this truth. We may not reduce it to the principles of a philosophical system or to mere political activity; neither may we forget it or betray it.

Perhaps one of the most evident weaknesses of contemporary civilization is its inadequate vision of man. Ours is, beyond a doubt, an age in which much has been written and said about man; it is an age of humanisms and anthropocentrism.

Yet, paradoxically, it is an age in which men experience profound anxiety in regard to their own identity and destiny and in which man has been abased to hitherto unimagined levels. It is an age in which human values have been trampled down as never before.

Man is cut off from God

How is this paradox to be explained? We may say that it is the paradox inseparable from atheistic humanism. It represents the

[37] *Evangelii Nuntiandi*, no. 77.

tragedy of man when he is cut off from an essential dimension of his being—his relation to the Absolute—and is consequently exposed to the worst possible diminution of that same being. The pastoral constitution *Gaudium et Spes* puts its finger on the root of the problem when it says: "Only in the mystery of the Incarnate Word is light shed on the mystery of man."[38]

Thanks to the Gospel the Church possesses the truth about man. This truth is to be found in an anthropology which the Church is constantly endeavoring to understand more fully and communicate. The basic assertion of this anthropology is that man is the image of God and not reducible to a mere fragment of nature or an anonymous component of the human city.[39] St. Irenaeus had this true status of man in mind when he wrote: "The glory of man is God, but the receptacle of all God's action and of his wisdom and power is man."[40]

To this indispensable foundation of the Christian conception of man I was referring in particular when I said in my Christmas Message: "Christmas is the feast of man. . . . Man, the object of calculation when considered from the viewpoint of quantity . . . but at the same time an individual being, unique and unrepeatable. . . . Someone eternally thought of and eternally forechosen; someone called and designated by his own name."[41]

The Church must proclaim the truth about man

In the face of so many other humanisms that are frequently the prisoners of a strictly economic, biological or psychological concept of man, the Church has the right and duty of proclaiming the truth about man that it has received from its teacher, Jesus Christ. God grant that no external coercion may keep it from doing so! God grant, above all, that it may not cease to do so because of fears or doubts, because it has allowed itself to be poisoned by other humanisms, because it lacks confidence in its original message!

[38] *Pastoral Constitution on the Church in the World of Today*, no. 22.

[39] See ibid., no. 12, par. 3, and no. 14, par. 2.

[40] St. Irenaeus, *Adversus haereses*, III, 20, 2–3.

[41] Pope John Paul II, Christmas message *Urbi et Orbi* (25 December 1978), no. 1: *L'Osservatore Romano* (27–28 December 1978).

Therefore, when a bishop of the Church clearly and unambiguously proclaims the truth about man as revealed by him who "was well aware of what was in man's heart,"[42] he should be sustained by the certainty that he is serving man in the best way possible.

This integral truth about man is the basis of the Church's social teaching, as it is the basis of genuine liberation. As seen in the light of this truth, man is not an entity subordinated to economic or political processes; instead, these are ordered to man and subordinated to him.

This truth which the Church teaches about man will surely emerge the stronger from this meeting of bishops.

SIGNS AND BUILDERS OF UNITY

Your pastoral service of the truth is matched by a similar service of unity.

Unity among the Bishops

This unity is to be above all a unity among yourselves, the bishops. As St. Cyprian wrote at a time when communion among the bishops of his own country was seriously threatened: "We must protect and preserve this oneness—especially we bishops who preside over the Church—in order to bear witness that the episcopate too is one and undivided. Let nothing lead the faithful astray or change the truth. The episcopate is one."[43]

This episcopal unity does not come from human calculation and maneuvering but from above: from service to the one Lord, from obedience to the inspiration of the one Spirit, from love for one and the same Church. It is a unity that derives from the mission Christ has entrusted to us, a mission that has been going on in the Latin American continent for almost five hundred years and that you are courageously continuing in a time of profound change, as we approach the end of the second millennium of redemption and ecclesial activity.

[42] Jn 2:25.
[43] St. Cyprian, *De ecclesiae catholicae unitate*, 5.

It is a unity that has its focus in the Gospel, the Body and Blood of the Lamb, and Peter living in his successors. These signs of the presence of Jesus in our midst are quite different each from the others but all are extremely important.

How you must live this unity, dear brothers, in the course of this conference which itself is a sign and fruit of a unity already in existence but also an anticipation and source of an even closer and stronger unity to come! You are beginning your work in an atmosphere of brotherly unity. May this unity be an evangelizing force!

Union with Priests, Religious and Faithful

The unity of the bishops among themselves is prolonged in their union with priests, religious and faithful. Priests are the direct collaborators of the bishops in the pastoral mission and the latter will be jeopardized unless this close unity between them and the bishops prevails.

Religious men and women are likewise especially significant factors in this unity. I am well aware of how important their contribution to the evangelization of Latin America has been and continues to be.

They came here in the very early years of the discovery and first exploration of almost all the countries. They worked here without ceasing at the side of the diocesan clergy. In some countries more than half, in others the great majority of the priests are religious.

This fact alone is enough to make it clear how important it is, here more than in other parts of the world, for religious not only to accept but honestly to cultivate an unconditional unity of purpose and action with the bishops. It is to the bishops that the Lord has entrusted the mission of feeding the flock. It is for them to map out the paths for evangelization. They cannot, must not, be deprived of the responsible and active, yet also docile and trusting collaboration of the religious, whose charism makes them workers all the more available for the service of the Gospel.

The laity, too, are a factor in this unity, whether through their individual involvement or as banded together in apostolic organizations for the spread of God's Kingdom. It is the laity who must, in close union with and obedience to their legitimate pastors, consecrate the world to Christ in their daily occupations and in their various familial and professional duties.

This precious gift of Church unity must be safeguarded among all those who make up the pilgrim people of God, as indicated in *Lumen Gentium*.

DEFENDERS AND PROMOTERS OF DIGNITY

III, 1. Anyone familiar with the history of the Church knows that at every period there have been admirable examples of bishops who were deeply committed to the furtherance and courageous defense of the human dignity of those the Lord had entrusted to them. It was the imperative contained in their episcopal mission that inspired these men, for in their eyes the dignity of man was an evangelical value that cannot be scorned without giving serious offense to the Creator.

This dignity is trampled on, at the individual level, when proper account is not taken of such values as freedom, the right to profess a religion, physical and psychological integrity, the right to essential goods, to life, and so on. It is trampled on, at the social and political level, when a man cannot exercise his right to participate or is subjected to unjust and illicit coercion or to physical or psychological torture and so on.

I am not unaware of the many problems that exist in this area in present-day Latin America. As bishops you cannot be unconcerned with these problems. I know you intend to reflect seriously on the relations and reciprocal connections between evangelization and the advancement or liberation of man and to consider what specific role the Church is to play in this extensive and important area.

Here is where we meet once again, but in their practical application, the themes we broached when speaking of the truth about Christ, the Church and man.

The Church and Social Justice

III, 2. If the Church takes a part in the defense or advancement of human dignity, it does so in the context of its mission. The latter, although religious and not social or political in nature, cannot fail to envisage man as an integral being. In the parable of the Good Samaritan the Lord has presented us with a model of attention to all of man's needs.[44]

He has also told us that in the last analysis he will identify himself with the disinherited—the sick, the imprisoned, the hungry, the lonely—who have been given a helping hand.[45]

The Church has learned from this and other pages of the Gospel[46] that an indispensable part of its evangelizing mission is action in behalf of justice and the tasks involved in advancing human dignity,[47] and that there are very strong links—anthropological, theological and of the order of charity—between evangelization and the advancement of man.[48]

Consequently, "evangelization cannot be complete . . . unless account is taken of the reciprocal links between the Gospel and the personal and social life of man."[49]

Let us also keep in mind, however, that the Church's action in such earthly areas as the advancement of man, development, justice and the rights of persons is meant always to be for the service of man and specifically of man as the Church sees him in the Christian vision of him that it makes its own.

The Church has no need, therefore, of recourse to systems and ideologies in order to love, defend and collaborate in the liberation of man, for at the heart of the message which has been entrusted to it and which it proclaims it finds its inspiration for acting in behalf of brotherhood, justice and peace, and against all forms of domination, enslavement, discrimination, violence, attacks on religious liberty, assaults on man and crimes against life.[50]

Commitment to the Gospel

III, 3. It is, therefore, not out of opportunism or eagerness for novelty that the Church, an "expert on mankind",[51] defends the

[44] See Lk 10:29–35.

[45] See Mt 25:31–46.

[46] See Mk 6:35–44.

[47] See the final document, *Justice in the World*, of the 1971 Synod of Bishops.

[48] See *Evangelii Nuntiandi*, no. 31.   [49] Ibid., no. 29.

[50] See the *Pastoral Constitution*, nos. 26, 27, and 29.

[51] Pope Paul VI, address to the United Nations Organization (5 October 1965).

rights of man. It is because of its *commitment to the Gospel*, which means, as it did for Christ, a commitment to those most in need.

Faithful to this commitment, the Church endeavors to remain free in relation to opposing systems, so that it may come down solely on the side of man. Whatever be the adversities and sufferings that afflict him, it is not by means of violence, the interactions of power or political systems but only by means of the truth regarding himself that man will advance toward a better future.

III, 4. Here is the origin of the Church's constant preoccupation with the sensitive question of property. An indicator of this concern is the writings of the Fathers of the Church during the first thousand years of Christianity.[52]

Clear proof is to be found also in the forceful teaching of St. Thomas Aquinas which has been repeated so often since.

In our own day the Church has appealed to the same principles in such wide-ranging documents as the social encyclicals of recent popes. Pope Paul VI addressed himself to this subject with notable force and depth in his encyclical *Populorum Progressio*.[53]

The voice of the Church, which echoes the voice of the human conscience in this matter, has been raised unceasingly through the centuries amid the most diverse sociocultural systems and situations. It should and must be heard in our age, too, when the increasing wealth of a few is paralleled by the increasing wretchedness of the masses.

No peace without social and economic justice

It is in this situation that the Church's teaching becomes especially urgent as it tells us that all private property is *mortgaged to society*. In regard to this teaching the Church has a mission it must carry out: it must preach, educate individuals and groups, form public opinion, direct those with authority over peoples. By doing so it will work in behalf of society.

This Christian and evangelical principle will finally lead to a more just and equitable distribution of goods, not only within each nation but on the world scene generally, and will prevent

---

[52] See, e.g., St. Ambrose, *De Nabuthae*, 12:53 (*PL* 14:747).

[53] Encyclical letter *Populorum Progressio* (26 March 1967), nos. 23–24; see also Pope John XXIII, encyclical letter *Mater et Magistra* (15 May 1961), no. 106.

the stronger nations from using their power to the detriment of the weaker.

Those who are responsible for the public life of states and nations will have to realize that peace, internal and international, will be assured only if there is a strong social and economic system that is based on justice.

Christ was not indifferent to this immense and demanding requirement of social morality. Neither can the Church be indifferent to it. In the spirit of the Church, which is the spirit of Christ, and in reliance on its extensive and solid teaching, let us set to work in this area.

The whole man

We must emphasize here, once again, that the Church is concerned with the whole man.

For this reason, an indispensable condition for a just economic system is that it foster development and the spread of public education and culture. The more just the economic system, the deeper the consciousness of the culture. This is very much in line with what the Council said, namely, that if man is to attain to a life worthy of himself he must not be content with *having more* but must aspire to *be more*.[54]

Therefore, brothers, drink from these genuine wellsprings. Speak the language of the Council, of John XXIII, of Paul VI. It is a language that reflects the experience, sufferings and hopes of contemporary mankind.

When Paul VI said that "development [is] the new name for peace",[55] he had in mind all the ties of interdependence not only within nations but outside of them, in relation to the rest of the world, as well. He was taking into account the mechanisms which, because they are impregnated not with authentic humanism but with materialism, are producing, on an international scale, the rich who are growing ever richer at the expense of the poor who are growing ever poorer.

[54] See the *Pastoral Constitution*, no. 35.
[55] *Populorum Progressio*, title for nos. 76 ff.

Moral and spiritual primacy

There is no form of economic regulation that is able by itself to change these mechanisms. In international life there must be an appeal to ethical principles, to the demands of justice, to the first commandment which is the commandment of love. Primacy must be given to the moral and the spiritual, to what springs from the integral truth about man.

I wanted to set these thoughts before you because I think them very important, although they are not meant to distract you from the main theme of the conference, namely, that we shall reach man and justice by way of evangelization.

The Church and Liberation

III, 5. In the light of what I have been saying, the Church sees with profound sorrow

> the sometimes massive increase of human rights violations in many parts of the world. . . .
>
> Who can deny that today individual persons and civil powers violate basic rights of the human person with impunity: rights such as the right to be born, the right to life, the right to responsible procreation, to work, to peace, to freedom and social justice, the right to participate in the decisions that affect people and nations?
>
> And what can be said when we face the various forms of collective violence like racial discrimination against individuals and groups, the use of physical and psychological torture perpetrated against prisoners or political dissenters? The list grows when we turn to the instances of the sequestration of persons for political reasons and look at the acts of kidnapping for material gain which so dramatically attack family life and the social fabric.[56]

The Christian concept of liberation

We cry out once again: Respect man! He is the image of God! Preach the Gospel so that this may become a reality! So that

[56] Pope John Paul II, message to the United Nations Organization on the thirtieth anniversary of the Declaration of Human Rights (2 December 1978).

the Lord may transform hearts and humanize the political and economic systems through the responsible involvement of man himself!

III, 6. Pastoral commitments in this area must be inspired by a correct Christian concept of liberation. The Church acknowledges its duty of proclaiming the liberation of millions of human beings and its duty of helping to make this liberation a solid reality,[57] but it also acknowledges a corresponding duty to proclaim liberation in the full and profound sense, as preached and made a reality by Jesus.[58]

This liberation consists not only in "deliverance from all that oppresses man but especially in deliverance from sin and the evil one, together with the joy of knowing God and being known by him."[59] It is a liberation which comprises reconciliation and forgiveness. A liberation which springs from our being the children of God, whom we can now address as "Abba! Father!"[60] and by reason of which we recognize in every man our brother and a person capable of having his heart transformed by a merciful God. A liberation which impels us, by the power of love, toward the communion whose supreme and fullest form we find in the Lord. A liberation which means the conquest of the various enslavements and idols man forges for himself and the growth of the new man.

This liberation, as the Church sees it from the viewpoint of its mission, is not reducible simply to the narrowly economic, political, social or cultural dimension of man, nor can it be sacrificed to the requirements of some strategy or other, to practice or to short-term effectiveness.[61]

Signs of liberation

In order to safeguard the originality of liberation in the Christian sense as well as the energies it is capable of releasing, we must at all costs avoid reductionisms and ambiguities as Paul VI asked: "The Church . . . would have lost her essential meaning. Her

[57] See *Evangelii Nuntiandi*, no. 30.
[58] See ibid., no. 31.   [59] Ibid., no. 9.
[60] See Rom 8:15.
[61] See *Evangelii Nuntiandi*, no. 33.

message of liberation would be radically altered and could easily be twisted and distorted to serve ideological systems and political parties."[62]

There are many signs that can help in discerning when liberation is Christian and when, on the contrary, it is fed rather by ideologies that deprive it of its consistency with an evangelical vision of man, things, and events.[63]

There are signs based on the content of what the evangelizers proclaim and others based on the concrete attitudes of these same evangelizers.

As far as content is concerned, note must be taken of its fidelity to the word of God, to the living tradition of the Church and to the Church's teaching authority.

As for attitudes, it is necessary to ask what sense of communion the evangelizers have with the bishops, first of all, and then with the other sectors of God's people; what contribution they make to the effective building of the community; what kind of loving concern they show for the poor, the sick, the dispossessed, the defenseless and the oppressed, and to what extent they see in such people the image of the "poor and suffering" Jesus and "make an effort to alleviate their wants and strive to serve Christ in them."[64]

Let us not fool ourselves: the humble, simple faithful intuitively understand, by a kind of evangelical instinct, when the Church is serving the Gospel and when it is evacuating the Gospel and letting other interests stifle it.

Importance of the Church's social teaching

As you can see, the various observations which *Evangelii Nuntiandi* made on the subject of liberation are still fully valid.

III, 7. The points we have been recalling constitute the rich and complex heritage which *Evangelii Nuntiandi* calls the social doctrine or social teaching of the Church.[65] It is in the light of the word of God and the authentic teaching of the Church that this doctrine comes into being due to the presence of Christians in the changing situations of the world and to their experience of the

[62] Ibid, no. 32.   [63] See ibid., no. 35.
[64] *Dogmatic Constitution on the Church*, no. 8.
[65] See *Evangelii Nuntiandi*, no. 38.

challenges these situations raise. This social teaching, therefore, contains principles to guide thinking as well as criteria for judgment and directives for action.[66]

A responsible confidence in this social teaching, even though some are trying to sow doubt and distrust of it; the serious study of it; the endeavor to apply it, teach it and be faithful to it: all this, in a son of the Church, guarantees the genuineness of his commitment to the sensitive and demanding tasks of the social order, as well as of his efforts for the liberation or advancement of his brothers.

Allow me, then, to commend to your special pastoral attention the urgent need of making your faithful aware of and sensitive to this social doctrine of the Church.

Special care must be given to the formation of a social conscience at every level and in all sectors. When injustices worsen and the painful distance between rich and poor only widens, this social teaching, if applied in a way that is creative and open to the wide-ranging areas in which the Church is present, should be a valuable means of formation and action.

This is especially true of the laity since "secular offices and tasks belong properly to laymen, though not exclusively."[67] We must avoid doing the laity's work for them and reflect seriously on whether certain kinds of substitution are still justified. Are not laypeople, because of their vocation in the Church, called to make their contribution in the political and economic sphere and to play an effective part in the defense and advancement of human rights?

SOME ESPECIALLY URGENT TASKS

You will be considering a number of pastoral matters that are very important. I do not have time to refer to all of them. I have already mentioned or will be mentioning some of them at my meetings with priests, religious, seminarians and the laity.

[66] See Pope Paul VI, apostolic letter *Octogesima Adveniens* to Cardinal Maurice Roy on the eightieth anniversary of the encyclical *Rerum Novarum* (14 May 1971) no. 4.

[67] *Pastoral Constitution*, no. 43.

IV, 1. The subjects to which I shall call attention here are extremely important, for various reasons. You will not fail to consider them along with the many others which your astuteness as pastors will suggest to you.

1. The family: Make every effort to develop a pastoral ministry to the family. Devote yourselves to this important area in the conviction that evangelization in the future will depend in great measure on the "church of the home". The family is the school of love, of knowledge of God, of respect for life and for the dignity of man. This pastoral ministry is all the more important because the family is subject to so many threats. Think of the campaigns in favor of divorce, of contraception, of abortion, that are destroying society.

2. Vocations to the priesthood and religious life: In the majority of your countries, despite a hopeful increase in vocations, the lack of these remains a serious and chronic problem. There is an immense disproportion between the increasing number of inhabitants and the ministers of evangelization. This fact is of inestimable significance for the Christian community. Every community must yield its own vocations, as a sign, in part, of its vitality and maturity.

There is need to reactivate an intensive pastoral campaign that will, on the basis of an appeal to the common Christian vocation and of an enthusiastic pastoral ministry to youth, provide the Church with the servants it needs. Vocations to the lay state are indispensable but cannot make up for the lack of clerical vocations. Moreover, fruitfulness in vocations to the consecrated life is one proof of the commitment of the laity.

3. Youth: What great hopes the Church sets on the young! What great energies the young of Latin America have and the Church needs! How close we pastors should be to them so that Christ and the Church and the love of their brothers may penetrate deep into their hearts!

V, 1. At the end of this message I cannot but invoke once more the protection of the Mother of God on yourselves and your work during these days. The fact that our meeting is taking place in the spiritual presence of Our Lady of Guadalupe, venerated in Mexico and all the other countries as Mother of the Church in Latin America, is for me a reason for joy and a source of hope.

May she, "the Star of Evangelization", be your guide in your coming deliberations and decisions! May she win for you from her divine Son the daring of prophets and the evangelical prudence of pastors, the perspicacity of teachers and the sureness of leaders and directors, the strength of soul to be witnesses and the serenity, patience, and gentleness to be fathers!

V, 2. May the Lord bless your labors! You have with you chosen representatives—priests, deacons, religious men and women, laypersons, experts, observers—whose collaboration will be of great help to you. The entire Church has its eyes on you, eyes filled with confidence and hope. Strive to meet these expectations in full fidelity to Christ, the Church and man.

The future is in God's hands but, in a way, God is placing the future of this new impetus to evangelization in your hands as well. "Go, therefore, and make disciples of all nations."[68]

[68] Mt 28:19.

II

THIRD GENERAL CONFERENCE
OF THE LATIN–AMERICAN EPISCOPATE AT PUEBLA

TO THE PEOPLES OF LATIN AMERICA:
THE PUEBLA MESSAGE

Our Word: A Word Of Faith, Hope and Charity

Ten years elapsed between Medellín and Puebla. Actually, with the Second General Conference of the Latin American Episcopate, solemnly inaugurated by the Holy Father Paul VI, of happy memory, there opened "a new period of the Church's life". [1] On our continent, marked by Christian hope and weighed down by problems, "God shed an immense light, which shines forth on the rejuvenated face of his Church." [2]

At Puebla de Los Angeles, the Third Conference of the Latin American Episcopate met to take up again the subjects previously discussed and to assume new commitments under the inspiration of the Gospel of Jesus Christ. The universal Pastor of our Church, Pope John Paul II, was with us at the opening of the work, showering on us pastoral attentions which deeply moved us.

His luminous words marked out ample and deep lines for our reflections and deliberations, in a spirit of ecclesial communion. Nourished by the strength and wisdom of the Holy Spirit and under the motherly protection of the Blessed Virgin, Our Lady of Guadalupe, we have carried out our great task with dedication, humility, and confidence. Bound for our particular churches, we cannot leave Puebla without addressing to the people of God in Latin America a word of faith, hope and charity which can be

Message of Pope John Paul II to the peoples of Latin America, given at the third General Conference of the Latin American Episcopate (February 13, 1979). Reprinted by permission from *L'Osservatore Romano*, English edition (26 February 1979) 10–11.

[1] See the opening speech of Paul VI.

[2] Introduction to the Medellín documents.

extended to all peoples of the world. In the first place, we wish to describe ourselves: we are pastors of the Catholic and apostolic Church, born of the Heart of Jesus Christ, the Son of the living God.

Our Question and Request for Forgiveness

Our first question, in this pastoral conversation, before the collective conscience, is the following: In our continent, are we living, in practice, the Gospel of Christ? This question, which we address to Christians, can be analyzed also by all those who do not share our faith.

Christianity, which brings with it the originality of love, is not always practiced in its entirety by us Christians. It is true that there exist great hidden heroism, much silent holiness, many marvelous acts of sacrifice. We recognize, however, that we are still far from practicing all that we preach. For all our shortcomings and limitations, we pastors, too, ask God and our brothers in faith and in humanity for forgiveness.

We wish not only to convert others, but also to convert ourselves together with others in order that our dioceses, parishes, institutions, communities and religious congregations may be, not an obstacle, but, on the contrary, an incentive to live the Gospel.

If we turn our eyes to our Latin American continent, what sight does it offer us? A thorough examination is not necessary. It is true that the gap between the many who possess little and the few who possess a lot, is increasing. The values of our culture are in danger. Fundamental human rights are being violated. The great initiatives in favor of man are unable to solve adequately the problems that demand our attention.

Our Contribution

But what have we to offer before the serious and complex problems of our time? How can we collaborate in the welfare of our Latin American peoples, when some people cling obstinately to their privileges at all costs, others feel discouraged, and again others promote initiatives to be able to survive and clearly assert their own rights?

Beloved brothers, once more we are anxious to declare that in dealing with social, economic and political problems we do not intend to do so as teachers on the matter, but as interpreters of our peoples, aware of their aspirations, particularly those of the most humble, who are the great majority of Latin American society.

What can we offer? Like Peter faced with the entreaty addressed to him at the gates of the temple, considering what great structural challenges are present in our society, we say: "We have no silver and gold, but we give you what we have; in the name of Jesus Christ of Nazareth, walk" (cf. Acts 3:6). And the sick man got up and proclaimed the greatness of the Lord. Thus Peter's poverty becomes riches and Peter's riches are called Jesus of Nazareth, who died and rose again, always present, by means of his divine Spirit, in the apostolic college and in the newborn communities formed under his direction. The act of healing the sick man indicates that God's power requires the greatest effort on the part of men in order to cause his work of love to ferment and bear fruit through all available means: spiritual forces, and the achievements of science and technique in favor of man.

What can we offer? John Paul II, in the opening address of his pontificate in St. Peter's Square, replies to us in an incisive, stupendous way, presenting Christ as the answer of universal salvation: "Do not be afraid! Open wide the doors to Christ! To his saving power open the boundaries of states, economic and political systems, the vast fields of culture, civilization and development."

It seems to us that here lies the potentiality of the seeds of liberation for the Latin American man, our hope to construct, day by day, the reality of our true destiny. Thus the men of this continent, the object of our pastoral concern, have an essential significance for the Church, since Christ assumed humanity and its actual condition, except sin. And, by so doing, he shared the immanent and transcendent vocation of all men.

Man struggles, suffers, and sometimes despairs, yet never loses heart, and seeks in the first place to live the full significance of his divine filiation. For this purpose it is important that his rights should be recognized, that his life should not be a kind of abomination, that nature, the work of God, should not be devastated contrary to his legitimate aspirations. Man demands, for reasons that are more than evident, that physical and moral violence, abuse of power, manipulation of money, abuse of sex, and, finally, the breaking of the Lord's commandments, should be eliminated; because what is contrary to man's dignity wounds God in a certain way. "All are yours; and you are Christ's; and Christ is God's" (1 Cor 3:23).

What interests us as pastors is the complete proclamation of the truth about Jesus Christ, the mission of the Church, and the nature, dignity, and ultimate purpose of man.[3] And therefore our message feels illuminated by hope. The difficulties we meet with, the imbalances we perceive, do not drive us to pessimism. It is true that the socio-cultural context in which we live is so contradictory, on the ideological plane and on the practical plane, as to lead not only to the shortage of material goods in the homes of the poorest but, what is even more serious, it tends to take away from them also their greatest treasure, which is God. This fact induces us to exhort all responsible members of society to revise their plans and, at the same time, imposes on us the sacred duty of struggling to maintain and deepen the sense of God in the conscience of the people. Like Abraham, we struggle and will struggle, "hoping against hope", that is, we will never stop hoping in the grace and power of the Lord, who established with his people an indestructible covenant, despite our breaches of trust.

It is moving to perceive in the soul of the people spiritual riches overflowing with faith, hope and love. From this standpoint, Latin America is an example for all the other continents, and in the future it will be able to expand its sublime missionary vocation beyond its frontiers. So *Sursum Corda*! Raise up your hearts, beloved brothers of Latin America, because the Gospel which we preach is such splendid good news as to convert and transform minds and hearts, since it can communicate the greatness of man's destiny, prefigured in the risen Christ.

Our pastoral preoccupations for the humblest members of the social body, some of whom are imbued with human realism, do not intend to exclude from our concern and from our hearts the other representatives of the social framework in which we live. On the contrary, they constitute serious and opportune warnings

[3] John Paul II, opening address.

in order that gaps may not increase, sins may not multiply, and the spirit of God not depart from the Latin American family.

And since we believe that the revision of the religious and moral behavior of men must be reflected in the political and economic spheres in our countries, we call upon all, without distinction of class, to accept and make their own the cause of the poor as though it were a question of accepting and making their own the cause of Christ himself. "As you did it to one of the least of these my brethren, you did it to me" (Mt 25:40).

Latin American Episcopate

Brothers, do not let yourselves be impressed by news that the episcopate is divided. There are differences of outlook and opinions, but we really live the principle of collegiality, completing one another, according to the capacities given by God. Only in this way shall we be able to face up to the great challenge of evangelization in the present and future of Latin America.

The Holy Father John Paul II indicated in his address at the opening of the Third Conference (in the fifth part), among other suggestions, three pastoral priorities: the family, youth and the apostolate of vocations.

The Family

We call, then, with special affection, the family of Latin America to take its place in the heart of Christ, transforming itself more and more every day into a privileged place of evangelization, of respect for life, and of community love.

Youth

We call cordially on the young to overcome the obstacles that threaten their rights to conscious and responsible participation in the construction of a better world. We do not wish them sinful absence at the table of life or sad abandonment to the imperatives of pleasure, indifferentism, or voluntary and unproductive solitude. The time of protest, expressed in exotic forms or by means of inopportune exaltation, is now over. Your capacity is immense. The time has come for reflection and full acceptance of the challenge to live fully the essential values of true and complete humanism.

Agents of the apostolate

With words of affection and confidence, we greet all those, of all categories, who generously exercise the apostolate in our particular churches. Exhorting you to continue your labors in favor of the Gospel, we call upon you to make an increasing effort for the apostolate of vocations, in the sphere of which there is space for the ministries entrusted to laity in virtue of their baptism and confirmation. The Church needs more diocesan and religious priests, as wise and holy as possible, for the ministry of the word and the Eucharist, and for the greater efficacy of the religious and social apostolate. It needs laity aware of their mission within the Church and in the construction of the temporal city.

Men of Good Will and the Civilization of Love

And now we desire to address all men of good will, all those who are engaged in tasks and missions in the most varied fields of culture, science, politics, education, work, the media of social communications, art.

We call upon them to be generous constructors of the "civilization of love" (Paul VI), inspired by the word, the life, and the full donation of Christ, and based on justice, truth and freedom. We are sure that in this way we will obtain your answer to the imperatives of the present time, to the hoped-for interior and social peace in persons, families, countries, continents and the whole universe.

We wish to explain the organic meaning of the civilization of love in this difficult but hopeful hour for Latin America. What does the commandment of love enjoin upon us? Christian love surpasses the categories of all existing regimes, because it brings with it the insuperable force of the paschal mystery, the value of the suffering of the Cross and the signs of victory and Resurrection. Love produces the happiness of communion and inspires the criteria of participation. Justice, as is known, is a sacred right of all men, conferred by God himself. It is integrated in the very essence of the Gospel message. Truth, illumined by faith, is a perennial source of discernment for our ethical conduct. It corresponds to our human condition and is an indispensable factor for the progress of peoples.

The civilization of love rejects violence, selfishness, waste, exploitation and moral disorders. At first sight this seems an expression deprived of the necessary energy to face up to the serious problems of our time. On the contrary, we assure you, there is no stronger word in the Christian dictionary. It merges with Christ's own strength. If we do not believe in love, we do not believe either in him who says, "This is my commandment, that you love one another as I have loved you" (Jn 15:12).

The civilization of love proposes to all the evangelical riches of national and international reconciliation. There is no act more sublime than forgiveness. He who is unable to forgive will not be forgiven (cf. Mt 6:12).

Renunciation and solidarity must have great weight on the scales of common responsibilities, in order that there may be a correct equilibrium of human relations. Meditation on this truth would lead our countries to revise, in harmony with the common good, in charity and without harm to justice, their behavior with regard to exiles and other consequent problems. There are numberless traumatized families in our continent.

The civilization of love condemns absolute divisions and psychological walls which violently separate men, institutions and national communities. Therefore, it defends with ardor the thesis of the integration of Latin America. In unity and in variety, there are elements of continental value which deserve to be appreciated and studied far more than purely national interests. Our countries of Latin America must be reminded of the urgent necessity of preserving and increasing the heritage of continental peace; because it would be a tremendous historical responsibility to break the ties of Latin American friendship, convinced as we are that there are juridical and moral remedies for the solution of problems of common interest.

The civilization of love rejects subjection and dependence, detrimental to the dignity of Latin America. We do not accept being a satellite of any country in the world, far less of its ideologies. We wish to live on brotherly terms with everyone, because we reject narrow and inflexible nationalisms. It is time for Latin America to tell developed countries not to keep us at a standstill, not to hinder our progress, not to exploit us; on the contrary, to help us generously to overcome the barriers of our underdevelopment, respecting our culture, our principles, our sovereignty, our identity, our natural resources. In this spirit we will grow united, like brothers, members of the same universal family.

Another point that worries and distresses us is the arms race, which does not cease to manufacture instruments of death. It brings with it the painful ambiguity of confusing the right to national defense with the ambitions of unlawful gains. It is not calculated to construct peace.

Ending our message, we respectfully and confidently call upon all those in charge of the political and social order to dwell on these reflections which have sprung from our experiences, the direct children of our pastoral sensitivity.

Believe us: we desire peace; and to reach it, it is necessary to eliminate elements that cause tensions between having and power, between being and its most just aspirations. To work for justice, for truth, for love and for freedom, in the framework of communion and participation, is to work for universal peace.

Final Word

And now the final word. At Medellín we ended our message with the following affirmation: "We have faith in God, in men, in the values and in the future of Latin America." At Puebla, taking up again this profession of divine and human faith, we proclaim: "God is present, alive, in Jesus Christ the liberator, in the heart of Latin America. We believe in the power of the Gospel. We believe in the efficacy of the evangelical value of communion and participation to bring forth creativity, and to promote experiences and new pastoral projects. We believe in the grace and strength of the Lord Jesus who instills life, who pushes us to conversion and solidarity. We believe in the hope which nourishes and strengthens man on his way to God, our Father. We believe in the civilization of love."

May our Lady of Guadalupe, the patron saint of Latin America, accompany us, solicitous as always, in this pilgrimage of peace.

III

INTERNATIONAL THEOLOGICAL COMMISSION

HUMAN DEVELOPMENT
AND CHRISTIAN SALVATION

Introduction

The problem of the relationship between human development and
Christian salvation is of considerable significance everywhere.
This is especially evident since the Second Vatican Council,
where the Church paid uncommon attention to issues of an
appropriate world order within the context of Christian responsibility. Within Latin America and elsewhere, it was different
types of liberation theology that increasingly won attention. The
International Theological Commission, in its annual meeting,
October 4–9, 1976, occupied itself less with individual treatises and
individual tendencies, more with basic issues touching the relationship between human development and Christian salvation.

The pages that follow should be regarded as an imperfect
abridgment of the principal results. This final report takes
account of the difficulties inherent in the issues studied and the
current status of theological discussion and research. The theological tendencies in question are many and varied, subject to
enormous changes; there is constant self-correction; they are
intimately linked with social and economic conditions and the
political situation in the world and in different geographical
areas. Nor should we overlook the disputes that such theological
treatises have occasioned on many sides because theology risks
being translated into politics and hurting the genuine unity of the
Church. Given this state of affairs, the International Theological
Commission wants to address itself to the discussion for a specific
purpose: to search out the potential and the risk in such tendencies.

Karl Lehmann
Chairman of the Subcommittee

Reprinted from *Origins* 7, no. 20 (3 November 1977) 306–13.

World Poverty and Injustice as Springboard for a Theological Movement

The Second Vatican Council reminded the Church of its ceaseless duty to "scrutinize the signs of the times and to interpret them in the light of the Gospel."[1] A special incentive to carry out this injunction was provided by the documents emanating from the Second General Assembly of the Latin American Episcopal Conference (CELAM) held in 1968 in Medellín, Colombia: the Church hears the outcries of poor peoples and makes itself the interpreter of their oppressive conditions. The Church's worldwide solicitude in response to the challenge hurled by oppression and hunger is shown not only by papal documents—*Mater et Magistra, Pacem in Terris, Populorum Progressio, Octogesima Adveniens*—but also by documents of the Synod of Bishops held in Rome in 1971 (*Justice in the World*) and in 1974. Pope Paul VI once again highlighted the Church's urgent duty in this regard with his apostolic exhortation of December 8, 1975, *Evangelization in Today's World*.[2]

These circumstances must be taken into account if the theological treatises on these issues are to be understood. Although they have a scholarly face, their primary source is not theoretical, scientific effort. They are not presented in the first instance as a "written" theology; they struggle to preserve close contact with the day-to-day existence of overburdened men and women and with the concrete injunction to action that challenges the Church in this factual situation. They intend to give public expression to the cries of our poor, anguished brothers and sisters—specifically, to hunger, disease, unjust profit, exile, oppression. Add to this the inhuman living conditions of all those who own only what they wear, sleep at night in the streets, live and die there, lack basic medical care. For Christians enlightened by the Gospel, these "signs of the times" are an exceptionally sharp stimulus to bend every effort, in the name of Christian faith, to free their brothers and sisters from inhuman living conditions. This attention to the needy, this affinity with all the oppressed, are

[1] *Gaudium et Spes*, 4.
[2] Cf. nos. 30–38.

singularly expressed and exemplified by the biblical words
"justice", "liberation", "hope", "peace".

This witness to solicitude for the poor, a witness supported by
the Gospel of Jesus Christ,[3] is something of a ceaseless spiritual
leaven in all the pertinent theological treatises; it obviously inspires their theological reflections and political options. A spiritual experience arouses innate forces whereby the pressures of
Christian love are transformed into commands effective for action by means of human reflection and scientific analysis.

Both elements, a basic spiritual experience and theological
and scientific reflection, are mutually complementary and consequently fashion a vital unity. But we must be careful not to
confound the two elements. No one, therefore, should condemn
these various theological systems if he is not listening at the same
time to the cries of the poor and seeking more acceptable ways to
respond. On the other hand, we must ask whether the types
of theological reflection currently in vogue are, in their actual
methodology, the only way of responding appropriately to
yearnings for a more human world of brothers and sisters. The
point is, every theology has service for its function, and so must
at times undergo needed changes and corrections, if these help it
to achieve its primary commission more effectively.

A New Type of Theology and Its Difficulties

The theological treatises of which we have spoken stem from
conditions in which human persons are oppressed, are slavishly
subject to others in economic, social and political life, and yearn
for freedom. This existential human story is not accepted as an
unchangeable destiny; it is understood as a "creative" process that
looks to a larger freedom in all sectors of life and ultimately to the
fashioning of a "new man". To change inhuman conditions is
seen as a divine demand, as God's will: Jesus Christ, who by his
redemptive action freed human persons from sin in all its forms,
offers a new basis for human brotherhood.

This way of thinking, which is the springboard for the theological treatises of which we are speaking, gives them a special

[3] Cf. Lk 4:18 ff.

form that is in a sense new. God reveals his mysterious plan in actual events; and the more intimately the Christian enters into concrete situations and the historical progression of events, the more appropriately he responds to God's word. In consequence, the Christian recognizes the profound unity that links the divine history of salvation accomplished through Jesus Christ to efforts undertaken for the welfare and rights of men.

Although secular history and salvation history should not be regarded as simply identical, still the relationship between the two is to be conceived in the first instance as a unity. Their distinction may not be extended to a dualism in which history and salvation would be represented as indifferent one to the other. In fact, human activity acquires an entirely new value in history, a theological value, in that it builds up a more human society; for the construction of a just society is, in a sense, the inauguration of God's Kingdom in anticipation.[4] Therefore Christian faith is understood principally as a historical praxis whereby sociopolitical conditions are changed and renewed.

This way of thinking contains many elements of great value; for it is indeed true that Christians should have a richer understanding of the total unity that their calling to salvation involves.[5] Nor can we doubt that faith, in its Scriptural sense, can be fructified and perfected only by deeds. Moreover, the Second Vatican Council reminds us[6] that the Holy Spirit is active in world history; even outside the visible Church the preludes to faith, that is, the truths and rules of right reason about God and the common good, which are a kind of foundation for the Christian religion, are found to some extent.[7]

Nevertheless, in some theological movements this elemental data is interpreted in a one-sided fashion that is open to objection. The unity that links world history and salvation history may not be so conceived that it tends to consolidate the Gospel of Jesus Christ, which as a supernatural mystery is altogether unique and

[4] Reference is made at times to *Gaudium et Spes*, 39.

[5] Cf. *Gaudium et Spes*, 10, 11, 57, 59, 61: *Ad Gentes Divinitus*, 8; *Populorum Progressio*, 15–16.

[6] Cf. *Gaudium et Spes*, 22, 26, 38, 41, 57; *Dignitatis Humanae*, 12.

[7] Cf. First Vatican Council, dogmatic constitution *Dei Filius* (DS 3005).

beyond human intelligence,[8] with secular history. Nor can it mean that the boundaries between Church and world are utterly effaced.

In a similar vein, the world in its historical existence is indeed the place where God's saving plan is unfolding—but not in such a way that the force and dynamism of God's word consist totally in its function of stimulating social and political change. And so faith's praxis is not reducible to changing the conditions of human society; for besides laying injustice bare, faith's praxis includes such things as conscience formation, change in mental attitude, adoration of the true God and of our Savior Jesus Christ in distinction from all forms of idolatry. Consequently, "faith as praxis" should not be interpreted in such a way that one's involvement in politics embraces and governs all human efforts and actions totally and "radically". Two points call for clarification here:

1. Political controversy, which is customarily linked with confrontation, should not be carried to the point where it obscures or obliterates peace and reconciliation as the objective and fruit of Christian activity, and what takes priority is an increase of antagonism and the onset of violence.

2. It must remain beyond dispute that for the Christian politics is not the final ground that gives ultimate meaning to all of life; it is not an absolute in the Christian eon; and so its nature is to be an instrument, a servant. Overlook this, and human freedom is threatened by movements that promote dictatorial control. Although theology is oriented in part toward praxis, its more prominent function is to seek understanding of God's word; for whatever engages it, theology must be able to distance itself from a concrete situation, which is almost always attended by various pressures and compulsions to action. It is from the principles of Catholic teaching on faith and morals that we can derive the light to make correct judgments about what has to be done to acquire eternal salvation without risk of losing the freedom of God's children. Only in this way is theology tied to truth; only in this way can it preserve the sovereign authority of God's word and

[8] Cf. ibid.

the altogether unique character of that word. And so we have to take special care not to fall into a unidimensional vision of Christianity that would adversely affect Christology and ecclesiology, our view of salvation and of Christian existence, even theology's proper function.

Prophetic charges of injustice and urgent appeals to make common cause with the poor have to do with situations that are highly complex in nature, have roots in history and depend on social and political realities. Even a prophetic judgment on the circumstances of a time calls for assured reasons or criteria. That is why the different theological treatments of liberation must deal simultaneously with theories that come from the social sciences, which study objectively what the "outcry of the people" expresses.

Theology, however, cannot deduce concrete political norms sheerly from theological principles; and so the theologian cannot settle profound sociological issues by theology's specific resources. Theological treatises which strive to build a more human society must take into account the risks that the use of sociological theories involves. In every instance these theories must be tested for their degree of certitude, inasmuch as they are often no more than conjectures and not infrequently harbor explicit or implicit ideological elements that rest on debatable philosophical assumptions or on an erroneous anthropology. This is true, for instance, of significant segments of analyses inspired by Marxism and Leninism. Anyone who employs such theories and analyses should be aware that these do not achieve a greater degree of truth simply because theology introduces them into its expositions. In fact, theology ought to recognize the pluralism that exists in scientific interpretations of society and realize that it cannot be fettered to any concrete sociological analysis.

Biblical—Theological Facets

Since the theological treatises we have been discussing often appeal to sacred Scripture, we should take care to uncover what the Old and New Testaments have to say about the relationship between salvation and human welfare, between salvation and human rights. Obviously, our reflections here must be incomplete. On the other hand, we must avoid the anachronism that would read contemporary ideas back into the Bible.

Old Testament

To determine the relationship between divine salvation and human development, practically everyone now cites the Exodus story. The reason is, the exodus from Egypt[9] is actually a salvation event of capital importance in the Old Testament: liberation from foreign tyranny and from works forced by public powers. Nevertheless, "liberation" in the Old Testament is not totally situated in the removal from Egypt and the return from exile; for the liberation is oriented to the covenant worship solemnized on Mount Sinai,[10] and apart from that orientation it loses its specific meaning. The Psalms themselves, when they deal with need and protest, with aid and thanks, reveal forms of prayer that express salvation and "liberation".[11] There distress is identified not only with social affliction but also with hostility, injustice, blameworthy fault, as well as with that to which this leads: the threat that is death and the void death represents. Less significance, therefore, is placed on felt needs in individual instances; more important is the convincing experience that only God can bring deliverance and salvation.

Consequently, one should not speak of Old Testament salvation in its relation to human rights and welfare without simultaneously revealing the complete theological argumentation: it is not man but Yahweh who effects change. Besides, as long as the exodus lasted, in the desert, it was especially for the spiritual liberation and purification of his people that God provided.

A moving instance of an effort inspired by God's revelation to improve conditions of human living is the rebuke to the social order sounded by the prophets, especially in Amos.[12] Later prophets take up and enlarge the theme initiated by Amos, as when they cry "woe" on those who own large estates.[13] In

[9] Cf. Ex 1–24
[10] Cf. Ex 24.
[11] Cf., e.g., Ps 18.
[12] Amos 2:6 f.; 3:10; 5:11; 6:4 ff.; 8:4 ff.
[13] Cf. Is 5:8 f.; Micah 2.

powerful language Hosea censures the absence of human solidarity.[14] Isaiah explicitly includes widows and orphans among
those who must be protected.[15] He threatens that the Lord will
take away from Jerusalem "the powerful and the strong", that is,
the more potent leaders in the society;[16] he complains about
possessions accumulating in the hands of a few[17] or, more
broadly, about the oppression of the poor by the rich.[18] But he is
clearly far from calling for revolt against the oppressors, even
though this theme is discoverable in Old Testament writings.[19]
Presentiment of impending disaster keeps a program for a more
equitable society from making its appearance.[20] The prophets
believe that there are many different ways of succoring society in
its needs. But instead of an optimism supposedly supported by a
theology of history, they show a large measure of skepticism on
man's ability actually to fashion a different world.

Such a change must be preceded by a way of acting that is
proper to interior conversion and justice. "Cease to do evil, learn
to do good; seek justice, assist the oppressed, defend the father-
less, plead for the widow."[21] It is God who must give men the
power to bring about a greater degree of justice in the social
sphere: in the last analysis Yahweh alone can efficaciously provide for human rights and welfare, especially of the oppressed.[22]
God works salvation beyond the good or evil designs of men.

In this connection, the prophets do recognize something akin
to the "corrupt system". As they see it, however, we may not
reduce everything to the point where evil is only a sign and effect
of society's unjust structures or where we could hope to correct
abuses simply by abolishing possessions. Over and above this,
we must keep in mind the personal element, which determines

[14] Hos 4:1 f.; 6:4, 6; 10:12.
[15] Is 1:17, 23; 10:1 f.
[16] Cf. Is 3:1 ff.; 1:21 ff.; 10:1 ff.
[17] Cf. Is 5:8.
[18] Cf. Is 1:21 ff.; 3:14 f.
[19] Cf. Jg 9:22 f.; 1 Kings 12.
[20] Note a beginning in Joel 3:1 f.
[21] Is 1:16 f.
[22] Cf. Is 1:24 ff.; Ex 3:7–9; Ps 103:6; 72:12 ff.; Dt 10:17 ff.

the process of "liberation" for the Old Testament. This is particularly exemplified and confirmed by the principle of individual responsibility.[23]

Some significant passages of the Old Testament disclose partial visions of a new society, no longer arranged along the lines of pervasive contemporary structures.[24] Many Psalms speak expressly of God as liberator of the oppressed and defender of the poor.[25] While freeing the people of Israel from oppression, God demands of them that they remove all human oppression.[26] God's lordship, once it comes, will eliminate all tyranny of man over man.

In the Old Testament, however, this hope is long not distinguished with sufficient clarity from concrete history and does not bear on realities which transcend that history. Even down to our own time, a fair number of ideologies of a "secularized" salvation look for these promises of God to be realized within the limits of history, and simply in consequence of man's activity; but this, we have seen, the Old Testament rejects. Lastly, we should recall that in the apocalyptic passages of the later Old Testament the hope of a life after this life and the theology of history commend in remarkable fashion man's experienced weakness and God's omnipotence.

New Testament

The New Testament takes up significant elements of the Old[27] or presupposes them.[28] As the discourse on the Beatitudes shows strikingly,[29] the Old Testament insistence on conversion and renewal of the human spirit is intensified, and in the New Testament these demands can be quite effectively realized by the power of the Holy Spirit. Still the impression remains—and it has been

[23] Cf. Ezek 18; Jer 31:29 ff.
[24] Cf., e.g., Is 55:3–5; Ex 34; 40–48; Jer 31:31 ff.
[25] Cf. Ps 9, 10, 40, 72, 76, 146; Judith 9:11.
[26] Cf. Ex 22:10; Lev 19:13, 18, 33; Dt 10:18; 24:14; Ps 82:2–4.
[27] Cf., e.g., Is 61:1 f., as cited in Lk 4:16 ff.
[28] Cf. Mk 12:29 ff. and Lev 19:18.
[29] Cf. 5:1–7:29, esp. 5:3–12.

stated time and again—that the New Testament is not primarily concerned about the social sphere and human togetherness.

Possibly the unique newness of the Christian message initially tempered concern for questions that involved worldly duties. The personal love of the incarnate God for his new people was so transcendently important that questions prompted by temporal existence could not take priority (recall only the expectation of God's Kingdom). With the spotlight on the mystery of our suffering and risen Lord, sheerly human needs could assume less urgency. The political situation of the Roman Empire prevented Christians from turning their minds freely and extensively to the world.

However, this is not the place to explain in detail how Jesus' Good News and New Testament ethics imparted many directive norms and patterns of human conduct which were capable of inspiring a "social critique". Enough that we think of the command to love neighbor and enemy,[30] of the exhortatory and threatening words to the wealthy and the glutted,[31] of the obligation to care for the poor and the weak[32] and the admonition to all to help others,[33] of avoiding the temptation to exercise control over others[34]—on the ground that all human beings are brothers and sisters.[35]

Moreover, the New Testament discloses in the faithful a disposition to welcome "institutional" forms of Christian charity. Examples are the contributions taken up for Jerusalem[36] and the arrangement for the ministries of "diaconate" and charitable aid.[37] But it is clear that such "institutional" helps, at least in the beginning, were restricted to the ambit of the Christian communities and were quite undeveloped.

The New Testament also attaches great significance to the element of liberation, but we must be uncommonly careful to

[30] Cf. Lk 6:35 f.; Mt 25:31–46.
[31] E.g., Lk 6:24 ff.; Mt 6:24; 1 Cor 11:20 ff.; Lk 12:16 ff.; James 2:1 ff.; 5:1 ff.
[32] Cf. Lk 6:20; 1 Cor 12:22 ff.
[33] Mk 10:21; Lk 12:33.
[34] Cf. Mk 10:42–45; Mt 20:25–28; Lk 22:25–27.
[35] Cf. Mt 23:8; 25:41 ff.
[36] Cf. 2 Cor 8:1 ff.
[37] Cf. 1 Cor 12:28; 15:15; Rom 12:7; 16:1; Phil 1:1; 1 Tim 3:8, 12.

uncover its genuine sense. St. Paul's words about the new freedom are closely linked to his message on justification; and so
liberation as such is not a theme severed from his other themes.
The salvific work of Jesus Christ opened even the inner chambers
of the human heart; so it is easy to be mistaken about what
constitutes true denial of human freedom, true slavery. The
announcing of justification shows with consummate clarity that
the human person is prey to evil powers.

Authentic, complete liberty is impossible without the primary
liberation[38] from death and perishability (*sarx*), from the power
of sin and from the law (note also the "elements of the world").
"It is with this freedom that Christ has set us free."[39]

Liberation from these powers, however, brings a fresh freedom, in consequence of which we can, in the spirit of Jesus
Christ, be effective in love so as to serve our brothers and
sisters.[40] Here surely we have a foreshadowing of what God will
himself accomplish as his gift to the just when he judges the
whole story of humankind. The justice of God, through the
Spirit and by his power, bestows a liberating action that enables
us to work what is good, an action that finds its perfection
through love.

And so, when the New Testament speaks of "the liberation
that brings freedom",[41] the freedom that is grace, moral stimulus, and eschatological promise, these utterances are inserted
into the proclamation of justification. Only if they rest on this
foundation do they acquire their full force and power. Only if we
bring our reflections to these depths can we understand and
actualize the stimulus the New Testament offers Christians for
liberating activity.

In the light of the New Testament, society is not genuinely
changed unless men are reconciled with God and with one
another. Only if men become a new creation by conversion and
justice can the conditions of human life be adequately and steadily
improved. Human rights and welfare, therefore, human liberation, are not situated in the category of "having", but primarily

---

[38] Cf. Rom 5–7.
[39] Gal 5:1.
[40] Cf. Gal 5:6, 13.
[41] Cf. Gal 5:1.

within the boundaries that comprise "being"—including, of course, the implications that flow therefrom for shaping all the situations of human living.

Systematic and Theological Reflections

God as liberator and man's liberating action

It has been noted that not all the Old Testament affirmations on liberation can be extended in every respect to the New Testament situation. The revelation given us in Christ divides the uninterrupted process of salvation history into two periods: promise and fulfillment. But both Testaments are at one in the conviction that God alone, precisely as supreme and utterly free Lord, administers human welfare; only he is properly liberator. This becomes clear, however, only when the needs of men and women are not reduced simply to their economic and material problems, only when we grasp the complete spectrum of their risk-laden, corrupt situation. Still, the unshakable proposition "God alone really frees" should not be interpreted as a kind of myth (as if we were talking about a *Deus ex machina*); such a myth can only increase the indolence, inactivity and apathy of those in straitened circumstances. Genuine faith does not condone inhuman living conditions, does not countenance them. God does not come to us in the violent hurricane of a revolution, but by his grace he strengthens the mind and heart of men so that they sharpen their conscience and, led by a living faith, build a more just world. To achieve this, however, the *whole* person must be freed from *all* the powers of evil. That is why an effectual change of mind and heart (*metanoia*) and a renewal of love for God and neighbor bring about actual liberation. But full liberation, according to Christian belief, is not accomplished in the course of earthly events, in history. For history leads to a "new earth" and to the "city of God"; consequently, until this fulfillment is realized, every liberating activity has a transitory character—and at the Last Judgment it will have to undergo its own ultimate testing.[42]

[42] Cf. Mt 25.

The relevance of our reflections, however, should not be restricted to spiritual reformation or incitement to assist individuals; for there is a kind of "injustice that assumes institutional shape", and as long as this obtains, the situation itself calls for a greater degree of justice and demands reforming. Our contemporaries are no longer convinced that social structures have been predetermined by nature and therefore are "willed by God", or that they have their origin in anonymous evolutionary laws. Consequently, the Christian must ceaselessly point out that the institutions of society originate also in the conscience of society, and that men and women have a moral responsibility for these institutions.

We may dispute how legitimate it is to speak of "institutional sin" or of "sinful structures", since the Bible speaks of sin in the first instance in terms of an explicit, personal decision that stems from human freedom. But it is unquestionable that by the power of sin injury and injustice can penetrate social and political institutions. That is why, as we have pointed out, even situations and structures that are unjust have to be reformed.

Here we have a new consciousness, for in the past these responsibilities could not be perceived as distinctly as they are now. From this perspective justice means a basic reverence for the equal dignity of all men; it means that radical human rights develop satisfactorily and are protected;[43] it means an assured equity in the distribution of those goods that are especially needful for human living.[44]

Concrete relationship between human development and divine salvation

Reflection on the relationship between the salvation which God effects and the liberating action of man reveals the need to determine with greater exactness the relationship between human development and divine salvation, between the building up of the world and eschatological fulfillment. As is clear from the proofs we have adduced, human activity and Christian hope may be

---

[43] Cf. *Schema Pontificiae Commissionis a Iustitia et Pace, The Church and Human Rights* (Vatican City, 1975).

[44] Cf. *Populorum Progressio*, 21.

4

neither utterly divorced—on one side the world of earth exclusively, on the other a life to come utterly severed from the world—nor seen in terms of an "evolutionary optimism", as if God's lordship and man's progressive construction of the world were one and the same thing.

Even the pastoral constitution *Gaudium et Spes* makes a distinction between the growth of God's Kingdom and human progress as between the work of divinization and the work of humanization, or as between the order of divine grace and the order of human activity.[45] Indeed it speaks first of the affinity between the two: the service of men on earth "makes ready the material of heaven's Kingdom."[46] The good fruits of our diligent activity—cleansed, however, of all sordidness, lit up and transfigured—we shall discover afresh in the Kingdom of God, so that it is not only love that will remain[47] but love's labor as well.[48] Eschatological hope, therefore, ought to find its expression even in the structures of secular life.[49] That is why the Council speaks not only of this world's passing away but of its transformation as well.[50] The earthly city and the heavenly city ought to penetrate each other, under faith's guidance, with due respect for their distinction and their harmonious union.[51] These ideas are summed up in the decree *Apostolicam Actuositatem* on the apostolate of the laity:

> Christ's redemptive work, while of its nature directed to the salvation of men and women, involves also the renewal of the whole temporal order. The Church has for mission, therefore, not only to bring to men and women the message of Christ and his grace, but also to saturate and perfect the temporal sphere with the spirit of the Gospel. . . . The two spheres, spiritual and temporal, distinct though they are, are so linked in the single plan of God

[45] Cf. *Gaudium et Spes*, 36, 38, 39, 40, 42, 43, 58; *Apostolicam Actuositatem*, 7.
[46] Cf. *Gaudium et Spes*, 38.
[47] Cf. 1 Cor 13:8.
[48] Cf. *Gaudium et Spes*, 39.
[49] Cf. *Lumen Gentium*, 35.
[50] Cf. *Gaudium et Spes*, 38, 39.
[51] Cf. *Lumen Gentium*, 36.

that he himself purposes in Christ to take up the whole world again into a new creation, initially here on earth, completely on the last day.[52]

These passages persuade us that the vindication of justice and participation in the process of transforming the world should be regarded "as a constitutive element of the preaching of the Gospel."[53] The words "constitutive element" (*ratio constitutiva*) are still the subject of controversy. If we look at their strict meaning, it seems more accurate to interpret them as meaning an integral part, not an essential part.[54] Besides, the texts cited from the Second Vatican Council have commonly been explained as favoring a *harmony* between eschatological salvation and the human effort to build a better world. It is useful, therefore, while maintaining unyieldingly the unity that links the two, to spell out again, with even sharper clarity, the distinction between them.

The very resistance of earthly situations to positive change for the better, the power of sin and some ambiguous effects of human progress[55] teach us to recognize with even greater clarity within the very unity of salvation history an abiding difference between the Kingdom of God and human development, as well as the mystery of the Cross, without which no activity becomes genuinely salvific.[56] But if, while preserving the unity, it is the difference that is highlighted, this does not introduce a so-called "dualism". In fact, this more penetrating vision helps us to carry out the task of promoting human welfare and justice with a greater measure of endurance, steadfastness and confidence; it can also keep us from being thrown into confusion if our efforts prove ineffective.

[52] *Apostolicam Actuositatem*, 5; cf. 7 also.
[53] Cf. 1971 Synod of Bishops, *De Justitia in Mundo* (Vatican Press, 1971) Introduction, 5.
[54] This is the interpretation that was given by the synod of 1974. [English translator's note: This footnote, translated here from the French version, does not appear in the Latin text sent to the members of the International Theological Commission on June 30, 1977, for final approval.]
[55] Cf. *Apostolicam Actuositatem*, 7 for greater detail.
[56] Cf. *Gaudium et Spes*, 22, 78.

This unifying connection and this difference in the relationship between human development and Christian salvation in their existential shape indeed demand further serious research; and this surely has a high priority among the tasks of today's theology. But the basic character of that unity cannot be overturned, for it is rooted at reality's very core.

On the one hand, existential history is in a way the locus where the world is so deeply transformed that it reaches as far as the mystery of God; and that is why love and its fruits abide. It is ultimately for this reason that there can be a link between salvation and human welfare, between salvation and human rights. But they are not linked to perfection, because the eschatological fulfillment "takes away" existential history.

On the other hand, the Kingdom of God "directs" history and utterly transcends all the possibilities of earthly fulfillment; it presents itself, therefore, as the action of God. This involves a certain break with that world, no matter what perfection we recognize therein. This discontinuity in our individual stories we experience as death, but the same discontinuity precisely as "transformation" touches the whole of history: it is the world's "destruction".

In our pilgrim state this "dialectic", which finds expression in these two irreducible principles, cannot be dissolved and ought not be removed. In particular, however, the eschatological fulfillment for which we still yearn (the "eschatological reserve") is the reason why the relationship between God's Kingdom and history cannot be described as either a monism or a dualism; and so from the very nature of this relationship we have to hold its definition in abeyance.

In any event, the relationship between the message of eschatological salvation and the shaping of historical time to come cannot be established univocally, by walking a single line, eyes fixed on harmony alone or difference alone. Perhaps this is what the words in Luke mean: "The Kingdom of God is not coming with outward show; nor will they say 'Lo, here it is!' or 'There!' For behold, the Kingdom of God is in the midst of you."[57] The *Pastoral Constitution on the Church in the Modern World* suggests

[57] Lk 17:20 f.

another consequence of this basic relationship between history and salvation: "We do not know when the earth and humanity are to be consummated; nor do we know how the universe is to be transformed."[58]

Here surely lies the formal solution to our problem—a solution commended by the principal acts of revelation. In the concrete working-out of this relationship, however, we can discover many ways of realizing it, ways that have different, distinct shapes. The correct choice of means appropriate to this solution in various periods of history and, for example, in areas that belong to the First, Second and Third Worlds will call for different procedures. What is effective in sections of Europe and North America that have a highly developed industrial economy does not have the same significance on continents and in areas of the world where most of the people are hungry. And still, however considerable the differences, we may not infringe on the above-mentioned basic relationship between human development and Christian salvation.

In this matter we have unambiguous criteria at hand. The basic relationship is disturbed, for example, if the practice of social and political liberation has such priority that divine worship, prayer, the Eucharist and other sacraments, individual ethics and all questions about the final destiny of man (death and eternal life), and the exhausting struggle within history against the powers of darkness[59] take second place. On the other hand, in situations of poverty and injustice those truths of the faith must be proclaimed and practiced in such a way as not to corroborate a frequent reproach: the Church disguises human distress, does no more than lull the poor in their very afflictions. Offering authentic relief is something totally different from raising hopes futilely comforting, hopes that only blunt the feeling of anguish.

Relationship between human development and salvation in the Church's commission

To commend the significance of the Church for the world is also to stress pointedly that the community which is Church is

[58] *Gaudium et Spes*, 39.
[59] Cf. *Gaudium et Spes*, 13b.

always concretely circumstanced and that in these circumstances political options have already been taken. The Church, though a special kind of community, must always remember that its life is ceaselessly lived on a stage where candidates for power compete with one another, where power is exercised in concrete ways, where power is linked to ideologies.

The Church "is not bound exclusively and inseparably to any race or nation, to any one particular way of life, to any customary pattern of living old or new."[60] In virtue of its origin, super-natural character, religious mission, and eschatological hope, it cannot be confounded with any sociopolitical system or linked with it by necessary, unbreakable ties.

If the Church must be careful not to be entrapped by the power seekers, no more ought it surrender to sheer neutrality or un-sympathetic detachment and retire to a purely nonpolitical role. It is a fact that in many parts of today's world the Church is so dreadfully restricted that its witness to faith is invited in other forms, forms no less prophetic; primary among these are suffer-ing in the footsteps of our Lord and silence by coercion.

The Church cannot allow itself the cunning stratagems that characterize politics, but it must take care to anticipate the politi-cal consequences of its actions and its omissions. It can share in the blame when it does not denounce the situation of the poor and the oppressed, of those who suffer injustice—much more if it covers such a situation over and leaves it unchanged.

And so the Church, on the model of the Old Testament prophets, should sharpen its conscience, so as to make a critique of the social order under the guidance of faith. A strong kinship with the poor ("poor" in its largest sense; e.g., those who are afflicted by any serious spiritual, psychological or material wants) and effective assistance to them have been from olden times among the principal functions of the Church and all its members. In our day, however, this task has become the pre-eminent witness to a living faith; for many outside the Church, it is an inestimable criterion of the Church's credibility.

To build up and shape the social and political order is a task committed in a special way to the laity.[61] But the Church as a

---

[60] *Gaudium et Spes*, 58; cf. *Lumen Gentium*, 9; *Gaudium et Spes*, 42.

[61] Cf. *Apostolicam Actuositatem*, 7; *Lumen Gentium*, 31, 37; *Gaudium et Spes*, 43.

whole—represented particularly by the ministerial functions of the supreme pontiff, bishops, priests and deacons—may not keep silent in conditions where human dignity and elementary human rights are crushed. This granted, the whole Church is under obligation to express its convictions quickly and courageously.

But in many individual circumstances it is possible for Christians to opt freely among different paths that lead to the one same goal.[62] In consequence, Christians cannot utterly avoid controversy on social and political issues. "Where Christians exercise different options and on the face of it are apparently in disagreement, the Church asks that they try to understand one another's positions and reasons with kindliness and appreciation."[63] Without concealing his own convictions, each should try by persuasion and encouragement to contribute to the realization of the common objective. Where opinions differ, therefore, Christians may never forget this maxim of Vatican II: "The bonds that unite the faithful are more powerful than anything that divides them."[64]

Nevertheless, the Church's unity is seriously imperiled if the differences that exist between social "classes" are taken up into a systematic "class struggle". Where you have those "class" differences, you can hardly avoid conflict. Christians are recognized in the first instance by the way they try to solve such tensions: they do not persuade the masses to destroy violence by counterviolence; rather, they try to effect change by, e.g., shaping the consciences of men, entering into discussion, initiating and supporting nonviolent action.[65] Nor may the Christian bypass the primary end: reconciliation.

We must also guard against the danger that social and political hostilities might supersede all else, so that, e.g., Christians of divergent positions no longer celebrate the Eucharist together or shut one another out of their Eucharist. The point is, political options may not become so contentious as to damage the universality of the Christian message of salvation. This message is to be

[62] Cf., at greater length, *Gaudium et Spes*, 43.

[63] Paul VI, apostolic letter *Octogesima Adveniens*, no. 50.

[64] *Gaudium et Spes*, 92.

[65] Obviously, we cannot give more extended treatment here to additional issues that concern recourse to force and violence.

carried to all, even the rich and the oppressors; for the Church ought not exclude any human person from its love.

The Church should constantly remind men that politics does not have a kind of absolute value, and should be increasingly concerned to strip politics of such value. An exclusive political option, intolerant of any other option, becomes despotic and subverts the very nature of politics. It is the Church's obligation— a duty it cannot forgo—to oppose the dictatorial claims of a state which would maintain that all the dimensions of human living fall under its sole control.

It is true that in such circumstances the Church at times finds it difficult or impossible to manifest its mind in the public forum. Still, it does its duty surpassingly well if, in imitation of its Lord, it responds to such situations by courageous protest, by silent suffering, even by martyrdom in its various shapes. But even in such extreme situations the Christian liberation that leads to freedom cannot be totally fettered. This is our sovereign comfort; here is the high point of our confidence.

Conclusion

In dealing with these questions, we become strikingly aware of the diverse situations that confront the local churches within the Church catholic; and this diversity is a cause for concern. Social, cultural and political differences can at times weigh upon us with such increasing heaviness that our common unity in faith, the centrality of faith, seems no longer capable of overcoming our tensions and our rendings.

In our discussions we too were able to observe with some clarity the varying situations in which different people live. Now, no one in the Church speaks simply for himself; and so all of us should listen to the cries of our brothers and sisters, all those all over the world who are treated with injustice, are oppressed by tribulations, suffer from poverty, are distressed by hunger. Here too we can learn from one another, so as to keep ourselves from repeating afresh the mistaken solutions that have plagued the history of the Church and of human societies (e.g., when politics is divinized).

In this effort it is the Spirit of Christ that links us all. In this connection, the Church's unity and catholicity amid the variety of her peoples and of human cultures is simultaneously a gift to us and a claim on us. What has been laboriously achieved, however, must not be facilely jeopardized. This is particularly the case with all issues touching the relationship between human development and Christian salvation.

A CHICAGO DECLARATION
OF CHRISTIAN CONCERN

The signers of this Declaration are members of the Catholic Community in Chicago.

For decades, the Church in Chicago nurtured a compelling vision of lay Christians in society. The vision they had was eventually accepted and celebrated by the Second Vatican Council. That same vision produced national movements and networks which generated a dynamic lay leadership. It attracted priests who saw their ministry as arousing the laity to the pursuit of justice and freedom; who served the laity without manipulating them.

Shall we passively accept that period of history as completely over, and with it the vision that proved to be so creative? While many in the Church exhaust their energies arguing internal issues, albeit important ones, such as the ordination of women and a married clergy, the laity who spend most of their time and energy in the professional and occupational world appear to have been deserted.

"Without a vision, the people shall perish." Who now sustains lay persons as they meet the daily challenges of their job and profession—the arena in which questions of justice and peace are really located? Where are the movements and organizations supporting the young toward a Christian maturity? Where are the priests sufficiently self-assured in their own identity and faith that they can devote themselves to energizing lay leaders committed to reforming the structures of society?

We wait impatiently for a new prophecy, a new word that can once again stir the laity to see the grandeur of the Christian vision

Published under the title "Declaration of Concern: On Devaluing the Laity" in *Origins* 7, no. 28 (29 December 1977). Reprinted by permission.

for man in society and move priests to galvanize lay persons in their secular-religious role.

We think that this new prophecy should retrieve, at least in part, the best insights of Vatican II. It was Vatican II that broadened our understanding of the Church. It rejected the notion that Church is to be identified exclusively with hierarchical roles—such as bishop and priest. The Church is as present to the world in the ordinary roles of lay Christians as it is in the ecclesiastical roles of bishop and priest, though the styles of each differ.

Vatican II did identify man's hopes for social justice and world peace with the Church's saving mission. The salvation of the world is no longer to be construed as applying only to individual persons but embraces all the institutions of society. The Church is present to the world in the striving of the laity to transform the world of political, economic and social institutions. The clergy minister so that the laity will exercise their family, neighborly, and occupational roles mindful of their Christian responsibility. The thrust of Vatican II is unmistakable:

> What specifically characterizes the laity is their secular nature. It is true that those in holy orders can at times be engaged in secular activities, and even have a secular profession. But they are, by reason of their particular vocation, especially and professedly ordained to the sacred ministry. Similarly, by their state in life, religious give splendid and striking testimony that the world can not be transformed and offered to God without the spirit of the beatitudes. But the laity, by their special vocation, seek the kingdom of God by engaging in temporal affairs and by ordering them according to the plan of God. They live in the world, that is, in each and in all of secular professions and occupations. They live in the ordinary circumstances of family and social life, from which the very web of their existence is woven. Today they are called by God, that by exercising their proper function, and led by the spirit of the Gospel, they may work for the sanctification of the world from within as a leaven. In this way they may make Christ known to others, especially by the testimony of a life resplendent in faith, hope and charity. Therefore, since they are tightly bound up in all types of temporal affairs, it is their special task to order and to

throw light upon these affairs in such a way that they may be made and grow according to Christ to the praise of the creator and redeemer.[1]

Although the teaching of Vatican II on the ministry of the laity is forceful and represents one of the Council's most notable achievements, in recent years it seems to have all but vanished from the consciousness and agendas of many sectors within the Church.

It is our experience that a wholesome and significant movement within the Church—the involvement of lay people in many Church ministries—has led to a devaluation of the unique ministry of lay men and women. The tendency has been to see lay ministry as involvement in some church related activity, e.g., religious education, pastoral care for the sick and elderly, or readers in church on Sunday. Thus lay ministry is seen as the laity's participation in work traditionally assigned to priests or sisters.

We recognize the new opportunities opened up to the laity to become deacons, but believe that in the long run such programs will be a disaster if they create the impression that only in such fashion do the laity mainly participate in the mission of the Church. We note that our misgivings are shared by the Apostolic Delegate to the United States, Archbishop Jean Jadot, who commented recently, "I believe in the laity. And the laity as laity. I was very, very impressed, I must say, by my experiences in Africa and my closeness and friendliness with some African bishops who don't want to hear about a permanent diaconate. They say it will kill the laity in the Church. It will kill the laity in the Church because it will reinforce the conviction already existing that to work for the Church you must be ordained."

Our own reaction to the Detroit "Call to Action" conference reflects a similar ambivalence. Without a doubt, it was historic, precedent-setting in its conception, in its consultative process, in helping all levels of the Church listen to each other and in facing challenges to growth affecting the inner life of the Church. But devoting, as it did, so much of its time to the internal affairs of the Church, the conference did not sufficiently illuminate the

[1] Constitution on the Church, par. 31.

broader mission of the Church to the world and the indispensable role of lay Christians in carrying out that mission.

During the last decade especially, many priests have acted as if the primary responsibility in the Church for uprooting injustice, ending wars and defending human rights rested with them as ordained ministers. As a result they bypassed the laity to pursue social causes on their own rather than enabling lay Christians to shoulder their own responsibility. These priests and religious have sought to impose their own agendas for the world upon the laity. Indeed, if in the past the Church has suffered from a tendency to clericalism on the right, it may now face the threat of a revived clericalism—on the left.

We also note with concern the steady depreciation, during the past decade, of the ordinary social roles through which the laity serve and act upon the world. The impression is often created that one can work for justice and peace only by stepping outside of these ordinary roles as a businessman, as a mayor, as a factory worker, as a professional in the State Department, or as an active union member and thus that one can change the system only as an "outsider" to society and the system.

Such ideas clearly depart from the mainstream of Catholic social thought which regards the advance of social justice as essentially the service performed within one's professional and occupational milieu. The almost exclusive preoccupation with the role of the "outsider" as the model of social action can only distract the laity from the apostolic potential that lies at the core of their professional and occupational lives.

Although we do not hold them up as models adequate to present-day needs, we do note with regret the decline and, too often, the demise of those organizations and networks of the recent past whose task it was to inspire and support the laity in their vocation to the world through their professional and occupational lives. We have in mind such organizations as The National Catholic Social Action Conference, the National Conference of Christian Employers and Managers, the Association of Catholic Trade Unionists, the National Council of Catholic Nurses, Young Christian Students, Young Christian Workers, and the Catholic Council on Working Life.

Although concerns for justice and peace are now built into

Church bureaucracy more so than when such organizations flourished, there is no evidence that such bureaucratization has led to further involvement of lay Christians. As a matter of fact, the disappearance of organizations like the above, and our failure to replace them, may have resulted in the loss of a generation of lay leadership.

As various secular ideologies, including communism, socialism and liberalism, each in turn, fail to live up to their promise to transform radically the human condition, some Christians seek to convert religion and the Gospel itself into another political ideology. Although we also yearn for a new heaven and a new earth, we insist that the Gospel of Jesus Christ by itself reveals no political or economic program to bring this about. Direct appeals to the Gospel in order to justify specific solutions to social problems, whether domestic or international, are really a betrayal of the Gospel. The Good News calling for peace, justice and freedom needs to be mediated through the prism of lay experience, political wisdom and technical expertise. Christian social thought is a sophisticated body of social wisdom which attempts such a mediation, supplying the middle ground between the Gospel on the one hand and the concrete decisions which Christians make on their own responsibility in their everyday life.

In conclusion, we address these words of hope and of deep concern to the members of the Church throughout the nation as well as to members of the Church in Chicago. We invite them to associate themselves with this declaration. We prayerfully anticipate that our words and theirs will prompt a re-examination of present tendencies in the Church and that out of such a re-examination will emerge a new sense of direction, a new agenda.

In the last analysis, the Church speaks to and acts upon the world through her laity. Without a dynamic laity conscious of its personal ministry to the world, the Church, in effect, does not speak or act. No amount of social action by priests and religious can ever be an adequate substitute for enhancing lay responsibility. The absence of lay initiative can only take us down the road to clericalism. We are deeply concerned that so little energy is devoted to encouraging and arousing lay responsibility for the world. The Church must constantly be reformed, but we fear that the almost obsessive preoccupation with the Church's structures and processes has diverted attention from the essential question: reform for what purpose? It would be one of the great ironies of history if the era of Vatican II which opened the windows of the Church to the world were to close with a Church turned in upon herself.

The Third Sunday of the Coming of the Lord, 1977

THE HARTFORD STATEMENT

AN APPEAL FOR
THEOLOGICAL AFFIRMATION

The renewal of Christian witness and mission requires constant examination of the assumptions shaping the Church's life. Today an apparent loss of a sense of the transcendent is undermining the Church's ability to address with clarity and courage the urgent tasks to which God calls it in the world. This loss is manifest in a number of pervasive themes. Many are superficially attractive, but upon closer examination we find these themes false and debilitating to the Church's life and work. Among such themes are:

THEME 1: *Modern thought is superior to all past forms of understanding reality and is therefore normative for Christian faith and life.*

In repudiating this theme we are protesting the captivity to the prevailing thought structures not only of the twentieth century but of any historical period. We favor using any helpful means of understanding, ancient or modern, and insist that the Christian proclamation must be related to the idiom of the culture. At the same time, we affirm the need for Christian thought to confront and be confronted by other worldviews, all of which are necessarily provisional.

THEME 2: *Religious statements are totally independent of reasonable discourse.*

The capitulation to the alleged primacy of modern thought takes two forms: one is the subordination of religious statements to the canons of scientific rationality; the other, equating reason with scientific rationality, would remove religious statements

Reprinted by permission from *Worldview* (April 1975) 39–40.

from the realm of reasonable discourse altogether. A religion of pure subjectivity and nonrationality results in treating faith statements as being, at best, statements about the believer. We repudiate both forms of capitulation.

THEME 3: *Religious language refers to human experience and nothing else, God being humanity's noblest creation.*

Religion is also a set of symbols and even of human projections. We repudiate the assumption that it is nothing but that. What is here at stake is nothing less than the reality of God: *We did not invent God; God invented us.*

THEME 4: *Jesus can only be understood in terms of contemporary models of humanity.*

This theme suggests a reversal of "the imitation of Christ"; that is, the image of Jesus is made to reflect cultural and counter-cultural notions of human excellence. We do not deny that all aspects of humanity are illumined by Jesus. Indeed, it is necessary to the universality of the Christ that he be perceived in relation to the particularities of the believers' world. We do repudiate the captivity to such metaphors, which are necessarily inadequate, relative, transitory, and frequently idolatrous. Jesus, together with the Scriptures and the whole of the Christian tradition, cannot be arbitrarily interpreted without reference to the history of which they are part. The danger is in the attempt to exploit the tradition without taking the tradition seriously.

THEME 5: *All religions are equally valid; the choice among them is not a matter of conviction about truth but only of personal preference or lifestyle.*

We affirm our common humanity. We affirm the importance of exploring and confronting all manifestations of the religious quest and of learning from the riches of other religions. But we repudiate this theme because it flattens diversities and ignores contradictions. In doing so, it not only obscures the meaning of Christian faith, but also fails to respect the integrity of other faiths. Truth matters; therefore differences among religions are deeply significant.

THEME 6: *To realize one's potential and to be true to oneself is the whole meaning of salvation.*

Salvation contains a promise of human fulfillment, but to identify salvation with human fulfillment can trivialize the promise. We affirm that salvation cannot be found apart from God.

THEME 7: *Since what is human is good, evil can adequately be understood as a failure to realize potential.*

This theme invites false understanding of the ambivalence of human existence and underestimates the pervasiveness of sin. Paradoxically, by minimizing the enormity of evil, it undermines serious and sustained attacks on particular social or individual evils.

THEME 8: *The sole purpose of worship is to promote individual self-realization and human community.*

Worship promotes individual and communal values, but it is above all a response to the reality of God and arises out of the fundamental need and desire to know, love, and adore God. We worship God because God is to be worshipped.

THEME 9: *Institutions and historical traditions are oppressive and inimical to our being truly human; liberation from them is required for authentic existence and authentic religion.*

Institutions and traditions are often oppressive. For this reason they must be subjected to relentless criticism. But human community inescapably requires institutions and traditions. Without them life would degenerate into chaos and new forms of bondage. The modern pursuit of liberation from all social and historical restraints is finally dehumanizing.

THEME 10: *The world must set the agenda for the Church. Social, political and economic programs to improve the quality of life are ultimately normative for the Church's mission in the world.*

This theme cuts across the political and ideological spectrum. Its form remains the same, no matter whether the content is defined as upholding the values of the American way of life, promoting socialism, or raising human consciousness. The Church must denounce oppressors, help liberate the oppressed, and seek to heal human misery. Sometimes the Church's mission coincides with the world's programs. But the norms for the Church's activity derive from its own perception of God's will for the world.

THEME 11: *An emphasis on God's transcendence is at least a hindrance to, and perhaps incompatible with, Christian social concern and action.*

This supposition leads some to denigrate God's transcendence. Others, holding to a false transcendence, withdraw into religious privatism or individualism and neglect the personal and communal responsibility of Christians for the earthly city. From a biblical perspective, it is precisely because of confidence in God's reign over all aspects of life that Christians must participate fully in the struggle against oppressive and dehumanizing structures and their manifestations in racism, war, and economic exploitation.

THEME 12: *The struggle for a better humanity will bring about the Kingdom of God.*

The struggle for a better humanity is essential to Christian faith and can be informed and inspired by the biblical promise of the Kingdom of God. But imperfect human beings cannot create a perfect society. The Kingdom of God surpasses any conceivable utopia. God has his own designs which confront ours, surprising us with judgment and redemption.

THEME 13: *The question of hope beyond death is irrelevant or at best marginal to the Christian understanding of human fulfillment.*

This is the final capitulation to modern thought. If death is the last word, then Christianity has nothing to say to the final questions of life. We believe that God raised Jesus from the dead and are "convinced that there is nothing in death or life, in the realm of spirits or superhuman powers, in the world as it is or in the world as it shall be, in the forces of the universe, in heights or depths—nothing in all creation that can separate us from the love of God in Christ Jesus our Lord" (Rom 8:38 f.).

VI

NEW YORK TIMES

POPE JOHN PAUL II:
A VOICE FOR BASIC CHRISTIAN CONCEPTS

To the Editor:

In reference to your January 30 editorial "A Voice Against 'Liberation Theology' ", I for one did not find Pope John Paul II's stand on priestly activity in politics "disappointing". It seemed a reaffirmation of some basic Christian concepts.

Nowhere in Jesus' teaching does he urge his disciples to minister to human wants and needs of a material nature. Nor does he call for the reform of social and political structures. (Surely the Roman Empire was oppressive.) Rather he instructed his followers to bring the "Good News" of Christ to all the nations that they might reform their moral and spiritual lives, thus inheriting everlasting life.

Surely there are enough people and institutions on this earth catering to the material and physical wants and needs of society. However, there are only a few ministering to the spiritual needs of mankind without getting sidetracked into political activism.

On the question of the usefulness of prayer: Prayer is the most powerful weapon a Christian possesses to overcome human problems, be it social injustice, hunger, poverty or any other trouble. In Jesus' words, "Ask and you shall receive."

It should follow then that the Pope, as the head of the Church started by Jesus Christ, should urge all priests not to get involved in social and political issues but rather to deal with the moral and spiritual needs of all mankind. As every Christian believes the soul and spirit are everlasting, this would seem a much worthier endeavor.

This letter, written from the spiritual point of view, might not make any sense to a nonbeliever. However, as you chose to

Reprinted from *The New York Times* (12 February 1979).

criticize the spiritual leader of Christ's Church from the human and physical point of view, I hope you will acknowledge this spiritual Christian rebuttal.

James M. Berkery, 3d

To the Editor:

Contrary to your editorial and several reports of recent days, the debate over "liberation theology" does not have to do with whether "Scripture justifies political action" or with whether priests "must confine themselves to the pulpit and altar."

"Liberation theology" is largely a Latin American phenomenon associated with the writings of men such as Gustavo Gutíerrez and Juan Luis Segundo, and with the revolutionary activities (praxis) of priests, some of whom have taken up arms in guerrilla movements. It is conventionally based upon an explicitly Marxist analysis of class struggle which its proponents believe should be normative for the Christian Church's teaching and life. As Pope John Paul made clear in Mexico, the issue is not whether the Church is for liberation. Clearly it is. The issue is how we define liberation.

Since Constantine, the Church has frequently attempted to establish through direct political action what it believed to be a just and Christian society, under auspices both right and left. When, last year, the first John Paul declined to be crowned with the papal tiara and the current Pope followed that precedent, a new era was signaled. The message is that the Church has abandoned its pretensions to direct political rule. It will no longer give its uncritical blessing to Caesar or to those who would be the new Caesars. It would be a sad regression for the Church that has broken its alliance with the Constantines and Francos of history now to resume its old habits in partnership with Marx.

A church that points toward the Kingdom of God, and thus lives in critical tension with all existing or proposed political orders, can better advance democratic pluralism and more effectively advocate the cause of the poor—who are ever oppressed by political saviors of both the left and the right. That, I believe, is the very progressive manifesto issued by John Paul this past week.

Richard John Neuhaus

To the Editor:

I wish you'd make up your mind. When the Catholic Church speaks out against abortion—which you and politicians have unaccountably removed from the moral order to the political order—it is accused of meddling in the affairs of the state. Now, when the Holy Father calls for an end to "liberation theology" and a return of priests to their religious vocation, you call that a disappointment.

Thank God for Pope [John] Paul's direct handling of this most important problem. At least he can see clearly that by allowing priests to get involved in political and social activities the Church would be reduced to another arm of the state. Each is necessary, but each involves a totally different sphere of activity. The Church seeks to provide for the spiritual welfare of man, the state for the temporal. When they work as they are supposed to, we have peace and harmony.

Rev. Thomas W. Prior

VII

POPE JOHN PAUL II

LIBERATION THEOLOGY INVOLVES "THAT TRUTH WHICH MADE US FREE"

1. Today, too, I wish to refer to the subject of the third Conference of the Latin American Episcopate: to evangelization. It is a fundamental subject, a subject that is always topical. The Conference, which ended its work at Puebla on February 13, bears witness to this. It is, moreover, the subject "of the future"; the subject that the Church must live continually and prolong in the future. The subject, therefore, constitutes the permanent perspective of the Church's mission.

To evangelize means making Christ present in the life of man as a person, and at the same time in the life of society. To evangelize means doing everything possible, according to our capacities, in order that man "may believe"; in order that man may find himself again in Christ; in order that he may find again in him the meaning and the adequate dimension of his own life. This finding again is, at the same time, the deepest source of man's liberation. St. Paul expresses this when he writes: "For freedom Christ has set us free" (Gal 5:1). So, liberation, then, is certainly a reality of faith, one of the fundamental biblical themes, which are a deep part of Christ's salvific mission, of the work of redemption, of his teaching. This subject has never ceased to constitute the content of the spiritual life of Christians. The Conference of the Latin American Episcopate bears witness that this subject returns in a new historical context; therefore it must be taken up again in the teaching of the Church, in theology, and in the apostolate. It must be taken up again in its own depth, and in its evangelical authenticity.

General Audience of Pope John Paul II (February 21, 1979). Reprinted by permission from *L'Osservatore Romano*, English edition (26 February 1979) 1, 12.

398

Relevant Subject

There are many circumstances that make it such a relevant subject today. It is difficult, here, to mention them all. Certainly it is recalled by that "universal desire for dignity" on the part of man, of which the Second Vatican Council speaks. The "theology of liberation" is often connected (sometimes too exclusively) with Latin America; but it must be admitted that one of the great contemporary theologians, Hans Urs von Balthasar, is right when he demands a theology of liberation on a universal scale. Only the contexts are different, but the reality itself of the freedom "for which Christ set us free" (cf. Gal 5:1) is universal. The task of theology is to find its real significance in the different concrete historical and contemporary contexts.

Knowledge of Truth

2. Christ himself links liberation particularly with knowledge of the truth: "You will know the truth, and the truth will make you free" (Jn 8:32). This sentence testifies above all to the intimate significance of the freedom for which Christ liberates us. Liberation means man's inner transformation, which is a consequence of the knowledge of truth. The transformation is, therefore, a spiritual process, in which man matures "in true righteousness and holiness" (Eph 4:24). Man, inwardly mature in this way, becomes a representative and a spokesman of this "righteousness" in the various environments of social life. Truth is important not only for the growth of human knowledge, deepening man's interior life in this way; truth has also a prophetic significance and power. It constitutes the content of testimony and it calls for testimony. We find this prophetic power of truth in the teaching of Christ. As a prophet, as a witness to truth, Christ repeatedly opposes non-truth; he does so with great forcefulness and decision, and often he does not hesitate to condemn falsehood. Let us reread the Gospel carefully; we will find in it a good many severe expressions—for example, "white-washed tombs" (Mt 23:27), "blind guides" (Mt 23:16), "hypocrites" (Mt 23:13, 15, 23, 25, 27, 29)—which Christ utters, aware of the consequences that are in store for him.

So this service of truth as participation in Christ's prophetic service is a task of the Church, which tries to carry it out in the various historical contexts. It is necessary to call by their name injustice, the exploitation of man by man, or the exploitation of man by the State, institutions, mechanisms of systems and regimes which sometimes operate without sensitivity. It is necessary to call by name every social injustice, discrimination, violence inflicted on man against the body, against the spirit, against his conscience and against his convictions. Christ teaches us a special sensitivity for man, for the dignity of the human person, for human life, for the human spirit and body. It is this sensitivity which bears witness to knowledge of that "truth which makes us free" (Jn 8:32). It is not permitted for man to conceal this truth from himself. It is not permitted to "falsify it". It is not permitted to make this truth the object of a "tender". It is necessary to speak of it clearly and simply. And not to "condemn" men, but to serve man's cause. Liberation also in the social sense begins with knowledge of the truth.

Man's Twofold Being

3. Let us stop at this point. It is difficult to express in a short speech everything involved in this great subject, which has many aspects and, above all, many levels. I stress: many levels, because it is necessary, in this subject, to see man according to the different elements of all the riches of his personal and at the same time social being; his "historical" and at the same time, in a certain way, "supertemporal" being. (History, among other things, bears witness to this "supertemporality" of man.) The being that the "thinking reed" is[1]—everyone knows how frail a reed is—just because it is "thinking" always goes beyond itself; it bears within it the transcendental mystery and a "creative restlessness" which springs from the latter.

We will stop for the present at this point. The theology of liberation must, above all, be faithful to the whole truth on man, in order to show clearly, not only in the Latin American context but also in all contemporary contexts, what reality is this freedom "for which Christ set us free".

[1] Cf. B. Pascal, *Pensées*, 347.

Christ! It is necessary to speak of our liberation in Christ; it is necessary to proclaim this liberation. It must be integrated in the whole contemporary reality of human life. Many circumstances, many reasons, demand this. Just in these times, in which it is claimed that the condition of "man's liberation" is his liberation "from Christ", that is, from religion, just in these times the reality of our liberation in Christ must become, for us all, more and more evident and more and more full.

Stronger than Evil

4. "For this I was born, and for this I have come into the world, to bear witness to the truth" (Jn 18:37).

The Church, looking to Christ who bears witness to the truth, must always and everywhere ask herself, and in a certain sense also the contemporary "world", *how to make good emerge from man*, how to liberate the dynamism of the good that is in man, in order that it may be stronger than evil, than any moral, social evil, etc. The third Conference of the Latin American Episcopate bears witness to the readiness to undertake this effort. We want not only to recommend this effort to God, but also to follow it for the good of the Church and of the whole human family.

BIBLIOGRAPHY

The purpose of this very limited bibliography is merely to give a brief indication of the literature and background of liberation theology itself as developed and criticized in this text.

1. Assmann, Hugo. *Theology for a Nomad Church*. Maryknoll: Orbis, 1975.
2. Bonino, José Míguez. *Christians and Marxists*. Grand Rapids: Eerdmans, 1976.
3. Bonino, José Míguez. *Theology in a Revolutionary Situation*. Philadelphia: Fortress, 1975.
4. Eagleson, J., ed. *Christianity and Socialism*. Maryknoll: Orbis, 1975.
5. Dussel, Enrique. *History and Theology of Liberation: A Latin American Perspective*. Maryknoll: Orbis, 1976.
6. Fierro, Alfredo. *The Militant Gospel*. Maryknoll: Orbis, 1975.
7. Gibellini, R., ed. *Frontiers of Theology in Latin America*. Maryknoll: Orbis, 1979.
8. Gheerbrant, A. *The Rebel Church in Latin America*. London, 1974.
9. Gutíerrez, Gustavo, S.J. *A Theology of Liberation*. Maryknoll: Orbis, 1973.
10. McFadden, T. S., ed. *Liberation, Revolution, and Freedom*. New York: Seabury, 1975.
11. Miranda, José Porfirio. *Marx and the Bible*. Maryknoll: Orbis, 1974.
12. Geffré, C., and G. Gutíerrez, ed. *The Mystical and Political Dimension of the Christian Faith*. New York: Herder and Herder, 1974.

13. MacEoin, G., ed. "Puebla: Moment of Decision for the Latin American Church". *Cross Currents*, no. 1, Spring, 1978.

14. Segundo, Juan Luis, S.J. *A Theology for the Artisans of a New Humanity*. Maryknoll: Orbis, 1974. 5 vols.

15. Torres, S., and J. Eagleson, ed. *Theology of the Americas*. Maryknoll: Orbis, 1976. Chapter 7: "The Latin American Theologians", 273–314.